Introduction
to the Study *of*
Religion

Introduction
to the Study *of*
Religion

Nancy C. Ring

Kathleen S. Nash

Mary N. MacDonald

Fred Glennon

Jennifer A. Glancy

ORBIS BOOKS

Maryknoll, New York 10545

The Catholic Foreign Mission Society of America (Maryknoll) recruits and trains people for overseas missionary service. Through Orbis Books, Maryknoll aims to foster the international dialogue that is essential to mission. The books published, however, reflect the opinions of their authors and are not meant to represent the official position of the society.

Published by Orbis Books, Maryknoll, NY 10545-0308
Manufactured in the United States of America

Scripture quotations are from the NRSV, copyright © 1989 by the Division of Christian Education of the National Council of the Churches of Christ.

Acknowledgments: Excerpts from "The Ass Is Transformed" from THE GOLD-EN ASS by Apuleius, translated by Robert Graves. Copyright © 1951 and copyright renewed 1979 by Robert Graves. Reprinted by permission of Farrar, Straus & Giroux, Inc. and Carcanet Press Limited (U.K.). Excerpt from YIMIKIRLI: WARLPIRI DREAMINGS AND HISTORIES, translated by Peggy Rockman Napaljarri and Lee Cataldi. Copyright © 1994 by Peggy Napaljarri, et al. Reprinted by permission of HarperCollins Publishers, Inc. Excerpt from "The Buddha's Enlightenment," from RELIGIONS OF THE WORLD, Nielson, et al. Copyright © 1983. Reprinted with permission of Saint Martin's Press, Inc.

Library of Congress Cataloging-in-Publication Data

Ring, Nancy C.
    Introduction to the study of religion / Nancy C. Ring . . . [et al.].
       p. cm.
    Includes index.
    ISBN 1-57075-183-8 (alk. paper)
       1. Religion. I. Title.
BL48.R455   1998
200—dc21

                                                    97-49093
                                                    CIP

Contents

Introduction

This book is an introductory college text book on the study of religion. The authors of this volume are colleagues in a department of religious studies. Over the years we have held countless conversations about religion with our students, and almost as many conversations with one another about teaching religion. Writing this book has given us an opportunity to continue our lively conversations, and the book itself represents an extension of those conversations.

Our basic goal is to help students think through basic questions that arise in the study of religion. What is the nature of religious experience, for example? In what ways is religion intertwined with our everyday lives, and in what ways is religion an experience set apart? How does religion shape the actions of individuals and communities? In what ways does language mediate our experience of the sacred, the ultimate? By what processes does religious change occur? And finally, does religion promote or inhibit human flourishing? The authors rely on examples from a wide variety of world religions to explore these questions. We teach at a Jesuit college, and our students tend to come from Christian backgrounds. Because it is often easiest to begin learning with what is familiar, we draw most frequently on examples from Christian traditions. We hope that we are also successful in leading students to think about traditions other than their own and that the book will be accessible to students from a wide range of backgrounds.

Students arrive in our classrooms with a variety of life experiences. Perhaps most of them fit the mold of traditional, late-adolescent, full-time college students, but we also teach part-time students, parents, workers who have been laid off, retired people, former military personnel, and others who never had a chance to complete a college education. As we wrote we tried to keep all these people, as well as others, in mind. We think that this book will also be useful to other groups who would like to think more systematically about religion: parish groups, for example, who are interested in expanding their understanding of the role that religion plays in other people's lives.

We have made every effort to make this volume easy to read and easy to use. At the end of each chapter, we include suggestions for further reading and for audiovisual aids. We expect that professors who use this book will select supplementary readings for students from these lists or from other texts that they find helpful. In addition, each chapter includes suggested activities that students may pursue on their own or that professors may assign as class activities. Many of these activities are research-based, and many of them culminate in a public presentation of some sort. We want you to continue the conversation that we have begun.

Each chapter also includes several activity sidebars, titled "Thinking about" or "Thinking with." We hope that as people read the book, they will take some time to reflect on the questions we have posed in these sidebars; perhaps some professors will assign these sidebars as quick homework assignments or use them to stimulate class discussions. The purpose of the sidebars is to help the students connect what are sometimes abstract concepts with their own life experience and ideas. All terms that appear in bold type are included in the glossary at the end of the book.

As we have worked on this volume, we have spoken not only to one another about its concepts but also to our friends and families, many of whom have taken the time to read and comment on the manuscript. We owe special thanks first of all to our students, who inspired us to collaborate on this text, and to our many friends and colleagues who gave us suggestions, advice, and encouragement and who read the text for us in its formative stages. We particularly want to thank David Andrews, Amy Glancy, Charles Goldsmith, Jo Ann Nelson, Barbara Olmstead, and Paul Petersen. We are grateful to Kathy Gervasi for technical assistance and to Penny Sandoval of Maryknoll, for her help in choosing illustrations. Finally, as any writer knows, editors play an enormous role in seeing a book through from inception to completion. We could have wished for no better editor than Susan Perry, whose care, astuteness, and insistence that we keep students central to our work governed our writing. Susan, we thank you.

During our many editorial sessions we would often ask each other, "How do you think this will work for the reader?" We hope that working with this volume will enable students to think through *for themselves* the importance of religion in human lives. We share many of our own ideas and refer students to classic works in the study of religion. We do not, however, deliver the final word. After all, our goal is to begin a conversation. We want to know what you think. Won't you join us?

PART I

HUMAN EXPERIENCE AND RELIGION

This book invites you to the study of religion, asking you to frame questions and think about evidence which we take from the religious behavior and beliefs of several cultures. It suggests that we can develop disciplined and imaginative ways of approaching the phenomena which we describe under the rubric of religion. Since we live today in a pluralistic world, our study is an invitation to open-mindedness, to a serious and enjoyable excursion into a variety of religious ways and the approaches that scholars have taken in studying them.

Why, at the end of the twentieth century, do we study religion? Many students and many citizens regard religion as a personal matter and are reluctant to have their faith placed under scrutiny. Others, interested in obtaining academic and professional training which will result in a secure job, would rather study something "practical," leaving religion to those who seek a career in ministry and to those who are embarked on some religious quest. There are, in fact, good practical reasons—as well as vocational and avocational reasons—for studying religion. Today religion plays a significant role in world politics, including conflicts between nations and ethnic groups. It is also a significant factor in the personal choices that people make. If you become a doctor, you are likely to find that your patients' religious beliefs influence their attitudes toward illness and its treatment. If you become a small business owner you will have employees who require certain days off to fulfill religious obligations. If you become a caterer you will need to take account of the dietary restrictions that are part of religious practice. The study of religion is an excellent way to enter the worlds of other people and thus to see your own world from a new perspective.

There are many ways to practice religion and many ways to study religion. We each bring our own experiences, our own convictions, and our own questions to the practice and study of religion. The first of the five parts of this book comprises three chapters concerned with human experience and religion. It asks us to think about our own experiences and also to consider experiences different from our own. In these first three chapters we consider the human quest for order and meaning, examine religious understandings of life, and assess ways in which scholars go about the study of religion.

Chapter 1, "Creating Order and Meaning," reflects on our experiences of organizing the undifferentiated landscape of our lives. We think about how we arrange the spaces where we live and work, how we organize the times of our day and week, and how we manage our relationships. The chapter calls on us to observe how the human imagination operates within particular ecological and cultural contexts. From these experiences we forge symbolic representations of life, as we experience it in the world, and of life as we want it to be. In order to see the religious imagination at work we explore two religious texts, one a hymn from the Hindu scriptures and the other a sacred story from the Haudenosaunee (Iroquois). Each text gives a vision of how the world should be and how we should live in it. Chapter 1 proposes that we think about religions as processes for creating order and meaning in an ultimate sense, and also that we think about them as processes for learning to be human.

Chapter 2, "Religious Understandings of Life," considers responses to the power and mystery of life. The chapter begins by exploring experiences of power and mystery in two communities: among the Warlpiri people of Central Australia—an indigenous community still living in its traditional land despite a disruptive colonial history—and among Jews—a community claiming a common religious heritage but today dispersed throughout the world. Each community sustains a relationship with a particular land. The chapter ponders the role of religion in the construction of personhood and the ways in which religions understand the human condition. Building on the previous discussion of order, we examine the distinction made between sacred and profane and consider the notions of the sacred, sacred space, and sacred time.

Chapter 3, "The Study of Religion," demarcates religion as an area of culture. The chapter begins with discussion of the ideas of nature, culture, and religion. These ideas are pursued in reflecting on a Zuni ritual in which a newborn child is presented to the sun. To discuss the ritual, of which a prayer given in the text is part, we find that it is necessary to provide considerable information about Zuni culture. Using the Zuni ritual as a point of reference, we examine some of the ways scholars go about the study of religion. Since some scholars are sympathetic to religion and some are not, we explore what is necessary for scholars in both situations to produce accurate and responsible descriptions of the religious expressions they study.

We use the word "religion" in both an abstract sense and a more concrete sense. As an abstract noun, "religion" signifies a human propensity to seek order and meaning within the mystery of life. By "a religion" or "religions" we mean particular traditions (for example, Judaism, Buddhism, Christianity, Hopi religion), which in their constellations of ideas and practices provide order and meaning for their followers, connecting them to what are considered the ultimate powers of life.

Chapter 1

Creating Order and Meaning

SHAPING HUMAN EXPERIENCE

We human beings are always trying to get our lives in order. We make lists and hatch plans. In small ways and large we strive to bring harmony and significance to our individual and communal pursuits. We sort our class notes, we count our money, and arrange our bills in an order of priority for payment. Periodically we tidy our closets and check our cars. We take stock of our friendships and work on repairing those which we value that have gone awry. We organize the space in which we live and the time we have for living. We designate certain spaces and times as private and others as public. We make places to play, places to work, places to pray. We establish times to relax, times to concentrate, times to be with those we hold most dear, times to engage with what we hold sacred.

Religion, some would say, is the human recognition that there is an ultimate order and meaning within the mystery of our lives. Others would say that religion is the human impulse to create order and meaning. The American poet, Wallace Stevens (1879-1955), captures something of the latter understanding in a poem called "The Idea of Order at Key West."[1] The poem belongs in a collection, published in 1936, called *Ideas of Order.*

Stevens suggests that we construct our own worlds of meaning through the use of imagination. In that sense we are all poets composing our lives. The Greek verb *poiein,* the origin of the word "poet," means "to make, to create, to compose." Stevens describes a woman walking and singing beside the sea. She cannot exactly replicate the noise of the ocean, but she can create something which suggests or approximates it. Her voice interprets and gives meaning to her experience of the sea. She, as it were, sings a world into being. She is a maker, an artificer. The poet writes:

She was the single artificer of the world
In which she sang. And when she sang, the sea,
Whatever self it had, became the self
That was her song, for she was the maker. Then we,
As we beheld her standing there alone,
Knew that there never was a world for her
Except the one she sang and, singing, made.

The poem concludes:

Oh! Blessed rage for order, pale Ramon,
The maker's rage to order words of the sea,
Words of the fragrant portals, dimly-starred,
And of ourselves and of our origins,
In ghostlier demarcations, keener sounds.[2]

Stevens recognizes that we create or assert order; from the chaos
and mystery of our lives we shape worlds of meaning. Others say that an
ultimate order is given to us, that it is part of the structure of human reality. On the one hand many people regard God as the first maker and the
source of order, while on the other hand, some say we human beings in
our search for order and meaning have created God and other religious
conceptualizations. Regardless of whether we see order as given or created we can probably agree with Stevens that a "rage to order," or a passion to overcome chaos, is central to the human condition.

The monotheistic religious traditions of Judaism, Christianity, and
Islam have a notion of a maker—called God or Allah—who gives order
to the universe and sustains all that exists in it. In contrast to monotheism, the main philosophical tradition within Hinduism—Vedanta—postu-
lates that there is only one reality and that the individual self is identified
with the absolute and with every other individual self. The indigenous
religious traditions—the traditions of native communities closely connected to a particular environment—present the search for order and
meaning in terms of sustaining a network of relationships. The indigenous traditions recognize many manifestations of life-giving power—gods,
spirits, ancestors—each of which contributes to the order of the world.

In comparing various religious understandings of the ordering of life,
scholars refer to experiences or manifestations of the sacred. Such experiences or manifestations are understood by those reporting them to
empower the life of an individual or community. The historian of religions Mircea Eliade (1907-1986) regards the sacred as a structure of reality which is manifested in particular historical circumstances.[3] Others
would say it is not a structure of reality, a given to which human beings
respond, but a human conceptualization of ultimate value and meaning,
and that at a further distance religion is an area defined for the purposes
of study. Eliade's former colleague at the University of Chicago, J.Z.

Smith, says, for example, that religion is "a creation of the scholar's study."[4] Although scholars may differ in their interpretations of the sacred, the notion that particular objects, times, places, and experiences provide an opening to that which bestows order and meaning is almost universal. The interrelated themes of order and meaning are never far from conversations about the sacred and religion. At issue is whether order and meaning are given or are created by human beings. People seek to connect with and participate in the fundamental power of life. Thus, they either recognize or create the order of the universe. Indeed "seeing" (gaining insight, recognizing the true situation) and "making" (structuring the world through intellectual and physical work) are complementary ways of undertaking the religious quest.

In periodic rituals religious communities may create the order of the world anew. The annual **Sun Dance**s of the Plains peoples of the United States and Canada, for example, are based on the understanding that human beings have a responsibility for sustaining the natural and social world. The performance of rituals at certain points in the year and at certain points in the life cycle facilitates carrying out of that responsibility. Rituals such as the Sun Dance permit people to connect with sacred power and to make it active in the world. For Islam the order of the world is revealed by God, and the tradition encourages recitation of the words of the **Qur'an**, the holy book of Islam, in which the revelation is recorded. For **Muslims** submission to God and proper relationship to neighbors are fundamental. It is, according to Islamic insight, acceptance of Allah and his law which brings order and meaning to the world. Despite differences in religious conceptualization and expression, the conviction of most people is that order—a system of life-giving connections—is possible, that our lives are potentially meaningful, and that they connect to a larger pattern of life beyond our immediate knowing.

In creating order in our lives we produce networks of relationships which connect us to the world, to our fellow human beings, and to whatever we consider to have greatest value. Some of us are more successful than others, of course, in creating order. At one extreme are people who are obsessive about order. They seem to want order for order's sake. We all know someone who has every piece of paper in its proper drawer, every pencil in its designated compartment, and the paper clips in their appointed box. We may liken the tidy-desk fanatic to the religiously obsessive person who follows every prescription of his or her religion to the letter. At the opposite extreme to the tidy-desk person is the disorganized-desk person, whose room is in such disarray that it may take some time to find papers and pencils. This person searches among clothes and books for pen and paper when something needs to be written. We might compare the person with a disorganized desk to the person who prays when the spirit moves her, recalls a prayer learned in childhood when she is in need of help, reports an awareness of the holy or the mystery of life when a child is born, and goes to church at Christmas. In the work of ordering our lives, and in our religious observances, most of us are somewhere between the extremes. We try to establish an order which is flexible and facilitates our living to the fullest, rather than an order which is controlling and burdensome.

Tidy rooms, messy rooms, or rooms that are somewhat ordered but still comfortable? Tidy lives, messy lives, or something in between? We want enough order to give predictability and coherence to our lives. We do not want so much order that it stifles our spontaneity and restricts our possibilities. Our "rage for order" is a desire to establish conditions in which we can live fully and authentically. However, even when we get things "just right" in our rooms and our lives, something will happen to challenge the order we have established—the gift of a beautiful carving challenges us to redecorate, the departure of a dear friend obliges us to rearrange our social network, the death of a loved one negates the very notion of order.

The opposite of order is chaos. Chaos is a state of being in which chance is supreme. It is, however, a state of potentiality. In many myths of origin storytellers contrast chaos (from Greek *chaos*, "an empty space"), a confused and unorganized state of primordial matter, and cosmos (from Greek *kosmos*, "order"), an orderly and harmonious world system. The stories of our individual lives, as well as the stories of communities, are made up of an ongoing reciprocity of chaos and cosmos. At certain stages in our journey everything lies in chaos around us, a confusing and mysterious mess. Yet, the chaos offers possibilities. We can make something of it; we can bring order to it. At other stages on the way everything is under control, well organized into a tidy world, perhaps too well organized. We may feel crushed by it; we may want to destroy the order, revert to chaos, and forge a new order.

Our order is constantly shifting and sometimes even falling apart, and we are constantly realigning and reconstituting it. Sometimes we accept an order established by others. A school or college has curricula and rules established prior to the arrival of a particular class. Each new class grumbles about the order, and some even boycott classes or protest outside the dean's office to get it changed. Religions, like other institutions, are constituted of practices and ideas which, in most cases, were put in place before the present generation was born. In its own way each generation remakes the tradition, challenging the old order and prescribing a new order.

Before we venture further into considerations of what religion is and how religion functions in our lives, we shall reflect on how college students "order" their lives. The exercise below will give us some ideas about the sense of order and meaning which we try to establish in our lives. If you are not a college student, just adapt the exercise to your own circumstances; for example, reflect on how your family "orders" its life. If you wish, discuss your responses with a classmate or friend.

Thinking about a Day in the Life of . . .

A. Imagine that you are sharing a dorm room with another student. First, think about some of the things you might do over a twenty-four hour period to bring order to:

  1. YOUR SPACE. Where do you put things? Where do you carry out various activities? Is lack of space a problem? If so, how do you resolve the problem? Are some spaces in your room special? How are they special?

  2. YOUR TIME. What do you fit into the day? How do you establish priorities? What do you do when there are too many things to fit into the available time? Are some times in the day special? Which times? How are they special? Are some times in the day difficult for you? If so, how do you cope with them?

  3. YOUR RELATIONSHIPS. With whom do you talk, work, play? Who is important to you? How do you sustain relationships? When there are conflicts, how do you choose between giving attention to people and giving attention to work and study? Are some relationships special? How are they special?

B. Think about how sharing a room with someone else influences your decisions and behavior. To what extent are your plans contingent upon the cooperation of your roommate? Is having a roommate calming or disruptive? How?

C. What principles or understandings guide you in making decisions about ordering your space, your time, and your relationships? How did you acquire or develop these principles or understandings?

ORDER AND MEANING

Through the exercise above we reflected on "making order and meaning" in daily life; now we move toward a consideration of religion as a process of "making order and meaning" in the largest possible sense. We shall be thinking about religions as systems which create networks of significant relationships. As you know from your consideration of order in daily life, a good order is not just a matter of "everything in its place." A life-giving, satisfying order is a harmonious network of connections to environment and people and, perhaps, to God and/or spirits. An important dimension of such order is that it be purposeful or meaningful. Most people regard "order for the sake of order" as empty and stultifying.

There are many ways to think about religion. Some scholars attempt to define religion; that is, they try to say what religion is in its essence. Others see too many difficulties in defining religion. If I say religion is "belief in God" and/or "practices for relating to God," they would ask how I classify a tradition that does not believe in God but carries out rituals to facilitate relationships with ancestors. If such a tradition is not a religion, what is it? Perhaps I could expand my definition to say religion is "belief in superhuman beings." I would then be including those who believe in a variety of supernatural beings, but I would be excluding from the domain of religion those who recognize a powerful mystery in the universe but do not conceptualize it in terms of gods, spirits, or other superhuman beings. Scholars who place a greater emphasis on describing than on defining will recount activities and institutions that could possibly be construed as "religion." They will, for example, describe the Mid-Winter Shalako Festival of the Zuni in which energy is danced back into the dormant earth, and they will report on the Easter liturgy in which Christians celebrate the resurrection of Jesus and the hope in life despite the evidence of death. We could elaborate on each of these rituals as a process of creating order in the lives of individuals and communities and, indeed, in the life of the cosmos. These are key rituals which encapsulate the Zuni and Christian understandings of the world. Scholars who define and scholars who describe also interpret. That is, they say something about what religion does in the lives of its practitioners; they elaborate on its role in creating meaning and order.

We began by thinking about order in our daily lives. We will continue by reflecting on the role that religion plays in "ordering" human experience: we consider how religion establishes fundamental understandings and structures for individuals and communities, and how religion facilitates and inhibits people's participation in the fundamental power of life. A Christian may understand that the world is basically a good place created by God but that it is also flawed by the sinfulness of human beings. Furthermore, she or he may believe that God has sent Jesus Christ to show us how to live in the world and how to overcome sin. Hence, Christianity provides an understanding of how the world is, and it provides certain structures, including the church, sacraments, and prayer, to help a person live in the world. Thus, Christianity is a set of ideas and practices which order the Christian's life. Yet, we must remember that order can be freeing or inhibiting. A good order can facilitate participation in life; it can lead us to live authentically. A bad order can unduly restrict participation in life; it can lead to a sense of alienation. For example, some religions place control in the hands of a few and stifle the participation of the many.

In authentically proclaiming their messages, religions may create disorder. There is a prophetic side to religion which calls the established order into question and highlights values and principles by which individuals and communities should re-order their lives. We find this challenge in the prophets of the Jewish scriptures, the Tanak. The prophets protest the hypocrisy of people who claim to be followers of the Israelite God but act unjustly toward their fellow human beings. We find it in the gospels of Matthew and Luke. Looking toward the end of an age and the way that followers of Jesus should live, they portray Jesus as saying, "Do not think that I have come to bring peace on earth; I have not come to bring peace, but sword" (Mt 10:34; Lk 12:51). In chapters 8 and 9 we shall be looking at changes which occur in the lives of individuals and communities as a result of challenging the religious and social status quo.

Hindu religious texts and practices emphasize the realization of the identity between the individual self and a cosmic principle of unity called **Brahman**. According to Hindu traditions, there is a religious and moral law, called **dharma**, governing all of life. Dharma is a principle of ultimate order, and those who attune themselves to it will realize their relationship to Brahman and their mode of participation in the life of the cosmos. Sometimes translated as "duty," dharma includes the carrying out of duties related to one's class and status. The Hindu worldview imagines cycles of rebirth, which are dependent upon one's actions in previous lives. Liberation from rebirth, or **moksha**, may be obtained by following three overlapping paths. These paths, which are given different emphases in the various Hindu traditions, are: **karma** marga, the path of work (with work usually interpreted as ritual or disinterested action); **jñana** marga, the path of light (with light interpreted as true knowledge); and **bhakti** marga, the path of love (with love interpreted as devotion to the divine). Thus, Hinduism suggests that there is an ultimate order to the world and provides its devotees with paths by which to order their individual lives so that they may also participate in the larger order.

If we look on religions—such as Judaism, Christianity, Native American religions, and Buddhism—as systems which enable people to order their lives in the world in an ultimate as well as immediate sense, we have made a beginning in the study of religion and religions. We have found an element which is common to religious traditions and which enables us, for purposes of study and comparison, to group diverse traditions together. As we progress in our study we shall think about how the order proposed by religious traditions becomes institutionalized in rituals, ethical codes, myths, and doctrines. We shall think about how and why the order changes over time, and we shall consider how the order can be helpful and harmful.

In keeping our houses tidy, our work in good shape, and our friendships intact, we try to bring order to the everyday world of home, work, and social interactions. In engaging in religious actions, we try to order our lives in relation to a larger world of which we have a sense, or which our religious tradition tells us is the eventual reality. The sociologist Emile Durkheim referred to the first area of our lives as the profane and to the second as the sacred. In both areas we are makers or, to use Wallace Stevens's old-fashioned word, artificers, creating through our actions and words the world in which we want to live.

Some people say there is no need to distinguish two worlds or two kinds of ordering activities. Why not, they ask, just see the world as a material whole? Why identify some acts of ordering as religious rather than as social? In place of sacred powers they would posit material causes and would reject the nonrational and the supernatural. Such questions lead at times to the drawing of a distinct line between the proponents of science and the proponents of religion. However, the defenders of science and the defenders of religion are not necessarily opposed. For objective scientists it can be difficult to find suitable methods for studying human subjectivity and social processes. There is no laboratory experiment to prove or disprove claims concerning the sacred. However, there is a wealth of rituals and myths and doctrines, and abundant accounts of ancient and contemporary religious experience, which enable us to explore the rage for order that is part of human history.

As we interrogate the constellations of human experiences and practices which we call religions, we accept that knowledge, whether it be "religious" knowledge or "scientific" knowledge, is socially constructed. That is, knowledge results from the ways that individuals and communities choose to study and interpret evidence which is before them. For religious people, their experience of the manifestation of sacred power is taken as part of the evidence. Both practitioners of religion and practitioners of the scientific method are attempting to bring cosmos out of the confusing and often overwhelming, but nevertheless fascinating and exciting, chaos of human experience.

When we are ordering that which is near to us (room, friendships, manner of working), we are dealing with matters which we understand relatively well; when we try to order our place in the ultimate scheme of things, we are dealing with matters of which we understand relatively little, matters which stretch our imaginations. Who knows what happens after death? Who knows what power or energy gives life to the world? There is, then, a qualitative difference in the two kinds of ordering activity. Religions grapple with difficult-to-answer questions. Like science, they use reason and imagination to create models of the world. Like poetry, they employ **symbol**s to describe ultimate realities. Like dance and drama, they act out in ritual their visions of the world as it is and as it may yet be. Along the way, religions pick up folk wisdom and songs and stories, some of which contradict each other, but all of which are concerned with how people should live their lives here and now. Although the complexes of ideas and practices which we call religions differ in their particular depictions of the world and of ultimate reality, they all sustain a concern that an empowering order should prevail in our lives.

For their adherents religious traditions provide some commentary on the mystery of the universe and on how to live with it. Islam, for example, proclaims that there is no god but God (no *allah* but *Allah*) and that Muhammad is the messenger of God. Then, the revelations recorded in the Qur'an lay out a system of ethical monotheism—a system which holds that there is one God and that this God requires a certain kind of behavior from human beings. Islam insists that all human beings are children of the one God and maintains that they should, therefore, act toward others as they would toward their brothers and sisters. The teachings of Islam are summarized in the **Five Pillars**, five devotional-ritual duties with social implications. These are: 1) *Shahada*, the proclamation of faith in God as the only god and acknowledgment of Muhammad as his messenger; 2) *Salat*, five daily prayer services acknowledging one's relationship to God and the human community; 3) *Zakat*, almsgiving, the support of those in the community who are in need; 4) *Sawm*, fasting during daylight during the holy month of Ramadan; and 5) *Hajj*, pilgrimage to Mecca for those financially and physically able to make the journey. Islamic spirituality elaborates on the beauty that God has inscribed in the universe and thus provides a framework to connect everyday experience with the divine. Muslims do not have to work it all out for themselves in each generation. The Qur'an, the Pillars, the community, and the weight of tradition are there to guide them.

Islam provides an order for life, and Muslims form their children within that order. If a person born into a religious tradition is to grow into an authentic member of the tradition, he or she needs to internalize what the tradition prescribes and practices. Of course, there are various understandings of what is "authentic." One Roman Catholic may say that the church's commandment to attend Mass on Sundays and Holy Days is to be observed with exceptions only for grave causes. Another may say it is a good guideline but that attendance at Mass is only one component in one's religious observance. Such differences in interpretation lead at times to divisions in religious traditions. Moreover, members of a religious tradition may take an image or a precept literally while others may understand it symbolically. One Christian reading the first chapter of Luke's gospel may take the author's description of Mary, the mother of Jesus, as a virgin in a literal, physical sense. Another may understand it as a representation of Mary's total availability to the plans of God and a depiction of an attitude of openness which should characterize all Christians in their relationship to God's Spirit, a metaphorical rather than a literal reading.

In sacred stories and songs and in religious doctrines, our faith communities provide us with understandings of the world; in rituals and ethical guidelines, they provide us with ways to engage the world. At certain points in our lives we may want to ask whether what we have received in our tradition accords with our particular experience. We may investigate, question, and even challenge the tradition in which we were raised. For example, in recent times many Jews and Christians, both women and men, have come to ask whether their scriptures and ritual practices discriminate against women. Some will say, "I don't want to belong to a religion that makes women subservient to men." Since religion is concerned with relationships, the way a religion looks at the relationship between men and women is significant. The person who starts out saying, "I don't want to belong to a religion that makes women subservient to men," has several options in dealing with the dilemma. One option is to submit to the discipline of the tradition and compromise his or her original position. A second is to leave the **synagogue** or church. A third is to accept that religions change over time and to recognize that in our time Jews and Christians are rethinking and reformulating their understandings of sex and gender. Some people will choose to stay with a religion and become advocates of change within the tradition. Our personalities and our early socialization have some role in determining which option we choose.

MAKING METAPHORS

Human beings think with symbols. We encode our experiences in words, in gestures, in images. We craft **similes** and **metaphors**, the former—signaled by "as" or "like"—making an explicit comparison, the latter implying an identity based on sensory and mental associations. We see a bird floating in the air, and it evokes a sense of freedom; we look forward to being "as free as a bird," when chores or end-of-semester exams are done. We observe the mountains, and they evoke permanence and stability; for many religions they suggest the abode of gods. We experience the rage and chaos of the storm; it provides an image in which to capture the turmoil of life. We carve statues and compose music. We tell stories and sing songs. We use sounds and marks and images to denote and connote experiences and intuitions. In symbols we articulate experiences which defy everyday language. We mentioned above the symbolic, rather than literal, interpretation of a gospel image, suggesting that the image of a virgin evokes an understanding of openness and commitment to God. The meaning and power of symbols depend on their contexts. In the context of Luke's gospel, for example, the virginity of Mary serves as a figure of speech, a metaphor, denoting the freshness and openness the Christian should bring to his or her service of the Lord.

In the Jewish scriptures the image of marriage is used in speaking of God's faithful relationship to Israel. In everyday life we use the image in expressions like, "He's married to his work," to suggest the restrictions our commitments impose on us. Whether marriage as metaphor denotes faithful companionship, restrictive contract, or something else depends on the context in which it is presented.

Religions, we could say, are systems of symbols in which the ideals, the aspirations, and the experiences of a community are represented. The symbolic process is part of the way we think. Usually it operates at a largely unconscious level but we can become more aware of how we think with symbols by reflecting on particular symbols (e.g., a flag, the cross, the mosque, the hammer and sickle) and symbol systems (e.g., Christian baptism, the Jewish **Sabbath** service, American Thanksgiving observances, national anthems). Symbols are powerful tools that groups employ in socializing their members. Religious leaders use symbols to encourage insight, to inspire, and to foster spiritual growth. They also use symbols to induce conformity and to brainwash their followers. We are so conditioned to accept the validity of the tradition in which we are raised that it may be difficult to recognize its manipulative tendencies. While

Pilgrims at the Ganges River, India. The Ganges is pre-eminent among the sacred rivers of India.

religious symbols—such as gods and spirits, creeds and hymns, shrines and icons—are shared by groups, they are also powerful repositories of meaning for individuals. From the repertoire of symbols a religion offers its members, each person will have favorites—hymns, saints, icons, passages of scripture—which help him or her in the human work of creating order and meaning.

Symbols carry meanings. If we drink water, it sustains our physical life. If we use water to wash, we experience it as cleansing and refreshing. If it rains for a long period of time and the rivers flood, washing away our crops and our houses, we experience water as destructive. Before birth we all had the experience of the watery abode of our mothers' wombs. Think of your own best and worst experiences of water. What adjectives would you use to describe the impact of water on you at those times? When we extract the word "water" from particular contexts, it exists as a natural symbol overflowing with meanings. It has the potential to evoke a range of emotions and thoughts which are related to the qualities of water and our experiences of water. Water is a symbol which suggests life itself, fertility, cleanliness, refreshment, destruction.

Devout Hindus make pilgrimages to mountain shrines and sacred rivers. At the Ganges River in India we see pilgrims washing away impurity and throwing the ashes of the dead into the stream. They pray that through their ritual cleansing they will deepen their union with the divine. The Ganges, which is said to flow from the toe of the life-giving god, **Vishnu**, is sacred to all Hindus. Hindus approach the waters of the Ganges, dirty and smelly though they may be today, with solemnity. Their gravity is in contrast to the cheerful, undignified splashing of water in the **Holi** festival. Holi is a popular Hindu spring festival which celebrates the death of winter and the birth of spring. Its theme of new life and regeneration is presented in joyful erotic images.

In northern India the Holi festival celebrates the affection between the god **Krishna** and his beloved Radha, the wife of a cowherd who, in the epic **Mahabharata**, leaves her husband to be with Krishna. Legend says that as an infant Krishna killed a demon who was in the service of the king of winter. In some parts of India, however, the festival is dedicated to Kama, the god of sexual love. Holi includes boisterous games in which the symbolism of water is employed in welcoming the new life of spring and, for the space of the festival, dissolving the usual class distinctions. The festival plays on water's fluidity and its fertilizing qualities, as spring rain and as seminal fluid, in the continuation of life. The eroticism in the stories about Radha and in the water games of Holi is criticized by some Hindus, while others see the love between Krishna and Radha as an example of the love between the divine and the human.

The meaning which we take from the symbol of water at a particular time depends on its context. For example, in ritual washings, which in the technical language of religion are called ablutions, water suggests cleansing and renewal. The word "baptism," which comes from the Greek verb *baptizein*, "to dip, to bathe" and would translate into everyday English as "washing," has these connotations. In his letter to the Romans Saint Paul goes beyond the symbolism of cleansing and suggests that the one baptized has been drowned. In Romans 6:1-4 Paul says that the Christian has died to the old life of sin and has a new life in Jesus Christ. Paul's symbolic way of speaking of baptism as drowning is reflected in the early Christian practice of baptism by immersion, a practice that continues in some Christian communities today. The religious imagination works with water, fire, trees, and other natural symbols. It also constructs pictures, stories, and rituals to convey its understanding of the world.

The symbolic process is part of the way we think. It is essential to the creation of art and literature, to scientific breakthroughs, and to religion. The sacred narratives—the good stories which have borne the test of time and which religious traditions pass on from generation to generation—are symbolic. They speak indirectly and evocatively, presenting us with images and metaphors in which to explore the human condition. Each offers its own characteristic understanding of the person in the world and gives guidance for individual and communal life. The ritual actions which religious traditions prescribe are also symbolic. They provide ways for their members to align themselves with what the traditions suggest is the real or ultimate nature of the world. These rituals, some of which focus on events in the individual life cycle and others of which celebrate the seasons or commemorate historical events, provide experiences of participating in the fundamental power of life. In some religious traditions icons—such as statues, paintings, and masks—are part of the symbolic system and evoke the power of God, saints, and spirits. We use our capacity to connect and focus our experiences of life in symbols to construct the symbolic systems which in the European intellectual tradition are known as religions.

CULTURES AND COSMOLOGIES

Human beings organize their relationships with their environment and with each other. They create communal designs for living which social scientists call **cultures**. "Culture," a word derived from the Latin *colere*, "to till," has at least two usages. The first refers to personal refinement, the result of much tilling, which is reflected in such things as a preference for classical music over popular, an interest in fine arts and philosophy, a taste for gourmet cuisine. The second usage, which concerns us here, is that of anthropology, the discipline which is most concerned with culture as shared and learned behaviors. Whereas we are born with certain biological capacities, we learn our particular culture from our families and our social groups. One of the first American anthropologists, Ruth Benedict (1887-1948), described cultures as "patterns for living."[5] A contemporary American anthropologist, James F. Downs, defines culture as "a mental map which guides us in our relations to our surroundings and to other people."[6] In the anthropological usage rap music or reggae is just as much a part of culture as opera. And, in the anthropological sense of culture, the indigenous peoples of the South Pacific have culture, as do North Americans, Africans, and all the people of the earth.

	DIACHRONIC		
S **Y** **N** **C** **H** **R** **O** **N** **I** **C**	1985	1990	1995
	Religion	Religion	Religion
	Science	Science	Science
	Technology	Technology	Technology
	Economics	Economics	Economics
	Music	Music	Music

Diachronic and synchronic axes of culture. A diachronic view shows changes occurring over time. A synchronic view shows how the different areas of culture connect with each other at a given time.

For purposes of exploring a culture we may, as it were, freeze it in time. We may stop the clock at a particular time so that when we look at the culture at that moment we can see how our economic transactions relate to our social patterns and how our religious observances have an impact on our production of fine arts. That is, we can see how the various components of culture are affecting each other at that moment. At the same time, however, cultures are constantly changing. Even as we stop to look at the current situation, some of the actors are moving and changing the pattern. The terms "synchronic" and "diachronic" refer to these two perspectives. A synchronic perspective is like a snapshot. It looks at the various parts of a system at a particular moment in time to see how the parts work together. Social scientists often take a synchronic perspective toward culture. They study how the various components of a culture fit together—how economy influences religion and vice versa, how social structure interacts with ideology, and so on. In contrast a diachronic perspective is more like a movie than a photograph. It shows how something changes through time. In the study of Christianity, a diachronic perspective on baptism looks at the changes over time in the ways that baptism has been practiced and understood, while a synchronic perspective looks at baptism in relation to a larger network of Christian beliefs and rituals. We can see that the two perspectives are complementary, and both are needed in the study of religion. However, in the division of labor within studies in religion some scholars focus on one and some on the other.

Each culture develops within a particular ecological context and makes use of the resources of that context. Yet, cultures differ from one another not only because of the availability, or lack of availability, of certain material resources, but also because of the different ways in which human beings make choices and exercise their imaginations. Many peoples have fish available to them. For example, the Solomon Islands peoples of the South Pacific have access to abundant marine resources. Therefore, it is not surprising that seafood is an important element in their diet. Nor is it surprising that Solomon Islanders have rituals for attracting fish to their hooks and nets. What might be surprising to those of us raised in other cultures is that traditional Solomon Islands societies conceive of fish spirits and have rituals which celebrate their relationship to fish.[7] Within each Solomon Islands community some marine species are of greater significance than others. For example, the people of Auki look upon sharks as guardians who take a particular interest in their welfare.

Many indigenous cultures have ceremonies which are similar in orientation to the fish rituals of the Solomon Islanders. In these rituals people celebrate their relationship to particular animals or particular plants. Communities may use the animal or plant as food and, thus, give thanks to it for making itself available to them. Hence, Native communities of the American Pacific Northwest give thanks to the salmon and Plains people to the buffalo. Pueblo women will give thanks to the clay—neither animal nor plant, but, even so, a gift of the earth—which they gather to

MARY N. MACDONALD

Contemporary fish carving from the Solomon Islands. Traditional Solomon Islands art includes ritual items such as carved masks and decorated items ranging from small combs and hooks to large canoes.

make pots. On the other hand, communities may avoid eating an animal or plant because they regard it as an ancestor or a close relative. Hence, the people of Auki in the Solomon Islands refrain from eating shark. In both cases communities are affirming that animals and plants are part of their essential network of life.

Like Solomon Islands communities, contemporary New England societies have a good supply of fish. However, New Englanders do not think about fish as their relatives. They do not celebrate their kinship with fish. New Englanders and Solomon Islanders exercise their imaginations about fish in different ways. Nevertheless, Christian groups in New England do, like traditional Solomon Islanders, employ ritual to acknowledge the fact that their well-being depends on fish. They recognize that they have a relationship to fish, even though they experience that relationship in different ways, emotionally and intellectually, from the Solomon Islanders. They think about fish not in terms of kinship, but in terms of God's care of them through the gift of fish. New England coastal communities have ceremonies, such as the annual blessing of the fishing fleet, in which they give thanks to God for the fish. In the fishing town of Gloucester, Massachusetts, the Portuguese-American community celebrates Saint Peter's Fiesta in the last week of June. A statue of Saint Peter, who was a fisherman when he was called to follow Jesus, is carried in procession. Along with an outdoor Mass and the blessing of the fleet the festival also includes entertainment and sporting events.

Solomon Islanders and New Englanders have fish in common. They share an attitude of thankfulness for the fish. Yet, just as they have different recipes for cooking the fish, they have different rituals for celebrating their relationship to the fish. Indeed, they have different views of the way the world is constructed and the way the world works. When we speak of a people's "worldview," a term which is a translation of the German *Weltanschauung* (*Welt* = world, *anschauung* = way of viewing, perception, intuition), we are referring to their characteristic philosophy of life or ideology, their way of imaginatively ordering the world, their conceptual framework.

The Solomon Islanders have a notion of a world in which people and animals are interdependent and in which a number of ancestral spirits and land spirits influence human lives. Given their worldview, it is appropriate that they give thanks to the fish for making themselves available to human communities. Most New Englanders have a notion of a world in which God is the ultimate source of all good. Thus, for them, it is God who gives fish to people. Therefore, their rituals focus on God as the giver of the fish rather than on the relationship between people and fish. They thank God for providing the fish and ask God to help them catch the fish. Given their worldview, it is appropriate that their thanks be directed to God. The ultimate world of the New Englanders is more hierarchically structured—fish are below people and people are below God. The ultimate world of the Solomon Islanders is more communally structured—fish are relatives playing their part in the ocean of life. Culturally and religiously the two groups have created different imaginative orders. They think about their lives in the world, or "imagine" them, in different ways. In the academic study of religion we do not say that one ordering/imagining is right and the other ordering/imagining is wrong. Both are ways of understanding the world and living in the world. Both constructions are viable possibilities for human beings; both, like all symbolic constructions, have limitations.

Not all cultures have a term which corresponds exactly to the Latin-derived "religion." The Latin word *religio* had political and moral overtones. In Ancient Rome *religio* expressed proper behavior and attitudes for a Roman citizen. The Roman statesman and scholar, Marcus Tullius Cicero (106-43 B.C.E.), and the Latin church father, Caecilius Lactantius (240-320 C.E.), who is dubbed "the Christian Cicero," give different accounts of the word's origin. Cicero said it came from the verb *relegere*, "to re-read" or "to pass on." Thus, he understood religion as "tradition." Lactantius said that the word "religion" came from the verb *religare*, "to bind fast." Thus, he understood religion as that which binds people to each other and to the gods or God. Both understandings are reflected in the way we use the word "religion" today. We think of religion as a way of ordering the world which is passed on from generation to generation and also as a process for connecting people to gods or powers and to each other.

While not all cultures have a concept of religion, all cultures have at least an implicit **cosmology**, an understanding of how the universe is ordered or structured. The word "cosmology" means "an account of the world," and the term has particular usages in philosophy and astronomy in referring to the structuring of the universe. In conversations about religion "cosmology" refers to the understanding of the world's structure which is found in a culture's significant rituals and stories. For scholars of religion cosmologies are starting points for the study of human experience.

We may enter a people's cosmology through listening to their stories and observing their actions. Hopi myths and rituals, for example, tell of nine potential worlds, of which four have already been inhabited by human beings. Hopi origin stories tell of the emergence of ancestor beings from three former worlds into the fourth world, in which, by following an inner voice or song, they were able to journey to the center where they now live. The Hopi place an emphasis on right thinking, conceived of as following the inner voice, the song in one's heart. Following the song is the way to negotiate one's life in the present world, and, in times of transition, to negotiate the route from one world to another. The members of a culture have a plan of the cosmos in their heads, and, the Hopi might say, a song of the cosmos in their hearts. It reverberates in their rituals and their stories. They transmit it, with adjustments at times, from generation to generation. In fact, a culture may have a number of variant cosmologies, and groups within the culture may understand the generally accepted cosmology in different ways.

Cosmologies are encoded in traditional narratives and rituals. They are also present, implicitly or explicitly, in scientific texts, philosophical treatises, and theological documents. They have their echoes in folk wisdom, in cultural mores, in etiquette. All cultures have their oral, and some their written, "texts," in which accounts of the physical and moral structure of the world are inscribed. All cultures employ rituals, scripted symbolic behaviors which echo and re-create the structure of the world and point to what the culture considers to be life-giving and ultimately significant.

EXPERIENCE AND IMAGINATION

People talk a lot about beginnings. We recall our first days in school, our first jobs, our first meetings with those who became our dear friends. We ask, "How did this custom begin?" "Who built this city?" "From where did these people come?" Sometimes our questions become more profound and we wonder, "Who or what started it all?" "How did human beings come to be such bundles of creativity and fragility?" However, we do not all frame our questions in the same way, and even those who do, arrive at different answers. The various peoples of the world have their own stories about why human beings and the world are the way they are. Like Spider Grandmother, a creator and storyteller in Hopi mythology, they have spun stories, which they project back to "the beginning." By placing the human situation in some ultimate perspective, these stories of beginnings assist people in thinking about their lives now. Perhaps you are familiar with the biblical accounts in Genesis 1-2 in which God creates the world. There are, in fact, two discrete creation accounts in Genesis, which differ in their presentations. What they share is the outlook that there is an ultimate being and source, existing before everything else, from which all creation receives the gift of life. These accounts will be discussed in detail in chapter 7.

We shall look now at two contrasting accounts which describe the shaping and ordering of the world in the beginning. Even as they tell of beginnings, such accounts are powerful in the here and now. At the same time as they encode traditional cosmologies, they prescribe how people should live. They can be a source of meaning and guidance; they can also be a source of frustration and alienation. In one account, a later hymn of the Hindu **Rig Veda**, a primeval being, *Purusa Sukta* (first person), is sacrificed and dismembered. From the many parts of his body come the various parts of the cosmos and of social life. The image of the one cut into the many gives us a monistic view of the world. Monism is the doctrine that all is one; monism denies the duality of matter and mind.

The other account comes from the **Haudenosaunee** or Iroquois. "Haudenosaunee," meaning "People of the Longhouse," is the name which the Six Confederate Nations of Mohawk, Oneida, Onondaga, Cayuga, Seneca, and Tuscarora give themselves. They think of their confederacy as a large house in which each nation occupies its allocated place. "Iroquois" is the term used by the French for the members of the confederacy. In the Haudenosaunee[8] story of the beginnings of life on earth, the curiosity of a woman sets in motion a train of events which leads to her grandchildren, Left-Handed-Twin and Right-Handed-Twin, shaping a physical and social world which contains both harmony and competition. Some say that the worldview of the Haudenosaunee account is dualistic, since it tells us that in the world, and in ourselves, we find two competing principles—straight-minded and crooked-minded—and suggests the importance of the straight mind overcoming the crooked. However, lest we oversimplify, the story also suggests that the world was shaped and continues in existence through the interaction of straight and crooked.

Before reading the two accounts we shall venture briefly into the culture and history of the peoples to whom they belong. As you read the accounts, ask yourself what insight each gives into the human condition. Although one is a Hindu story and one is a Haudenosaunee story, both have something to say to all of us because both are stories about our human condition. Both answer the question, "How did we come to be like this?" and both give guidance as to how we are to live here and now. In entering into the worlds of the stories we find differences of time and culture, yet we also find perspectives on the human situation which apply to our own lives.

THE ARYANS AND VEDIC RELIGION

The Rig Veda[9] is a collection of 1,028 hymns which was made between approximately 1200 and 900 B.C.E.[10] The hymns are written in an archaic dialect of Sanskrit and are ascribed to various seers. The Sanskrit word *veda* means "sacred knowledge" or "wisdom." It is derived from the same Indo-European root as the English words "wit" and "wisdom." *Rig* is a transliteration of the Sanskrit word for "praise." Hence, this is a collection of hymns of praise and wisdom. The Rig Veda is the oldest of four Vedas which belong to the Vedic religion which preceded Hinduism. They have become part of the scriptures of Hinduism. The Vedas were the sacred hymns of invaders who entered the northwest of India from Persia around the middle of the second millennium B.C.E. The invaders called themselves Aryans or "lords." The Indo-European languages of South Asia descend from their language which is also called Aryan.[11]

Literary and archaeological evidence suggest that the religion of the Aryans included rituals in which a drink prepared from the *soma* plant was offered to the gods and consumed by worshipers, sacrifices in which food and animal offerings were made to the gods, and the recitation of hymns. The chief priest would draw material from the Rig Veda for his recitations. In time the Vedic religion of the newcomers merged with indigenous Indian traditions to produce a variety of practices and ideas which we speak of collectively as "Hinduism." For Hinduism the Vedas constitute that which was heard, and thus revealed, in the beginning. The Vedas are the basis of Hindu religious authority although the commentaries written upon them offer a wide variety of interpretations. The Vedas were transmitted by oral recitation, being passed from teacher to student, for more than two thousand years. Then over a period of several hundred years they were written down, so that by the fifteenth or sixteenth century C.E., the Sanskrit text as we know it today had been established.

The Rig Veda has several hymns which describe the shaping of the world. Some of the older hymns present the creation of the world as the result of a cosmic battle, while other hymns—including the one given below, "Purusa Sukta" (Hymn 90 from Book 10)—show the world and the people in it being brought into being through a process of sacrifice. A hymn from the Chandogya Upanishad, a philosophical part of the Vedas, which we shall explore in chapter 6, employs the metaphor of an egg hatching. In "Purusa Sukta," which is sometimes referred to as the Hymn of Man, the gods cut up the primal person and, from the parts of his body, shape the physical and social world. This is one of the later hymns of the Rig Veda and the only one in which the four social classes or castes are mentioned (v. 12). Creation by dismemberment is a common theme in Indo-European mythology. The cutting up of Purusa Sukta produces four castes. The mouth becomes the priests (the Brahmin caste) with the duty of speaking to the gods; the arms become the warrior caste; the thighs become the farmers and tradespeople; and the feet on which all else rests become the laborers.

PURUSA SUKTA: A HYMN OF PRAISE

1. A thousand heads hath Purusa, a thousand eyes, a thousand feet.
On every side pervading earth he fills a space ten fingers wide.
2. This Purusa is all that yet hath been and all that is to be;
The Lord of Immortality which waxes greater still by food.
3. So mighty is his greatness; yea, greater than this is Purusa. All creatures are one-fourth of him, three-fourths eternal life in heaven.
4. With three-fourths Purusa went up: one-fourth of him again was here.
Thence he strode out to every side over what eats not and what eats.
5. From him Viraj was born; again Purusa from Viraj was born.
As soon as he was born he spread eastward and westward o'er the earth.
6. When Gods prepared the sacrifice with Purusa as their offering,
Its oil was spring, the holy gift was autumn; summer was the wood.
7. They balmed as victim on the grass Purusa born in earliest time. With him the Deities and all Sadhyas and Rsis sacrificed.
8. From that great general sacrifice the dripping fat was gathered up. He formed the creatures of the air, animals both wild and tame.
9. From that great general sacrifice Rcas and Sama-hymns were born: Therefrom were spells and charms produced; the Yajus had its birth from it.
10. From it were horses born, from it all cattle with two rows of teeth: From it were generated kine, from it the goats and sheep were born.
11. When they divided Purusa how many portions did they make?
What do they call his mouth, his arms?
What do they call his thighs and feet?
12. The Brahman was his mouth, of both his arms was the Rajanya made. His thighs became the Vaisya, from his feet the Sudra was produced.
13. The Moon was gendered from his mind and from his eye the Sun had birth;
Indra and Agni from his mouth were born, and Vayu from his breath.
14. Forth from his navel came mid-air; the sky was fashioned from his head;
Earth from his feet, and from his ear the regions. Thus they formed the worlds.
15. Seven fencing-sticks had he, thrice seven layers of fuel were prepared, When the Gods, offering sacrifice, bound as their victim, Purusa.
16. Gods, sacrificing, sacrificed the victim: these were the earliest holy ordinances. The Mighty Ones attained the height of heaven, there where the Sadhyas, Gods of old, are dwelling.

(Rig Veda 10:90)[12]

> In order to follow the process of world formation which the hymn describes, several terms need explanation. *Viraj* (v. 5) is the female principle of creativity; *sadhyas* (v. 7) are demigods; *rsis* (v. 7) are wisdom teachers; *rcas* (v. 9) are verses; *sama*-hymns (v. 9) are chants. *yajus* (v. 9) are verse meters; the *rajanya* (v. 12) is the warrior caste, also called *kshatriya*; the *vaisya*, or *vaishya*, (v. 12) is the caste engaged in business and agriculture; the *sudra* (v. 12) is the caste of laborers; *Vayu* (v. 13) is the wind; *Indra* (v. 13) is the Aryan god of war and storm; and *Agni* (v. 13) is the fire god of Vedic times. In ritual, Agni takes the form of sacrificial fire and mediates between gods and men. He is particularly concerned with order and ritual.

THE HAUDENOSAUNEE AND LONGHOUSE RELIGION

The second account, a Haudenosaunee narrative, is still passed on in oral form from generation to generation. For hundreds of years the five original nations of the Haudenosaunee—the Mohawk, Oneida, Onondaga, Cayuga, and Seneca—have occupied separate territories in New York State and Canada. Today the Oneida also have territory in Wisconsin. At some stage prior to European settlement, the five nations formed a confederacy. The Tuscarora joined later to make what we now refer to as the Six Nations. A confederacy narrative tells that warfare was a way of life among the five nations. According to this story it took the efforts of a peace maker, Deganawidah, who came from the Huron people to the north, and an Onondaga chief, Hayenwatha (Hiawatha), to establish peace among them. Deganawidah is so revered that many today will not pronounce his name. The confederacy strengthened the nations against outside enemies and encouraged peace among themselves.

Traditionally the Haudenosaunee were agricultural and hunting people. Therefore, their ritual cycle is related to the seasonal cycle of crops and game. For example, in the summer, after the corn, beans, and squash are ripe, they hold the Green Corn Festival to rejoice and give thanks. In winter, after hunting is over for the year, they hold their New Year or Mid-Winter Festival, a celebration which emphasizes cleansing and new life. The Haudenosaunee creation account, confederacy narrative, and thanksgiving address complement each other, each echoing themes of right-mindedness, thankfulness, competition, and balance.

In the time since European contact, more than forty versions of the Haudenosaunee creation story have been written down in English. The following account is based on them, particularly on a version composed by Hazel Hertzberg. When a story is transmitted orally, the storyteller is able to accommodate the basic story to the circumstances of the community for whom it is told. Knowing the situation of the audience, the storyteller may, for example, highlight points which are pertinent for them at the time the story is told. It is not surprising that so many written versions of the Haudenosaunee story may be found, since those who wrote them down heard the story told for different communities by different storytellers. Thousands upon thousands of tellings of the story have resided not on written pages, but in the lives of those who heard them and used them as a framework for thinking about our situation as human beings in the world.

SHAPING THE WORLD: A HAUDENOSAUNEE STORY

In the beginning, in the Sky World, lived a husband and wife. The wife was expecting a child and craved various delicacies as pregnant women are wont to do. Her husband was kept busy fetching them for her. In the middle of the Sky World grew a Great Tree with huge roots and many branches. Those who lived in the Sky World were not permitted to take leaves or wood from the tree or to injure it in any way. The woman wanted some of the bark from one of the roots of the Great Tree, but her husband was reluctant to take it. Eventually he gave in to his wife's desire and scraped away some soil to bare the root. In fact, the floor of the Sky World was not very deep and he made a hole, which revealed an empty space beneath. He was afraid and would not take any of the root.

The woman was curious. She looked down through the hole and saw the ocean. Then, she fell. Perhaps she slipped. Perhaps her husband pushed her. As she fell she grasped at the edges of the hole and pulled away bits of the small roots of the tree and parts of the things growing in the soil under the tree. When the birds saw the woman falling, some of them came to her aid and, flying wingtip to wingtip, made a raft to support her. Other birds flew down to the ocean and called to the ocean creatures for help. The great sea turtle agreed to receive her on his back and, so, the birds placed her there.

The woman wanted to plant the bits of root and plant material which she had brought from the Sky World. The diving birds and animals took it in turns to dive down into the ocean to see if they could find some soil which could be placed on the turtle's back to enable the woman to plant the things from the Sky World. Finally the muskrat was successful but he was completely out of breath and almost dead when he emerged from the ocean. They hoisted him up onto the turtle's back, sang and prayed over him, and breathed air into his mouth until he recovered. The woman took the soil and placed it in the middle of the turtle's back. Then she walked around in a circle, moving in the direction that the sun goes. This is still the direction for dance rituals. The soil spread out, and the earth grew until it was big enough for her to plant the roots she had brought from the Sky World. These grew and thus we have plants in the Earth World.

The woman who had fallen from the sky was after some time delivered of a daughter. The child knew nothing of the Sky World, but she knew the animals and birds and ocean creatures who had helped her mother. One day, after the girl had grown up, a man appeared. Some say he was the West Wind and had been sent from the Sky World. The girl was so surprised to see him that she fainted. The man lay two arrows across her body, one sharp and one blunt. When the girl awoke she continued, as before, to walk with her mother around the earth which had been formed on the turtle's back. Soon it became clear that she was pregnant. In fact, she was pregnant with twins.

While still in their mother's womb, the twins began to quarrel. They even argued about the way they should be born. The right-handed twin wanted to be born in the usual way that babies are born, emerging through his mother's birth canal. The left-handed twin said he could see light in the opposite direction and wanted to go that way. He could not be born through his mother's mouth or nose, but he forced himself out through her left armpit and killed her in the process. When Right-Handed Twin, who had been born in the normal way, saw what had happened, he accused Left-Handed Twin of murdering their mother. However, their grandmother, who tended to favor Left-Handed Twin, told them to stop arguing. They buried the woman, who now is referred to as "Our Mother," and "Corn Mother." From her grave grew the staple foods of the Haudenosaunee. From her head grew corn, beans, and squash, which are referred to as "Our Supporters, the Three Sisters." From her heart grew sacred tobacco, which is used in ceremonies to send messages and thanks to the Sky World.

The two brothers represented two different ways of living in the world, and they were always competing with each other. Right-Handed Twin always told the truth and always did things in a reasonable way. Left-Handed Twin lied and did things in unusual ways. Right-Handed Twin, people say, had the straight mind, and Left-handed Twin had the crooked mind. The brothers shaped the world as we know it now. They took clay and molded it into animals. Right-Handed Twin made the deer, and Left-Handed Twin made the mountain lion which kills the deer. Then Right-Handed Twin made the ground squirrel, which was able to dig a hole and get away from the mountain lion. Left-Handed Twin responded by making the weasel, which is able to pursue the ground squirrel into its hole. Right-Handed Twin then made the porcupine, and, of course, the weasel could not kill it. However, Left-Handed Twin made the bear, and the bear was not afraid to flip the porcupine over on its back and tear out its stomach.

Just as Right-Handed Twin and Left-Handed Twin competed with each other in making animals, so they competed with each other in making plants. Right-Handed Twin made fruits and berries which the animals could eat. Left-Handed Twin made plants with thorns and poisons, and he made medicines, some for healing and some for harming. Right-Handed Twin made human beings and, therefore, he is called "Our Creator," and "The Master of Life." However, it is said that Left-Handed Twin also had some part in this creation, and it is he who is responsible for the rituals of sorcery and healing. Together the twins built a world which embraced both competition and cooperation. Even when they were adults they still argued with each other. Eventually their arguments led to a series of contests and to the departure of both of them from the world they had shaped.

First they gambled. They took wild plum pits which they had burnt on one side, so that they were white on one side and black on the other, and tossed them in a bowl to see how they would fall. In this way they gambled all day, but neither was the winner. Then they played lacrosse all day, but neither was the winner. Then they fought with clubs, but neither won. Each knew deep in his mind that he had a weak point. They talked about this as they dueled and the deep mind of each entered into the deep mind of the other. However, the deep mind of Right-Handed Twin lied to his brother while the deep mind of Left-Handed Twin told the truth. Finally they both knew that Right-Handed Twin would vanquish Left-Handed Twin and so it was. Left-Handed Twin took a stick for the final contest. Right-Handed Twin took a deer antler. With one touch of the deer antler he destroyed his brother and threw his body off the edge of the earth. Left-Handed Twin now lives somewhere off the edge of the world. People say that the day is the domain of Right-Handed Twin and night the domain of Left-Handed Twin.

After killing his brother, Right-Handed Twin went home to Grandmother. She was angry over what he had done and said he was a murderer. He told her she had always favored Left-Handed Twin, and in his fury he cut off her head. He threw her body into the ocean and her head into the sky where still she keeps watch. People call her, "Our Grandmother, the Moon." Today Right-Handed Twin lives in the Sky World. People burn sacred tobacco in order to honor him and to send thanks to him. Left-Handed Twin lives in the world below. At Mid-Winter and other festivals, the day is dedicated to rituals honoring Right-Handed Twin, and the night is given to social activities, to feasting and singing and dancing under the auspices of Left-Handed Twin. Thus, the balance the twins built into the world is reflected in the structure of rituals even today.

Thinking with Stories

Storytelling and ritual performance provide opportunities to think about our situation in the world. We might even say that storytelling and ritual performance are ways of thinking, because they tell or enact possible ways of understanding ourselves and our world. They provide models with which, or against which, we can test our experience. In telling of beginnings the Vedic hymn and the Haudenosaunee story call on us to think about our life in the world here and now.

1. Summarize the cosmology (account of the world's structure) to be found in the Vedic hymn and the Haudenosaunee story.
2. What does each account suggest about social order?
3. What does each account suggest about the power of life?
4. Religious rituals and texts contribute some insight into the human situation and raise issues for further reflection. What insights do the Vedic and Haudenosaunee accounts provide for you? What issues do they raise?

Each of us makes his or her own world within—and sometimes against—the cultural pattern that our forebears transmitted to us. We inherit religious images, such as those in the Vedic Purusa hymn and the Haudenosaunee creation account. These images help us to shape our human experiences and to reassure ourselves that they have meaning. These images are so influential that most of the time we take them for granted. However, in studying religion our task is to move beyond the attitude of "taken for grantedness" and to ask what understandings of life are embodied in religious conceptualizations and practices.

RESOURCES

Activities

1. Divide the members of your class into several groups, and ask each group to watch one of the episodes in the PBS series, "The Wisdom of Faith with Huston Smith." Have each group report on the worldview, symbols, and values of the tradition(s) being discussed. How does Huston Smith approach traditions other than his own? (You could modify this exercise for use with the *Long Search* series or other documentaries, or you could make use of library resources to prepare reports on the worldview, symbols and values of selected traditions.)

2. Divide into several groups, and have each group prepare a thumbnail sketch of the search for order and meaning as it is exemplified in the following traditions (or traditions of your choice): Hopi religion, Dogon religion, Hinduism, Buddhism, Judaism, Islam, Christianity, Sikhism, Shinto, Confucianism.

3. a. Join an Internet list in which people discuss religious issues. What is the focus of the list you joined? What ideas about religion and human experience are expressed by those posting messages to the list? Do the discussants have a positive or negative attitude toward religion? How is this manifested?
   b. Visit Web sites which provide material on a religious issue in which you are interested. What resources did the sites provide? In making use of the Internet, as in making use of a library, one cannot take information at face value. It is necessary to establish the qualifications of the person providing information and to check the information against other sources.

4. Make use of your library to:
   a. Find out more about Vedic religion and its relationship to modern Hinduism.
   b. Find out more about present-day Haudenosaunee religion.

5. Choose a poem which you consider to have a religious theme. Discuss the symbols in the poem and the messages which it conveys.

6. Choose a natural symbol (water, fire, tree, mountain, animal, fish). Find out how the symbol has been used in secular and religious contexts (in literature, art, ritual, etc.). Then with other students prepare a multimedia presentation on the symbol.

Readings

The Bible. Since biblical texts are referred to throughout *Introduction to the Study of Religion* it would be useful to have a Bible at hand while reading the book. For example, when reflecting on the creation stories, one could turn to the Book of Genesis. *The New Oxford Annotated Bible with the Apocrypha* (New York: Oxford University Press, 1991) would be a good choice. It employs the New Revised Standard Version translation (NRSV), gives an introduction to each of the books of the Bible, and provides notes to the text. Another suitable edition would be *The Catholic Study Bible* (New York: Oxford University Press, 1990) which uses the New American Bible translation.

Paula Cooey, William R. Eakin, and Jay B. McDaniel, eds. *After Patriarchy: Feminist Transformations of the World Religions*. Maryknoll, NY: Orbis, 1991. The contributors grapple with the possibilities and problems of developing religious communities which transcend sexism.

Frederick M. Denny. *Islam and the Muslim Community*. San Francisco: Harper and Row, 1987. A short, comprehensive introduction to Islamic doctrine, institutions, and spiritual practices, and to the diversity of the Muslim community.

Mircea Eliade, ed. *The Encyclopedia of Religion*. New York: Macmillan, 1987. This encyclopedia, the most complete and up-to-date encyclopedia on religion available in English, is a good starting point for research on particular topics in religious studies.

Mircea Eliade. *The Sacred and the Profane: The Nature of Religion*. New York: Harcourt, Brace & World, 1959. A classic introduction to the history of religion, this book delineates the idea of the sacred in several cultures.

David M. Knipe. *Hinduism: Experiments in the Sacred*. San Francisco: Harper San Francisco, 1991. A general introduction to Hinduism which introduces the main religious concepts and the diversity of Hindu practice.

Adrienne Salinger. *In My Room: Teenagers in Their Bedrooms*. San Francisco: Chronicle Books, 1995. Through photographing forty-three teenagers from New York state in their bedrooms, Adrienne Salinger produces impressions of the order and disorder of their lives. Each full-page color photograph is accompanied by an extract from Salinger's interview with the teenager.

Huston Smith. *The World's Religions*. San Francisco: Harper, 1991. This is a revised and updated edition of Smith's 1958 classic, *The Religions of Man*. He presents Hinduism, Buddhism, Confucianism, Taoism, Islam, Judaism, Christianity, and Primal Religions. An illustrated version is available.

Jonathan Z. Smith. *Imagining Religion: From Babylon to Jonestown*. Chicago: University of Chicago Press, 1982. In a series of essays on various expressions of religion, Smith makes a case that religion be seen not as the result of divine intervention in human affairs but as a product of the geographically and historically located human imagination.

Elisabeth Tooker, ed. *Native North American Spirituality of the Eastern Woodlands*. New York: Paulist Press, 1979. This volume makes available texts of myths, dreams, visions, speeches, healing formulas, rituals, and ceremonies of native peoples of the Eastern Woodlands of North America. It includes a chapter on Iroquois ceremonies.

Audiovisuals

The Image Bank for Teaching World Religions. The Image Bank is a collection of annotated slides prepared as a resource for teachers. A computerized index to the Image Bank Collection may be ordered from The Center for the Study of Religions, Harvard University, 42 Francis Street, Cambridge, MA 02138. Individual slides or the whole set may also be ordered.

Image Bank slides suitable for use with chapter 1 include:

The Hindu Holi Festival (Slides 0491-0514),

Christian Baptism (Slides 0866-0868 on lake baptism; Slides 0870-0874 on baptism by immersion),

Dakota Sun Dance Paintings by Short Bull (Slides 3700-3701),

Blessing of the Whale Boats (Slides 2644-2645).

Hinduism: 330 Million Gods. Commentator Ronald Eyre. London: BBC, 1979. An episode in the *Long Search* series in which the commentator, with the help of an Indian tourist guide/pundit, a British-educated religious studies scholar, a sanyasi (renouncer), and various other people, explores the idea of the divine in India. The *Long Search* series comprises thirteen episodes on the religious traditions of the world. Although it is a little dated, the series does a good job of introducing the diversity of religions.

The Wisdom of Faith with Huston Smith: A Bill Moyers Special. PBS, 1996. Available from Films for the Humanities and Sciences, P.O. Box 2053, Princeton, NJ 08543-2053.

Huston Smith, the son of American missionary parents, was born and grew up in China. He has devoted his life to the study and practice of religion. In five one-hour programs, each presented with art, architecture, music, and poetry from the traditions being presented, Smith discusses the wisdom which humankind embodies in its religions. The programs are: I. Hinduism and Buddhism, II. Confucianism and Yoga, III. Christianity and Judaism, IV. Islam and Sufi Mysticism, V. A Personal Faith: Religions as Windows on Truth.

NOTES

1. From *Collected Poems* by Wallace Stevens. Copyright 1936 by Wallace Stevens and renewed 1964 by Holly Stevens. Reprinted by permission of Alfred A. Knopf, Inc.

2. Stevens, 129-130.

3. Mircea Eliade, *The Sacred and the Profane: The Nature of Religion* (New York: Harcourt, Brace & World, 1959).

4. Jonathan Z. Smith, *Map Is Not Territory* (Leiden: Brill, 1978).

5. Ruth Benedict, *Patterns of Culture* (Boston: Houghton Mifflin, 1934).

6. James F. Downs, *Cultures in Crisis* (Beverly Hills: Glenco Press, 1971), 35.

7. On Solomon Islands societies see Raymond Firth, *We, the Tikopia* (London: Allen and Unwin, 1936); Ian Hogbin, *A Guadalcanal Society: The Kaoka Speakers* (New York: Holt, Rinehart and Winston, 1965); Roger Keesing, *Kwaio Religion: The Living and the Dead in a Solomon Islands Society* (New York: Columbia University Press, 1982). Hogbin's chapter on religion includes a discussion of shark spirits and fishing rituals.

8. For further information on the Haudenosaunee see Hazel W. Hertzberg, *The Great Tree and the Longhouse: The Culture of the Iroquois* (New York: Macmillan, 1966); Dean R. Snow, *Iroquois* (Cambridge, MA: Blackwell, 1994); Elisabeth Tooker, *The Iroquois Ceremonial of Midwinter* (Syracuse: Syracuse University Press, 1970); Elisabeth Tooker, ed., *An Iroquois Source Book*, 3 vols. (New York: Garland Publishers, 1985-86); Anthony F.C. Wallace, *The Death and Rebirth of the Seneca* (New York: Knopf, 1970).

9. For background and commentary see Wendy D. O'Flaherty, *The Rig Veda: An Anthology* (Harmondsworth: Penguin, 1981); Ralph T.H. Griffith, trans., *The Rig Veda*, in *Sacred Writings*, ed. by Jaroslav Pelikan (Delhi: Motilal Banarsidass, 1992).

10. It is usual in religious studies today to use C.E. (common era) to designate years which in the past were given as A.D. (anno Domini = in the year of Our Lord) and B.C.E. (before the common era) to designate years which in the previous nomenclature were given as B.C. (before Christ). The use of C.E. and B.C.E. recognizes that the Gregorian calendar is in general use, but does not privilege it on religious grounds over other calendar systems, such

as the Muslim calendar which is used by most Arab countries, and the Hindu and Jewish calendars which are used for religious purposes.

11. In the nineteenth century the term Aryan came to be used synonymously with "Indo-European." The French diplomat and ethnologist Comte Joseph Arthur de Gobineau (1816-1882) spread the idea that those who spoke Indo-European languages were superior to "Semites," "yellows," and "blacks." Among de Gobineau's followers the Germanic peoples came to be seen as the purest Aryans. Although the idea of an Aryan race was discredited by anthropologists, it was taken up by Adolph Hitler and the Nazis as the basis of their policies for disposing of non-Aryans.

12. The translation of the *Rig Veda* by Ralph T.H. Griffith (1826–1906) is used here. Griffith prepared a complete translation of the *Rig Veda* and it has appeared in several editions, including Volume 6 of the *Sacred Writings,* edited by Jaroslav Pelikan (New York: Book-of-the-Month Club, 1992). A contemporary translation of the "Purusa Sukta" hymn by Wendy Doniger is published in *The Rig Veda: An Anthology* (Harmondsworth and New York: Penguin Books, 1981).

Chapter 2

Religious Understandings of Life

THE POWER OF LIFE

Human beings desire life and, yet, they suffer diminishments of life, and they experience death. Religious communities grapple in their teachings and practices with the paradox of life and death. Religions express the human desire to understand and to engage the power of life. They speak of the power of life in terms of the sacred, the holy, the transcendent, the absolute, the good, the beautiful, the true, the energy to effect change. The religious imagination gives the power of life location and character. The Aztec look to the heavens from whence the sun and the rain send their warmth and moisture to the earth. Confucianists, Shintoists, and many indigenous communities turn to ancestors, to whom we are in debt for both biological and cultural life, to give them wisdom and strength. The Plains peoples of North America imagine the power of life to be dispersed throughout nature. Theists see it centered in a God or gods. Zen Buddhism teaches that we can experience the real power of life by living intensely in the present.

Conceptualizations of life-giving power and of power which is inimical to life differ, but there is an understanding common to religious communities that we are part of a powerful mystery of life. Religious texts speak of that mystery and what they deem to be appropriate responses to it; they also struggle with the facts of illness and suffering. Religious rituals provide opportunities to connect with the mystery and commit to living in accord with it; they grant absolution to sinners and afford solace for those who suffer a weakening of their own life or the loss of loved ones.

The symbolic formulations in which communities capture a sense of the power and mystery of life suggest that there is something "more" than the world that we know through our five senses. Religious words and actions and images bear a surplus of meaning and feeling, which points to the "more." Just as individuals and communities conceive of life and the ultimate power of life in various ways, so they devise various ritual ways to tap into the power of life. For example, the **Aborigines** of the Central Desert of Australia understand that their world was shaped by ancestors in the beginning time. They have daily, seasonal, and life-cycle rituals to link them to the originating time/space and to continue its empowering processes in the here and now. In contrast to the Australian Aboriginal representation of life-giving power, Jews conceive of a God who dwells in a realm apart but graciously intervenes in the history of his people. In their annual **Passover** ritual Jews stand with their ancestors and celebrate God's power and love in freeing them from Egypt long ago and continuing to free them from whatever inhibits their life today. They too have daily, seasonal, and life-cycle rituals which, above all, connect them to God and the orienting events in their history.

In this chapter we explore understandings encoded in an Aboriginal initiation story and in the Jewish Passover Seder ritual. Both the Warlpiri story of the Aborigines and the texts and actions which comprise the Passover Seder suggest that life is good and blessed and that human beings participate in the fundamental power of life. A dialogue of the two accounts uncovers areas of commonality and difference. Such a dialogue reveals that the Central Desert peoples of Australia and the Jewish community, with its origins in the Middle East but spread today throughout the world, have ideas about relationship to land which shape their religious experience. In the search for an ultimate order and meaning the communities think with similar and with different images. Both focus on land, although they conceive of it in different ways. The Jewish community tells of a God who chose them and established them in a particular land. The Warlpiri community of Central Australia tells of kangaroo ancestors who traced out the boundaries of the land in whose life they participate. Both communities seek to develop appropriate relationships with what they understand to be the fundamental power of life.

Even as human beings seek life, they experience suffering, evil, and death. On the surface of it we say that sickness, hunger, aging, loneliness, and grief diminish life. We say that children should not be tortured and murdered. We say that all people should have food and shelter. Yet things are not the way we want them to be. Since religions purport to provide frames of reference to give human experience purpose and meaning, suffering and death put them to the test. Buddhism addresses the test by asserting that suffering is an intrinsic structure of transitory existence. The point with which the Buddha begins his discourse on life is the universality of suffering. From the fact of suffering the Buddha moves to an analysis of its causes (desire and ignorance) and to the prescription of a path which will lead to nonattachment and wisdom. For the theistic religions suffering raises the problem of theodicy: of reconciling the existence of evil with a God who is held to be all-powerful, all-knowing, and all-good.

Religions suggest that this world of the senses, with all its unsatisfactory aspects, is not all that there is. They propose that we are in some way presently alienated from ultimate reality. Some religions teach that death is a path to true life. As individuals we may refuse to recognize the inevitability of death in our own case (most of us recognize it in general), we may resign ourselves to it, or we may accept it willingly. Our attitude is often governed by our religious formation. The images that a religious community employs in setting life and death within a larger design may seem unusual, or strange and confusing, to outsiders. However, we can uncover something of their import if we take the time to reflect on these images in their historical and cultural contexts.

LAND IN WARLPIRI EXPERIENCE

The Warlpiri (Walbiri) of Central Australia understand that they belong to the land, and for them the land is imbued with sacred power. The Warlpiri tell of ancestors who in the original space/time traveled from place to place, shaping the land and establishing the laws by which people would live. Some of the ancestors of whom they tell have animal forms, and some have plant forms. The power of the founding ancestors is still available to people through the telling of their stories and the performance of rituals which replicate their actions of long ago. The Warlpiri do not talk about "religion," but they talk about the original shaping work of the ancestors and of their ongoing work in molding the land and community. The term **hierophany** is used in religious studies to refer to appearances of the sacred. In the Warlpiri case songs, journeys, dances, dreams, paintings, rituals, storytelling, and places where the ancestors stopped on their mythic journeys are all opportunities for hierophany. They are occasions for people to participate more intensely in their myth history and to experience the power of a sacred geography.

Jukurrpa, the term the Warlpiri use in speaking of the journeys of their ancestors and also in claiming their connection to the path taken by the ancestors, is usually translated as "dreaming." Each person has his or her own dreamings, inherited from both mother's and father's sides of the family. Notice that the story is about two kangaroos, not one, and that the storyteller speaks of them affectionately as "my two kangaroos." Dreamings are mental and emotional maps which situate the person in relationship to the ancestors, to other people, and to the land. The story of the Two Kangaroos is a male **initiation** myth which is told in a simple form to children and in a more detailed form to candidates for initiation. Notice the humor in the transformation of the small rat-like animal into a noble kangaroo. What happens in the story is comparable to what happens in all our lives. We start out as puny rat-like creatures focused on our own needs, but through the care and instruction of our elders, we grow physically into adults and socially into citizens. Notice also that the tale has been transcribed and translated from an oral account. Hence, we need to imagine the storyteller, with his gestures and pauses and emotional overtones, and the audience, for whom the territory through which the characters journey is home.

The Warlpiri story tells of kangaroo ancestors who marked out the territory of the storyteller's dreamings, brought water places (soaks or soakages) into being, planted fruit-bearing shrubs, and gave people the songs to use for initiations. The power of the ancestral figures is, in Warlpiri conceptualizations, embedded in the landscape. Providing water, the condition of physical life, in the desert country of Central Australia is regarded as the work of powerful and benevolent beings. The two kangaroos, however, give not only physical life but also the ritual means to produce social life. Traces of their journey are to be found in the landscape, and rituals are carried out at places where they stopped along the way. Those who follow their tracks invoke their power for the here and now.

The account which follows was narrated in 1990 by Henry Cook Jakamarra.[1] Read the story as though you were the storyteller telling of your heroes, punctuating the story with gestures, and outlining the kangaroos' journey with marks in the desert sand. Since the context of the story is most likely unfamiliar, you might need to read it a few times. Remember that the story is about land and initiation—about the Warlpiri association with a particular area of land in Central Australia and about the possibility of transformation into a real kangaroo-person.

THE TWO KANGAROOS: A WARLPIRI INITIATION STORY

These are my two kangaroos. There they went, along the east side. The two kangaroos travelled along the east side. They went, where, where, am I trying to remember? They went to Parntarla. They stayed at Parntarla. Then they departed. They stopped again. They went to Lawarri next. They stayed at Lawarri. There they stayed, the two kangaroos belonging to that place. These two places belong to them, Lawarri and Parntarla. These places belong to them both. They are the two who belong to these places. They brought many places into being, many soakages in the surrounding area.

They stayed. Then they left. A little later on they set off, then they stopped. You know, in the old days they walked about during the Dreaming. There they were travelling, the two of them. They travelled south, along the west side to the Granites, then back along the east to Yurlpuwarnu, along the east side again. From the Granites they went along the west side again, near the Granites. Then they left the Granites. Then one of the two kangaroos was taken away. He was carried away in a big flooded stretch of water. Thus he was taken away. The other looked for him all around.

"Now I will have to travel alone. What has happened? Maybe he was carried off by all that water? The water has been running everywhere, it has spread out everywhere. That lake, that lake has swallowed him up."

He was taken from there, one of the two was taken away. Then, from that place the one who was left, went away. He went off, and put the other one out of his mind.

He looked around. "What is this sitting here?"

It was a type of little mouse, a little rat, somewhat related to a mouse but slightly different, called a wulyu-wulyu. He approached it and picked it up. He looked at it closely.

"Ah, it has two ears, two ears and it has a tail, it has two feet, and it has a tail." He looked at it carefully. In particular he looked at its tail.

"What will I do with this creature? I'll take it with me, I'll take it along." He carried it to Mulyu, he carried it to Mulyu. There he remade it, completely. He made it into a kangaroo. Now that he was a kangaroo, he started to hop about. Where did he go? He went away. Now that he was a kangaroo, now that he had been completely remade into a kangaroo, he went away.

Now there were two kangaroos. One had come from the little animal we call wulyu-wulyu. The two kangaroos stayed in that place for a considerable time, in that place which belongs to them. The two kangaroos stayed there for a long time.

"Let's go on a journey."

"Yes."

The one that had spoken was probably the older brother, I am not sure, probably the older brother. The other was now also a real kangaroo, the one that had been made from a little rat. At first it hopped around on all fours, on all four legs. It went. It stopped. It went on.

"I am going on a journey, I am going on a journey."

"Yes, yes, on a journey, then, yes."

"All right, you go in front, like that."

He made the little one, the one made from the little rat, travel in front of him. The other one followed him. In this way, he went along. Then they found another place, called Nyurrijardu, which is a very important place. They created that place, the two of them, and there they stayed for a while. They were the two belonging to that place. In that southern part of the country there are all those places that belong to them, all those soaks, there in the south.

Then they travelled east to Jalyirrparnta. They slept there, they stayed out there. Then they went on into the south for a long time. They also visited a soak on the way. Now what is that name I am looking for? Somewhere behind Jalyirrparnta. Warrarna, Jupurrurla's father, knows that place. I have never visited that particular country.

From there they went to another soak, further away, to Kuyujarra, Kuyujarra. I do not know of another soak there, either to the south or the north. To Kuyujarra. From Kuyujarra to Yintawalyarri. From Yintawalyarri they went along the west side to Warnirriparnta. They went a long distance away, along the west side. There they encountered another dreaming. At that place, the Pirlarla dreaming follows the same path.

Then they arrived at Lirrawarnupatu. At Lirrawarnupatu, they mistakenly made contact with that other dreaming. From Lirrawarnupatu they went to Japiya-jarra. In that area, many, many soakages, some very big, lie across the basin there. I learned about those places when I was growing up, a little at a time. I can follow this dreaming as it goes along the west side, as it has been told to me, as it has been shown me.

The two kangaroos continued their journey. They went into Japiya-jarra. From there, now, into another country, into Yintaramurru, which is in the west. White people call that place Mount Singleton. That country, in the west. They went away over there. There they put down bush tomato plants, the fruit which we call ngayaki which is like jarlparrpa as well. In that country they deposited the bush tomato plants.

They came back this way. At Yarrpawangu, there is a stone knife, a stone knife at Yarrpawangu. From there they went back to eat the bush tomatoes. They went back to Yintaramurru. From there they went on to Butcher Creek. And from there they went further still. They went away for a long time. From there we will leave them as they go from Butcher Creek to Yanjiwarra. At Yanjiwarra those two sang the kurdiji (initiation) songs for others. Then they left there, just the two of them. They went away towards that place, they climbed up towards Pikilyi, from Yanji-warra. They climbed up towards Pikilyi. That is as far as I will take the story, as far as Pikilyi.

That is all.

FREEDOM IN JEWISH EXPERIENCE

For the Jewish community, as for the Warlpiri, relationship to a particular land is an important element of identity. According to archaeological evidence there have been people living in Australia for more than fifty thousand years. Prehistorians say that there have been people in Israel for an even longer period, for some one hundred thousand years, and that the ancestors of the Jews were established there by the thirteenth century B.C.E. In the Book of Genesis, the first book of the **Bible**, we read the story of the Jewish people's establishment in the land they call their own. Genesis tells that God led the patriarch Abraham, his wife, Sarah, and their family, from Ur of the Chaldees to a land which he promised them, the land of Canaan (Gen 12). The biblical account narrates that, after some years in Canaan, a famine occurred, and Abraham's grandson, Jacob, brought his family into Egypt where they remained for four hundred years and became enslaved to Pharaoh, the king of Egypt (Gen 42-50). In the Book of Exodus, the second book of the Bible, we are told that the Lord had compassion on his people and delivered them out of this slavery and brought them back to the promised land. That land, referred to today as Eretz Israel, has become a symbol of freedom for Jews. The story of God's intervention to release the Hebrews from slavery in Egypt has become central to Jewish self-understanding. God is the hero of Exodus, and he acts on behalf of his people.

If we study the history of the land of Israel we find that during most of the time that Jews lived in Israel, other nations governed them. From 1550 to 1200 B.C.E. Egypt had jurisdiction over Palestine but lost control with the coming of the Sea Peoples. One faction, the Philistines, became a significant power to be subdued by the Israelites under Kings David and Solomon. Solomon's reign in the tenth century B.C.E. is remembered as a golden age for Israel, and during it the First Temple of Jerusalem was built. His death brought division of the kingdom into two—Israel in the north and Judah in the south. The ancient Canaanites had developed a linear alphabet; this was adopted by the Israelites around 1000 B.C.E. From that time on, the stories of the Israelite ancestors and their legal and religious codes began to take written form and, as will be discussed in chapter 7, underwent revision until the present canon of the Tanak was established. Jewish teachers and, later, writers reflected on the saga of their relationship to the land, on the graciousness of God in giving it to them, on his interventions to restore it to them, and on their own transgressions which merited such punishment as loss of the land.

The northern state of Israel fell to the Assyrians in 722 B.C.E. while the southern state of Judah survived as an Assyrian vassal until 625 B.C.E., when Assyria lost power to Babylon. The Babylonians destroyed Judah in 587 B.C.E. and took many of the priests and scholars into exile in Babylon. Under the Persian ruler Cyrus II (c. 550-529 B.C.E.) the exiles returned to Jerusalem and built the Second Temple. After the invasion of Alexander the Great (356-323 B.C.E.) Palestine came under Greek suzerains. It enjoyed a period of independence from 141 B.C.E., following a revolt led by Judas Maccabeus, until 65 B.C.E. when dissension in the ruling family led to civil war and Roman intervention. The Romans crushed subsequent attempts at revolt. After a final revolt in 135 C.E. the Jewish population of Palestine was dispersed and drastically reduced, and Israel ceased to exist as a separate state even though Jews continued to live there.

Members of **diaspora** communities in North Africa and Europe still remembered the land of their ancestors, a land they understood to have been given to them by God. Connection to the land of Israel remained a part of Jewish identity. In the centuries which followed the establishment of Roman hegemony, Palestine became part of the Byzantine Empire and then fell to the Ottoman Turks. After World War I it became a League of Nations mandated territory governed by Britain. European Jews, fleeing antisemitism, began moving there from the 1880s. The Zionist Movement, under the leadership of the Viennese journalist Theodor Herzl (1860-1904), advocated the establishment of a Jewish homeland. In the 1930s Jews fleeing Hitler's persecutions joined them. Finally, in 1948, following the partition of Palestine into Arab and Jewish areas, the United Nations created the modern state of Israel.

Today Jews live in all parts of the world, so it is not surprising that they have a variety of ideas about the land of Israel. Some maintain that every true Jew should live in the present-day geographical equivalent of the promised land. Others do not see the modern state of Israel as equivalent to the biblical promised land. Rather, they see Zion as the ideal land of freedom in which people live in faithfulness to God and loyalty to each other. They take it upon themselves to build Zion wherever they might be. However, since the **Holocaust**, in which almost six million Jews were murdered by the Nazi leadership during World War II, the land of Israel has also come to be seen as a safe haven, a place in which Jews might govern themselves and live free of the anti-Judaism which marked their life in the European diaspora. Today the United States, with some six million Jews, has the largest and most diverse Jewish community in the world. Many American Jews see it as a duty of solidarity to give material support to Israel.

Despite different understandings of the relationship between symbolic Israel and the modern state of Israel, the image of God as savior and liberator who intervenes to free his oppressed people is central to Judaism. Each year Jews echo the theme of God's saving love as they gather to celebrate Pesach or Passover, a springtime festival of new lambs which Judaism has transformed into a historical commemoration. Passover brings into present consciousness the liberation from bondage in Egypt. At Passover Jews pray for freedom for themselves and for all the peoples of the earth. Their own experiences of persecution and loss of freedom make them sensitive to oppression. In their sacred narratives, telling of a God who intervenes to save Israel, they point, however, to the possibility of universal liberation. Although the symbolic structure of Judaism has been shaken by the events of the Holocaust, nevertheless, millions of Jews gather each year to celebrate Passover and thus to assert the value and possibility of freedom.

Passover is celebrated in the home on the first new moon of the Spring equinox with a Seder, a meal which follows a particular order. The word "seder" in fact means "order." The Seder arranges readings from the Bible, prayers, songs, and the consumption of symbolic foods in an orchestrated order. Passover is the most widely observed Jewish holiday. The Passover home service enables all Jews to remember their heritage and to become part of the ongoing movement from slavery to freedom. The sequence of the Seder meal, along with all the prayers and readings and songs used in the service, is published in a text called the **Haggada**. Some parts of the Haggada are passages from the **Torah**, the first section of the Tanak; some parts were composed by rabbis around two thousand years ago; other parts date from the Middle Ages.

A plate containing six symbolic foods is placed on the Seder table. The foods are: *karpas*, a mild green vegetable such as parsley, which symbolizes the new growth of spring and which is dipped in salt water or vinegar to recall the tears of the enslaved Hebrews; *maror*, a bitter herb such as horseradish, to suggest the bitterness endured by the slaves; *hazeret*, another bitter herb such as romaine lettuce, pointing to a double portion of bitterness; *haroset*, a sweet mixture of fruit, nuts, and wine said to resemble the mud and mortar that the slaves molded into bricks, which suggests that even harsh slavery is tempered with sweetness and optimism; *zeroah*, a roasted lamb shank bone to recall the Exodus

A seder plate and blessing cup belonging to Rabbi Daniel Jezer and his wife, Rheah Jezer. The names of the six symbolic foods are written in Hebrew on the plate.

account of the last meal eaten by the slaves as they prepared to leave Egypt and also to recall the days of the Temple in which a lamb was sacrificed and then roasted for the family passover meal; *baytzah*, a roasted egg, symbolic of new life and of the second festival offering brought to the Temple, and also seen as symbol of mourning for the second temple. Three pieces of unleavened bread (*matzot*) are set on the table and are consumed throughout the course of the meal. The bread is unleavened because in the Exodus account it is said that the Hebrews left Egypt in such haste that there was not time to wait for bread to rise. The ritual meal begins with a blessing which recalls God's creation of the world, his choice of Israel, the distinction he makes between sacred and profane, and the distinction he has established between the days of work and the Sabbath and festival days. A ritual washing of hands follows, and then the leader—traditionally the head of the household—distributes the *karpas* which he has dipped in salt water or vinegar. Then the middle one of three sheets of unleavened bread, the second *matzot*, is broken.

To prompt the telling of the Exodus story the youngest child present asks four questions to which the company makes an initial response. The readings, prayers, and songs spread throughout the evening constitute a longer response to the questions. We shall read a section from near the beginning of the Passover service. It includes the four questions with the company's response, an anecdote concerning why the Exodus story is narrated at night, and a passage which concerns the instruction of four sons: one wise, one wicked, one simple, and one too young to even ask questions. At the same time as the Haggada narrates the story of God's intervention to save the Hebrews and to make of them a nation, it speaks of the need to pass on the tradition and to accommodate the teaching of it to the disposition of the student. The Jewish liturgical renewal of recent years has produced several new scripts for the Seder which accommodate themselves to the situations of people today. Some of the new scripts give attention to humanist and feminist issues and to the relationship of Judaism and other religions.

FROM THE PASSOVER SEDER

Child: How is this night different from any other night? On any other night we eat leavened and unleavened bread. Why on this night only unleavened bread? On any other night we eat all kinds of herbs. Why on this night only bitter herbs? On any other night we do not dip our herbs into anything even once. Why on this night do we do it twice? On any other night we eat either sitting upright or reclining. Why on this night do we all recline?

(The leader uncovers the dish of matzot and places it on the table.)

Company: We were slaves to Pharaoh in Egypt and the Lord our God brought us out from there with a mighty hand and an outstretched arm. If the Holy One, Blessed be He, had not brought our fathers out of Egypt, then we and our children and our children's children would still be enslaved to Pharaoh in Egypt. Therefore, if all of us were wise, all mature, all versed in the Torah, it would still be our duty to tell the story of the Liberation from Egypt. The more one dwells upon the details of the Exodus, the more he is praised.

It once happened that Rabbi Eliezer, Rabbi Joshua, Rabbi Eleazer ben Azariah, Rabbi Akiba, and Rabbi Tarphon gathered together in Bene Berak and they discussed the Exodus throughout the night until their disciples came and said to them: "Our teachers, it is time to recite the morning Shema."

Rabbi Eleazer ben Azariah said, "I am like a man of seventy and yet I did not understand why the story of the departure from Egypt would be related at night until Ben Zoma explained the reason: It is said, seven days shall you eat unleavened bread 'so that you may remember the day when you came out of the land of Egypt all the days of your life' (Dt 16:3). Had the text stated 'the days of your life' it would have meant the days only, but 'all the days of your life' includes the nights also. The sages further maintain that 'the days of your life' refers to this world while 'all the days of your life' is taken to include the days of the Messiah.

Blessed be the Omnipresent, Blessed be He. Blessed be the One who gave the Torah to His people Israel. Blessed be He. The Torah speaks of four kinds of children: the wise, the wicked, the simple and the one who is too young to ask.

What does the wise son ask? "What mean the testimonies, the statutes, and the ordinances, which the Lord your God commanded you?" (Dt 6:20). It is then your duty to tell him all the laws of the Passover down to the last detail of the Afikoman.

What does the wicked son say? "What does this service mean to you?" (Ex 2:26). Since he says 'To you' and not 'to himself' he excludes himself and thus denies God. Refute his arguments and tell him: "This is done because of that which the Lord did for me when I came out of Egypt." 'For me' and not for him, implying that if he had been there he would not have been redeemed.

What does the simple son ask? "What is this?" (Ex 13:14). You shall say to him: "By strength of his hand, the Lord brought us out of Egypt, from the house of bondage."

To the son who is too young to ask, you shall tell him, for it is said, (Ex 13:8), "On that day you shall tell your son, 'This commemorates what the Lord did for me when I came out of Egypt.'"

Thinking about Our Place in the World

Both the Warlpiri story and the section of the Passover Seder picture what we might call sacred geographies. That is, they describe places in which powerful life-giving events occurred.

1. Draw maps to summarize the sacred geographies pictured in the two accounts.
2. How do members of the Warlpiri community and the Jewish community today connect themselves to the sacred power which is evoked in their mythic geographies?
3. Draw a map or picture showing your place in the world. Are there sources of power and energy which you need to include?
4. What do the Warlpiri story, an initiation myth, and the Passover Seder, a liturgy structured around scripted questions posed by children, suggest about the education of children?

Construed in a large sense, as a quest for significance or as a structuring of a world of meaning, religion is, according to some scholars, a defining characteristic of human life. The historian of religions, Mircea Eliade, we have already observed, talks about the sacred as a structure or modality of human consciousness. That is, he sees the sacred as one mode of human awareness, a mode which apprehends a transformative power of life. Eliade contrasts this modality with another which he calls the profane.[2] By profane ("prior to the temple") he means that which is not yet sacred, not yet aware of the transformative power of life. For Eliade religion is the process in which the sacred irrupts into the profane and transforms it, making it holy or powerful, filling it with true life. Another way of thinking about religion, which we shall explore in chapter 3, is to consider religion as an awareness expressed in symbols of participation in the fundamental power of life.

MARYKNOLL PHOTO LIBRARY/J. BEECHING, M.M.

Mosque, Egypt. Most mosques have an outer courtyard for ablutions and a large unfurnished inside area for worship. Muslims are called to prayer from a tower, called a minaret, attached to the mosque.

SACRED SPACE AND SACRED TIME

Human beings are aware of space and time. We notice our closeness to, and distance from, other things and other people. We notice the succession of events and the cycles of the seasons. We are people of particular places and particular times—contemporary Warlpiri of the Central Desert, ancient Hebrews in Egypt, Americans of the twentieth century, Solomon Islanders of the late nineteenth century. Our experience of ourselves is conditioned by the time and place in which our larger community lives and by the particular times and places in which each of our lives is lived. To some extent our time and place is given, and to some extent we create it. We work with time and place to structure our lives, to bring order to our existence.

We have offices and factories for work, classrooms for study, kitchens for cooking, bedrooms for sleeping, chapels for praying. We have times in our daily schedule to sleep, to eat, to study, to play, to worship.

Each of these places and times has its own quality. The locker room and dance hall feel different from the synagogue and church. The time of a lecture feels different from a time of eating or a time of praying. There are times that we call "relaxing," times we call "boring," times we call "powerful," times we call "painful." There are beautiful places and ugly places, inviting places and repulsive places, places we call "stressful," places we call "peaceful," places we call "disturbing," places we call "exciting." In special spaces and times we sense the potential to change ourselves and our communities for the better. For some people a library is such a space. It is a quiet space, conducive to reflection, which contains materials that carry us beyond the more restricted space of our daily lives, beyond our local communities, beyond the boundaries of our nations, to the larger world. It is a space of possibilities.

We characterize some places and times as religious or sacred because they are places and times, distinct from the other places and times of our lives, in which we are more aware of our relationship to the power of life. On the Sabbath Jews take a day in the weekly cycle to refresh themselves and to rejoice in their relationship to God and community. It is a time taken out of ordinary time and separated from it by Sabbath conventions. Jews also take a place, the synagogue—a place within, but separated from, profane space—and set it aside for worship, study, and community activities. Characterized primarily as a gathering place, the synagogue affords opportunity to dwell on, and in, relationship to God and community. Sacred space may be a natural space which becomes sacred to a religious community because God or ancestral spirits have manifested themselves in it, or because it has been the place in which a paradigmatic figure such as the Buddha achieved insight. Sacred space may also be architecturally created space such as a Shinto shrine, a Mayan temple, or a mosque.

Some Christians give time each day to prayer and Bible reading; these are sacred times within the daily cycle. Similarly, spaces set aside for the Bible and for religious objects are sacred places within the home. They have a different feeling from the places where we put our pots and pans and clothes. Jews and Christians pray that the power of God, the grace, which is encountered in sacred times and places will come to transform all of life. Buddhism looks on such times and places as opportunities to gain insight into reality. Buddhism, its followers say, is not a religion of God but a religion of wisdom, enlightenment, and compassion. For **Taoism** sacred times and places are windows into the natural way of all things. For indigenous traditions such as that of the Warlpiri they are opportunities for empowering the whole of life.

The biblical book of Qoheleth, often referred to in English as Ecclesiastes, outlines a succession of the times of our lives. Qoheleth is a proper noun meaning "speaker in the assembly," and suggests one who conducts a school or assembly. The word Qoheleth has been translated into Greek as "Ecclesiastes." The writer was probably a Jewish wisdom teacher writing in the third century B.C.E. who had been influenced by

MARYKNOLL PHOTO LIBRARY

Shinto Temple at Matsuyama, Province of Ehime, Japan. The torii *(gateway) leads to the shrines for the* kami *(spirits).*

Greek thought. He writes of the shallowness or vanity of life and echoes a distaste for conventional wisdom. Qoheleth describes the seasons of our lives without finding a completely satisfying order or meaning. He even makes us wonder whether the search for order and meaning is futile. His observations could come as easily from a gentile as from a Jew, from an atheist as from a theist. However, Qoheleth situates the perennial human problem of the shortness of life and the difficulty of knowing how to act within a Jewish religious context. Qoheleth's God may be more remote and inflexible than the God we encounter in other parts of the Hebrew Bible but he is God nevertheless and it is he who has given life to human beings. Qoheleth gives people the common-sense advice that, "it is God's gift to man that every one should eat and drink and take pleasure in all his toil" (3:13), yet he concludes that human wisdom is not sufficient to comprehend the work of God.

TIMES (ECCLESIASTES 3:1-11)

> For everything there is a season, and a time for every matter
>   under heaven:
>   a time to be born, and a time to die;
>   a time to plant, and a time to pluck up what is planted;
>   a time to kill and a time to heal;
>   a time to break down, and a time to build up;

> a time to weep, and a time to laugh;
> a time to mourn, and a time to dance;
> a time to throw away stones, and a time to gather stones together;
> a time to embrace, and a time to refrain from embracing;
> a time to seek, and a time to lose;
> a time to keep, and a time to throw away;
> a time to tear, and a time to sew;
> a time to keep silence, and a time to speak;
> a time to love, and a time to hate;
> a time for war, and a time for peace.
>
> What gain have the workers from their toil? I have seen the business that God has given to everyone to be busy with. He has made everything suitable for its time; moreover he has put a sense of past and future into their minds, yet they cannot find out what God has done from the beginning to the end.

People live through the stages of their lives in particular ecological and social contexts. There is no "human life" in the abstract but only human lives lived out in various circumstances. There are people with their various drives and desires connected to each other in social networks, connected to their land with its plants and its animals. There are people in relationships which may be cooperative or competitive, encouraging or exploitative. Religions posit an ultimate context, a large scheme of things, a cosmos or world. When they help us locate ourselves within that world and make life-giving connections to all else within it, they are inspiring and freeing. Tragically, though, religions have a negative side. Religious leaders may use their authority to dominate and control their followers. Adherents may take hope in an afterlife as reason to suffer unjust working and social conditions in the present. Patriarchal traditions may interpret their dogmas to the detriment of women.

In chapter 1, following Mircea Eliade, we encountered the word "hierophany," which means "manifestation of the sacred." Sacred times, sacred places, sacred objects, and sacred persons facilitate hierophany. A hierophany is a point of contact between life, which stands in need of meaning and empowerment, and anything (the sacred, the holy, the true, the good, the beautiful) that is able to transform it. Hierophanies occasion reverence and also fear on the part of believers. That which is potentially life-giving is also potentially life-destroying and needs, therefore, to be approached with caution and reverence. Hence, rituals which cultivate the manifestation of the sacred may be surrounded with taboos in order to avoid an unregulated release of power.

Some religions emphasize a separation between the sacred and the profane; others stress their mutuality and, hence, the accessibility of the sacred to human experience. However, even for traditions which stress the separation of sacred and profane, notions of transcendence and immanence are not mutually exclusive. Those who stress transcendence say that we may "climb across" (tran-scend) from our everyday experience to the experience of another realm. In this view ultimate power, the transcendent, is located primarily beyond our ordinary experience. Traditions emphasizing transcendence say that the Creator, or the company of the gods, or the spirit of creativity, or the power of life, lies beyond the limits of ordinary experience but may, on occasion, enter directly into our existence. We might, through a spiritual journey or mystic experience, cross to the realm of the transcendent, or the transcendent may graciously come to us.

In contrast to understandings ordered by an emphasis on trancendence, in the so-called "nature religions" the power of life is conceived of as immanent, as "remaining in place." "Immanent," like the words "remain," and "mansion," comes from the Greek *menein*, "to remain." In religious discourse "immanence" suggests that the sacred, or the power of life, is to be found in the world of ordinary existence. For example, Purusa Sukta, the primal person or divine being conceptualized in the Vedic hymn we considered in chapter 1, is diffused throughout the universe. Or, in the Solomon Islands, to recall our discussion of relationships to fish, *mana*, a quality which empowers technical processes and relationships, is accessible and manifests itself within the realm of community life. Mana has, in fact, become a technical term in religious studies denoting supernatural power of various kinds.

PERSON, SELF, AND EXPERIENCE

We experience ourselves in space and in time and in relationship with others. Just what is the self or the person who realizes such experiences? A body, mental states, spiritual substance? Our understandings of self and personhood are conditioned by our cultures. Ethnopsychologists, those who study the relation of psychology and culture on a comparative basis, consider self-awareness to be a human universal and the "self" to be the individual, but never fully individuated, human being. They define the person as the culturally constructed point of intersection between the subjective and the social. Some cultures permit the person to be more individually than communally defined; others see the person as part of a network of relationships. Even cultures which define the person in more social terms may permit considerable idiosyncrasy.

The English empiricist and moral and political philosopher, John Locke (1632-1704), defined a person as "a thinking intelligent being, that has reason and reflection, and can consider itself as itself, the same thinking thing, in different times and places; which it does only by that consciousness which is inseparable from thinking and essential to it."[3] Someone who in his early life shared Locke's understanding of the person as basically "a thinking intelligent being" was the French Protestant missionary, Maurice Leenhardt (1878-1954), who worked in New Caledonia, a French colony in the South Pacific adjacent to the British Solomon Islands, early in this century. Leenhardt was to find his notion of person challenged by the ideas of the indigenous people of New Caledonia. In *Do Kamo*,[4] a book whose title means "the true person," he presents the idea of the New Caledonians that the person has identity only in relationship to a land and to a community. On his return to France, Leenhardt taught at the Sorbonne. He influenced scholars such as Lucien Lévy-Bruhl and, as studies in cross-cultural psychology advanced, *Do Kamo* became a classic in the cross-cultural discussion of personhood.

In Maurice Leenhardt's European Protestant upbringing, the person was seen as an autonomous being whose dignity lay in the ability to make free individual decisions. In New Caledonia he encountered a notion of person in which authentic identity partook also of the social and mythic worlds. That is, the true person experienced himself or herself as connected to kin, to ancestors, to land, and to tradition. The notion of the person embedded in the landscape and the community, a notion similar to the one we encountered in the Warlpiri story about the two kangaroos, so entranced Leenhardt that he spent the rest of his life thinking about it and writing about it. Leenhardt's life is truly a record of learning to appreciate ways of thinking, and ways of being religious, that were radically different from those he learned in his own upbringing.

As Leenhardt listened to the stories and analyzed the complex social structures of the Melanesians among whom he lived, he sensed that these people dwelt in a mythic landscape that extended beyond his French-conditioned imagination. He perceived that they understood the self not so much as an individual entity but more as one locus of a larger pattern of life. It seemed they allowed the mythic to exert a living influence on the present time and place. In trying to capture this understanding Leenhardt coined the term "living myth." He observed that not only did the New Caledonians have rules about marriage, and stories that set out patterns for relations between the sexes, but that the complementarity of male and female was even echoed in the spatial arrangements of New Caledonian gardens and villages. "The couple," he wrote in his analysis of the New Caledonian landscape, "is inscribed in the earth."[5]

In the New Caledonia of the late nineteenth century, the French with their nickel mines and the missionaries with their Christian stories and rituals were still newcomers. The true person, *Do Kamo*, was intrinsically a part of a cosmos which included land, people, ancestors, animals, plants, and spirit beings. The authentic person was powerfully connected to the world of his or her culture's making. As a missionary and a French citizen Leenhardt had qualms about what was happening to this "person" as a result of French annexation of the land and the introduction of Christianity. He saw that the dialectical relationship between the person and the person's Melanesian world was in danger of being lost to consciousness. The true person was in jeopardy of becoming an alienated person.

Thinking about Personhood

1. What are the advantages of thinking, as Leenhardt did in childhood and young adulthood, of the true or authentic person as someone conscious of his or her individuality and capable of making individual decisions?
2. What are the advantages of thinking, as the New Caledonians described by Leenhardt did, of a true person as a locus in a network of relationships connecting land, tradition, and others?
3. How would you describe the true or authentic person in your community? What accommodations for variations in values and behaviors does a multicultural situation require you to make in describing the true or authentic person?

Religions suggest that, in one way or another, we can overcome all that inhibits our existence and attain a fullness of life. Or, looking at it from another perspective, Buddhists might say that religion is a path by which we can attain an emptiness of life, a state of not clinging to life. Religions also suggest that if this fullness or emptiness is not achieved in this world, then it may be achieved in another. Religions provide their followers with central symbols on which to focus their vision of life and with ritual means and moral guidance for achieving that vision. At their best religious understandings of life are open-minded and life-enhancing, encouraging and inspiriting; at their worst they are narrow-minded and life-destroying, discouraging and dispiriting. At both ends of the spectrum religions afford their members ways of putting individual and communal lives, and life itself, into an ultimate perspective, and of participating in whatever the tradition understands to be the fundamental power of life.

RESOURCES

Activities

1. Assign groups within the class to visit houses of worship of various religious traditions. Groups should give attention to arrangement of the sacred space and to ritual and instruction taking place there. Each group will report on what they learned about the worldview and values of the religious community.
2. Read the story of the Two Kangaroos again. Describe the characters and outline the plot of the story. What does the story say about life and death? What does it say about relationship to land? What can we learn from Warlpiri understandings of life?
3. Obtain a copy of the Haggada, the liturgical text used for the Passover service from which the extract in this chapter is taken. After reading the service

answer these questions: What is the structure of the Seder? What understanding of the human condition does the Seder narrate and enact? What can we all learn from Jewish understandings of life?

4. Choose a story which helps you to understand your life. Is it a story which is generally recognized as religious? Do you regard it as religious? Why, or why not? How does it portray authentic life?

5. Describe an example of religious architecture. How has the space been arranged and embellished? What messages does it convey? What mood does it create? What does it suggest about the power of life? Consult books and articles on religious architecture to obtain the vocabulary and framework for describing the building you have chosen.

6. Work with a group to prepare a multimedia presentation on religious architecture in your community.

Readings

Charles Birch, William Eakin, and Jay B. McDaniel, eds. *Liberating Life: Contemporary Approaches to Ecological Theology*. Maryknoll, NY: Orbis, 1990. The contributors to this volume draw on their religious traditions in seeking an ethics of life which will respect life in its many forms and will encourage justice and peace in human communities.

Martin Frishnan and Hasan-Uddin Khan, eds. *The Mosque: History, Architectural Development and Regional Diversity*. New York: Thames and Hudson, 1994. A discussion of the spiritual and aesthetic principles of Islamic architecture along with an exploration of the development and diversity of mosque architecture.

Abraham Maslow. *Religions, Values, and Peak-Experiences*. Columbus: Ohio State University Press, 1964. Maslow, the founder of humanistic psychology, discusses the role of religion in helping the person to become a "self-actualizing individual."

Stephen Muecke. *Textual Spaces: Aboriginality and Culture Studies*. Sydney: University of New South Wales Press, 1992. A study of misunderstandings and miscommunication in relationships between Aborigines and European Australians since colonization.

Peggy Rockman Napaljarri and Lee Cataldi, collectors and translators. *Warlpiri Dreamings and Histories*. San Francisco: HarperCollins, 1994. A collection of Warlpiri stories. The collectors explain, "The narrative is simultaneously an account of the creation of the places in the story, an account of the mythical but human behavior of the ancestral figures, and a mnemonic map of the country with its important, life-giving features for the purpose of instructing a younger listener. These elements make up Warlpiri Jukurrpa, commonly translated as the Dreaming."

Chaim Potok. *The Chosen*. New York: Fawcett Crest, 1967. This story of two Jewish boys and their fathers in the Williamsburg section of Brooklyn during World War II introduces the diversity of Jewish tradition and its profound influence from generation to generation.

Joseph Telushkin. *Jewish Literacy: The Most Important Things to Know about the Jewish Religion, Its People, and Its History*. New York: William Morrow and Company, 1991. An accessible introduction to Judaism arranged in fifteen areas.

Anzia Yezierska. *Bread Givers*. New York: Persea Books, 1975, original edition 1925. An autobiographical novel which brings a woman's viewpoint to the Jewish immigrant experience in New York City in the early twentieth century and raises enduring questions about the position of women in religious traditions.

Audiovisuals

The Image Bank for Teaching World Religions. The Cycle of the Jewish Year (Slides 3469-3634),

Islamic Architecture in India and Pakistan (Slides 0400-0410, 0570-0572, 0577, 1240, 1636-1638, 2090, 2160-2164, 4780),

Shinto Temple Activities, Japan (Slides 0109-0115).

Sabbath of Peace. Commentator Eli Wallach. New York: Jewish Chatauqua Society, 1979. A presentation of the course of a Sabbath and a discussion of its significance in Jewish life.

Walbiri Fire Ceremony. Australian Institute of Aboriginal Studies, distributed in the U.S. by University of California Extension Services, Berkeley, CA. Documents the fire ceremony by which the Walbiri (Warlpiri) negotiate relationships between moieties.

Women of the Sun. Hyllus Maris and Sonia Borg, produced by Bob Weis, 1982, Generation Films, distributed in the U.S. by University of California Extension Services, Berkeley, CA. Four television dramas, each concerning a period in the experience of Australia's Aboriginal people since the arrival of white settlers. The chief protagonist in each drama is a woman.

NOTES

1. Henry Cook Jakamarra, "Marlujarrakurlu: The Two Kangaroos," in *Yimikirli: Warlpiri Dreamings and Histories*, collected and translated by Peggy Rockman Napaljarri and Lee Cataldi (San Francisco: HarperCollins, 1995), 46-53.
2. Mircea Eliade, *The Sacred and the Profane*, trans. Willard R. Trask (New York: Harcourt, Brace and World, 1959).
3. John Locke, *An Essay Concerning Human Understanding* (first edition, London, 1690). Edited with an introduction by John W. Yolton (London: Dent, 1965).
4. Maurice Leenhardt, *Do Kamo: Person and Myth in the Melanesian World* (Chicago: University of Chicago Press, 1979).
5. Maurice Leenhardt, *Gens de la Grande Terre* (Paris: Gallimard, 1937).

Chapter 3

The Study of Religion

NATURE, CULTURE, AND RELIGION

We turn now from reflection on the ways that human beings order their lives, and the ways that religions assist them in doing so, to the ways that scholars study the ordering process they call religion. In talking about the ways in which we structure our lives we have used the terms "culture" and "religion." Implied in our discussion has been a third term, "nature." "Nature" and "culture" are complementary frames, reciprocal mental constructs, which many scholars use in their study of religion. They are concepts which help us to talk about our life in the world and, therefore, they are useful to us in the study of religion.

"Nature," in our usual way of speaking, is what is given. Nature includes land, water, sun, sky, trees, animals, people in their biological being. "Culture," on the other hand, is what human beings create. Culture includes technical processes for obtaining food and shelter, conventions for interacting with other people, and ideas about the structure of the world. Religion is part of culture. The constructs of "nature" and "culture" can be used to frame discussions about the lives of human communities and about the creative activity of human beings. However, the terms have their limitations. Much of what we call "nature" (rolling meadows, herds of cattle) is not "given" but is the result of human decision making and activity. Moreover, human life is both natural and cultural. Nature requires that we eat; culture dictates how we prepare food and the conventions to be observed in eating it.

As we have seen in our discussion of communities in the Southwest Pacific, people can think about their life in the world without resort to the mental constructs of nature and culture. That is, we can draw boundaries and forge linkages with other constructs, for example, that of kinship. The indigenous people of New Caledonia of whom Leenhardt wrote, the Solomon Islanders whose relationship to fish we considered, and the Warlpiri on whose initiation story we reflected, construct the interrelationship of land and animals and people in terms more like kinship than like nature and culture. Then, some people construct their world as a vast organism. Each way of thinking about the human and cosmic condition yields its particular insight but falls short of saying the last word.

Even cultures with similar material resources available to them and cultures in similar ecological niches differ considerably from each other. They differ because of the varied ways that human beings use their imaginations in symbolically structuring their worlds. In fashioning human communities we live with the possibilities and constraints of our ecological contexts. We are not

MARY N. MACDONALD

The Three Sisters, a carving by Onondaga artist Gene Thomas, which incorporates the staple foods of corn, beans, and squash.

going to be farmers if we have no land. We may well become hunters of game if we live in a forest where there are animals. Yet, just living in a forest where there are animals does not determine that we shall be hunters. We may choose not to eat certain animals, or we may choose to be vegetarians and not to eat animals at all. Regardless of our ecological contexts we are, as Wallace Stevens reminds us, the makers of the worlds in which we live. Our exercise of imagination results in diversity in our understandings of the world and in the symbol systems we use to express our relationship to the world. We create different economic systems, different social structures, and different understandings of the human condition and the fundamental powers of life.

Culture, as anthropologist Ruth Benedict says, is a pattern for living. Anthropologists tell us that cultures provide us with ways to live and reasons for living. The social sciences understand culture to be a pattern which embraces the domains of:

1. economy (the use of the resources available to us to sustain our physical existence–from Greek *oikos*, "house," and *nomos*, "manager"),

2. social life (our conventions for relating to others, including marriage and kinship rules, processes of warfare and alliance making, strategies of cooperation), and

3. ideology (ideas about how the world is constituted and the use of symbols to reinforce those ideas and to facilitate engagement with the world).

Within this threefold schema religion and philosophy and literature all belong in the domain of ideology. They have to do with understanding the human situation and the context in which human beings find themselves. Of course the three domains overlap. Yet, seeing them as separate provides a tool to help us think about the ways that people create order and meaning. If a community supports its physical existence by growing corn, the chances are that corn will be part of the exchange network by which social relationships are sustained and part of its symbolic system in which understandings of human life are imaged and articulated. This, as we shall see, is the case for the pueblo peoples of the American Southwest such as the Hopi, Tewa, and Zuni.

CULTURE—A SHARED PATTERN FOR LIVING

In the understanding which is couched in terms of "nature and culture," nature is a context, a resource, and a locus of power. Human beings as they create their cultures, including the domain of religion, develop characteristic attitudes toward nature. They may seek to subdue nature, to harness its power to satisfy their desires—cutting forests for farmland, using swift-flowing streams to generate electric power. They may seek to work with nature, to use its products without destroying their sources—fishing and hunting in ways that do not destroy habitats or herds. People may strive with or against nature; they may respect nature or fear nature. Whatever their attitude they are obliged, on occasion, to accommodate themselves to nature, to live with the fact that nature will demolish the order they have created. Despite their careful efforts there will be floods and blizzards. We are not obliged to frame our understandings of the world and of ourselves with the "nature and culture" dichotomy. We may choose to see our human communities as part of nature. Or, we may choose to see our human cultures as parallel to, and in interaction with, other communities or cultures, such as those of plants and insects and animals. Today many people like to use the image of a web of life, which is common in a number of indigenous traditions, when they work at bringing order to their experience of the world.

Each culture is a pattern for living, created within a context of constraints and possibilities. It is transmitted from generation to generation, and the pattern changes over time. Changes may result from external or internal causes. The Solomon Islanders and New Caledonians, to whom we referred in chapters 1 and 2, have changed their ways of life over the past century as the result of colonial incursions and Christian missions: both external causes. Many of their communities have forsaken subsistence agriculture, hunting, and fishing, for wage labor or have come to supplement their subsistence economy with wage labor in colonial and neocolonial enterprises such as plantations and mines. Around the time that colonial officials and traders reached the Solomon Islands and New Caledonia, missionaries, the majority of whom were Pacific Islanders, also arrived. Hence, for better or worse, new religious options were added to the repertoire of indigenous myths and rituals. Today most people in these neighboring areas of Melanesia have appropriated biblical stories and Christian practices and consider themselves to be Christians.[1]

While cultures develop their own characteristic ways of understanding the human condition, modern circumstances bring people from different cultural backgrounds together within the same nation and even within the same city. Hence, people may be, at the one time, exposed to several worldviews, each employing its own metaphors, each proposing a model for understanding the human condition. Sometimes a person of one culture marries a person of another culture. Such multicultural situations call for respect, and they afford opportunities to stretch our imaginations as, along with our fellow human beings of various cultural backgrounds, we try to comprehend and negotiate our time and place in the world. In order to reflect on religion in multicultural contexts, openness and a willingness to dialogue are essential.

Cultures propose different understandings of what it means to be human, and they educate the potential human being so that it may approach the cultural ideal of personhood. That area of culture which we refer to as religion is employed in inculcating such understandings. Religion provides guiding narratives and paradigmatic rituals to encourage the development of the person and community. Via word and ritual, religion transmits its vision of true humanity from generation to generation. The vision is, of course, challenged and modified. It is experienced by some as true and harmonious and by others as false and alienating.

The Zuni of the Southwest of the United States encapsulate their understanding of the world in rituals and storytelling and prayers. The matrilineal Zuni live in a multistoried adobe pueblo, into which they incorporated six or seven earlier pueblo communities after conflicts with the Spanish in west central New Mexico. They tell that their ancestors emerged from underground and then journeyed to their present location. Their relationship with rain beings called "dwellers in the clouds" (*uwan-ammi*) and their messengers (*kachinas*) was established at that time, and priesthoods, including twelve rain priesthoods charged with responsibility for moisture of four different kinds, were instituted. Unlike traditions in which religious expertise is attributed to individual shamans, the Zuni, a long-settled agricultural people whose traditional way of life remains largely intact, have developed groups of ritual practitioners. In English we would call them societies or priesthoods. Each priesthood has responsibility for an area of ritual performance.

A **shaman** is a religious practitioner who is able to induce a trance experience in which he or she is believed to contact spirits; this ability depends more on innate and individual qualities. A **priest**, one authorized by the community to carry out ritual, depends more on training in traditional practices. Religious officiants fall somewhere along a spectrum between the shamanic and the priestly. In traditional Native America, priestly religious practitioners tend to be found in communities with a primarily agricultural economy. Shamanic religious practitioners are more likely to be found in communities with a primarily hunting economy. Modern industrial societies, in which book education is highly valued, tend to have religious practitioners who, like Zuni priests, have undergone a long period of training followed by a form of investiture. However, these societies, which prize individualism, also have a number of charismatic religious practitioners who claim a personal religious empowerment more like that of a shaman.

Despite the incursion of modern life Zuni ceremonialism continues today with *kachinas* and clowns dancing in the plazas each summer as part of the process of maintaining right relationship between the people and the *uwanammis*. Zuni ritual regulates the annual cycle of the corn; it also regulates the cycle of human life. The prayer that the Zuni say for an infant on the eighth day of its life, as it is taken outdoors for the first time and presented to the sun, suggests that corn is the stuff of life. Like many Native American peoples the Zuni refer to corn, beans, and squash as "our three sisters." On the morning of the infant's presentation its head is washed by its father's female relatives. Corn meal, which is used in Zuni prayers and healing rituals, is placed in its hands. Then, at the moment of sunrise the child is taken out and, symbolically, placed on the road of life, linked to its ancestors, and introduced to the sun who does his part to ripen the corn and other crops on which human life depends.

In the Zuni prayer for the presentation of a newborn child to the sun, good wishes are addressed to the child, and corn meal ("prayer meal") is given to the sun. The prayer expresses the community's desires for the child and, moreover, like the Warlpiri initiation songs, its powerful and evocative words have a role to play in the shaping of the person. The infant has been born; it has biological life. However, the infant is not yet a cultural and religious person. For the child to become an authentic Zuni person, it must be introduced to the sun and set on the road of life. Then, as the girl or boy proceeds on life's way, there will be more prayers and rituals and stories to instruct it and shape it until the child becomes a real person. Notice that in the Zuni idiom the sun and stars are spoken of in kin terms—"our sun father," "our night fathers."

ZUNI PRAYER FOR PRESENTATION OF INFANT

Now this is the day
Our child,
Into the daylight
You will go out standing.
Preparing for your day,
We have passed our days.
When all your days were at an end,
When eight days were past,
Our sun father
Went in to sit down at his sacred place.
And our night fathers
Having come out standing to their sacred place,
Passing a blessed night
We came to day.
Now this day
Our fathers,
Dawn priests,
Have come out standing to their sacred place.
Our sun father
Having come out standing to his sacred place,
Our child,
It is your day.
This day,
The flesh of the white corn,
Prayer meal,
To our sun father
This prayer meal we offer.
May your road be fulfilled
Reaching to the road of your sun father,
When your road is fulfilled
In your thoughts (may we live)
May we be the ones whom your thoughts will embrace,

For this, on this day
To our sun father.
We offer prayer meal.
To this end
May you help us all to finish our roads.[2]

Thinking with Corn

1. What experiences have you had with corn and corn products? Have you eaten it, cooked with it, used it for decoration? Is it a regular part of your diet?
2. What sayings and images do you have that depend on the qualities of corn? What times and places does corn evoke for you?
3. What experiences do the Zuni have with corn in sustaining their natural, cultural, and religious life? How do these experiences differ from your experiences with corn? What foods and/or drinks sustain your natural, cultural, and religious life?
4. What qualities of corn are evoked in the Zuni prayer given above?

STUDYING RELIGION

"Religion" is a term that ordinary people use when they talk about gaining access to whatever it is they consider ultimately life-giving. In addition "religion" is a term that scholars use when they study people's ideas and practices concerning whatever they consider ultimately life-giving. We have been discussing religion as the area of culture which orders life in an ultimate sense. Human beings link themselves to other people in social networks. They recognize a relationship to other sentient beings and to the world in which they live. These relationships may be life-giving or, at times, life-inhibiting. Human beings also link themselves to whatever they regard as most empowering. Christians, Jews, and Muslims appeal to God. Melanesians nurture relationships with their ancestors and their land spirits. Buddhists seek *nirvana*, release from all the attributes of sensory existence. Taoists attune themselves to nature. When scholars study all these quests for life in its fullness, they do so under the rubric of religion. They may be assisted in their study by insights from history, anthropology, and other disciplines, but religious studies is also seen as a discipline in its own right.

The modern study of religion grew out of the **Enlightenment**, a philosophic movement which questioned traditional authority and emphasized the use of reason. In eighteenth-century Europe the Enlightenment motivated people to think for themselves. A consequence was that many people abandoned the teachings of their churches and synagogues, saying that they wanted to reason things out for themselves and not to accept blindly what was passed on from generation to generation by priests and rabbis. For Enlightenment thinkers the scientific method, not tradition, was the way to true knowledge. Even those who remained within their faith traditions were affected by the spirit of the Enlightenment, some trying to understand religious teachings in humanistic ways, others becoming defensive about religious teachings that seemed to be opposed to reason.

The Enlightenment encouraged scholars to be more critical in their study of religion, to make use of tools from the study of languages and literature, and to employ scientific and historical methods. For example, biblical scholars came to rely more on archaeology and philology in establishing contexts for the religious texts they sought to explicate. The Enlightenment began a movement which has taken the study of religion beyond the confines of religious institutions to the larger academy. Today people study religion not only because they might themselves be religious and, therefore, want to know more about something which is important to them, but also because religion is a part of the experience of humankind and, as such, is worth studying. The modern critical study of religion looks not only to the positive contributions that religion has made, but also to the suffering it has caused and the destruction it has wrought.

Contemporary religious scholarship makes a distinction between natural religion and revealed religion. This distinction appears in the work of Immanuel Kant (1724-1804), one of the pioneers in the modern study of religion. Kant understood natural religion as a sensibility or faculty common to all people, an aspect of the human spirit, whereas he understood revealed religion as a set of beliefs and practices passed on within a community which claims to have received them from God. Obviously claims that a religion is revealed are made by people inside a tradition. They accept the content of the revelation in a commitment of faith; then they devote themselves to explicating it. For example, a Christian who accepts that Jesus is Lord and Savior will say that he or she does so on faith. However, in explicating what it means to say that Jesus is Lord and Savior, the person might use psychological analysis to tell us why human beings are in need of salvation and historical and literary analysis to situate Jesus and his message in a particular time and place. She might present archaeological evidence identifying sites connected with Jesus' ministry.

Scholars not belonging to the religious tradition they are studying may be more concerned to look at how the religion functions than to explicate its basic tenets. Hence, they ask: Does a particular religious belief or practice, or a religious tradition as a whole, help people to lead happy and generous lives? Does it stifle their creativity and result in guilt complexes? Whether they are insiders or outsiders, scholars are concerned both to obtain accurate descriptions of the insiders' experiences of

MARY N. MACDONALD

Mayan Temple, Pacbitun, Belize. This major ceremonial site was first occupied around 1000 B.C.E. Archaeology is expanding our knowledge of many ancient religions, including that of the Maya.

religion and to assess the ways that religion functions in the lives of individuals and communities.

Tu Wei-ming, a professor of Chinese history and philosophy at Harvard University, teaches and writes about Confucianism and contributes to discussions of the role that religion plays in the modern world. Tu was born in mainland China, studied in Taiwan, and has taught for several years in the United States. He says that when he first studied Confucianism, an ethical system based on the teachings of **Confucius** (551-479 B.C.E.), he approached it as a historian. Next he adopted a philosophic stance, analyzing the ideas and the concepts in the teachings of Confucius and his followers. More recently, he says, he has examined it as religionist, seeing it as a religious system which holds out the possibility of perfecting human nature through self-effort. Tu told interviewer Bill Moyers that he had come to look on Confucianism as "a process of learning to be human," and that he took the Confucian mandate of heaven to be "one's ability to go beyond anthropocentrism,"[3] the ability to go beyond human self-interest. Taking this Confucian concept as a starting point, he can bring Confucianism into dialogue with other religious traditions and see what *they* say about going beyond human self-interest. Tu Wei-ming's work is important as a bridge between Eastern and Western approaches to the study of religion, and also as a bridge between practitioners of religion and scholars of religion.

Since the Enlightenment the study of religion has taken three major directions. The first, an outcome of the Enlightenment stress on reason, suggests that religion is part of the world of ideas, a matter of thinking, concerned with truth and wisdom. The second, which is a development from the first, proposes that religion is part of the moral order, a matter of discrimination and behavior, concerned with goodness. The third, which places the other two in a wider context, says that religion is part of aesthetics, a matter of a feeling for relationships and patterns, concerned with order and beauty. The three perspectives, corresponding to the classical triad of "the good, the true, and the beautiful," are interconnected. It might seem that by framing our discussion in this book in terms of the human propensity to order our individual and communal lives, we have adopted a primarily aesthetic perspective. However, in the following chapters we shall also be examining the efforts of religious people to find truth and live good lives.

DEFINING RELIGION

In thinking about an area of experience, such as religion, in a systematic way, we can be helped by definitions. Definitions set boundaries for what it is we are studying, and the attempt to define obliges us to clarify our ideas. Definitions are not, however, value-free; they tell us a lot about the interests and orientations of the people who make them. For example, the French writer, philosopher, and social activist, Jean-Paul Sartre (1905-1980), characterizes religion as "an attempt to escape responsibility." His definition is part of a pattern of ideas about human freedom and responsibility which leads him to a negative evaluation of religion. On the other hand, the Christian theologian and philosopher Rudolf Otto (1869-1937) defines religion as "the experience of the Holy." As a young student of **theology** Otto had studied the life of the Protestant reformer, Martin Luther (1483-1546), and had become intrigued with the human response to what he called the *mysterium tremendum et fascinans*, the "awe-inspiring and attracting (appealing/enchanting) mystery." Luther, of course, saw himself standing before an awe-inspiring and fascinating mystery which he called God. Otto speculated that in traditions other than Christian there were comparable concepts. In his writings he referred to them as "the numinous," the "wholly other," the "transcendent," or, his preferred term, "the Holy."

In studying religion as a general field, and in studying the religions of Oceania in particular, the following working definitions have been used:

1. Religion is awareness expressed through symbols of relationship to, or participation in, the fundamental power of life.

2. Religions are symbol systems which facilitate relationship to, or participation in, what the members understand to be the fundamental power of life.

The first definition presents religion as a disposition, a way of apprehending the powerful and life-giving mystery of the world and engaging with it. The second definition recognizes that religions, as human constructions, are usually developed by communities and so become systems which communities share but which may admit of variation in individual or group usage. These definitions allow that the practitioner of religion may believe in God or spirits or the influence of ancestors but does not require that he or she do so. Using these definitions one could study Taoism and Confucianism as religions because both are systems of symbols which encourage and facilitate participation in the fundamental power of life, even though they do not posit the existence of a god. If one's interests were more theological, or more psychological, or more philosophical, a different definition could be crafted.

Defining is an analytic Enlightenment way of going about the study of religion. A definition circumscribes an area of experience and thus sets it out for further investigation. The recent *Harper Collins Dictionary of Religion* (San Francisco, 1995), edited by Jonathan Z. Smith, proposes that religion be understood as "a system of beliefs and practices relative to superhuman beings." The believer has faith in the superhuman beings of the definition. The nonbeliever may not ascribe objective reality to the superhuman beings but recognizes their significance to the members of a religious community. The focus on superhuman beings excludes Nazism, Marxism, and secularism as religions, whereas someone could conceivably make a case for including them under my working definition. Taken at face value the definition also excludes the religion of Taoists and Confucianists and many Buddhists, who look on their faiths more as ways of wisdom than as ways of devotion to a superhuman being.

Definitions of religion tend to take one of two directions. Some, including mine and that of J.Z. Smith, focus on religion as a system of symbols, or a system of beliefs and practices, embedded in human experience. Others focus on religion as experience of the transcendent. For the theologian working within a religious tradition, and for scholars such as Mircea Eliade, experience of the transcendent is taken for granted as part of the human condition. It is accepted as a structure of reality. There are, however, other scholars of religion who would neither affirm nor deny the reality of the transcendent. While they regard formulations such as God, sacred, holy, mana, and transcendence as important encapsulations of human experience, these scholars say they cannot think of any way in which claims of transcendence can be proved or disproved. Hence, they may "bracket" their own belief or disbelief and proceed to study how religion functions in human communities. Or, like Tu Wei-ming, they may seek to discover in ancient formulations some wisdom for going beyond anthropomorphism to a larger view of life in the world. Both the scholars who doubt that transcendence is anything more than a human way of speaking of the mystery of life and scholars who wholeheartedly profess faith in a transcendent reality recognize the importance of the transcendent to faith. All of them report on the ways it is conceptualized and made part of religious practice.

Thinking by Defining

Analyze the definitions which follow, and if possible discuss them with another person. After reading each definition consider: Does the definition accord with the way you have been accustomed to think about religion? Why, or why not? Would you be able to use it as a framework for describing the religious experience of people you know? Why, or why not?

1. Religion is a "feeling of absolute dependence." Religion is "the consciousness that the whole of our spontaneous activity comes from a source outside of us."
   (Friedrich Schleiermacher, 1768-1834, theologian)

2. Religion is "an institution of culturally patterned interaction with culturally postulated superhuman beings."
   (Melford Spiro, contemporary anthropologist)

3. "Religion is the aspect of depth in the totality of the human spirit." "Religion is an expression of ultimate concern."
   (Paul Tillich, 1886-1965, theologian and philosopher)

4. Religion is "the recognition of all duties as divine commands."
   (Immanuel Kant, 1724-1804, philosopher)

5. Religion is "a set of symbolic forms and acts that relate man to the ultimate conditions of his existence."
   (Robert Bellah, contemporary sociologist)

We saw that the European philosophical movement known as the Enlightenment stressed reason. On the one hand, it prompted those who valued religion to show the reasonableness of their faith and to use scholarly tools in studying religion. On the other hand, the Enlightenment prompted scholars to study religions as social phenomena without respect for the reasonableness of their particular truth claims. In the wake of the Enlightenment the modern social sciences, such as anthropology, sociology, and psychology, developed. Social scientists, such as sociologist Emile Durkheim, psychologist William James, and anthropologist E.E. Evans-Pritchard, have given attention to the ways that religion operates both functionally and dysfunctionally in individual lives and in communities. The social sciences have, for example, considered the role of religion in politics, in economics, and in class and gender construction. Archaeology has made a large contribution to our study of prehistoric cultures and led most scholars to the conclusion that all known societies have had some forms of religious expression.

SYMBOLIC FORMS

Some scholars, including Ernst Cassirer (1874-1945) of the University of Marburg, have thought that the Enlightenment project carried out by people like Kant was incomplete because it stressed reason but neglected the consciousness of symbolic forms. Cassirer, whose three-volume work *The Philosophy of Symbolic Forms* has influenced contemporary religious studies, believed that there was more to thinking than the exercise of formal logic. He saw his reflections on symbolic awareness as extending the work of Kant. Cassirer gives place to both mythical consciousness, which emphasizes participation in life, and scientific consciousness, which analyzes parts of life. An awareness of and openness to symbolic language is, in his view, basic to any philosophy. Most people working in religious studies would say that it is basic to the study of religion.

Human beings communicate with symbols, that is, with words, gestures, and objects that evoke or stand for other things. Symbols carry meaning. They help human beings to interpret their experience. We saw that in Zuni experience corn has come to represent the very stuff of life to the extent that special corn meal, known as prayer meal, is used in most rituals. Similarly, in the experience of Christians bread and wine have come to symbolize the fullness of life and self-giving. The present-day French philosopher Paul Ricoeur points out that symbols are multivalent. That is, they carry multiple meanings which will be revealed according to the way we approach them and according to our own life experience. It is not only, Ricoeur would say, that we interpret symbols but that the symbols provided by our religious and cultural traditions help us to interpret ourselves.[4]

The twenty-third psalm from the biblical Book of Psalms presents us with reciprocal images of shepherd and lamb in order to have us reflect on the relationship of God and God's people. Many Jews and Christians have learned this psalm by heart as children. Even those who have grown up in surroundings where sheep are rare and those who have grown up in places like Australia and New Zealand, where flocks of sheep are so huge that the relationship of sheep and shepherd is very different from that of the psalmist's Israel, have been schooled in the significance of the hymn's central image. In reading the psalm note its evocative quality and the concreteness of its language.

PSALM 23

The Lord is my shepherd, I shall not want.
   He makes me lie down in green pastures;
he leads me beside still waters;
   he restores my soul.
He leads me in paths of righteousness
   for his name's sake.

Even though I walk through the darkest valley,
    I fear no evil;
for you are with me;
    your rod and your staff–
    they comfort me.

You prepare a table before me
    in the presence of my enemies;
you anoint my head with oil;
    my cup overflows.
Surely goodness and mercy shall follow me
    all the days of my life,
and I shall dwell in the house of the LORD
    my whole life long.

MARYKNOLL PHOTO LIBRARY/J. TOWLE, M.M.

Teenager Bette Tuso, an Aymara Indian of Peru, cares for a new lamb in her Andean village.

Would we be able to express the sentiments of the psalm in more straightforward, less symbolic language? "God cares for me" does not say as much as "The Lord is my shepherd." Children can uncover some facets of the psalm's imagery; adults are able to plumb further depths. As children the psalm may help us to trust and to see the world as basically a benevolent place in the hands of God. As teenagers who have suffered losses, we may uncover other aspects of the shepherd's care for the sheep and may become attentive to our need for healing. As adults the image of the valley of death may move us to reflect on our own mortality and our experiences of alienation. As we accept responsibility for caring for others—as parents, teachers, community leaders—we may come to identify with the shepherd. In other words, the meaning of religious symbols is not limited to one-to-one correspondences. Symbols are evocative, drawing on our life experience and the shared history of the communities which employ them.

A symbol is something that stands for something else. A distinction may be made between representational symbols and presentational symbols. Some would call this a distinction between signs and true symbols. Representational symbols or signs point to or stand for something else but do not necessarily participate in the realities for which they stand. Presentational symbols are necessarily connected to that which they symbolize. A green light is a representational symbol. It means "Go," because we have arbitrarily agreed that it means "Go." We could just as easily have agreed that a red light means "Go." Religious symbols are more likely to be presentational. For example, in Christian iconography the church is presented as a ship, a barque. A ship is a temporary home, transporting its passengers over calm and stormy seas to their destination. In the context of early Christianity the church, a community set upon by a dangerous world but yet secure in its faith, could seem like a ship tossed by the seas. Thus, the early Christians came to see the ship as a symbol of the church because it had qualities analogous to those of the church.

A presentational symbol is something which suggests something else by virtue of analogous qualities. It "presents" the other through its own qualities. The analogous qualities may be colors or shapes or patterns of behavior. In the association of the shepherd with God in the twenty-third psalm, a comparison is made between the way a shepherd cares for and protects the flock and the way God cares for and protects his people. Think of symbols in which you represent your relationships with friends and family. What does each of the symbols suggest? Is there anyone you would call a shepherd—or a bus driver or doctor or coach—not because that is the person's actual occupation but because of qualities or attributes which suggest such an occupation?

The meaning of symbols is determined by the contexts in which they are located. Very often they are part of rituals or part of religious narratives. Religious symbols, such as the sharing of food in the Eucharist or the image of the shepherd and the sheep, point to the fundamental power of life, to the sacred. They draw us beyond our everyday lives into the power and mystery of life. To put it another way, symbols suggest an ultimate order and meaning which we are encouraged to create in the world. Moreover, since symbols are usually shared by groups, they serve as rallying points, vehicles to articulate and reinforce group loyalties.

Thinking with Symbols

Symbols may awaken our consciousness to new ways of thinking about ourselves and our world. Take any religious symbol with which you are familiar, or on which you would like to do some research, as a basis for reflection. It may be a statue of the seated Buddha, which suggests peace and enlightenment. It may be a wampum belt, used by the Haudenosaunee to send messages and to seal commitments. It may be an image from a prayer or poem, a character from a hero myth, or a ritual action.

1. What do you know about the symbol's religious context?
2. What does the symbol suggest to you? How does it appeal to your senses (sight, touch, taste, smell, hearing)?
3. How does your interpretation of the symbol coincide with, and differ from, that of the tradition to which it belongs?
4. How does the symbol interpret you? How does it help you think about your own life, your relationships to other people, the world about you, the mystery of life?

In this section of our conversations about religion we have explored religion as an area of human experience. We have suggested that religion is a symbolic process which enables us to make connections to the world beyond ourselves, to think about and get in touch with the fundamental power of life, to bring order and meaning to the time and space in which we live. We have seen that people who study religion may or may not be religiously inclined themselves. Those who are religious and who study religion want to better understand the nature and practice of religion. Those who are not religious are, nevertheless, fascinated with the role that religion has played and continues to play in the world. In succeeding sections we shall explore ways that people act religiously and the ways that people talk about their religious experience. We shall see how religions assist and also inhibit the quest for authenticity. And, we shall see the resilience of religious traditions in re-creating themselves from age to age. The study of religion on which we have embarked is very much a study, as Wallace Stevens might say, of the "idea of order" in the experience of human communities.

RESOURCES

Activities

1. Arrange a debate within the class to defend and oppose the following statement: "We live in a multicultural and multireligious world. It is, therefore, impossible to hold particular religious commitments without slighting the commitments of others."

2. Construct a working definition of religion. Write a page commenting on each significant phrase in your definition. Modify your definition as you reach the end of each chapter in this book. As you modify a part of the definition write a note indicating why you made the change. Think about the definition as a practical tool which will help you by circumscribing the area of human life which you are exploring.

3. In the Public Television series *Cosmos* (1980) the eminent popularizer of science, Carl Sagan (1934-1996), makes a case for the scientific method as the way to plumb the mysteries of the universe. In his last book, *The Demon-Haunted World: Science as a Candle in the Dark* (New York: Random House, 1996), Sagan reiterates that good science is our only hope in understanding the world. Sagan does not deny that religions may have some insight into the human condition, but he clearly regards science and religion as opposed worlds. Consult works by Sagan in order to understand his point of view, and then write a page summarizing "Sagan's Point of View." Think about how a religious person who also takes science seriously might respond to Sagan's point of view, and then write a paragraph of "Response to Sagan."

4. Rewrite the twenty-third psalm, or another psalm, in everyday language. (If you choose a long psalm rewrite only part of it.) Which version do you prefer? Why? Post your rewriting of the psalm to your class computerized bulletin board if you have one. If not, make copies to distribute in class.

5. Identify the specializations of the members of your Religious Studies department or its equivalent. How does each of these scholars go about the study of religion? You may work in groups and interview the scholars to find out how each understands his or her contribution to the study of religion.

6. Imagine that you are a non-Christian scholar who has been sent to report on a celebration of the Lord's Supper at a local church. Write a report saying (a) what you observed, and (b) how you interpreted it. You will need to actually attend a celebration of the Lord's Supper in order to carry out this activity. If it happens that you are a Christian you will need to set your own presuppositions aside in recording your observations.

Readings

John Elder and Steven C. Rockefeller. *Spirit and Nature: Why the Environment Is a Religious Issue.* Boston: Beacon Press, 1992. A discussion of current ecological issues and religious responses to them.

Carlo Ginsburg. *Clues, Myths, and the Historical Method.* Baltimore: The Johns Hopkins University Press, 1989. Historian Ginsburg reflects on how we construct knowledge and what we might do to retrieve a "history" which is fuller and richer than that which our current methodologies make available to us.

John Hick. *An Interpretation of Religion*. New Haven: Yale University Press, 1992. A philosophical approach to the study of religion which suggests that religions may be looked upon as culturally conditioned responses to the mystery of being.

Jacob Olupona, ed. *African Traditional Religions in Contemporary Societies*. New York: Paragon House, 1991. A collection of papers by African scholars discussing indigenous sacred ways in modern contexts.

Robert A. Orsi. *The Madonna of 115th Street: Faith and Community in Italian Harlem 1880-1950*. New Haven: Yale University Press, 1985. A narration of the religious experience of an Italian immigrant community in New York City.

Priscilla Pope-Levison and John R. Levison. *Jesus in Global Contexts*. Louisville, KY: Westminster/John Knox Press, 1992. Exploration of the symbol of Jesus in a variety of cultures, with particular attention to materially disadvantaged peoples and the perspectives of women.

Charles E. Rosenberg. *No Other Gods: On Science and American Social Thought*, rev. ed. Baltimore and London: Johns Hopkins University Press, 1997. Rosenberg, a social historian of medicine, examines the ways in which our conception of knowledge and our search for knowledge are conditioned by the culture of which they are part.

Arvind Sharma, ed. *Women in World Religions*. Albany, NY: SUNY Press, 1987. A presentation of the traditional and contemporary situation of women in the world religions.

Lawrence E. Sullivan, ed. *Native American Religions: North America*. New York: Macmillan, 1989. A selection of essays on Native American religions taken from the 1987 *Encyclopedia of Religion*.

Tu Wei-ming. *Confucian Traditions in East Asian Modernity: Moral Education and Economic Culture in Japan and the Four Mini-Dragons*. Cambridge, MA: Harvard University Press, 1996.

Audiovisuals

Image Bank for the Teaching of World Religions.

Presentation of infant to tutelary *kami*, Japan (Slides 0089-0103),

Mayan temples (Slides 4037-4056).

Hopi: Songs of the Fourth World. Produced and directed by Pat Ferrero. Wayne, NJ: New Day Films, 1983. This documentary presents the traditional worldview and way of life of the Hopi. It shows how their religion and art are integrated with experiences of a particular landscape and community. Their relationship to corn, their staple crop and a central religious symbol, is highlighted. Through interviews with a number of Hopi people the documentary describes Hopi experiences with the Anglo world and the changes that these have brought to the community.

Searching for God in America. Hosted by Hugh Hewitt. PBS, 1996. Consists of eight thirty-minute programs in which Hewitt interviews religious leaders about their commitments and about the spiritual quests of contemporary Americans.

Those interviewed are the Rev. Charles Colson (Evangelical), Rabbi Harold Kushner (Jewish), the Rev. Cecil Murray (African Methodist Episcopal), Father Thomas Keating (Catholic), the Rev. Roberta Hestenes (Presbyterian), Dr. Seyyed Hossein Nasr (Muslim), Elder Neal A. Maxwell (Mormon), His Holiness the XIV Dalai Lama (Buddhist).

Sir Edward Evans-Pritchard: Strange Beliefs. Available from Films for the Humanities and Sciences, P.O. Box 2053, Princeton, NJ 08543-2053. This fifty-two minute film examines the career of the first trained anthropologist to work in Africa. Evans-Pritchard's reports on the religious beliefs and practice of the Azande and the Nuer challenged religious studies scholars to take seriously the religious worlds and sentiments of "primitive" peoples.

Tu Wei-ming: A Confucian Life in America. Available from Films for the Humanities and Sciences, P.O. Box 2053, Princeton, NJ 08543-2053. This thirty-minute film introduces the modern Confucian scholar, Tu Wei-ming, a professor at Harvard University, who explores Confucian teaching from the points of view of both secular humanism and religion.

NOTES

1. For a history of Christianity in Oceania see Charles Forman, *The Island Churches of the South Pacific* (Maryknoll, NY: Orbis, 1982); John Garrett, *To Live among the Stars: Christian Origins in Oceania* (Suva: University of the South Pacific Press, 1982).

2. Ruth Bunzel, *Zuni Ritual Poetry* (Washington, D.C.: Smithsonian Institution, Bureau of American Ethnology, 47th Annual Report, 1929), 635.

3. Bill Moyers, *A World of Ideas II* (New York: Doubleday, 1990), 110.

4. See, for example, Paul Ricoeur, *Interpretation Theory* (Fort Worth: Texas University Press, 1974).

PART II

RELIGIOUS ACTION

Leaving the familiar surroundings of our hometowns, families, and friends to face the unknown worlds of college or work can intimidate, confuse, even scare us. To help calm our fears we fill our rooms and apartments with treasures from home: pictures of friends and family, a stereo and favorite compact disks, a comfortable blanket and pillow. Through sight, sound, and touch these treasures symbolize what we find meaningful in our lives and help us to order our new environments. Yet we cannot stop there. To make the transition to college or work life we seek to make new friends, to familiarize ourselves with the campus or workplace, and to discern the expectations of our new institutions. Fortunately, returning students or co-workers are there to orient and to guide us. Eventually we develop a routine that helps us to order our new worlds: we fix our rooms and apartments to make them comfortable and to express our personalities, we set our schedules to accommodate our work patterns, and we develop relationships and engage in activities that reflect our values and interests.

As the previous chapters make clear, the search for order and meaning is not a passive enterprise. Finding meaning and purpose in a world often filled with ambiguity, suffering, and confusion requires some action on the part of us all, as individuals and as members of communities. The next two chapters discuss two types of action: ritual and ethical. Ritual and ethics are symbolic and practical actions that help us make sense of our lives, to give life order and direction, to relate us to one another in harmony with the worldviews we affirm.

Chapter 4 explores the nature of religious ritual as a form of symbolic action which provides meaning and order for religious people. The chapter begins with a review of the nature of ritual action, the distinctiveness of religious ritual, its symbolic/expressive dimensions, and its personal and social functions. We follow this with a discussion of three types of religious rituals: life-cycle rituals, life-crisis rituals, and periodic rituals. Life-cycle rituals refer to those rituals that are chronological, occurring over the lifetime of an individual. These rituals celebrate and commemorate key transitions in the life of an individual and reflect a certain structure which we can analyze in the context of birth, adulthood, marriage, religious vocation, and death. Life-crisis rituals enable individuals and communities to cope with natural and human calamities, including illness, accident, and death. Periodic rituals are rituals that celebrate seasons in the year or commemorate specific historical events. These rituals provide an opportunity for reflection, to take stock, and to redirect individual and communal life. We discuss the rituals associated with **Kwanzaa** to illustrate these functions.

The focus of chapter 5 is on the nature of ethical action—a form of practical action which religious traditions prescribe as in keeping with their perception of the ultimate ordering of life. The chapter begins with a general discussion of ethics followed by consideration of the relationship between religion and morality. We contend that religion and morality are intricately connected; one cannot be religious without being moral. The focus then turns to the ways in which religion provides ethical action with its source, sanction, and goal. In particular, we look at how religion provides norms for both moral conduct and moral character. Under the rubric of norms for moral conduct, we explore three types of moral obligations that religions provide: laws, ends, and responsibilities. The section on norms for moral character includes discussions of the development of moral conscience/consciousness, moral affections and virtues, and illustrations of how these are embodied in moral exemplars. This is followed by a discussion of how religions not only provide norms for individuals but also societies. We conclude the chapter, and the section, with a detailed discussion of the interrelationship between ritual and ethical action.

Chapter 4

Ritual Action

Rituals are symbolic, routine, and repetitive activities and actions through which we make connections with what we consider to be the most valuable dimensions of life. They are often associated with significant events or places in our individual and communal lives. Rituals set aside specific times and places and provide us opportunity to ponder their meaning and to connect emotionally. The birthday candles, the cake, the giving of gifts—all celebrate the value of a person's life and make room for reflection upon what that life has meant over the past year and the year ahead. The bedtime rituals between parents and children—sharing a favorite story, giving a kiss and a hug, saying a prayer—solidify the parent-child bond and affirm the importance of family.

Ritual actions enable us to maintain continuity with significant persons and events from the past. The ceremonial first pitch in baseball's Fall classic, the World Series, is often thrown by a member of the baseball Hall of Fame, a person remembered for his contributions to the sport. The Hall of Fame itself in Cooperstown, New York, is the place that enshrines the great ones of baseball, such as Babe Ruth and Hank Aaron, and enables fans to celebrate and to pay homage to their accomplishments. Traditional African families build shrines on the burial sites of those considered to be Ancestors, deceased prominent members of the family or community, to honor their spirits and to seek their favor in the ongoing life of the community.

Rituals, further, commemorate significant events in the life of our communities and provide a means for renewing the meaning of those events among us. For example, the Fourth of July holiday and its rituals celebrate the beginnings of America. Community picnics and fireworks displays pay tribute to the sacrifices made by the revolutionaries, the prolific display of flags celebrates the emergence and the unity of the nation, and the playing and singing of patriotic songs declare anew the values of freedom and equality. In the Passover ritual, Jews celebrate the freedom of their Hebrew ancestors from Egyptian oppression and their development as a people. During the Passover Seder, participants sing songs and the leader asks specific questions about the ritual foods and the Exodus event that prompt reflection on the meaning of being chosen as God's covenant partners.

Rituals can be exciting and dramatic, engaging all of our senses. Many Christians enjoy attending the midnight worship service on Christmas Eve even if they seldom attend church on other occasions. The sights of the sanctuary decorations and colorful clerical vestments, the smells of incense and pine, the sounds of ringing bells and beautiful voices, serve to heighten the significance of the Christmas season. In the Yoruba festival of *Odun Egungun,* the sounds of the rhythmic drums, the sights of the colorful masks, the smells of the sacrificial food, and the whirling motions of the dancers remind the community of the presence and power of the ancestors.

Rituals help us individually and communally to make sense of life's transitions, providing some structure to ease movement from the familiar to the unknown. Becoming an adult is a significant event in our lives. We move from the familiarity of dependence and the protection of childhood to assume the mantle of responsibility in the adult world. To aid in that transition, among the Yupik, an indigenous people of Alaska, fathers instruct their sons on the skills needed to kill their first seal. The ability to hunt seals is an essential attribute of a man and an important component of the community's survival. At the ceremony following the kill, the boy shares his kill with the entire community. This symbolizes that the boy has also developed the generosity to provide for others.

Moreover, although rituals have formalized patterns, they are still subject to change. Ritual actions often adjust to changes in values or worldviews. For example, wedding vows once included the promise to obey for women. This reflected a patriarchal structure of the family in which the husband was the head of the household and the wife played a subordinate role. Because of changing gender roles and the affirmation of equality between the partners in the marriage covenant, however, most wedding ceremonies today have dropped this vow. Some have gone a step further to emphasize the equality of the partners by having the parents accompany both the bride and the groom.

Like all symbolic action, our rituals can have different meanings depending upon the context or our experiences. The rituals associated with Christmas bring many Christian families together, providing opportunities for gathering with relatives and friends and for reaffirming the faith tradition they share. For Jews, however, Christmas rituals can be a source of frustration and alienation, partly because of the religious prejudice some Christians still harbor against Jews, and partly because of the pressure to embellish what were once quite simple Hanukkah rituals.

Moreover, to some extent, Jews have to participate in Christmas rituals even against their inclinations because they are so much a part of our culture. Similarly, Italian Americans celebrate Columbus Day, stressing the significance of the Italian-born explorer's discovery of the New World. The celebration of Columbus's birthday, on the other hand, reminds some Native Americans of their oppression and exploitation by Europeans, whose lust for resources and power resulted in the near destruction of indigenous traditions and civilizations, a catastrophe hardly worth celebrating.

RELIGIOUS RITUAL

Religious rituals share many of the features of ritual described above; some of the examples used are drawn from religious contexts. Some people who study religious ritual, however, want to distinguish it from other rituals. They see ritual as a critical component of religion and thus note the distinctiveness of religious ritual. Various definitions of religious ritual are available. Consider the following examples:

> [R]ites are the rules of conduct which prescribe how a man should comport himself in the presence of . . . sacred objects.
> —Emile Durkheim

> A religious ritual can be defined as an agreed-on and formalized pattern of ceremonial movements and verbal expressions carried out in a sacred context. —James C. Livingston

Although different, each definition suggests that there is a regularity or pattern to religious rituals ("rules," "formalized pattern") and that they are social in origin ("prescribe," "agreed-on"). Of course, all ritual activity can be described in this manner. What makes religious ritual distinct is its intention. Religious rituals connect our individual and communal efforts to order life and create relationship with what we perceive as ultimate or sacred orderings ("sacred objects," "sacred context").

When many of us define religion, we generally include beliefs and rules for living that provide some sense of meaning and direction for our lives. Missing in our definitions is any mention of practices. When pushed, we often speak of how the traditional rituals with which we grew up no longer provide meaning, order, or connection with a sense of ultimacy. For many of us, just the thought of having to attend another religious service raises concern. We look around and see people participating in these rituals who have no sense of the meaning dimension attached to them. In fact, we sometimes describe the rituals and practices we grew up with as a part of "organized" religion. We feel that we can still be "spiritual" without observing religious ritual.

Upon further exploration, we admit that what alienates us are particular rituals not ritual itself. We engage in other practices that provide meaning for us. We may pray freely instead of using the formal prayers we learned. We may hike though the woods to get in touch with our perception of the sacred. In other words, although we may not define our practices as religious rituals, they share similar ends. Our practices enable us to express our spirituality and provide a way to order our lives in concert with our sense of perceived ultimacy.

SYMBOLIC/EXPRESSIVE DIMENSIONS OF RITUAL

The previous chapters speak of the significance of symbols and signs. In that vein, religious ritual is significant action. Religious ritual expresses the connection with our perception of ultimacy or the sacred in the universe. Religious ritual expresses our deepest understandings of the world. Here the connection between ritual and **myth** emerges. Many religious rituals act out the great myths and stories of our religious traditions. They help to express a community's worldview and understanding of the ultimate ordering in the universe. As a result, many rituals are dramatic and performative. Christmas pageants have become ritualized for many churches. The children of the church practice for weeks as they assume the various roles surrounding the Christmas myths. The adult volunteers provide costumes and props: robes for the shepherds, wings for the angels, and gifts for the magi. Young people are given the important roles of Mary and Joseph. The magi come bearing their gifts. The drama sets the stage for the retelling of the myth. Often the congregation joins in by singing key Christmas carols. "Angels We Have Heard on High" accompanies the angel's announcement to the shepherds of the birth of Jesus. "We Three Kings" follows the entrance of the magi bearing their gifts. And "Silent Night" often concludes the dramatization.

Thinking about Ritual

Write down your own definition of religion. Using the categories we have discussed concerning religion in the text thus far, what components are present? What components are missing? What do you think about the rituals of your youth? Do they still provide meaning for you? Have they lost their meaning? Have you substituted other practices in their place to help you understand or get in touch with what you perceive to be ultimate in the universe? What are those other practices? How do they provide meaning for you?

Religious rituals are often expressive of our imaginative capacities. Religious rituals open the door for imagining another realm and for new possibilities. The meditation rituals associated with Zen Buddhism are a good example. The person who meditates recites a **koan** received from a master, a phrase or saying that defies the logic or worldview dominant in society. An example would be: "What did your face look like before your parents were born?" The purpose of reciting or reflecting on this word or phrase is to imagine a different world, to break free from cognitive constraints of one's culture, and so to achieve some sense of enlightenment. Similarly, the singing of spirituals by slaves in the United States helped them get through the day by providing some hope. "Sometimes I hangs my head an' cries, But Jesus going to wipe my weep'n eyes." The spirituals spoke about a world different from the pain and suffering they knew and enabled them to envision a life beyond slavery.

Many talents and abilities are expressed in religious ritual actions. Music, dance, art, and architecture often play critical roles. Many great works of music were composed to set the mood and tone for religious celebrations. The music of Johann Sebastian Bach (1685-1750) is a good example. Although he may be best known for his Brandenburg concertos, written for the private enjoyment of a prince, the vast majority of Bach's works express his deep religious faith. Bach spent most of his life as an organist and music director for churches in Germany. During his twenty-seven years as director of music at Saint Thomas' Church in Leipzig, Bach wrote hundreds of masses, oratorios, motets, and cantatas in which he displays a wide range of religious sentiments, from joyful celebrations of life to reflective meditations on death. Through his musical talents he explored the deep mysteries of his Christian faith and enabled his listeners to do the same. As a Lutheran, Bach realized that, regardless of one's chosen occupation or vocation, one could express one's love for God. That is why he signed each piece, *Sola Deo Gloria*, which means "to the glory of God alone."

Some of the world's great architectural achievements are dedicated to religious purposes. Cathedrals are good examples. The beautiful **stupas** associated with the Golden Temple in Bangkok, Thailand, are others. Initially, stupas were mounds of earth built over the remains of great persons as places of remembrance and worship. Mounds were built at places where the Buddha visited or preached, or where some relic was found. With the development of the notion of merit, and the belief that the power of the great person is still present with the relic or place, people began to make pilgrimages to the stupas. With the rise of the cult associated with Buddhism, larger, more ornate stupas were built. In Bangkok, the golden stupas house various sculptures of the Buddha (golden Buddha, emerald Buddha, reclining Buddha) which are the objects of religious veneration and devotion. These bell-like structures (they are dome-shaped in India) have elaborate carvings of mythic beings from popular local beliefs. The reverence paid by visiting pilgrims is not like the worship

FRED GLENNON

The Golden Temple in Bangkok, Thailand.

of a god. Instead, the pilgrims pay respect to the Buddha's attainment of enlightenment, the experience of full insight into the nature of reality as suffering; and they commit themselves to follow the Buddha's example.

Religious rituals also express our embodiedness in the world. They often transform routine bodily experiences, such as eating, drinking, bathing, and experiencing pain, into symbolic experiences of spiritual potency and ultimacy. Christians of all denominations imbue the routine acts of gathering to break bread and drink wine (or grape juice) with cosmic significance when they connect it with God's saving grace in the life, death, and resurrection of Jesus. Similarly, many religious traditions associate the act of bathing with purification and cleansing before coming into the presence of the sacred. Native Americans of the Plains bathe before pursuing a vision quest, preparing themselves for the connection with the sacred they are about to undertake. In preparation for the Sun Dance, Oglala Sioux pierce their bodies with leather thongs as they dance and gaze into the sun. The pain they experience reflects the pain associated with the birth and rebirth of creation.

Suggesting that religious rituals are expressive and symbolic or provide a sense of meaning does not mean that they always do so. Sometimes we lose sight of the meaning of our religious rituals. For example, Ash Wednesday marks the beginning of Lent for Christians, a time of reflection, prayer, and fasting in honor of Christ's sacrifice for the church. Having ashes placed upon one's head symbolizes one's commitment to reflect, pray, and fast. Many people walk around on this Wednesday with ashes on their forehead. When asked why they have ashes placed on their head each year, most simply respond that they do it because of their tradition. Others say, "Ashes to ashes, dust to dust." In doing so, they are attempting to suggest the symbolic meaning of the ritual activity. When asked what that statement means, however, many are unable to tell.

If we cannot express the purpose or aim of the ritual action, then why do we do it? Is it a waste of time? Some theorists of religious ritual conclude from this that ritual activity is action and that the ritual has intrinsic value even if we cannot connect it with any explicit meaning. One does the ritual even when one does not find meaning. Its significance comes from orthopraxy, right action, not orthodoxy, right thought. The ritual may have secondary effects, such as creating bonds between participants and reinforcing solidarity, but these are not their intention.[1]

PERSONAL AND SOCIAL FUNCTIONS OF RITUAL

Others who study religious rituals speak of their personal and social functions. The function of ritual for individual and social harmony is beautifully summarized by the Confucian scholar, Hsun Tzu:

> It is through rites that Heaven and earth are harmonious and sun and moon are bright, that the four seasons are ordered and the stars are on their courses, that rivers flow and that things prosper, that love and hatred are tempered and joy and anger are in keeping. They cause the lowly to be obedient and those on high to be illustrious. He who holds to the rites is never confused in the midst of multifarious change; he who deviates therefrom is lost. Rites—are they not the culmination of culture?[2]

This view illustrates the potential of ritual to help individuals find a sense of meaning and direction for their lives. They are able to make connections with the broader communities out of which they emerge.

Finding meaning and purpose in our lives is an important element of human experience. Religious communities have developed rituals to enable members to make this discovery and to celebrate its occurrence. For example, the Oglala Sioux developed the vision quest ritual. Through the vision quest a young person receives guidance and direction for his or her life. After undergoing some purification rituals, a guide takes the person seeking the vision to a distant sacred hill. The only provision the person may take is a blanket and a sacred pipe. While on this hill the seeker prays for a vision from the spirits. The spirits may speak to the seeker through animate or inanimate objects, such as a bird, a tree, or a rock. The experience lasts from two to four days. When the time is over, the guide retrieves the seeker and the community celebrates the seeker's adult status.

A hajj. Pilgrims circling the Ka'ba in Mecca, Saudi Arabia.

Religious rituals enable us to make connections with our heritage and history. They provide an understanding of the historical significance of our faith and a sense of belonging to a broader, even cosmic, community. One of the five pillars of Islam, the foundations of Islamic life, is the pilgrimage to Mecca (*hajj*). Those who take this journey travel to a sacred place, where Muslims believe Adam and Eve lived, where Abraham and his son Ishmael built the *Ka'ba* as the first house of worship for Allah, and where Muhammad and his followers prayed. They re-enact the rituals of significant persons in their tradition: they run in search of water like Hagar, Abraham's maidservant, did for her son Ishmael; they circumambulate the *Ka'ba* seven times on three occasions like the monotheistic worshipers of old; and they make a blood sacrifice of a consecrated animal as Abraham did when God tested his faith. Pilgrims get to see and meet fellow believers of all races and languages. They experience the unity and equality of the *Umma*, the worldwide Muslim community, in all of its rich diversity.

Religious rituals often provide benefits for us as individuals and for our communities. This dual function can be seen in the Buddhist ordination ritual. At the individual level, the ordinand receives a sense of mission, vocation, and purpose; he becomes a member of the *Sangha*, the community of monks who live together and participate in the practices and rituals that line the path leading to enlightenment. At the communal level, the ordinand's spiritual energies are released for the benefit of the community, especially for his relatives and those ancestors who may be suffering in hell. By renouncing all worldly pleasures, he becomes a storehouse of spiritual power that others can draw upon. Some communities believe that the sexual renunciation of the monks enhances the fertility of the entire community. For this reason the ordination rituals are often done prior to the rainy season.

TYPES OF RELIGIOUS RITUAL

There are many types of religious rituals. Some occur at significant moments in the life of the individual or community. They tend to be chronological: the key actors in the ritual engage in such rituals only once in their lifetime. Some religious rituals, however, are more cyclical: they occur periodically in the course of a year. Researchers do not agree on any one typology; instead they use a variety of typologies and classifications. As with any typology, there is the danger of oversimplifying.

Life-Cycle Rituals

Life-cycle rituals occur throughout our lives, celebrating key transitions, especially birth, initiation into adulthood, marriage, vocation, and death. Many of these events are marked by **rites of passage**. Rites of passage involve a variety of significant actions and rituals to mark the process of moving from one status in our lives or communities to another.

French anthropologist and ethnologist Arnold van Gennep (1873-1957), in his classic work, *Rites of Passage*, speaks of three phases associated with a rite of passage: *separation, transition (liminality)*, and *incorporation*. The *separation* phase is marked by symbolic behaviors or actions that stress the separation or detachment of the individual or group undergoing the rite from a previous status. For example, the vision quest often begins with purification rituals, such as bathing or time spent in the sweathouse. The person then leaves the tribe and goes to a place alone to await the vision. These activities separate the person from his former status within the community.

The *transition* or *liminal* phase prepares the person for the next status she will assume. This phase is ambiguous: she no longer possesses the old status but the new status has not been conferred. She is, in the words of symbolic anthropologist Victor Turner (1920-1983), "betwixt and between." The behavior and actions done in this phase prepare the person for her new status. The liminal phase is crucial because during this phase the person is outside of the structures of ordinary life and potentially exposed. The stage is set for new experiences of the sacred. In the vision quest, the person seeking the vision has no status within the community. He is left to his own devices with just his blanket and his pipe. At this stage, the person has no real direction for his life, he is seeking it from the spirits who will come to visit him. The spirits often come in the form of animals or birds, melting away the distinctions that are normal within the community.

The final phase of *incorporation* involves a variety of rituals and actions that confer the new status upon the person and welcome her back into the community. The guide retrieves the person seeking the vision and brings him back to the community. The person receives a new name, often associated with the animal form the spirit takes. There is a celebration and feast commemorating the new status of the person as an adult in the community. If the person is also a medicine man, then he becomes the apprentice of an experienced medicine man. Finally, the person receiving the vision shares the wisdom of that vision with the entire community.

The three phases are not developed to the same extent in every ceremony or rite of passage. Some ceremonies stress one phase over the other. For example, with birth rites, the phases of separation and incorporation are more significant than the transition or marginal phase. Rites of initiation into adulthood, however, often have longer transitional phases. Thus, while all rites may express some aspects of these three phases, the latter are not always equally important or developed by all religious peoples or cultures.

The birth of a child is a significant event in our lives, our families, and our communities; and numerous rituals accompany it. Friends and family give baby showers for the expectant couple, offering gifts for caring for the child (including books on how to parent). The parents select a name that has some significance for the couple or connects the child with the broader family. The family sends out a birth announcement, including a picture of a rather wrinkly newborn. In all of these rituals, the family commemorates the importance of this event for their lives and their families.

Similarly, religious communities have developed rituals to celebrate the event of the birth of a child and to connect it with its communal and cosmic significance. Often, there are separation and purification rituals attached to the celebration of the birth. One aspect of the traditional baptism ritual in Catholic churches is that it represents the washing away of Original Sin—the propensity of disobedience toward God that is inherent in the human condition and that was transmitted to humanity through the disobedience of Adam. Baptism, by imparting the life of Christ's grace, purifies the child from that condition and initiates the child into a community that pledges to provide nurture in the Christian faith. Some churches have the baptismal font in a separate building. Infant baptisms in some Protestant churches follow a similar pattern. The baptismal liturgies speak of the baptismal font as the place where the old person of Adam is washed away and the child becomes a new person in Christ. Then they challenge the parents, the godparents, and the congregation to provide appropriate Christian care and nurture.

In some traditional African religions, the heads of newborns are shaved to symbolize the cutting off of anything bad—shaved off with the old hairs—and the separation of the baby from its mother's womb. The communal significance of the birth can also be seen in the separation and naming rituals attached to it. Because the family's continuation is dependent upon the survival of the child, families separate their children from contact with others for a period of time and say prayers to insure the survival of the child. The naming of the child in some instances reflects the belief that the ancestors, important persons in the life of the family, are often reborn into new children. This is significant because ancestors are spiritually potent and can provide help to the community. A family presents the names of ancestors to the child until the child stops crying. When this occurs, the family chooses a name that reflects the belief that this ancestor has been reborn in that child.

Thinking about Birth

Think about the birth of your child (real or imagined). How do you feel about the experience? How have you prepared for it? What will you name the child? How will you involve family and friends in the experience?

Now think about your religious community. How do they welcome children into the community? Are there specific rituals, like baptism, attached to this event? Are these rituals private? public? both? What words are spoken by the leaders of the ritual? What role does the child play? What role do the parents play? What role does the congregation play?

Initiation rituals associated with moving into a new status are common occurrences. Graduation events celebrate the move from adolescence to the adult world of work and family. College campuses with fraternities and sororities are familiar with initiation ceremonies through which pledges become full members in the community. Ceremonies mark inductions into academic and athletic honor societies, such as Phi Beta Kappa and the Baseball Hall of Fame. What all these rituals have in common is that they reflect significant achievement and membership in a new status.

Religious rituals associated with initiation into adult status in the community reflect this same significance. There is usually some separation or gathering together, instruction in the ways of the religion or group, and a public ceremony welcoming the new members. From their youth, Jewish boys and, in some communities, girls receive instruction in the Hebrew language and Jewish tradition in preparation for their formal membership in the Jewish community. At about the age of thirteen, the age at which Jews believe their intelligence and self-consciousness have matured sufficiently, the boys and girls become a **bar/bat mitzvah**, literally a "son/daughter of the commandment." At this time, the community expects them to perform all the commandments and to take responsibil-

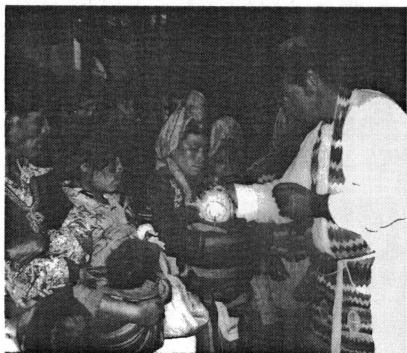

MARYKNOLL PHOTO LIBRARY/P. GAUDVIS

Infants being baptized in Guatemala.

ity for their religious behavior. During the ceremony, the young people publicly read from the Torah in the synagogue, symbolizing their new status as members of the religious majority, and the parents and the community say blessings in their honor. The service is followed by a celebration welcoming the young people as members of the religious majority.

In cultures where the lines between religion and society are less clearly drawn, the rituals attached to the transition to adulthood are significant because of their connections with the whole meaning of adulthood: not only do those initiated assume adult religious responsibilities and privileges, but they also assume the responsibilities of marriage and family. Male and female **circumcision** in some African cultures is reserved for this time. The cutting away of the foreskin of the penis or the removal of part or all of the clitoris allows blood to be spilled and connects the individual with the ancestors and the community. The young people are gathered together, circumcised by an adult skilled in the procedure, then separated from the community for a period of instruction on the responsibilities and expectations of religious and sexual adulthood. During this time, they are often dressed alike, representing their commonality and liminal status. At the end of the training period, the whole community welcomes them back with a public ceremony celebrating their new status.

Newlyweds at San Miguel Acatan, Guatemala.

Marriage is another significant stage in the life cycle that has various rituals attached to it. Historically, marriage brought families, rather than two individuals in love, together. Marriages were arranged to reinforce kinship ties or to enhance the social and economic status of the families involved. Traditional societies also stressed procreation in marriage as a central means for the survival of the community. In some modern societies, romantic love and personal happiness have become the primary motivations for marriage. In spite of this, however, the economic, social, and communal significance of marriage continues to play a role, and it is reflected in various marriage rituals.

In the United States, friends and families often hold wedding showers for the couple, where the couple receive gifts of dishes, cookware, and other items they will need to set up their own household. The activities surrounding the marriage ceremony take months of preparation and planning. The couple must decide when and where to have the ceremony and reception, whom to invite as participants and guests, what costumes, flowers, and music to adorn the event, and how to orchestrate each activity. The presence of flowers and children historically represented the promise of fertility. Leaving the home of the parents, entering the door of the church, and being carried over the threshold of the new home all signify the change in the status of newlyweds from adolescents, sons and daughters of their parents, to adults where they will establish a household and family of their own. Arnold van Gennep writes, "The door is the boundary between the foreign and the domestic worlds in the case of an ordinary dwelling, between the profane and sacred worlds in the case of a temple. Therefore to cross the threshold is to unite oneself with a new world."[3]

For many religious traditions the significance of marriage is not simply about the personal connection made between two people. There is also the importance of children for the life and well-being of the community. In Jewish tradition, marriage receives spiritual significance because the creation myths suggest it is ordained by God as the ideal human relationship and because it is the appropriate context for fulfillment of the first commandment: "be fruitful and multiply." Traditional Jewish marriage rites begin with the engagement, which at one time was a formal commitment to marry but is now a social occasion where the couple announces their intention to marry. The engagement period marks the separation from their formal single status and preparation for what is about to take place. The liminal status of their situation is reflected in the marriage contract, **kettuba** The contract provides a sense of equality between the partners; they covenant together and it protects them. The seven blessings reflected in the nuptial prayer connect the couple being married to the mythic couple, **Adam** and **Eve.** In this moment, there is an immediacy with the sacred reflected. The conclusion of the ceremony is marked by the groom's stomping on a drinking glass and the communal welcoming of the couple into the life of the community. In past times, the couple were taken to a room where they would sexually consummate their marriage. Today, the period of privacy is brief and symbolic. The couple is then welcomed into the community and expected to fulfill the first commandment, "be fruitful and multiply." They fulfill the obligations associated with house and home.

Religious communities often associate certain activities and rituals with entrance into religious vocation. The structure or order of those rituals can be similar across different religions. Future religious leaders may experience some sense of call or vocation, or the mantle of leadership may be passed on from one generation to another. (It is quite common to discover that ministers have parents and grandparents who are also ministers.) Sometimes this occurs because the person or the community attaches religious significance to a specific event, experience, or vision/ dream. The community often validates the experience and provides a period of training for the person in the ways of religious leadership and the performance of religious rituals. Upon completion of the training, the community has a public ritual to celebrate the transition into religious leadership and to affirm the person's calling. Finally, the newly appointed religious leader undergoes some time in apprenticeship with an experienced religious leader to learn the practice and nuances associated with religious leadership.

Buddhism ordains monks in two ways. First, there is lower ordination. In many ways, this is a rite of passage from youth to adult re-

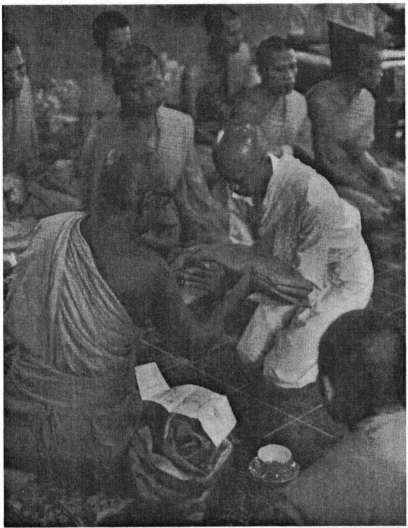

MARYKNOLL PHOTO ARCHIVES

In this Buddhist ordination ceremony, the young ordinand comes to the monastery to live where he will receive instruction in the Buddhist doctrines and way of life. Here he is receiving his robes.

sponsibility that is similar to a Jewish *bar/bat mitzvah* or a Catholic confirmation. In **Theravada Buddhism,** all persons must eventually follow the monastic path if they are going to reach enlightenment. The first ordination is an attempt to provide early training and instruction in the way and teachings of Buddhism. The young men who become ordained generally do not remain monks; most stay monks for about four months. They engage in monastic rituals, such as walking the streets begging for food, and they perform some priestly functions, such as the blessing of houses.

But generally they assume the role of apprentice and learn Buddhist doctrine. Ordination associated with religious vocation is known as the higher ordination. This time commitment to the monastic community is for life; one has dedicated onself to become an **arhant** (worthy one).

Both forms of ordination follow the pattern typical of rites of passage: separation, transition, and incorporation. The ordinands die and are reborn ritually. The ordinand leaves behind family and friends to live at the monastery. He leaves his clothes, shaves his head, undergoes a ritual bath, and receives a new name. All of these elements reflect the separation phase, the separation from a past life. The transition phase includes instruction in the ways of the monastic order. The ordinands vow to keep the **Ten Precepts** of Buddhism, which include the **Five Precepts** observed by all Buddhists plus the precepts not to take food from noon to the next morning; not to adorn their bodies with anything other than the three robes; not to participate in or be spectator to public entertainments; not to use high or comfortable beds; and not to use money. Those of higher ordination also commit themselves to keep the 227 rules of the monastic code. Any infractions of the rules are confessed publicly in the presence of other monks. They study together and learn the practice of meditation. They are taught how to perform the various rituals and blessings for the lay community.

Incorporation occurs in two stages. First, friends and relatives in the lay community provide cloth for the robes the ordinands will receive from the monks. Eventually, those undergoing lower ordination return to their communities. A public ceremony and celebration accompany this event. Those of higher ordination in Theravada Buddhism commit themselves to celibacy and remain in the community for life. Their interactions with the lay community are still important. The laity provide food and other basic material needs of the monks. These gifts enable the monks to practice the monastic path, to become models of spiritual and moral ideals, and to generate spiritual power. Rituals and the exercise of this spiritual power through blessings bring prosperity to the lay people. In **Mahayana Buddhism**, after their training at the monastery, most monks marry and serve as priests to local congregations, performing rituals for families who belong to the temple.

The final life-cycle rituals we will discuss center on dying and death. When someone we love dies, the loss generates a variety of emotions: shock, denial, anger, grief. Not only do we experience loss, we also confront our own mortality. To deal with our loss and anxiety, cultures develop funeral rites. These rites not only honor the dead, they also provide aid and comfort to the living. Wakes and funerals provide opportunities for people to come together and remember the significance of the dead in their lives, their families, and their communities. These rites also provide opportunity and social space to weep together, to express anger, grief, and anxiety, and to prepare one another for life without the deceased.

Similarly, religions have generated a vast array of funeral rites to honor the dead, prepare the person for passage into the next life, and provide aid and comfort to the bereaved. A common practice in Jewish and Islamic funeral rites is the bathing, preparation, and dressing of the body. As in other life-cycle rituals, the bathing and cleansing mark the separation phase, the dead become separated from the living. The preparation and dressing signify the transition or liminal phase of the ritual. Often the person is dressed in a simple white cloth. This notes the common status of the dead. There is no division of wealth before the creator of the world. At this point, all are equal. For Jewish men, the prayer shawl (*tallit*) they received at their *bar mitzvah* and used as their wedding canopy, becomes their burial gown. Similarly, many Islamic men are buried in the white linen robe that they wore when on the pilgrimage (*hajj*) to Mecca. Both traditions stress burial as the norm, reflecting the biblical notion of "ashes to ashes, dust to dust," an allusion to reincorporation with the source and substance of their creation. Both traditions also stress the importance of burial taking place as soon as possible, preferably on the day of death. The mourning period is marked by the suspension of normal social activities during the period. In Judaism, the mourning period is marked by seven days; in Islam, the period is three days. The mourning period allows the living to face the separation that death brings.

Some religious traditions believe that not all of the deceased pass immediately into the next life. They become the "walking dead" of Buddhist tradition or *wanagi yuhapi* (ghost) of Oglala Sioux. This reflects a liminal phase where the dead are "betwixt and between" the realm of the living and the realm of the dead. If left there, they can generate problems for the living through various mischievous and malevolent acts. To keep this from happening and to aid the living dead to move into the heavenly realm, the family performs a variety of rituals.

Thinking about Life-Cycle Rituals

Think about a life-cycle ritual that you have observed or in which you have participated. Describe the ritual. Look at your description and ask yourself the following questions: Was there a time when the participants were separated from the rest of the community? What were they doing? What was that experience like? Was there a feeling of community among the participants? Did they wear special clothing? How did the ritual conclude? What symbols were used? What words were spoken? How did the rest of the community respond to the ritual participants? How were they welcomed?

Life-Crisis Rituals

Disorder and chaos threaten the meaning and order we have created in our lives through the inevitable life crises we encounter. To counter their effects we develop various rituals to help us cope and to get us through. Baseball players who are in a batting slump often develop specific rituals designed to get them out of it. They may wear an article of clothing they wore when they were on a hitting streak, they may change their eating habits before a game, or they may pray.

Religious communities also develop rituals aimed at helping individuals and communities deal with human and natural calamities, such as an accident, a sudden illness, a drought, a death, or war. For example, a key component of some indigenous religious worldviews is that there is a balance or harmony in human life and in the universe. Crises, whether natural or human in origin, reflect a break in that balance. A fundamental way to restore the balance is through ritual activity. Whether through sweat, music, or dance, the rituals seek to restore the harmony in the world and, in so doing, bring an end to the affliction suffered by the community or the individual.

The practice of divination, using certain signs to understand the cause or cure of an affliction, is a common practice. When a catastrophe or problem emerges unexpectedly, we often ask, "Why is this happening to me?" We want to know what we did. We may even decide to call an expensive psychic hotline or have our palm read to get some answers. Many indigenous cultures have developed elaborate systems of divination, and they value the role of diviner. The Ndembu of Africa believe that most individual and communal misfortunes are a result of moral problems within the community. A diviner's task is not to tell the future but to scrutinize the past and to disclose the spiritual and moral causes for the crisis. By asking a series of questions of the people involved, the diviner seeks to construct a picture of the events and the relationships involved that led to the misfortune. Because each relationship in Ndembu life carries certain moral responsibilities, the diviner is able to identify potential moral conflicts that might be the source of the crisis. In addition, the diviner uses a winnowing basket filled with approximately twenty objects which symbolize relationships, problems, and motives common to Ndembu society. By shaking the basket, certain objects rise to the top and these provide clues which the diviner uses to discern the cause of the crisis.

Healing rituals seem puzzling in this day of modern medicine. But the rituals continue. Lighting a candle, mentioning the names of the sick during the worship service, and saying brief prayers are all rituals practiced by Christians today in hopes of aiding the healing process for themselves and for their loved ones. In some traditional Jewish communities, people will change the name of a person who is deathly ill or dying in hopes that the new name will trick the Angel of Death into believing that the person is already dead thus providing the person with a new lease on life. In the rituals, people are doing, they are being agents in the process, and the hope is that their action will have some effect.

In some evangelical traditions in the United States, healing services are fairly common. Those who participate in these services take seriously the promise of Jesus that, if they are faithful followers, they too will be agents of God's healing power to others. The power of touch is especially important to them. Either through the special connection the person leading the service has with God's Spirit, or through the power of the faithful community, laying on of hands is a common healing practice in which the healing power of the Holy Spirit passes through the individual or community to the sick.

As society recognizes the complex nature of suffering, pain, and disorder, religious communities develop new healing rituals. In her book *Women-Church*, Rosemary Ruether discusses various rituals that Christian women have developed to provide healing from the sexual and physical violence to which they have been subjected, including rape, incest, and wife battering. The women-church movement seeks to liberate women and men from the chains of the patriarchal subordination of women to a community where men and women are equal partners. Such liberation requires the development of new liturgies that reject the violence so much a part of that subordination and bring healing for the victims and the community. The rituals reaffirm the importance of healing traditions which recognize the emotional and spiritual aspects of an illness or injury. This is especially true in the suffering caused by sexual violence, which creates emotional scars for the victims and often isolates and alienates them from community. The "rite of healing from rape" Ruether describes incorporates many elements of traditional healing rituals, including ritual bathing, anointing with oils, and laying on of hands. It also includes rituals for purifying and rededicating the woman's home if the rape took place there. What is significant about these rituals is that they recognize that the violence has created disorder for the woman with her world. The rituals bring communal recognition of the violence, seek to reincorporate the woman back into community, and empower her to create new order by integrating the event into her life without shame or blame.

The importance of rituals in life crises came home to me as a young chaplain in a hospital in Louisville, Kentucky. I was working in the Emergency Room when I received a call requesting that a chaplain come to the Delivery Room to comfort a woman who had delivered a premature, stillborn infant. When I arrived I discovered that the mother of the child wanted me to baptize the child, the thought of which terrified me. Not only had I never performed a baptism, but my Baptist tradition taught me that baptism is a rite reserved for persons professing their faith in Christ, something infants could not do. I explained this to the nursing staff, who, although listening sympathetically, proceeded to dress me in a surgical gown and to provide me with a basin of water. Apparently, they had done this before. As I entered the room, I saw an eighteen-year-old African-American woman lying in a bed and holding a beautifully formed but lifeless child. As I spoke with her, we talked about her sorrow and about the hopes she once had for her child. I finally asked if there was anything I could do for her. After giving the child a name, she looked into my eyes and requested that I baptize her child so that her spirit and her daughter's spirit could be at peace with God. Confused and uncertain, I took her child in my arms, placed my fingers in the water basin, and baptized her daughter in the name of the Creator, the Christ, and the Comforter. Baptists say that there is nothing sacramental about the ritual of baptism, no saving grace comes from it. Perhaps. In that ritual act in that Delivery Room, however, I experienced the presence of the Sacred in a way I have not since, an experience I can only describe as grace. As I looked at the woman, I could see that she had experienced it as well. The peace the woman requested had come to her, to her daughter, and, unexpectedly, to me.

Periodic (Cyclical) Rituals

Periodic rituals are rituals that celebrate seasons in the year or commemorate specific historical events. As with all rituals, there are often several layers of meaning attached to them. The rituals associated with Easter have various religious and secular meanings. The specifically religious dimensions include the rituals associated with Holy Week, Good Friday, and Easter morning. In them, the new life and salvation God brought about through the life, death, and resurrection of Jesus the Christ are celebrated. Easter also includes rituals associated with spring and the birth of new life. Some Christians believe that the dogwoods bloom only during Easter, even though the dates for Easter change. The Easter bunny, the decorated eggs, the colorful flowers, and the bright clothes all reflect and celebrate the new life that appears after the winter season has ended.

New Year rituals also have multiple levels of meaning. They are rituals of thanksgiving and gratitude for all that the sacred has provided. But they are also periods of penitence and renewal, full of recognition of past wrongs and promises to change in the year ahead. The festivals and celebrations provide an opportunity to reflect, to take stock, and to redirect one's life.

An intriguing recent ritual development within the African-American community is the Kwanzaa celebration, which begins on December 26 and ends on January 1. Kwanzaa was developed as a cultural holiday by African-American historian Dr. Maulana Karenga in 1966. He did so in the aftermath of the riots that took place in Watts, a predominantly African-American community in Los Angeles, in August 1965. The riots lasted for four days, in response to an alleged incident of police brutality. Thirty-four people were killed, hundreds more were injured, and more than two hundred million dollars in property damage was incurred. As a result, the African-American community joined together to rebuild Watts and to make it a stronger community. Karenga's goal in developing the holiday was to bring a sense of pride and unity among African-Americans by setting aside a special time for this purpose. Although not connected to a specific religious tradition, the ritual embodies many features of the harvest festivals in the traditional African cultures Karenga researched. It is a time for African-Americans to join together to honor the traditions of their ancestors. More importantly, it is a time for participants to take stock of the past year and to prepare themselves for the year ahead with the hope of improving their lives and their communities. Thus, Kwanzaa reflects the elements of many religious festivals associated with the New Year.

The reflective dimension of the holiday centers on the **seven principles** (in Swahili, *nguzo Saba*). The principles include unity (working together as a people), self-determination (accomplishing goals set), collective work and responsibility (working together to solve problems), cooperative economics (maintaining individual businesses to profit the community), purpose (a plan for life), creativity (making the community and world better), and faith (trust in the rightness of our efforts). The principles provide the basis for reflection and discussion during the festival. Such reflection, it is hoped, will lead to actions throughout the year that will enhance the lives of the individuals and communities who take part.

Various rituals are attached to the festival, involving all of the senses. Many adults fast from sunrise to sunset in order to purify and prepare themselves. Participants wear colorful traditional African clothing to commemorate their African heritage. Seven candles representing the seven principles are lit, one each day. A black candle is placed at the center, and it represents unity. It is lit on the first day of the celebration. Three red candles, placed on the left side of the black candle, represent purpose, creativity, and faith. Three green candles, placed on the right side of the black candle, represent self-determination, collective work and responsibility, and cooperative economics. Fruit and vegetables are also displayed, representing the connection with the African harvest festivals. Ears of corn represent the children and are displayed even by childless couples to reflect the African belief, "It takes a village to raise a child."

Each day one candle is lit for its principle. Discussion of that principle takes place in the glow of the candle. On the sixth day, there is a feast among families and friends, and gifts are exchanged. The gifts given are meant to improve the life of the recipient, such as books about African culture. Before the feast, all of the candles are lit, and the principles they represent are discussed. Then there is time for stories, songs, and dances. Many of the stories center on the lives of significant African-Americans. After the festivities, there is a time for all to commit themselves again to the seven principles. A unity cup filled with water, the essence of life, is passed and everyone sips. Then drums are played, signaling the beginning of the feast. The final day of Kwanzaa is New

Year's Day. The gifts given the previous day are opened, and the day is spent reflecting and planning on ways to put the seven principles into place in the year ahead.

SUMMARY

From this discussion of religious ritual, we can see the tremendous use of ritual activity to help participants find meaning, order, and relationships in their lives. Religious rituals encompass every facet of life, from daily practice and annual celebrations to significant transitions and crises in the lives of individuals and communities. These symbolic actions re-enact and make conscious religions' understanding of reality and enable participants to make their lives meaningful by connecting to their perceptions of the ultimate ordering of life. Symbolic action, however, is but one form of significant, ordering action. Religions also prescribe practical or ethical actions that are in keeping with the worldview as well.

RESOURCES

Activities

1. Research and observe a religious ritual in which you have never participated. (This can be done individually or in groups.) The research will enable you to understand the meaning of the symbols and activities you observe. Write a reaction/reflection paper in which you describe the rituals and what they mean for the participants. In addition, compare/contrast the ritual with a similar ritual from your own tradition.
2. Divide the class into small groups (assigned or self-chosen) and create your own religions. Be sure to include a religious worldview and a religious ethos that corresponds to that worldview, including ritual performances and symbols.
3. Healing has been the subject of various Hollywood films. Select one of those films (for example, *Leap of Faith*). Write a reaction/reflection paper or do an oral report which answers the following questions: What religious rituals common to evangelical Christian traditions do you notice? What individual and communal life crises are depicted in the film? How are they dealt with? What do you think the film is attempting to say regarding them?
4. Recall a crisis you have experienced in the past. Write a reflection paper or journal entry that answers these questions: What did you do? What actions helped you to make sense of the experience? What actions provided comfort? What were the actions of those around you? Were they helpful? If you feel comfortable, you may want to share this with the class by posting it on your computerized bulletin board if you have one.
5. Research specific celebrations on your college campus, such as Founder's Day, that commemorate the beginnings of the institution. What rituals are associ-

ated with them? What members of the community, past and present, participate in those rituals?

Readings

Catherine Bell. *Ritual Theory, Ritual Practice*. New York: Oxford University Press,
1992. This books looks at theories of ritual and how they function in academic
discourse. Bell questions whether ritual should be associated with action rather
than thought. Instead, she sees ritualization as always strategic and, hence,
political.

Tom F. Driver. *The Magic of Ritual*. San Francisco: HarperCollins, 1991. In this
book, Driver argues for a theological reclamation of ritual's transformative
capabilities. He argues that ritual has the ability to evoke moral and social
transformation because of the way ritual both changes things and is subject to
change.

Emile Durkheim. *The Elementary Forms of Religious Life*. New York: The Free
Press, 1965. Durkheim maintains that ritual and belief are what constitute religion. He contrasts the religious realm, the sacred, with the secular realm, the
profane. Because of this dichotomy, he defines ritual in a way that makes it
fundamentally religious, a step with which other ritual theorists disagree.

Ronald L. Grimes. *Readings in Ritual Studies*. Upper Saddle River, NJ: Prentice-
Hall, 1996. This collection of essays seeks to illustrate and foster the interdisci-
plinary discussion of ritual studies that has developed by including writers
from a variety of disciplines, including religious studies, anthropology, theology, history, psychology, and the arts. In addition, the volume includes selections from theorists who shaped the field, such as Durkheim, Eliade, and
Freud.

Angela Shelf Medearis. *The Seven Days of Kwanzaa*. New York: Scholastic
Books, Inc., 1994. This book is a readable account of the history, principles,
and practices associated with the African-American celebration of Kwanzaa.

Rosemary Radford Ruether. *Women-Church: Theology and Practice of Feminist
Liturgical Communities*. San Francisco: Harper, 1988. The book reflects the
perspective of religious feminists who seek to reclaim aspects of their religious
tradition, but who see the need to reform its patriarchal roots. It discusses special liturgies for moments of crisis and healing, especially from sexual violence
and abuse, with the hope of providing resources for the liturgical work of religious communities.

Victor Turner. *The Ritual Process*. Ithaca, NY: Cornell University Press, 1977.
This book provides a detailed discussion of the concepts of *liminality* and
communitas Turner developed to expand van Gennep's understanding of the
phases of rites of passage.

Arnold van Gennep. *Rites of Passage*. Chicago: University of Chicago Press, 1960.
In this book, van Gennep develops his understanding of the three phases of
rites of passage: separation, transition, and incorporation. He contends that
transition from one social status to the next requires some means of negotiat-
ing them, namely rites of passage.

Audiovisuals

Ritual: Three Portraits of Judaism. Produced by Brenda J. Goodman and Oren Rudavsky. Interfaith Broadcasting Network, 1990. Judaism has rituals for blessing each day, rituals for blessing each life, and rituals for blessing the annual cycle. In this documentary we observe daily rituals in the life of a woman seminarian, a periodic or holiday ritual (Sukkoth) celebrated by a family, and a life-cycle ritual (circumcision) which involves a community of family and friends. Each ritual links the individual to God and to the Jewish community. The documentary illustrates the engagement of the senses, as well as the mind, in ritual.

The Five Pillars of Islam. Available from Films for the Humanities & Sciences, P. O. Box 2053, Princeton, NJ 08543. The five pillars of Islam are discussed, described, and put into historical context. The film places them in an international context and also introduces the conflict between traditional teaching and the effects of industrialization.

Holy Places and Pilgrimages. Available from Films for the Humanities & Sciences, P. O. Box 2053, Princeton, NJ 08543. This film, part of the *Religions of the Book* series, explores the meaning of holiness and its implications for ritual practice and holy places in the religions of Judaism, Christianity, and Islam.

NOTES

1. Frits Staal, "The Meaninglessness of Ritual," in *Readings in Ritual Studies*, ed. Ronald L. Grimes (Upper Saddle River, NJ: Prentice-Hall, Inc., 1996), 483-494.
2. Hsun Tzu, "On Rites," in *Essential Sacred Writings from Around the World*, ed. Mircea Eliade (San Francisco: Harper & Row, 1977), 234-235.
3. Arnold van Gennep, "Territorial Passage and the Classification of Rites," from *The Rites of Passage*, excerpted in *Readings in Ritual Studies*, ed. Ronald Grimes (Upper Saddle River, NJ: Prentice-Hall, 1996), 532.

Chapter 5

Ethical Action

Ethical or moral action is another way we order our lives and engage our world. Ethics help us to answer the significant human questions: What must I do? What kind of person should I become? How should I act in relationship to others? How do I connect to the world? The moral feelings, habits, values, and codes that we develop individually and communally help us to discern directions for our behavior and relationships.

Where do our ethics come from? Like language, morality is social. We derive the feelings, habits, values, and codes of ethical action from the social and institutional circumstances in which we live. They, of course, reflect the worldview, the picture of how things are and ought to be, of our particular culture or tradition. For example, European philosophical ideas that continue to influence our political and economic institutions posit the freedom of the individual as the ultimate value of society. The rights of the individual to life, liberty, and property are inalienable. This view answers the question, "What should I do?" negatively: do no harm. Individuals are free to do as they please so long as their actions do not harm or interfere with the ability of others to do the same.

Anthropologists note the connection between our worldviews and our ethical actions. Worldviews not only serve the ordering process by helping us make sense of how things are, they also suggest how life ought to be lived. The power of myth, a key element in a community's worldview, demonstrates this connection. Myths are both models of the world and models for the world; they are both descriptive and prescriptive. For example, the Horatio Alger myth in American culture, the story of an individual who moves from rags to riches, supports the worldview that America is a land of opportunity. There are no restrictions to social mobility. The myth also serves to encourage a certain way of life: hard work and persistence are virtues that all Americans should emulate.

In many cultures, ethical action is that action that conforms to the moral **code** generated by the community and reflected in the worldview. Members understand ethical action in this way. "What should I do?" is answered with "What is the relevant rule or principle?" Children's initial experience with ethical action is usually abiding by the rules or facing the consequences of failure to do so. Families, schools, and religious organizations all socialize children to these codes. As children grow and develop cognitive skills, parents introduce them to the rules of the house which are designed to respect persons, pets, and property: no hitting or biting, no playing with matches, and no writing on the walls. When they get to school, teachers and principals introduce children to a similar set of rules that reflect the need for order in the broader social context. This reflects most of our initial experience of ethical action.

Moral codes, and the values embodied in them, begin external to us. They are out there and we confront them. They exist before us, we abide by them, and they go on existing after us. The hope of most communities, however, is that we will internalize the moral codes and values, make them our own. They become a part of our moral **conscience**. Parents hope their children will someday do the right thing without the need for punishment or reward. They admonish their children to let their conscience be their guide. The Old Testament prophet Jeremiah reflects this hope of internalizing the moral code when he proclaims, "But this is the covenant that I will make with the house of Israel after those days, says the LORD: I will put my law within them, and I will write it on their hearts; and I will be their God, and they shall be my people" (Jer 31:33).

If we could imagine a society where a single worldview and ethos dominated all cultural and institutional life, ethical action might be simple, and certain types of moral problems might never emerge. We live in a culturally pluralistic society, however, where communities have different worldviews and institutions embody different values. Moral ambiguity and conflict are everywhere. In the American context, this conflict is no more evident than in the debate over abortion. Believing in the humanity and sanctity of the life of the fetus, a belief drawn from their religious communities, many Christians form picket lines outside abortion clinics to protest with words and gestures the killing of unborn children. Across the street, stressing the values of freedom and the sovereignty of the individual over her own body—values that are embedded in American culture, religion, and politics—an equally vocal group of Christians seeks to protect the right of women to choose. Both groups claim that the weight of morality is on their side.

Sometimes, the moral conflict and ambiguity occurs within us. This is often referred to as **moral perplexity**. When faced with an ethical choice or dilemma, we are sometimes unsure of which course of action to take. We cannot make one choice over another without experiencing some moral blame. For example, a Congressional representative may vote in favor of closing a military base in her district because she feels it is in the best interests of the country as a whole. The closing, however, may

MARY N. MACDONALD

A foe of abortion picketing outside a Planned Parenthood office.

result in some dislocation or joblessness within her district. When she returns home, she may question the moral worth of her decision when visited by her unemployed constituents and their families.

The moral perplexity we experience arises from the competing values or obligations that social and institutional contexts place upon us. They demand commitment and loyalty. For example, imagine that you work as a resident assistant (RA) for a small Catholic college. One of the requirements of being an RA is to provide educational programs for the students living in the residence hall. Several of the other RAs want to have a program on birth control because most of the students have become sexually active and they wanted to know the best ways to prevent unwanted pregnancies. As a Catholic you believe the church's teaching that artificial forms of birth control are inappropriate because they violate the procreative purpose of sexuality. Although you agree that unwanted pregnancy would be a terrible burden for a college student to bear, you feel that providing a program on birth control would suggest to students that having sex without intending procreation was morally acceptable.

All the RAs except you vote to have the program and, because you are an RA, you are expected to participate in the planning and implementation of the program. What should you do? Regardless of the choice you make, you are likely to feel conflicted or to experience guilt. These feelings illustrate the difficulty of resolving the moral conflicts created by competing values and loyalties.

RELIGIOUS ETHICS

Religions provide not only a worldview but also an ethos, a way of being in and relating to the world. They present their followers with a way of life that is considered to be in keeping with the ultimate ordering of life. Religious ritual is one aspect of this ethos; religious ethics is another. The connection with the ultimate or sacred ordering is a central dimension of religious ethics. Historian of religion Joachim Wach (1898-1955) suggests:

> To recognize an order in the universe (as profound religious experience would prompt [humanity] to do) means that in [their] every act [humans] would strive to sustain that order. Where this order is interpreted as an expression of a divine will, the divine commands will have to be obeyed. They may be obeyed because they are commands, because they promise rewards, because they are believed to be conducive to well-being, success, or happiness, and finally because they are deemed to be expressive of the nature of the Supreme Reality.[1]

If, as a result of religious experience, we see an order in the universe, we would in all our actions strive to sustain, enhance, or restore that order. Thus, religion can become a fundamental source for our ethics.

In today's secular society, we may not see the intricate connection between religion and ethics clearly. We may think that religion and ethics are really separate and distinct human endeavors that do not necessarily go together. It may be possible for us to have ethics without religion. In support of our view, we can point to numerous ethical decisions we have made that had nothing to do with our religious beliefs. We tell the truth because we feel that lying undermines the possibility for genuine relationships. We tutor disadvantaged children in reading and math because we think that all children deserve a good education regardless of economic status. What do these actions have to do with religion? The answer may be nothing or everything depending upon the source of these underlying values.

While it may be possible to have ethics without religion, we would contend that the reverse is not true. Religions help people focus on or provide answers to human questions of ultimacy, including questions about morality: What must I do? What kind of person should I be? How should I relate to others and to the nonhuman world? Religions suggest possible answers to these questions based upon their perceptions of the ultimate ordering of life. Thus, what distinguishes secular morality, ethical ideals or norms without conscious religious support, from religious ethics is that the latter are grounded in some perception of ultimacy or sacred ordering.

RELIGION AS THE SOURCE OF ETHICS

In discussing the relationship between religion and morality in the Jewish and Christian traditions, religious ethicist John Reeder contends that religions attempt to synthesize the worldview and ethos of the religious community, providing the moral order with its source, its sanction, and its goal or salvation.[2] Religions provide the norms for both conduct and character for their practitioners. By advocating particular moral principles, laws, and virtues, religions prescribe what religious people and communities should do and the kind of people they should become. Thus, they encompass both moral doing and being.

Thinking about Religious Ethics

As a way of seeing whether or not you have done religious ethics, do the following exercise. First, think about an ethical situation you faced recently. Write the situation out in a paragraph or two. Then write what decision you made or what course of action you took in this situation. When you are finished, look at your decision or action and ask yourself the following questions: Why did you take this course of action? What beliefs and/or values motivated your action? List those beliefs and values as much as you are able. Now looking at your list of values and beliefs, put a mark next to those that came in full or in part from the religious tradition or community in which you grew up. The religious dimension can be from parents or directly from the religious organization. How much did your religious background influence the moral action you took? To the extent that your religious background influenced you, you have done religious ethics.

Moreover, religions sanction particular ways of doing and being as most in keeping with the perceived ultimate ordering in the universe. Religions help their practitioners to believe that their way of living in relationship to one another and to the world is not simply what ought to be but also what is "really real." How many children have been told that the reason they should respect their parents is because this is what the Bible says? By invoking the name of the sacred text parents declare that this is not simply what they think is good behavior, but also what God wants. The reverse is also true: acting contrary to what the Bible says can bring about divine judgment. Such examples are a part of what sociologists of religion define as religion's legitimating role, an explanation and justification of society's moral order. Religions enable people to answer the question of why a particular moral order is in place. Often this legitimation comes in the form of a religious community's founding myths.

Recall the Indian and Iroquois creation myths discussed in chapter 1, the *Purusa Sukta* and the Haudenosaunee creation story. Both accounts provide not only understanding of how the world came to be, but also some indication of the moral worlds their respective communities inhabit. The first account, *Purusa Sukta*, has been used by Hindus to justify a particular social order, the caste system of India. There are four castes identified in the myth: the Brahmin (priests), the Rajanya (warriors/rulers), the Vaisya (merchants/artisans), and the Sudra (unskilled workers). These castes are hereditary; one remains in the particular caste into which one is born. These castes also have specific religious and moral duties and responsibilities associated with them, known as *dharma*. This is important because these duties connect to the religious understanding of **reincarnation** and *karma*. Reincarnation refers to the cycle of birth and rebirth in which all creatures are enmeshed. *Karma* refers to the cause and effect nature of the universe. By fulfilling the duties associated with one's caste faithfully, a person generates good *karma*, and will be rewarded by a better life when one is reborn. Failure to fulfill one's duties has the opposite effect. This connection, in effect, justifies or legitimates the caste system. Those born into higher castes deserve their status because they have earned it by their good deeds; those born into lower castes deserve their position as well.

This example not only illustrates how religion sanctions morality, it also points Reeder's third tie between religion and morality, salvation. The religious goal—salvation, liberation, enlightenment—is often achieved as a result of moral actions. By fulfilling the responsibilities of *dharma*, the religious and moral duties associated with each caste, Hindus believed they would attain higher positions and social status in future lives. Ultimately, they are able to break free of the cycle of birth and rebirth through the three paths noted in chapter 1. It is the path of *karma marga*, the path of works, that most people would follow. Works include religious as well as moral duties, but fulfilling one's moral responsibilities is required as well in order to achieve the goal of Hinduism.

To suggest that religious traditions are the source, sanction, and goal of religious ethical action does not necessarily answer the moral questions that concern us. We want to know what we should do and what kind of persons we should be. How does religion help us here? From the examples given above, it is clear that religion provides particular norms for human conduct and human character. The next two sections will focus on the norms religions provide.

NORMS FOR MORAL CONDUCT

For many of us, thinking about morality and ethics occurs most when deciding what we ought to do in specific contexts or situations. Religious ethicists call this the ground level of reflection, trying to discern the appropriate action in the heat of the moment. It is this question of oughtness that leads many to suggest that our primary experience of ethics is as an ethics of obligation. When we seek to act morally we are looking for particular norms or principles to guide our action. As the source and sanction of ethical action, religions have provided such norms for the ethical and moral action of their followers. These norms are generally of three types: laws, ends, and responsibilities. They may appear singly or in some combination in different religious traditions. In all cases, however, followers experience these norms as obligations: they are expectations that followers must abide by in their lives.

Law

As we noted previously, for many of us our early moral experiences are with laws or rules. In response to the basic moral question, "What should I do?" we ask, "What is the relevant rule, principle, or law?" Using our reason, we discern which rule applies, and we follow the appropriate rule. What makes the action right is that our behavior conforms to the rule. The virtue that is praised here is the virtue of obedience: the actor is obeying the moral law in this situation.

Clearly, this approach to ethics is nonconsequential. What this means is that one abides by the rule, law, or principle regardless of the consequences. For example, those who oppose abortion for religious reasons point to the sanctity of human life as a fundamental, God-given principle. From this they derive a basic rule or law: it is morally impermissible to do any action that undermines the sanctity of human life. Abortion violates this principle and is, therefore, an immoral practice. Abortion opponents may agree that having a child may be financially ruinous for the person or the family involved. They may feel sympathy for the woman who does not want the child and offer counseling on adoption. The bottom line, however, is that the consequences for the woman or the family or even society are ultimately immaterial. What matters, abortion opponents argue, is that the child has a fundamental right to life and we ought to respect that right.

In modern moral philosophy, law as the norm for moral action is connected with the experience of duty. Most people at one time or another experience ethical action in the form of duty. In our relationships with others we develop certain obligations and responsibilities that people expect us to fulfill. Sometimes, we may not want to meet those expectations. Fulfilling our obligations may not be enjoyable, or we might rather do something else. Yet we keep our obligations even though we do not feel like it because we know it is the right thing to do. For example, we make a promise to a friend that we will help her move into her new apartment on Saturday afternoon. Saturday morning, another friend calls to say she has free passes to an afternoon movie matinee and asks us to come. Our preference that morning is to go to the movie; the weather is rainy and we really want to see that movie. Because of our promise to our other friend, however, we decline the invitation and spend the day moving furniture and getting wet. By keeping our promise, we have done our duty. Duty is often understood in contrast to inclinations to do differently. In fact, it is the presence of these other inclinations and desires that make duty so forceful.

Many researchers in religious ethics refer to this dimension of religion as code. As we see in the examples of the Ten Commandments, the Five Precepts, and the Golden Rule, many religions codify the ethical actions they prescribe. Why? Part of the reason is that codes are easy to remember and are helpful in the moral socialization process. Children growing up morally can learn a set of rules or codes that they can cherish. Many children in the Jewish and Christian traditions can recite the

Ten Commandments; many more can recite the Golden Rule. Codes also embody the collective wisdom of the group or the deity. If the worldview and the ethos of a community are mutually reinforcing, then we can expect that a rule expresses the community's wisdom regarding how life ought to be lived.

THE FIVE PRECEPTS

(Buddhism)

"I undertake to observe the rule to abstain from taking life; to abstain from taking what is not given; to abstain from sensuous misconduct; to abstain from false speech; to abstain from intoxicants as tending to cloud the mind."

(*Buddhist Scriptures*)

THE GOLDEN RULE

(Christianity)

Do unto others what you want them to do to you. (Mt 7:12)

THE TEN COMMANDMENTS

(Judaism and Christianity)

You shall have no other gods before me.

You shall not make for yourself an idol.

You shall not make wrongful use of the name of the Lord your God.

Remember the sabbath day and keep it holy.

Honor your father and your mother.

You shall not murder.

You shall not commit adultery.

You shall not steal.

You shall not bear false witness against your neighbor.

You shall not covet your neighbor's possessions. (Ex 20:2-17)

Theistic religions (those that believe in a transcendent being or beings) see the moral order in the universe as coming from that being(s). Two important ways the transcendent being makes the moral order known are by issuing divine commands and by revealing divine character. Most theistic religions have elements of a Divine Command moral system; the moral rules or principles are directly related to the commands of the deity. This idea is captured in the Hebrew scriptures in various places, including the prophet Micah: "He has told you, O mortal, what is good; and what does the Lord require of you but to do justice, and to love kindness, and to walk humbly with your God?" (Mi 6:8). Obedience to the divine command is considered the fundamental expression of one's religious piety and devotion.

Of course, people have questioned the validity of divine command as a basis for morality. In his dialogue, *Euthyphro*, Plato suggests two possible ways of construing the connection with the deity: either God commands a certain act because it is right, or an act is right because God commands it. If the former is true, then the basic standard of morality is logically independent of God's commands. In the context of the biblical passage quoted above, God requires followers to do justice and to love kindness because justice and kindness are good in and of themselves.

Divine revelation or authority ("He has told you ... what is good") may provide the basis for understanding these moral duties or the motivation for accepting and doing them. Yet they would still be good even if God did not require them. If an act is right because God commands it, on the other hand, then there is no independent reason to do what God commands except that God commands it, which, for some, makes morality seem arbitrary. For example, if God required injustice and cruelty of followers, then justice and kindness would lose their moral value. Certainly we can point to numerous religious texts and stories which make the deity seem capricious. Whatever we may think about Divine Command theory, however, should not keep us from exploring those religious groups that affirm divine command as a foundation for ethics.

Related to divine command is divine character. One of the ways theistic religions connect their moral laws with the ultimate moral ordering in the universe is by suggesting that the deity reflects these laws in its own being. In the Deuteronomic code—which includes the Ten Commandments—found in the Hebrew Bible the people of Israel are commanded to care for the the sojourner, the widow, the orphan, the poor and all of the marginalized members of the community. Part of the rationale for this is that it reflects the same care and concern that God expressed for the Hebrew people when they were enslaved in Egypt. Similarly, in the prophetic literature, the call for the people to embody justice, righteousness, and steadfast love is a call to imitate their God. In the words of the psalmist, "Gracious is the Lord, and righteous; our God is merciful" (Psalms 116:5).

In the case of divine command, the moral question, "What should I do?" is answered by the question, "What does the deity command?" Then the person performs that action that follows the appropriate command. Here again, obedience is the primary virtue. We may know some religious people who have this approach to ethics. When confronted with a moral situation, they pause to pray, asking what God would want them to do. One of the appeals of this ethical stance is that it provides a measure of certainty about their moral action, connecting it with the ultimate moral ordering. If they can discern what God commands, through Bible study or prayer, then moral decision making seems relatively simple. They can do what God commands without regard for the consequences of their actions.

Some would contend that Islamic ethics are an example of a divine command moral system. This makes sense when you understand that the word Islam means "submission." A Muslim is one who submits her or his life totally to the will of God. An action is not inherently right or wrong, but rather is either commanded or forbidden by God. The key is that the Muslim submits all of her life to God, and the emphasis is on conformity to God's law. How do you know what God wants? The connection with the revealed dimension of religion becomes apparent. The divine will is revealed in the Qur'an, the sacred text of Islam, which has the status of the "word of God." It is the ultimate judge between what is good and what is evil. Because the divine laws entailed in the Qur'an tend to be stated in general principles, rather than detailed commands for specific situations, the need arose for specific interpretations. It was in this context that the Islamic law, *shari'ah*, developed.

The *shari'ah* is a collection of interpretations and extrapolations developed by learned members of the Islamic community to make laws for people to abide by. It has its source in both the Qur'an and the *hadith*—the record of customs derived from the words and deeds of Muhammad—both of which are considered divinely inspired. Because the *shari'ah* is human interpretation and humans cannot fully know and comprehend God's transcendent law, the *shari'ah* does not carry the same status as the Qur'an and is subject to debate among legal scholars. However, in Islamic societies it does carry the status of law, and people are expected to obey. The duties included are both individual and collective. The actions are further divided into five categories: obligatory, recommended but not obligatory, permitted, disapproved, and forbidden.

Even though much of ethical thinking is duty oriented, and thus rules and principles are critical, people continue to be frustrated with moral rules. The source of their frustration is often that rules seem to be restrictive and oppressive. They contend that many rules lose sight of the bigger picture or do not always apply in a given situation. However, many religious traditions affirm rules and laws, not because they are a problem, but because they are grateful for the guidance. This is expressed in the Jewish notion, "The reward for keeping one *mitzvah* is another!"

Not all religious affirmation of moral laws is in the form of Divine Command theory. Many accept the difficulties of knowing exactly what the divine will is, even in sacred texts. Instead, they will suggest that there is a significant set of rules or principles that people can know through the use of reason. These rules and principles represent the collective wisdom of the community, or are part of the structure of reality itself, and ought not to be violated easily. Moral action is that action which conforms to the moral law that is discernible through the use of reason. This moral law has its foundation in divine law and thus has a connection with the transcendent moral order in the universe. This is certainly behind those systems of ethics that affirm **cosmic law** or **natural law**.

The concepts of cosmic and natural law enable us to comprehend the notion of a moral order in the universe. Certain ways of acting are more in keeping with that order than others. They contribute to the balance and harmony. Acting contrary to that order causes chaos and disruption. Nontheistic religions (those that see the sacred as impersonal) suggest that the source of morality comes from some sense of order inherent in the cosmos. As the previous chapter noted, some Eastern religions, such as Hinduism, see a religious and moral law that governs all of life. Hinduism and Buddhism refer to this law as the *dharma*, although they have some different ideas about it. Chinese religions, including Confucianism and Taoism, refer to this cosmic law as *Tao*, which means the "way" or order that underlies all reality. Although there are spiritual and metaphysical aspects of the *Tao*, both religions stress the ethical dimensions of it. By discerning and following the *Tao*, individuals and society find the ethical guidance they need to live in harmony with nature and to achieve the ends they seek, including order, prosperity, and peace.

A well-known proponent of natural law was Saint Thomas Aquinas (1225-1274). In the nineteenth century, the Roman Catholic hierarchy found in Aquinas the basis for its moral and social norms. For Aquinas, law always has some good, generally the good of the individual or the community, in mind. Underlying all of the created order is the eternal law, through which God is guiding all things in the universe toward their intended end. This guidance has the significance of law. The natural moral law is that law embedded in all rational creatures, namely humanity, which directs us toward our own right ends or good. We discover those ends by reflecting on human nature through the use of our reason. On the one hand, human beings share certain ends with other creatures, such as self-preservation, the union of males with females, and the education of offspring. On the other hand, as uniquely rational creatures, human beings also have a natural inclination to know the truth about God and to live in society. Once we have discovered those ends, then we can discern the means for achieving them. This understanding of God's intent for us, built into our nature by God's creative activity, Aquinas referred to as natural law. Thus, those rules or principles of reason that guide us to promote human good and avoid evil carry the weight of natural law. For example, most human societies have laws or principles against unjustified killing of human beings. Many societies call such actions murder. For Aquinas, such laws are natural laws, because they preserve human life and do not harm it.

Ends

The notion that somehow laws are in keeping with the ultimate order in the universe and that they reflect what is good for human life and flourishing leads to a second norm for ethical action: ends. As John Reeder notes, people often follow religions because of some goal: salvation, liberation, or the like. Many times, achieving those ends is dependent upon moral behavior. Human beings are valuing beings. This means that we have certain ideas about goods that we think make human life meaningful and worthwhile, and so we pursue those values. Codes, laws, and principles embody certain values deemed worthy by the community. For example, the rule not to kill other persons embodies the notion that life is intrinsically valuable and not simply there for someone else's use.

The idea of acting morally to gain a desired goal or value is a common experience for us. As children, many of us acted a particular way deemed moral by our parents or other adults for some reward or to keep from being punished. The same is true for children when their moral action is tied to their religion. Children have done the right thing from a desire to gain God's blessing or out of fear that God would punish them if they did not. Of course, parents hope that eventually their children will act morally because of some other moral end, such as world peace, loving community, or justice. In other words, the ends are moral or a moral state of affairs.

The term most often used for this approach to ethical obligation is teleology. The word comes from the Greek word, *telos*, which means "end." The response an ethics of ends provides to the moral question, "What should I do?" is "What ends am I seeking to achieve? What are the best means for achieving them?" Then the person uses the most efficient means for achieving his ends. Unlike law, the moral action has more to do with the actions and their consequences than with the intention of the actions. That is why this approach has been labeled consequential. No matter how good the intention of the actor is, if the action does not result in the goal or end sought, the morality of the action is called into question. For example, a person stops to help an accident victim and in the process of helping ends up causing more serious injury. We understand and appreciate the intention of the helper, but we judge his actions by their consequences as well.

With regard to the goal of religious morality, John Reeder says that religions provide both moral ends and also ends that transcend morality. For example, the biblical record advocates the norms of justice and mercy because they will generate a specific kind of moral community, enabling all members of the community to experience meaningful, fulfilling, and moral lives. So visions of community are moral ends that require certain moral actions to achieve them. This understanding was evident in the Civil Rights movement in the United States. Martin Luther King, Jr., and others advocated nonviolent resistance as the means to achieve their end, the "beloved community." The beloved community entailed the norms of equality, justice, and peace for all. To achieve that end using means that were destructive was inappropriate. Violence was destructive of the very community they were hoping to achieve. Thus violence could not be accepted as a means to that end, and participants in the struggle were trained in the principles of nonviolent resistance.

In religious ethical action, the goal can also be the promise of a trans-moral state. When we Christians describe heaven, the goal of our religion, we often depict a state of being that is beyond morality. We envision a society where there are no wants or needs, where there is no sexuality, no economic relations, no political structures. We are tired of having to make moral decisions, of having to do the right thing, of having to be a particular type of person. For us, heaven means salvation and liberation from the trials and tribulations that the moral condition brings to us. We want a world where we no longer face moral decisions or questions. We want a return to the premoral bliss of our childhood. For those who accept a particular reading of the second creation account in the book of Genesis, we

Martin Luther King, Jr., addresses a large rally in front of the United Nations protesting the Vietnam War.

want a return to the Garden of Eden, before the man and the woman ate fruit from the tree of the knowledge of good and evil.

The goal of Buddhism is liberation from the suffering that is endemic to the cycle of birth and rebirth in the universe. People refer to this liberation as *nirvana*. *Nirvana* is difficult to describe. In fact, most do so only negatively. They describe what *nirvana* is not. It is the experience of non-being, the loss of self, the loss of desire and craving. Clearly, critical to achieving the experience of *nirvana* is to follow the **Eightfold Path**, which will be discussed shortly. Some of the actions required to achieve liberation are moral, such as not killing living creatures. In Mahayana Buddhism, the ideal person for entry into *nirvana* is the **boddhisattva**, a person who chooses to delay entry to this state in order to help all living creatures reach this end, a person full of compassion for others. Yet the goal of Buddhism clearly transcends morality. Breaking free from the cycle of birth and rebirth means breaking free from the human condition itself and all that it involves, including the moral condition.

A final way of looking at the teleological approach to religious ethics is to explore the metaphors of "path," "way," or "road," used by many religious traditions to speak of moral obligation. We often hear of moral action as action that is on the right path or going the right way. The image of path carries with it the notion of destination. Those who follow the path are seeking some end or goal; they are going somewhere for a purpose. One of the **Four Noble Truths** of Buddhism is that the end to suffering comes by following the Eightfold Path. This path consists of various religious and moral practices aimed at achieving this end. The end or goal determines the kind of actions deemed moral. The requirements of *sila*, or morality, include right speech, right conduct, and right livelihood. Right speech refers to not speaking falsely about others. The notion of right conduct embodies the remainder of the Five Precepts, not killing, not stealing, not engaging in sexual immorality, and not using intoxicants. Right livelihood means not earning one's keep by work that violates these precepts, such as prostitution, pornography, or the sale of alcohol. The problem with each of these activities is that they lead to desiring and craving, the source of suffering in human life and the stumbling block to the goal of liberation from this suffering. Engaging in them leads to a perpetuation of the cycle of birth and rebirth. Thus, the path one follows is intricately connected to the destination at which one arrives.

Thinking about Moral Obligations

To help you grasp the notion of ends as moral obligation, write out four or five of the most important goals in your life. Next to each of the goals, write out what values are implicit in those goals. Do they reflect what you think is most important in life? Reviewing those goals and values, think of the ways that they determine the actions you do today. Do you choose some activities over others because they are more in keeping with your goals and values, even though you might want to do those other activities? Do you ever experience your decision to do certain activities as an obligation, in that you feel you have to do those activities or you will not accomplish your goals? Do you ever feel remorse or regret when you fail to do those actions you know are more in keeping with your goals or values?

Responsibility

Laws and ends are not the only way we conceive of our moral obligations. Sometimes, we understand our obligations as responsibilities. According to ethicist Albert Jonsen, the word "responsibility" carries two basic meanings: to answer and to promise. "To answer" refers to accountability, being answerable for one's behavior; "to promise" refers to commitment, the trustworthiness and dependability of the agent for some enterprise.[3] For example, when a parent comes into a room where a lamp has been broken and asks her children, all of whom are looking quite innocent, who is responsible, she has in mind responsibility as accountability. She wants to know who is to blame for breaking the lamp. On the other hand, when a parent gives the keys to the family car to her child because she believes him to be a responsible driver, she is thinking of responsibility as commitment. Her child is dependable and worthy of the trust placed in him.

From the perspective of responsibility, the moral question, "What should I do?" is answered by discerning, "What is going on? What is the context and the situation I find myself in? To whom am I responding? What is the most appropriate action?" A responsible person is one who understands that she is enmeshed in a web of relationships, that she is connected in various ways to the broader communities of which she is a part and to which she is committed. She understands that her actions have implications for these other relationships, and she seeks to act in ways that will nurture and develop these relationships rather than harm them. Such action requires that the person be morally discerning, spending time to understand the context and the implications of her actions. What makes an action moral is that it is fitting or appropriate for the context and the community rather than "right" or "good." A primary virtue here is accountability. The agent is willing to stand by her actions, to take responsibility for them, and to accept the consequences of her actions. Responsibility as commitment also defines the character of the person. The person is willing to be accountable because she is acting in accordance with her promises.

To help us understand this approach to ethical obligation, let us consider the following example. A woman in danger of being injured by her husband runs to a neighbor's house and asks the neighbor to hide her. Being a compassionate person, the neighbor agrees. Ten minutes later, the husband comes knocking on the neighbor's door and asks if his wife is there. What should the neighbor do? If the neighbor tells the truth, the woman might be harmed. If the neighbor says the wife is not there, then the neighbor violates the principle of not lying. Most people would suggest that the neighbor should tell the man the woman is not there. The reason is that following the rule would have consequences that would be considered more immoral than telling a lie. In other words, the context has become critical. This does not mean that the rule is not important or can be ignored whenever a person chooses. Rules or moral codes are still important and affirmed. It is just that rules are not the only factor in moral decisions. One must also consider the context and the implications for all involved, choosing that action which is most appropriate and for which one is willing to be held accountable.

The connection between responsibility as obligation and the assumption of certain roles in the community should be clear. When we take on a role, such as a job or parenthood, we assume responsibility for faithfully fulfilling our duties. The marriage covenant is a good example. People who enter into the covenant of marriage bind their lives together and make promises to one another for fidelity, nurture, and support. The person willingly assumes the responsibilities that go along with these promises. Not all of our responsibilities are necessarily chosen, of course. We are born into families and communities, and their nurturance requires certain actions on our part. For example, as our parents age, they lose some of their independence and may require assistance. The primary responsibility for their care falls upon us, their children. We may not have chosen to be their children, but because we are enmeshed in relationship with them, we feel obliged to care for them; and society expects us to do so as well.

Responsibility as obligation often becomes clearest in those situations that are morally ambiguous. Consider an example of voluntary passive euthanasia, in which a person with a terminal illness asks to be allowed to die. A man has a form of cancer that is being treated through the use of radiation and chemotherapy. The therapy, however, does little to stop the progress of the cancer. Eventually, the therapy becomes overly burdensome, physically, emotionally, and financially, to the patient and his family. He asks his doctor to stop treatment and allow him to die with some dignity and without bankrupting his family. The doctor, whose focus is life not death, feels morally obligated to persuade the patient to continue the therapy. But the doctor is unsuccessful, and he eventually supports the patient's decision. In thinking about the situation, it is difficult to say that the doctor, the patient, and his family made the "right" decision or a "good" decision, terms that are connected to obligation as law and ends. These terms seem strangely inadequate in light of the moral ambiguity inherent in this context. Rather, they reached an "appropriate" or "fitting" decision for this situation, enabling the patient to maintain his own sense of moral integrity, while at the same time fulfilling his responsibilities to his family.

In the Jewish and Christian traditions, understanding one's moral obligations as responsibilities is best exemplified in the notion of covenant community. A covenant is an agreement between two parties based upon mutual promise and commitment, i.e. the making and keeping of promises. Covenant structures all of our communal lives; all of our relationships rely on trust and the mutual promise of fidelity. All people participate in covenants, by birth and by choice. Families, voluntary associations, and political communities are all covenantal in structure. For example, while the family has a natural basis in sex and parental love, its essence is found in the promise making and promise keeping between husbands and wives, parents and children. When members of the family fail to keep their promises or fulfill their obligations to one another, the experience of community disintegrates, in spite of the bonds of nature and affection.

The Jewish and Christian conception of covenant is always theocentric: our promises and commitments to one another are made in the presence of and in response to God. Among the Israelites all human relationships were covenant relationships based upon the fundamental covenant between God and humanity. The biblical account of the covenant at Sinai demonstrates that the people were connecting their lives to one another and to their God. The obligations and responsibilities that they pledged to one another covered all aspects of life together and were made in response to the moral ordering of God. Moreover, they included all members of the community, from the powerful to the most marginal members, such as widows, orphans, and the poor (Ex 22:22-27). The covenant even extends to the strangers and resident aliens who come into the community (Ex 22:21; 23:9; Dt 24:17-22).

The Yoruba of West Africa have an ethical system in which covenant plays an important role. The relationships between persons and the relationships with the spiritual realm, including ancestors and divinity, have their basis in covenants. The covenants tend to be reciprocal, in that the parties bind themselves to one another by bilateral obligations. E. Bolaji Idowu describes the Yoruba conception of covenant.

> It is believed that to be trusted by a friend, to be bosom friends, to eat together, or to be received hospitably as a guest, is to enter into a covenant which involves moral obligations. A covenant between two parties means, negatively, that they must think or do no evil against each other's body or estate, and positively, that they must co-operate in active good deeds towards each other in every way.[4]

Thus, relationships among the Yoruba and within other African communities are characterized by a reciprocity of responsibilities and duties which seek to preserve and enhance the lives of the individuals and communities involved.

NORMS FOR MORAL CHARACTER

Discussion of moral norms limits our focus to the actions themselves, the *doing* of ethics. We also make moral judgments about people, however, as when we say someone is a moral or ethical person. When we make these judgments, we are making judgments about character, the *being* of an ethical person or community. Being and doing are obviously related. It is because a person is a certain type of character that we know that she will do a certain type of action. The difference is that the moral judgment of character focuses more on the inner motivations—the traits, habits, or dispositions a person has to act a certain way—than on the actions themselves. For example, when we say that someone is a good person or has a moral character, we are declaring that when moral situations arise, that person tends to do the right thing, the moral thing. They are predisposed to act in moral ways because they have a certain way of being in the world. Often our description of those persons includes various virtues or emotional traits, such as compassion, caring, wisdom, or courage. In part, our moral character is determined by us, by the choices and decisions we have made over the years that shape our moral orientations and perspectives. In part our moral character is determined by our environment, the social, cultural, and institutional contexts in which we grow up.

For many of us, one of the institutional influences on our moral character is religion. Religious morality speaks as much about character as it does about conduct. For example, in Yoruba religion ethics is best described by the term "character" (*iwa*). The focus of Yoruba ethical teachings is on the essential nature or being of the person. People are either good characters or bad characters. To help us understand this aspect of religious ethics, we will discuss three elements connected to the formation of moral character: moral development, moral conscience and consciousness, and moral emotions and virtues. We will conclude with a discussion of moral exemplars, persons who embody the moral character deemed significant by their respective religious communities.

Moral Development

When we ponder the moral character of a person, we are making a judgment about the person at that particular moment. Moral character, however, has a history as well. The notion of moral development suggests that human beings are not born morally mature; rather, their capacity for moral and ethical action grows and develops gradually with other capacities as they get older. For many, a key component of moral development is cognitive development, the reasoning process one uses to make judgments. For example, if we find a five-year-old boy and girl together exploring one another's genitalia, we generally do not judge them by the same standards of sexual ethics we might judge a sixteen-year-old boy and girl doing the same thing. The reason is that we feel that the five-year-olds do not know any better. Their cognitive capacity to understand their actions has not developed sufficiently to warrant such a judgment. We might use the opportunity to instruct them on appropriate versus inappropriate behavior with one another, but until they are older, we feel that they cannot fully understand the nature of their actions.

The concept of cognitive moral development is often mythically portrayed in religious traditions. Many creation myths regarding humanity reflect the movement from some premoral condition to the condition of morality. The second creation myth in Genesis can be seen in this light. Often the second creation myth (Gen 2:4-3) is seen as a fall from some state of moral perfection to a state of moral imperfection. The Genesis story can also be seen as a story depicting the movement from a premoral state into a moral state. The prohibition against eating of the tree of knowledge of good and evil means that Adam and Eve relate to one another initially without having any concepts of good and evil. They are in a state of premoral bliss. After eating of the fruit, however—after desiring moral knowledge—they now enter the moral condition. This is symbolized in their recognition of their nakedness. Their sexuality becomes conscious to them, and the need for moral structure (the fig leaf) enters into their cultural understanding. They begin the moral history of humanity. From that point forward, the direction of Genesis and Exodus could be seen as a movement to establish some moral dimensions to life, culminating in the giving of the law at Sinai. The movement reflects the struggle of living within a moral universe.

Moral Conscience or Consciousness

Related to cognition is the notion of moral conscience or consciousness in moral development. Most people claim to have a conscience, some inner sense of what is right and wrong that leads them to do the right thing most of the time. This is implicit in such questions as, "Didn't your conscience bother you?" which parents often ask children they catch doing something wrong. In fact, people who don't have a conscience are referred to disparagingly as psychopaths or sociopaths. Some religious traditions suggest that human beings are born with an innate moral sense. We have the capacity from birth to know the difference between right and wrong. Many identify this innate faculty as the conscience. It is a faculty we believe is universal among people. When we suggest, "Let your conscience be your guide," we are assuming that people have the capacity for conscience and that it will lead them to do the right thing. In so doing, we imply some type of unity between moral knowing and moral doing.

There is some debate about whether or not this innate capacity for moral discrimination or conscience needs development. Mencius suggests that people are basically good. If left to our natural inclinations, or allowed to follow the dictates of our conscience, we will do the right thing. Others are not so sure. They suggest that the conscience is shaped by our social and cultural location. Sigmund Freud suggested that the conscience, which he called the superego, is primarily the internalization of parental and societal restrictions that act to keep our sexual and aggressive tendencies in check. Theologian Walter Conn suggests that conscience is not simply some innate human faculty or the internalization of a moral code. Rather, conscience also refers to moral consciousness, a consciousness that can be informed, self-critical, and can move toward self-transcendence. Conscience enables moral consistency in that there is coherence between our moral knowing and moral doing. A person does not *have* a conscience, a person *is* a conscience.

An example from literature that illustrates the self-transcendent dimension of conscience can be found in Mark Twain's *The Adventures of Huckleberry Finn*. Huck helps Jim, Miss Watson's slave, escape into free territory. Throughout the experience, Huck battles his conscience, a conscience formed by a community that accepted slavery as a way of life and labeled helping runaway slaves as a crime. In a memorable scene after Jim's capture, Huck wrestles his conscience over whether to write a letter to Miss Watson informing her of Jim's whereabouts. Huck ponders: "The more I studied about this the more my conscience went to grinding me, and the more wicked and low-down and ornery I got to feeling." He was afraid he might go to hell. He decides to pray but realizes that he cannot until he writes the letter. After doing so, he feels "clean of sin" for the first time in his life. Before praying, however, Huck reflects on the relationship he developed with Jim in the course of their journey. He realizes that Jim was more than a slave, Jim was his friend. Then he picks up the letter and reflects: "I was a-trembling, because I'd got to decide, forever, betwixt two things, and I knowed it. I studies a minute, sort of holding my breath, and then says to myself: 'All right, then, I'll go to hell'—and tore it up." This marks a step in Huck's moral development, from unquestioned acceptance of society's norms to critical moral consciousness in the face of new experiences and insight.

Of course, it is important to realize that when we say our consciences ought to be self-critical—that we ought to include moral consciousness and awareness in our understanding of conscience—we need to be sure what things are included. What are the sources that inform and shape our consciences? Conn writes:

> While it may be true that a person must follow his own conscience, and I for one think it is, it will not be enough on that symbolic day of judgment for him to say, simply, "I followed my conscience." For ... he will surely be asked not only how faithfully he *followed* his conscience, but also how authentically he *formed* it.[5]

Conn's point is that, when we judge people who claim to have followed their conscience, we have a normative view of conscience. It is not simply some faculty that everyone has. Rather, it is a moral consciousness that grows and develops and is always self-critical. This means that the mature conscience is always expanding and deepening its understanding by critical engagement with and openness to various sources of moral wisdom and insight.

For example, some of the Nazi doctors who participated in Hitler's euthanasia program claimed they did so "in good conscience." Karl Brandt, the chief medical administrator in Germany at the time, was charged with responsibility for carrying out various human experiments, including exploding a man's brains out of his ears in a high compression chamber. He spoke these words to the Nuremberg Tribunal:

> Somewhere we must all take a stand. I am fully conscious that when I said "Yes" to Euthanasia I did so with the deepest conviction, just as it is my conviction today, that it was right.... I bear a burden, but it is not the burden of crime. I bear this burden of mine, though with a heavy heart, as my responsibility. I stand before it, and *before my conscience* as a man and as a doctor (emphasis added).[6]

Even though they claimed "good conscience," Brandt and other doctors were hanged for "crimes against humanity." These doctors provided moral justification for their actions, citing both compassion for those unworthy of life and a commitment to the betterment of humanity. Before their conscience, they felt free of guilt. The decision to hang them for crimes against humanity reflects the judgment that they had not allowed their consciences to be fully or appropriately developed.

From the perspective of religious ethics, an informed conscience is always one that is shaped and open to the wisdom that comes through the religious tradition, wisdom that has its source in some divine or transcendent order. When the prophet Jeremiah suggests that God will write his law upon the hearts of his people, the point is that the moral consciousness of the person will be directed by God. Similarly, the Jewish tradition contends that the study of written and oral Torah is the path to a fully formed conscience and a moral life. Both the impulse to do good and the impulse to do evil exist in the human heart. God has given the study of Torah as the antidote to the evil impulse.

For Buddhism, the moral conscience can find wisdom in the Five Precepts and the Eightfold Path. The Eightfold Path is a guide to action to achieve the goal of Buddhism, enlightenment. The first two precepts, right views and right aspiration, reflect the consciousness expected of persons seeking to live rightly. Right views means that one accepts the Four Noble Truths about the cause and cessation of suffering. One is not deceived by one's immediate desires and cravings but knows that desiring is the source of suffering in the world. Right views also means understanding that change and becoming—including the impermanence of the self—are at the heart of reality. Right aspiration, purpose, or thought means negatively, freeing oneself from all sensual and material cravings and desires; positively, it means embracing thoughts of nonviolence, detachment, and compassion. These cognitive aspects of the Eightfold Path are a means to generating right living among people.

The notion of a conscience that is informed by religious tradition, a transcendent ordering in the universe, is reflected in the defense Martin Luther King, Jr., provides for breaking segregation laws in his "Letter from Birmingham Jail." People wanted to know how King could advocate obeying some laws and not others. The answer he provided was that some laws were just, others were unjust. "Any law that uplifts human personality is just. Any law that degrades human personality is unjust." By recognizing a transcendent basis for law, King was suggesting that moral consciousness must be shaped by more than human convention. For King, the source of that transcendence was his religion. "A just law is a . . . code that squares with the moral law or the law of God." But in the practice of civil disobedience, to accept the penalty is not just to act on the individual's own conscience, it also has the goal of raising the moral consciousness of the community as well. "I submit that an individual who breaks a law that conscience tells him is unjust, who willingly accepts the penalty of imprisonment in order to arouse the conscience of the community over its injustice, is in reality expressing the highest respect for the law."[7]

Emotions and Virtues

At this point, the reader may feel that the discussion about religious ethics and moral character has been too cognitive. Too much focus has been placed on the development of moral consciousness. Not all moral or ethical action, however, is conscious action, applying moral codes to specific contexts. There are emotional and dispositional dimensions to our moral being in the world as well. Sometimes, our ethical actions flow from the moral dispositions, feelings, and virtues that constitute our character. When a moral situation arises that calls for action, we simply respond without conscious reflection. It is a part of who we are. For example, when we come across a child who is hurt and there are no other adults around, our immediate response is to attend to the needs of the child. We do not ask ourselves whether we should help or not, or what moral principle applies in this situation. Instead, we respond from our hearts with compassion because we have become caring people.

The power of emotions which religions instill within us is that they can move us from indifference to action. They can be the motivations or triggers that lead us to put our beliefs or dispositions into action. Many ethicists have seen this power in the moral affection, or emotion, known as sympathy. Sympathy is fellow-feeling, an affective identification with the situation of others, especially situations that involve sorrow or suffering. Our ability to feel someone else's pain or suffering is often a precondition for us to do something to relieve it. Without sympathy, we may never get interested enough to act. For example, several years ago, a group of musicians, aware of the plight of the people in several African nations, spawned the "USA for Africa" campaign. They were "moved," "affected" to the point of action on behalf of those in need. One might argue that they became aware of their obligation to all of humanity because we live in an interdependent world. Some of the words in the song they dedicated to this work, "We Are the World," may affirm this interpretation. Or one could say that a sense of guilt or shame for the situation in Africa was responsible. For some this is surely true. But to hear the originators of the program tell it, what moved them was their concern for these hungry people, their identification with the pain and suffering these Africans were experiencing, an affective response which we would identify as sympathy. The response of millions of people who provide aid and assistance when a natural catastrophe strikes a community can be identified as sympathy as well.

Within the Jewish and Christian traditions, the human capacity for sympathy operates as a mediator or symbol for construing the experience of the sacred. Many key myths and symbols portray God as a sympathetic power. The Bible contains numerous stories about God's intervention on behalf of the lowly and the poor who have cried out to God. The biblical account of the Exodus suggests that God heard the cries of the Hebrew slaves and was moved to act to liberate them from their bondage in Egypt. "The Israelites groaned under their slavery, and ... their cry for help rose up to God. God heard their groaning, . . . and God took notice of them" (Ex 2:23-25). The covenant law called upon the Israelites to care for the stranger and the sojourner, for they can identify, sympathize, with what it is like to be strangers and sojourners. "You shall not oppress a resident alien; you know the heart of an alien, for you were aliens in the land of Egypt" (Ex 23:9). The Christian tradition's understanding of the person and work of Jesus the Christ is that God identifies with our sufferings and sin and acts decisively to redeem us. "For God so loved the world that he gave his only Son, so that everyone who believes in him may not perish but may have eternal life" (Jn 3:16). Even today, many Jews and Christians conceive of God as being concerned for their well-being.

Emotions can also lead us to restrict our actions. We often experience emotions when we do the right thing *or* when we go against the dictates of our conscience. In the former instance, we may feel pride, joy, or contentment; in the latter case, we may feel guilt or shame. Our emotions lead us to do some self-assessment or assessment of others. We take stock of ourselves, see what things need to change, and act to make those changes. (Of course, we may deny the wrongdoing and repress the feelings, which, psychologists tell us, can lead to a variety of unhealthy behaviors.) The point is that the emotions we experience are the triggers. When someone else does something wrong, we may feel anger or outrage at the person or events. For example, whenever we feel unfairly treated, we experience a sense of anger at the person who, we feel, has mistreated us. We are suggesting that this person has violated an important value in the life of the community. Here, again, the emotions trigger a response on our part or on the part of the community.

Within indigenous religious traditions, this connection between emotions and moral judgment is seen in the concept of taboo. Ethicist John Ansah tells us that in some African cultures, taboos form an extremely important part of their ethical code. "They are charged with a high degree of religious fervor, being associated with divine power."[8] By claiming something is taboo, the community generates such an emotionally charged aura around the action that the breaking of the taboo can trigger emotions of shame or guilt on the part of the individual and outrage or abhorrence on the part of the community. For example, taboos associated with sexual conduct are so highly respected that deviations from them are deeply detested. This level of emotion is understandable when we realize that in the African worldview, such offenses can have disastrous consequences for the society as a whole, such as epidemics, drought, or famine.

In addition to emotions, religious traditions emphasize virtues as norms for moral character. Many of us have a narrow concept of virtue. We see virtue primarily as a type of self-restraint, especially with regard to human wants and desires. We are virtuous when we do not give in to our seemingly insatiable desires for fame, fortune, and sex. The dictionary reflects this view when it includes "chastity, especially in a woman," as one of the definitions of virtue. But the basic moral meaning of virtue signifies strength, power, and excellence. Moral virtues are certain excellences, skills, habits, and traits that develop over time and which dispose us, intellectually and emotionally, to act in ways that are in keeping with our understanding of the moral ordering of the world. Not only do virtues make us ready to act in morally good ways, they make it easy for us to do so; it becomes part of our nature. Virtues also generate emotions of joy and intrinsic satisfaction when we act morally, thereby reinforcing these moral habits. If we have developed the virtue of generosity, we readily and easily act generously when the opportunity arises, and we feel happy when we do.

As conceptions of the good life or moral order differ among religious communities, so do their accounts of the virtues. The Greeks affirmed four virtues: wisdom, courage, temperance, and justice. When acquired, these virtues enabled persons to find happiness. Christianity stressed these same moral virtues, but added the theological virtues of faith, hope, and love, which all people need to find their true happiness in God. These virtues are infused into believers by the Spirit of God working within them. In Buddhism, the virtues include self-restraint and compassion, which lead to enlightenment for the self and others. The Yoruba religious tradition of Africa upholds the virtues of honesty and loyalty because of their significance for maintaining relationship and community.

One way religious communities contribute to the cultivation of virtue is through their stories of what the good life or moral ordering is all about and the virtues or "habits of the heart" needed to achieve it. For example, the Gospel of Luke includes the story about the Good Samaritan. In this story, a man asks Jesus what he needs to do to achieve salvation. Jesus tells him that salvation is achieved through living out the two-fold command to love God and to love one's neighbor. The man responds with a question, seeking to limit his ethical obligations: "Who is my neighbor?" Instead of answering this question, Jesus responds with the story of the Good Samaritan, a story that stresses the moral character of the hero over the fulfillment of the commandment. Briefly, three individuals encounter someone who has been robbed and beaten and is lying by the roadside. The Good Samaritan is the one who stops and goes out of his way to insure that the victim receives the care and assistance needed to restore him to health. After telling the story, Jesus asks which of the three persons who passed by embodied the norms of love and care essential to being a neighbor. It is the Samaritan who is the neighbor; it flows from his being because he has the covenant written on his heart.

It is not always easy to differentiate between moral affections and virtues. For example, compassion is an emotion that a person may feel for others, but it is also a habitual response on the part of a person. It is cultivated over time and held up as a virtue by various religious traditions, especially Buddhism. In Buddhist scriptures, **the Buddha** exemplified his deep sympathy and compassion for the suffering that all living things experience: in the face of temptation by the Evil One (Mara) to disappear into nirvana at the time of his enlightenment, the Buddha delayed so that

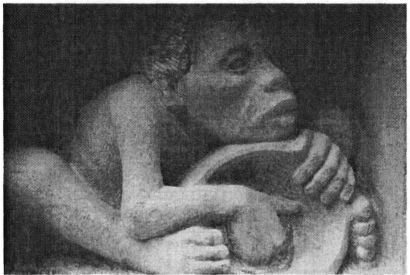

CNS PHOTO BY DIANNE NORDQUIST, *SAINT CLOUD VISITOR*

A sculpture by Joseph O'Connell illustrating the verse from the Gospel of Matthew: "I was hungry and you gave me food."

he could teach the path of enlightenment to others. In doing so the Buddha modeled the depth of compassion which all Buddhists should emulate.

In Mahayana Buddhism, compassion becomes a central moral trait. Mahayana Buddhists are critical of Theravada Buddhists who hold up what appears to be a selfish ideal, the *arhant* (worthy one), who achieves enlightenment in monastic isolation. By contrast, Mahayana Buddhists point to the pattern of life exemplified in boddhisattvas (Buddhas-to-be), who sacrifice their own welfare through countless lives out of compassion for the suffering of other living creatures. Moreover, they postpone their own liberation until all are liberated. In many ways, bodhisattvas are like ship captains who will not leave a sinking ship until they are sure that all of the passengers and crew are safely on lifeboats.

One final element that must be stressed here is that all communities charge certain institutions or groups with the task of assisting others in their character formation. In the United States, the family is given the primary role for the moral development and character formation of children. This is one reason why so many people contend that the rise in immoral behavior is directly related to the dysfunction of many families, which for various reasons no longer provide the moral training needed to develop moral children. Others would contend that, while families play a central role, moral development is the responsibility of the whole community. The African proverb "It takes a village to raise a child" reflects this perspective. Thus, many communities charge their schools with the task of values education as well as academic preparation, including a community service requirement for graduation to stress the importance of service to others.

Religions have played and continue to play a significant role in moral development in many cultures. They are communities of character. Alexis de Tocqueville noticed how religion cultivated "habits of the heart"— habits that included benevolence and concern for others—that limited the effects of growing self-interest and excessive consumption taking place in nineteenth-century United States.[9] Today, the various religious traditions struggle to continue that tradition. Religious instruction by lay and clergy leaders at churches, synagogues, mosques, and temples also includes instruction in the ethical obligations and virtues cherished by those traditions. Similarly, in African traditional religious communities, while the locus of moral development and character formation is with the family, the religious leaders are also given responsibility for the moral development of children. Rituals associated with initiation into adulthood include instruction in the proper use of sexuality and other adult responsibilities.

Moral Exemplars

Moral exemplars are those persons or communities that live a life deemed pre-eminently moral. They embody the norms of conduct and character advocated by the community most fully. Many religious communities hold up their founders as moral exemplars in their scriptures. The Qur'an describes Muhammad as "a fine example" (33:22), full of "high moral excellence" (68:4). We have already noted the model provided by the Buddha. Some would contend that this general attitude of compassion holds the same status as *agape* (love) for Christians. Jesus describes the nature of this love in John's Gospel: "No one has greater love than this, to lay down one's life for one's friends" (Jn 15:13). Here again, Christians recognize that the best exemplar of this love is Jesus. The notion of moral exemplar or ethical model may be reflected either in a specific individual or group, or in a way of life that is esteemed highly by the tradition. In both instances, what is key is that the person lives out the life he or she believes is right and good. They model that way of life in their own actions, and that way of life is deemed to be ultimately connected to sacred orderings.

Mohandas K. (Mahatma) Gandhi (1869-1948) is a good example of a contemporary religious moral exemplar. Although this claim about Gandhi can be made for many reasons, no reason is more evident than in his dealings with the "untouchables" in Indian society.[10] Untouchables were at the lowest level of Hindu society. They were outside of the caste system. An untouchable is someone who must not touch anything a caste Hindu has touched. In fact, if a caste member does come into contact with an untouchable, he is considered polluted and must purge himself through some kind of cleansing ritual. Obviously, such a status means that many taboos developed within Indian society against contact with untouchables. This was not simply religious discrimination but discrimination carried over into every facet of life, resulting in a great deal of poverty and deprivation. For some, this state of affairs seems unfair. But, in light of the Hindu notions of reincarnation and karma, many Indians believed untouchables deserved their lot. The idea of doing anything to eliminate their misery was problematic.

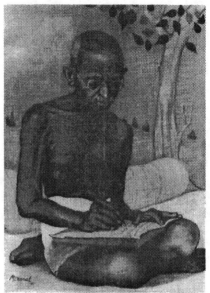

PASTEL BY RICHARD DE MENOCAL, COURTESY OF ROBERT ELLSBERG

Work for social justice and reflection on Hindu traditions are united in the life of Mohandas Gandhi.

Gandhi refused to accept untouchability and chose by word and example to eliminate it. He called untouchability a "hideous system" and a "canker eating at the vitals of Hinduism." He felt that early Hinduism did not support this system. He went so far as to proclaim that if Hinduism required untouchability, then he would declare himself "an open rebel against Hinduism itself." He recognized that independence for India is meaningless so long as Indians kept one fifth of its population in servitude. "Inhuman ourselves, we may not plead before the Throne for deliverance from the inhumanity of others." Understanding the way language influences reality, Gandhi began to call them by a different name, *Harijans*, which means children of God.

Even as a youth, Gandhi defied his mother's orders and played with an untouchable boy. He fought untouchability in South Africa as well. Later in life, Gandhi associated with untouchables, even allowing an untouchable family into his ashram, or community. This created a great deal of furor for benefactors of the community, and financial support was withdrawn by many. When the possibility that the community would run out of funds emerged, Gandhi responded, "Then we shall go to live in the untouchable quarter." Gandhi eventually adopted a woman, Lakshmi, as his own daughter, thus making him the father of an untouchable. He said, "I do not want to be reborn, but if I have to be reborn I should be reborn an untouchable so that I may share their sorrows, sufferings, and the affronts leveled against them in order that I may endeavor to free myself and them from their miserable condition." He even cleaned the bathrooms of the ashram. As a result of his action, and the esteem given to him as the title Mahatma, "great souled one," indicates, untouchability began to lose some of its curse for the thousands of Hindus who came to visit and eat with him. Many others followed Gandhi's example and began to hire these "children of god" into their homes. Thus, in both word and deed, Gandhi was a model and an example for many people throughout India and the world.

SOCIAL ETHICS

Thus far, the discussion has focused on moral or ethical action for individuals seeking to be faithful to their religious tradition and to uphold or create the moral order within that tradition. Religious ethics, however, are also social ethics in that they relate to the way institutions and societies organize and structure themselves. Like interpersonal ethics, social ethics address the moral order within the community. Social ethics provide norms for both the ethical action and character of social institutions. The assumption is that if we structure social institutions according to socially acceptable moral norms, then persons who participate in those institutions will develop accordingly. For example, children who grow up in families that have an openness toward others may develop as children who have an openness toward others. This is part of what is meant about the "habits of the heart" mentioned above. Ethical institutions are important for generating ethical people. The difference is that social ethics look at the moral patterns within society and its institutions.

The fundamental norm for social ethics is justice. When we throw out the word "justice," we are often unclear what it means. More often we are clearer about what is unjust than just. This can be seen among children. If you have three children and only two candy bars, and you decide to give the candy bars to the two older children, the youngest may not be able to tell her parents about a notion of equality as an inherent component of a conception of justice. She can, however, say quite emphatically, "That's not fair!" Of course, she might not think that way if she has learned that age is a significant criterion for the distribution of material goods; that is, the older you are the more benefits you should receive.

Justice as a norm for society often centers around the notion of distributive justice. Distributive justice refers to the proper distribution of social benefits and burdens: because society has benefits and burdens to distribute, they have to be distributed fairly. Aristotle argued that distributive justice requires treating equals alike and treating unequals differently. For example, two students take the same test and answer the same number of questions correctly. Justice requires that they receive the same grade. The teacher discovers, however, that one student studied hard to make her grade, while the other student stole a copy of the test with all the answers the day before. Justice requires that the teacher give them different grades. Deciding what is a fair or just distribution requires that we understand the appropriate criteria by which the goods are distributed.

In Hindu caste society, and in European feudal society, a legitimate criteria for the distribution of society's benefits and burdens was ascription. What this means is that certain benefits and burdens follow one's station or status in the community. Recalling the Vedic creation account from chapter 1, we see that there were certain rewards that went with being born to the Brahmin, or highest, caste. They had certain privileges, opportunities, and responsibilities that went along with their position in society. The distribution of society's goods that favored them was considered just and fair because it was in keeping with the moral order inherent in the universe, an order that is hierarchical. In contrast, the Jewish and Christian traditions speak about a distribution of goods based upon need. The justice of a community or society depended upon all members of the community having their basic needs met, especially the poor and the marginalized. By providing for their need, the members of the community would undergird their basic equality before God.

As with personal ethical obligations, the right action, justice as law, may be connected to a specific goal or end. For many religious traditions, justice is often connected to some vision of community. Within the Jewish and Christian traditions, there is a concept of covenant community to which God has called all creatures. The vision inherent in this concept is of a community in which all members of the community participate meaningfully in society and in which the well-being of all people is assured. It is a vision of community that fully values all persons, especially those who are marginalized. This collective sense of well-being has been referred to as the common good.

The common good has been a critical component of official Catholic social thought in recent times. The common good refers to the communal nature of human existence. Humans were created for community, not isolation, and this means that the good of each person is bound up with the good of community. Catholic teaching contends that the common good is a social reality in which all persons should share through their participation in it. On the one hand, participation means that each person should contribute to the common good to the best of his or her abilities, not simply attend to individual goods. It is a part of each person's moral obligation. On the other hand, participation means that all persons in the community should benefit from the enhancement of the common good. In his **encyclical** *Mater et magistra* (1961), Pope John XXIII (1881-1963) says that the common good is "the sum total of conditions of social living, whereby persons are enabled more fully and readily to achieve their own perfection" (MM 65). Unless everyone shares in the benefits of social advance, the common good can be a source of domination and exploitation. To keep this from happening, Catholic teaching advocates the guarantee of basic political and social rights that specify basic levels of material and higher goods that no citizen is allowed to fall below, including food, shelter, and education. Moreover, because the human community has become globally interdependent, efforts must be made to secure the universal common good, not just the good of nations.

Catholic teaching on the common good does not limit itself to the boundaries of the human community, however. Pope John Paul II has advocated including the protection of the environment in his discussion of

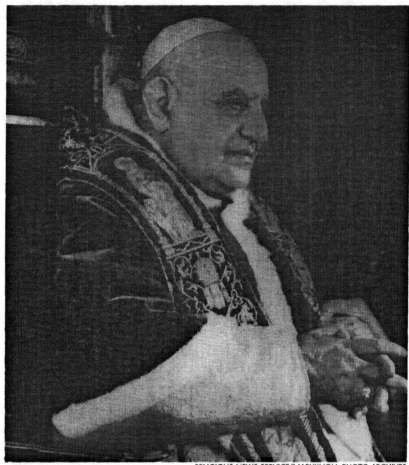

RELIGIOUS NEWS SERVICE/MARYKNOLL PHOTO ARCHIVES

One of the most popular popes of modern times, John XXIII. His official portrait.

the common good in his encyclical *Sollicitudo rei socialis* (1987). Human technology will have disastrous effects on the environment, and on humanity, unless it is guided by moral values or ends. Although including the biosphere in deliberations about the common good transcends the human community, it still does not go far enough. Ultimately, Catholic social teaching contends, the full common good is realized only in the communion of all God's creatures with God and with each other in God. This is the highest good for humanity and transcends any good that can be achieved politically, economically, or culturally.

Whether or not a religious tradition has a social ethic depends on the attitudes of the tradition toward the world. If a religion affirms this world as good, and urges its members to live within it, then there is the need for a social ethic and norms for life in the world. We have seen how this is true for the Catholic tradition in our discussion of Catholic social thought on the common good. This is also true for Islam, which holds that the world is a theater for human service to God. Not all religious traditions find significance in this world, however. As we have noted, historically Buddhists thought of this world as a place of suffering and sought release from it. The goal of religious and moral action is to eliminate desire, the craving for the things of this world. The goal is to reach nirvana which, in Theravada Buddhism, is done through monastic withdrawal from this world. This rejection of the world can be seen in the following quote from the *Dhammapada*, a classic text of early Buddhism. "Whoever looks upon this world as a bubble, as a mirage, is not seen by the King of Death. . . . Come, look at this world, like a painted royal chariot; fools sink in it, the knowing have no attachment to it."[11] As a result, some would contend, Buddhism has been slow to develop a social ethic (although this is changing).

THE RELATIONSHIP BETWEEN SYMBOLIC AND PRACTICAL RELIGIOUS ACTION

Most people have a keen sense of the intricate connection between ritual and ethics. Those of us who have a negative opinion of ritual often relate it to our feeling that many who engage in ritual fail to live up to the ethical norms of their religion. Like the biblical prophet **Amos**, we understand that the rituals we practice should correspond with our actions in our everyday lives. Without fully understanding the implications, we recognize that just as important as orthodoxy (right belief) is orthopraxy (right action). Moreover, we realize that orthopraxy encompasses both ritual and ethics. In the Jewish and Christian traditions, this connection is reflected in the two-fold commandment to love God and to love one's neighbor. Holding the two forms of action together fulfills all the law and the prophets. Thus, ritual and ethical action are mutually reinforcing. Rituals support a particular moral way of life, embody values and relationships, and remind us of our moral responsibilities and commitments. How religious rituals accomplish this is through their pedagogical, their redemptive, and their transformative functions.

RITUAL AND MORAL PEDAGOGY

Theodore Jennings, Jr., reminds us about the pedagogical character of ritual. Ritual's repetitive dimension imparts knowledge to its participants and invites our imitation or response. In the performance of ritual, we learn not only how to conduct a ritual, but also how to conduct ourselves outside of the ritual act. This teaching provides a pattern of doing. Ritual is important "in forming a way of being and acting in the world." In fact, Jennings suggests, "Ritual serves as a paradigm for all significant action."[12] We can see this pedagogical dimension of ritual in a variety of ways.

As part of the ethos—the acceptable ways of behaving and living—of an individual or community, ritual action is often symbolically supportive of a particular moral way of life. For example, storytelling is ritualized in many cultures. On the one hand, the stories remind people of the significant events and people in the life of the community, thereby reinforcing the worldview. On the other hand, they hold up certain virtues or qualities that a person in the community who wants to live rightly should develop. This is especially true in stories about heroes. The heroes in the stories become moral exemplars, people who embody the moral character the community cherishes. For example, during the Jewish festival of Purim, the story of Esther is read in the synagogue. This story recounts how the Jews were saved from persecution and death by the courage and shrewdness of Esther and her cousin Mordecai.

Some rituals remind us of our moral commitments and responsibilities. The rituals associated with the holidays of Thanksgiving and Christmas remind people of the good fortune they have and prompt them to share it with others. The "giving tree" ritual developed in many Christian churches and by the Salvation Army reflects this connection. In the ritual activity of Christmas gift-giving, the "giving tree" reminds people of the value of charity and meeting the needs of others and provides a formalized way of practicing that virtue. A similar ritual among the Oglala Sioux is the "giveaway ceremony." The ceremony is done in conjunction with a significant event in the life of the individual or family or as an attempt to find spiritual renewal. In this ceremony, a family may give away some or most of its valued possessions to others, especially the poorest members of the community. This provides a ritualized way for practicing the value of sharing and for demonstrating concern for the well-being of others. It also inhibits concentrations of wealth.

Rituals also embody values and relationships. Having the "man of the house" sit at the head of the table and carve the turkey on Thanksgiving Day, even if he has no role in the preparation and cleanup of the meal, embodies certain values and gender roles. The Native American ritual of giving thanks to the animal for surrendering its life for the health and well-being of the tribe suggests the valuable place of all living creatures in the web of life and the importance placed on humanity's relationship with the rest of nature. Female circumcision rituals practiced in some African cultures reflect the belief that the value of sexuality for women is more procreation than pleasure. They also point to the subordinate position of women.

The pedagogical significance of ritual can be seen in moral development. Rituals often include recitation of myths, proverbs, or creeds that reinforce the moral worldview of the community. For example, school children in the United States often say the pledge of allegiance to the flag. The concluding phrase of that pledge is "with liberty and justice for all." These are moral norms that the community wishes all members of the community to abide by, and so they are included in their daily rituals.

The repetition of this ritual suggests this ordering to the minds of the people. Rites of initiation in many religious traditions include training and instruction in moral behavior. The puberty rites of African traditional religions include lessons in the values of the society, special instructions on the roles the participants will have as adults, and how they are expected to behave sexually.

In addition to having a cognitive dimension, ritual action enables participants to perform actions that produce feelings of fellowship and social solidarity. Victor Turner's description of the transition or *liminal* phase in rites of passage is a good example. He suggests that participants in the rite experience a common bond or feeling of *communitas* that they do not encounter outside the ritual experience. As a result, there is a sense of community and social solidarity that takes place among the initiates which enables them to become aware of the interconnectedness and equality between them. This can be seen clearly in the pilgrimage experience associated with Islam. The people on the pilgrimage wear a common white garment. All distinctions of rank and ethnic background are lost. Together they circumambulate (walk around) the Ka'ba in Mecca. In undergoing the ritual, the participants understand and feel the unity and solidarity that make up the *Umma*, the world community of Islam.

RITUAL AND MORAL REDEMPTION

The intricate relationship between ritual and ethics can also be seen in the redemptive character of ritual. When we act in ways contrary to the moral order affirmed by our religious traditions, we can experience a sense of guilt and confusion. Conscience may come into play here, as we feel that our actions have become disruptive to the moral order. In some indigenous religious traditions, when the harmony in the universe is out of balance, there is an assumption that someone or some group has acted contrary to the moral order of the universe. The only way to set things right, to restore the balance, is by means of ritual action, which may include some divination process as to the cause of the malaise.

Religions have provided people with a variety of rituals to help assuage their moral guilt and to restore them to community. Many indigenous religious traditions use the sacrifice of vegetables or animals as a way of appeasing the offended party, especially if that party is the deity or some other transhuman being. Other traditions, including Judaism and Christianity, affirm the importance of the private and public confession of wrongdoing. We have heard people say, "Confession is good for the soul." What they mean is that confession allows people to give voice to their wrongdoing, to take ownership of and responsibility for it, and to make amends. The Call to Confession liturgy and the Jewish holy day of Yom Kippur, discussed in detail in chapter 10, are good examples of confession rituals that enable people to experience moral redemption.

Ritual and ethical action are also connected when there is moral ambiguity. The Vietnam War was an ambiguous event in the life of the American community. People felt it was both just and unjust, moral and immoral. The war created a rift in the American psyche and experience, bringing division to families and communities. Soldiers who went to war believing that what they were doing was right experienced a sense of betrayal when they returned home. In other wars, soldiers returned to parades and celebrations; Vietnam veterans returned to public scorn and ridicule. The construction of the Vietnam War Memorial has become a way to heal the rift in the community. Many people make pilgrimages to the site of the memorial in Washington, D.C. They touch or trace the names of friends and family members who died during the war. They weep together. They leave flowers. Whether one was in favor of or against the war, the memorial provides a public statement about the ambiguity of the war and offers the promise of symbolically restoring the bonds of community broken during that time.

The *mizuko kuyo* ritual in Japan serves a similar redemptive function. Abortion has been legal in Japan since 1948. It is the most effective form of birth control in a nation where other forms of birth control are not discussed widely. Women seeking abortion feel it is the right thing to do, especially before they marry or after they have borne their complement of two children, because it accords with the norms of their society. Yet they cannot escape the fact that the unborn child is understood by Buddhism to be a living human being. Women may still feel pangs of guilt and grief over the loss of the child, even though they willed it. They experience a form of spiritual malaise which needs healing.

The *mizuko kuyo* ritual means offering up prayers for the nourishment of the spirit of the unborn child. It also is a service intended to console the parents, especially the mother. There is wide variety in the practice of the ritual because of the sectarian nature of Japanese Buddhism. The service may take place once, monthly, or on the anniversary of the death of the fetus. The service can be private, although mostly it is a service said for many *mizuko* at the same time. The priest conducts the service at the altar on behalf of those requesting the service. One or more names of the Buddha or boddhisattvas are invoked. Some parts of sutras (Buddhist scriptures) are chanted. During the service, offerings of food, flowers, incense, and the like are made to the Buddha on behalf of the child. Some sculpted representation of Jizo, a boddhisattva seen as the protector of young children, or an infant is left on the temple grounds. A Buddhist name is given to the child posthumously. A mortuary table is placed in the temple or placed in the family shrine. Sometimes a priest gives a sermon to place the experience in a wider context.

This ritual relates to Japanese Buddhist cosmology in two ways. First, *mizuko* literally means "water-child" or "child of the waters." To

Jizo dolls at a Buddhist monastery in Japan. Dolls include traditional as well as modern, robot-like types. (Reprinted with permission, William R. LaFleur, Liquid Life: Abortion and Buddhism in Japan *[Princeton University Press, 1992].)*

refer to a fetus as a "child of the waters" means that its status is fluid and in flux. This notion accords with the Buddhist notion of the impermanence of the self and its understanding of reality as becoming. If, for some reason such as too many children or an inability to care for a newborn, a woman decides to abort a fetus, her decision means returning the child to the heavenly realm from which it came until it can be reborn into a better situation, a situation where the child is welcomed and nurtured instead of seen as a burden. Thus, abortion is viewed as a moral course of action, although recognizing the difficulties and the pain it brings to the woman who undertakes the action.

Second, Buddhist cosmology recognizes that there is ambiguity in all existence. Anything can be malevolent, but it is not inherently so: these same forces can be turned to good for those who seek wisdom and goodness. In Buddhist doctrine, there are various worlds for the dead, some of which are not pleasant. Without proper veneration, there is potential that the spirit of the unborn child may become a demon. The *kuyo* service provides a means for transforming potentially dangerous or malevolent forces to helpful and beneficial forces for the living.

Non-Japanese viewers of this ritual may see it as strange. But it deals with the issue of moral ambiguity and perplexity head-on. It recognizes that what is at stake in many moral decisions is the quality of life against life. No matter which choice we make, we experience guilt. This and similar rituals enable people to confront the dark side of human experience directly instead of glossing over its ambiguities and difficulties. It seeks to re-establish harmonious moral order, but only after the roots of disharmony have been confronted and displaced.

> ### Thinking about Ritual and Moral Redemption
>
> To explore the connection between ritual and moral redemption, think of a time when you did something wrong (or ask several friends to do so). What feelings, if any, did you experience as a result of your wrongdoing? How did you express those feelings? What activities did you find helpful in dealing with or channeling these feelings? What actions did you do to make amends for what you did? What did you do to help you feel good about yourself again? Thinking about those activities, do you find that you repeat them in other instances of wrongdoing?

RITUAL AND MORAL TRANSFORMATION

A final dimension of the relationship between ritual and ethical action is in the transformative character of ritual. Not only does ritual action affirm the moral order, sometimes it also reorders or recenters the moral universe, transforming the lives of participants. It is easy to see the transformative dimension of ritual. In the performance of rituals associated with birth, the status of the participants is changed. When people perform marriage ceremonies, their status is transformed from single to married, and it has communal significance. When an individual prays for healing, they often want some state of affairs to be different. They hope that through their ritual action, some transformation will take place.

The question is, How is this transformative dimension related to morality? How can ritual effect moral change in the lives of individuals and communities? At a basic level, ritual is performative. What this means is that it enables us to see ourselves as agents, enacting some event or state of affairs. We bring something into being. For example, many students take advantage of weekend retreat opportunities afforded to them by their colleges. Usually they go off campus to a quiet place away from the grind of college life and spend the time reflecting and meditating individually and communally. Many students return to campus feeling refreshed and renewed. Some students, however, experience far more. They speak of how the retreat allowed them time to rethink their goals, values, and priorities. They declare that they have a new outlook on life and that their actions and behaviors will take new directions. In other words, they have changed, a transformation has taken place.

Tom Driver suggests, "When we understand ourselves as agents active in a world made up of other purposive beings, our sense of self and responsibility is heightened."[13] His point is that the doing of ritual has a moral effect; it helps us to understand our connection with others and forces us to some moral action. A good example is the Islamic practice of almsgiving. By giving money and alms, the Islamic person is doing something about poverty and inequality. Their actions are attempting to make a transformation in the world. They suggest that poverty and inequality are not acceptable, even though they are widely accepted in the world at large. Almsgiving also has the effect of helping people realize that their lives are more than material possessions.

The early Christian baptismal formula not only had a pedagogical function, it also symbolized moral transformation.[14] The initiates would gather together apart from the community. Their separation reflected not only a separation from the group, but also from former professions and ways of life. Prostitutes, gladiators, and charioteers were not allowed to become Christian unless they had abandoned their former ways of life. In response to ethical instruction, especially from portions of the *Didache*, a manual on faith and practice of the early church, the initiands would renounce the Devil and vow to live in accordance with Christian teaching. Even the baptismal formula developed in Paul's letters indicated the transformation process, dying to the former self and rising to newness in Christ. In going into the water, sometimes the initiands were held down to symbolize drowning and death and then raised to new life. What is important to note is that this new life was not simply a religious transformation, but a moral transformation as well.

The connection between ritual performance and the transformation of society can be seen in the Civil Rights movement in the United States. The marches, the sit-ins, and the singing were all ritualized actions, formal and repetitive, performed by the participants. These rituals were often preceded by worship and prayer. But these actions were not done to simply draw attention to the structures of segregation and injustice prevalent in society. Rather, they were geared toward the transformation of that society toward a vision in which all persons, regardless of race, would be treated with respect and dignity. Moreover, that vision, which Martin Luther King, Jr., called the "beloved community," included the oppressor as well as the oppressed. More importantly, the participants lived out that vision in their rituals. People of different races worshiped together, marched hand-in-hand, and refused to confront violence with violence. As a result, these actions pricked the nation's collective conscience, forced the elimination of legal segregation, and led to a greater degree of social justice for all citizens.

It should be clear that sometimes the transformation that takes place through ritual can also affect the ritual itself. This is what occurs when people see the sense of community built into the Christian ritual of communion, and they redirect the rest of the service to reflect this new vision: distinctions are broken down, a common humanity before God is affirmed and declared. In many traditions, there is the passing of the peace following the communion ceremony, reaffirming this inherent equality before the eyes of God. This inherent equality has led many to argue for equality in other ways as well. When the ritual affirms the equality of all, it becomes difficult to justify the prominent place of men in the ritual or division between the races.

Similar ritual transformations are current practice in the women-church movement. New rituals and liturgies are being developed to celebrate women's experiences in the world, which have too long been ignored because of the patriarchal structure of the church and worship leadership. Inspired by the affirmation of mutuality and equality, they generate rituals that practice this new way of looking at the world. Instead of having worship leaders on a raised platform, the rituals are done in circles. Even the candles are ordered in circles to reflect this relational worldview. Participation in the ritual is meant to reaffirm a different way of looking at the world, and it has political dimensions. Many of the litanies speak of the problems of violence, sexism, and patriarchy inherent in society, and they seek to practice a different order. They also advocate for participants in the rituals to seek change in the society at large.

SUMMARY

Ritual and ethical action help us to order our lives in meaningful ways, individually and socially. Without such symbolic and practical actions, our lives would seem chaotic and confusing. The chaos impinging upon our lives, chaos that comes with changes in our lives—such as moving away from home, changing jobs, or going to college—has the potential to overwhelm us. Fortunately, we are able to gain control over this chaos and find meaning in our lives through the actions we take. As we have seen, however, many religious traditions use stories, metaphors, and myths to enable us to understand and to motivate us to perform the ritual and ethical actions critical to finding such meaning. They are a part of the language that makes up our religious traditions. Thus, it is to language that we now turn our attention.

RESOURCES

Activities

1. Do an analysis of a religious social-justice organization. Visit a local religious organization seeking to promote social justice, gather information regarding the underlying values and beliefs of the organization, and analyze how well the structure (ethos) reflects the organization's purpose (worldview). Present your findings in a written or oral report.
2. Gather the moral questions of members of the class or study group. At the beginning of the session, ask students to write questions regarding any ethical concerns they have. Place the questions in a brown paper bag. Periodically draw questions from the bag that the entire class will attempt to answer together using the materials from the text.
3. Interview eight to ten people about the ritual activities that help them cope with the moral difficulties they experience. Analyze the responses to discern the types of ritual activities respondents use to help deal with their moral failures.

4. Have a debate over the following statement: Morality without religion is impossible. Have teams research each position thoroughly and provide time for each group to make its case.
5. Watch several films that raise significant moral issues (*Philadelphia* and *Disclosure* are good examples). Do an analysis of the films looking for the filmmaker's approach on the moral issue in question. Is the emphasis on moral conduct? Moral character? Both?

Readings

Denise Lardner Carmody and John Carmody. *How to Live Well: Ethics in the World Religions.* Belmont, CA: Wadsworth Publishing, 1988. An introductory textbook in the ethical convictions of the major world religions written primarily for undergraduates. The text explores the ethical understandings of family life, work, social justice, and nature of all the major religious traditions.

Cromwell S. Crawford, ed. *World Religions and Global Ethics.* New York: Paragon House, 1989. An excellent collection of essays on the ethical traditions of a variety of religions, including African traditional religion, Buddhism, Hinduism, Christianity, Confucianism, Judaism, and Islam.

Ronald Green. *Religion and Moral Reason.* New York: Oxford University Press, 1988. A comparative study in religion and ethics in which Green seeks to show the moral intentionality that animates religious belief. The text also explores the connections between religious ritual and ethics in a variety of religious traditions.

William R. LaFleur. *Liquid Life: Abortion and Buddhism in Japan.* Princeton: Princeton University Press, 1992. This book explores the meaning and practice of *mizuko kuyo*, the Buddhist abortion ritual in Japan.

Robin W. Lovin and Frank E. Reynolds. *Cosmogony and Ethical Order.* Chicago: University of Chicago Press, 1985. A collection of essays which brings together religious ethicists and historians of religion in an attempt to further the discipline of comparative religious ethics, by exploring the ethical orderings present in a variety of religious cosmogonies.

H. Richard Niebuhr. *The Responsible Self.* New York: Harper and Row, 1963. In this book, published posthumously, Niebuhr outlines the meaning of responsibility as a basic category for understanding human moral obligations. He contrasts this perspective with the experience of moral obligation as law and as ends.

John P. Reeder, Jr. *Source, Sanction, and Salvation: Religion and Morality in Judaic and Christian Traditions.* Englewood Cliffs, NJ: Prentice-Hall, 1988. This book provides a framework for understanding religion as the source, sanction, and goal of religious ethics. Although restricted to the Jewish and Christian religious traditions, some of the themes are applicable to other religions as well.

Audiovisuals

Contemporary Issues in World Religions. 2 cassettes. ABC News/Prentice Hall, 1995. These videos provide short, news-oriented stories on such issues as abortion, women in the priesthood, and female circumcision. They are excellent discussion starters.

Religion and Race in America: Martin Luther King's Lament. Available from Films for the Humanities and Sciences, P.O. Box 2053, Princeton, NJ 08543. The film examines the issue of religion and race by visiting four churches, speaking with experts and with members of each congregation. The film examines a church that holds separate services for whites and blacks, a black couple who attend a predominantly white church, a white woman who attends a black church, and an interracial church.

Islamic Conversations. Available from Films for the Humanities and Sciences, P.O. Box 2053, Princeton, NJ 08543. This series of films provides insight into the views of influential Muslim thinkers on such subjects as violence and holy war, democracy, the rights of women, multiculturalism, and religious authority.

The Great Religions and the Poor. Available from Films for the Humanities and Sciences, P.O. Box 2053, Princeton, NJ 08543. Part of the *Religions of the Book* series, this film explores the beliefs of Judaism, Christianity, and Islam regarding the poor, taking a comparative look at the traditional concept of the poor.

On Values: The Roles of Faith, Family, and Freedom in America Today. Available from Films for the Humanities and Sciences, P.O. Box 2053, Princeton, NJ 08543. This series of three films looks at the relationship between religion and civic life, the changing nature of the family, and the dynamics of the culture/ values war in the American context.

Gandhi, starring Ben Kingsley.

NOTES

1. Joachim Wach, *The Comparative Study of Religions* (New York: Columbia University Press, 1958), 115.

2. John P. Reeder, Jr., *Source, Sanction, and Salvation* (Englewood Cliffs, NJ: Prenctice Hall, Inc., 1988).

3. Albert R. Jonsen, "Responsibility," in *The Westminster Dictionary of Christian Ethics*, ed. John MacQuarrie and James Childress (Philadelphia: Westminster Press, 1985), 545-549.

4. E. Bolaji Idowu, *Olodumare: God in Yoruba Belief* (London: Longmans, 1962), 150.

5. Walter E. Conn, *Conscience: Development and Self-Transcendence* (Birmingham, AL: Religious Education Press, 1981), 206.

6. *Trials of War Criminals Before the Nuremberg Military Tribunals*, in Edward Zukowski, "The 'Good Conscience' of Nazi Doctors," *The Annual of the Society of Christian Ethics* (1994): 56-57.

7. Martin Luther King, Jr., "Letter from Birmingham Jail," in *Why We Can't Wait* (New York: New American Library, 1964), 82-84.

8. John K. Ansah, "The Ethics of African Religious Tradition," in *World Religions and Global Ethics*, Cromwell S. Crawford, ed. (New York: Paragon House, 1989), 249.

9. See Robert Bellah, et al., *Habits of the Heart* (Berkeley: University of California Press, 1985), 223.

10. The following paragraphs are drawn from the biography by Louis Fischer, *The Life of Mahatma Gandhi* (New York: Harper & Row, 1950), 138-147.

11. *The Dhammapada*, trans. Thomas Cleary (New York: Bantam Books, 1995), 59-60.

12. Theodore W. Jennings, Jr., "On Ritual Knowledge," in *Readings in Ritual Studies*, ed. Ronald L. Grimes (Upper Saddle River, NJ: Prentice Hall, 1996), 324-334.

13. Tom F. Driver, *The Magic of Ritual* (San Francisco: HarperCollins, 1991), 1974.

14. The discussion that follows relies on the intepretation given by Ronald Green, in "Religious Ritual: A Kantian Perspective," *Journal of Religious Ethics* (1979): 235-236.

PART III

RELIGIOUS LANGUAGE

We are born storytellers. We turn momentary setbacks into comedy as we explain to skeptical classmates how the new puppy mistook copies of a group report for a bowl of *Kibbles and Bits*. When a sudden failure or unexpected tragedy bulldozes our world, we recount yesterday's triumphs in order to reassert our sense of self and to lend some coherence to a crumbling universe. Like the woman in Wallace Stevens's poem in chapter 1, we use language to make sense of our experiences. As the following example indicates, we use stories to transform threat into safety.

> The wind has been howling around the house for hours. Leaves skitter across the porch. Is someone running? The limb of the big oak tree in the side yard rubs up against the window. The light at the corner of the yard throws shadows that dip and sway on the walls. I think I hear voices, far away, fading. The house creaks and groans. Will it collapse? Will someone find me if it does? Then lamp light floods the world. Mom, checking that I am still here. We settle down together in the warm quilts, and she tells me a story. The house will not collapse; no one is running on the porch. Out of the uncertainty and danger I fear, my mother's voice weaves a world in which I am small and safe, where shadows smile and the wind sings.

Through language we create and share stories that reveal who we are and how we fit into the world around us. At the same time we inherit stories which teach us about our families and our societies, about values and traditions. Over the years, for example, the United States has portrayed itself as "the peacekeeper of the world." Much like the solitary law officer of the Old West who rides into town and singlehandedly vanquishes the outlaws who threaten its citizens, the United States has sent troops into Vietnam, the Persian Gulf, and Bosnia, promising to drive out oppressors or restore order. This national story sanctions the allocation of tax dollars to support troops and offers military personnel a meaningful way of framing long months away from home. Proponents of this story challenge its critics to "Love it [the United States] or leave it!"

Motion pictures and television also shape our imaginations and help us tell our stories. Thanks to characters like Luke Skywalker and Princess Leia, Captain Kirk and Mr. Spock, we imagine worlds in which justice, wisdom, and compassion are possible. Darth Vader and Lex Luthor, on the other hand, plunge us into worlds organized around greed, instant gratification, and a disdain for life. On the surface *Star Wars*, *Batman*, even *The Lion King* may seem to be nothing more than light entertainment. Their continuing popularity suggests, however, that each film expresses a powerful mythic structure that stirs the imaginations and the hearts of its viewers.

In European-based societies, the Bible has influenced both cultural and individual stories. The Hollywood cinema draws on this material for themes and plots. An obvious example is Cecil B. DeMille's *The Ten Commandments*; more subtle illustrations are Quentin Tarentino's *Pulp Fiction* and Tim Robbins's *Dead Man Walking*. In the United States, politicians appeal to biblical morality and justice and use covenant language to frame their platforms. Biblical narratives also play a significant role in the stories, both told and sung, of colonized indigenous peoples who heard them from their European colonizers. At the same time, religious literatures of non-European traditions (for example, Native American, Mesoamerican, African, Islamic, Buddhist, Hindu) offer valid ways of ordering the world; they speak for women and men whose concerns and experiences do not coincide with those of European-based societies.

One objective of this section is the practice of responsible reading. In many cases we begin with the Tanak or the Bible and then move to other scriptures. Some of these texts may sound very familiar. Even if you can recite them in your sleep, imagine that you are reading them for the first time. Forget what you know; suspend any initial boredom or disinterest. Instead, read the text carefully, paying close attention to language, detail, character, and plot. Use your imagination; listen to speech and silence. Remember that religious texts seldom contain a clear account of "what really happened"; they are, rather, "representations of particular value systems"[1] that are culturally determined rather than eternally mandated. They may shape, adjust, or change our thinking. We need to be aware of how this is happening and what values are at stake.

Reading responsibly is a learning ritual. Some people may resist a text's point of view, turning away in anger from passages limiting a woman's activity or laws condoning slavery. On the other hand, there may be such a close fit between the text's value system and our own that we need to talk about it with others, especially those whose concerns the text ignores. Such conversations uncover how the text views the relationship of the sacred to the human world and its representations of gender, class, and race. We can learn whether our reading of the text is an invitation to live more fully or an excuse to resist transformation. This approach may raise more questions than it answers and may challenge some deeply held beliefs and opinions. It may also clarify our thinking and show us new ways to order our lives. If we read them carefully, religious texts provoke change, which gives birth to new stories, new texts.

Parts I and II introduced us to the importance of storytelling in different religious traditions. We saw how creation stories help people locate themselves within an ordered universe and how stories accompany ritual action to remind people about their ancestors and to set their history within the activity of the sacred. Now we look more specifically at religious language. In chapter 6, we discover that the message language intends to convey lies somewhere between its figurative and literal meanings. We identify language as hyperbole, paradox, and negation; these aspects allow us to talk about mystery and power, a dimension both within and beyond human experience. Religious traditions use language to create myths, parables, and stories. We consider myths of origin, alienation, destiny, and challenge, and we practice reading them responsibly. Because religious language includes gesture and dance, drumming and singing, gardening and cooking, we also examine some of the ways in which religions speak about the sacred nonverbally. We examine how calligraphy and basket weaving become ways to create order and to remember the holy.

In chapter 7, we consider the processes through which these narratives and stories have been preserved and handed down from one generation to another. Collections of these stories have become canonical scripture, that is, normative for belief and practice. We explore what "scripture" means in both oral and written religious traditions. The ways in which religions use their scriptures as a standard against which to measure correct behavior and the reverence they show their holy books and scrolls indicate that these texts mediate the sacred. Using the New Testament as a case study, we examine the formation of Christian canons. Finally, we consider how traditions construct more formal, conceptual statements, such as creeds and doctrines, which practitioners use to order their behaviors and beliefs.

NOTE

1. David M. Gunn and Danna Nolan Fewell, *Narrative in the Hebrew Bible* (New York: Oxford University Press, 1993) p. 191. Gunn and Fewell's treatment of language and narrative influences Part III.

Chapter 6

Talking about the Sacred

INTRODUCTION

We live in a web of language. We use it to convey facts ("It's raining"), to give directives ("Meet me at the mall!"), to express opinions ("As a sport, baseball is far superior to football"), to declare love ("I can't live without you!"). Language also helps us tell others about ourselves and our experiences. Language, however, stands between us and these experiences because any description is already an interpretation, an ordering, of experience. As we are well aware, the description is not the experience itself.

Far from being neutral and transparent, language reveals and shapes our experience. According to novelist Iris Murdoch:

> We can no longer take language for granted as a medium of communication. Its transparency is gone. We are like people who for a long time looked out a window without noticing the glass—and then one day began to notice this too.[1]

Language makes our experience available to us for reflection, sharing, and discovery; it also conceals elements of experience, because no single account of an event in our lives expresses or embodies all of its nuances, subtleties, and meanings. A single experience has as many meanings as there are stories told about it and people to tell them. For example, on a weekend trip you witness an act of selfless courage; a woman risks her life to save a man from drowning. As soon as you return home, you call a friend and relate your experience. Your act of speech has already shaped what you witnessed and has distanced you from the original event. The only way you can get at that experience is by means of the language that you use about it. The "raw," uninterpreted version is lost forever; what remains are the narratives that the witnesses to the event construct. Like them, you have created a model, a world, through which you understand courage or risk or meaning.

What we see and how we respond depends on the quality and clarity of the language we use to create the story, the "world" that mediates significance for us. If, for example, we use language to construct a world that does not include all individuals, we may find ourselves eliminating them from our definitions of human being and citizen, convincing ourselves that they are invisible and unimportant; we may identify their differences as a threat and respond to them with anger and violence. Language is personal and political; it shapes our private and our public worlds.

FIGURATIVE LANGUAGE

Because language is pliable enough to shape into worlds of meaning, we can also stretch it to include what is unusual. Introduced to a new idea, a new person, or an unfamiliar object, we immediately connect the unfamiliar with what we already know. We describe a new dessert as "food for the gods" or dismiss a singing group because it sounds worse than a family member singing in the shower. The research of educational psychologists on learning styles verifies this structure of the human mind: we learn or understand better when we can connect or associate new material with what we already know. We have more difficulty learning concepts for which we have few associations.

Thus we use language to establish meaningful connections between what we already know and what is still unfamiliar to us. We mentioned before that language is the glass through which we experience our lives. It does not offer a direct correspondence between the word and what it signifies; the word "rose" is not the flower itself. Language, then, is seldom literal. It is mostly figurative. This is true even for scientific language, which some people consider more exact and trustworthy than religious language. Out of language both scientists and religious practitioners construct worlds, models that describe their experiences, models both like and not-like these experiences. A scientist's lab report about the new compounds formed by the interaction of certain chemicals describes the interaction; however, the report is not that interaction, nor is it the newly formed compound. It is a model or pattern that represents or points to both realities. Entomologists describe animal societies with metaphors like "caste" and "xenophobia," following models of human society. Geneticists personify genes and speak of their "wisdom." These formulations presume that animals and genes are similar but not identical to human beings and the ways they function. In the sciences and in religion, we search for understanding by stretching language, by correlating the familiar with the unfamiliar, by creating relationships of aptness and similarity. Because language is so elastic, our world is full of possibility in

MARY N. MACDONALD

"For now we see in a glass, dimly...." (1 Cor 13:12). Once we become aware of the lens through which we experience ourselves and others, our relationship to language changes. We become aware that it shifts and creaks, unable to bear too much burden.

which truth "is an artifact whose fundamental design we often have to alter," rather than something delivered by God or nature.[2] Truth, then, may not be "out there" at all; truth, whether religious or scientific, may be nowhere until we use language to give it substance and location.

There are several kinds of figurative language. Hyperbole, for example, represents exaggeration carried to the extreme. If a friend declares, "One more meal in the caf and I'm dead," we recognize that this com-

MARYKNOLL PHOTO ARCHIVES

We frequently project human qualities onto dangerous and powerful natural forces. We make nature humanlike by seeing gods present within it, creating a metaphoric worldview in which humanity, the gods, and nature are interdependent upon and continuous with one another.

plaint is more serious than others; however, we rush for pizza, not medical assistance. Irony conveys the opposite of what the speaker intends. Instead of telling her class outright that only a few members scored high on a recent test, while the majority ranked in lower percentiles, a professor observes, "I didn't realize I was dealing with rocket scientists!"

Metaphor is another kind of figurative language. We use metaphors to describe those things about which we know little or to make the foreboding familiar. We create metaphors when we construct a relationship between two ideas or experiences and crowd similarities into that relationship. Metaphors represent insights about how dissimilar ideas may be related. An insensitive, unresponsive person has a heart of stone. Using an image from horticulture, a parent may marvel how, after a troublesome first year at school, a daughter has blossomed intellectually and socially. Soldiers in combat have described war as "hell." A single metaphor can sometimes express a complete worldview, a social relationship. For some indigenous people of the Andes mountains of Argentina, "the mountain is a human body . . . its land is a human body. People feed the mountain body with gifts and sacrifice, and the mountain reciprocates with food for all the people."[3] This metaphor establishes familiarity and continuity between villagers and the mountains looming over them; the language reflects the villagers' experience of the mountains as benevolent and humane.

RELIGIOUS LANGUAGE

The phrase "religious language" describes our use of ordinary vocabulary in religious contexts, just as we often use religious vocabulary in ordinary contexts. For example, we read about the "myth of progress," the "church of Baseball," the "ritual of negotiation," in articles about economics or sports or labor relations. Religious language, however, concerns itself with those dimensions of human existence in which the ultimate and the holy manifest themselves. Religious language is rooted in human experiences of what ultimately matters. It is complex. It carries meaning about the ordinary and about the sacred. It speaks about the world and about human experience in such a way that the sacred within them becomes apparent. In the Gospel of John, Jesus of Nazareth uses such language in his conversation with the Samaritan woman at the well (Jn 4). Her physical thirst for water is also a spiritual thirst; the fresh water that Jesus offers is also the "living water" that sustains eternal life. In Matthew's parable of judgment, the hungry and the naked, the homeless and the imprisoned are simultaneously the suffering Christ crying out for help (Mt 25:31-46). Religious language is a way in which the mystery within human experience reveals itself.

Language about the sacred is "speech about the unspeakable, speech at the limits of language."[4] Such language is the language of metaphor. Some metaphors express analogy, that is, a similarity between two unlike entities. For example, an important Christian description of the sacred is "God is love." This metaphor suggests that Christians experience God's love in human love, that the sacred manifests itself in the love that people have for each other. This type of religious language asserts that there is continuity between the human and the divine, that the human is a helpful, if inadequate, model for understanding mystery. Buddhism has a similar understanding: "It is precisely the Original Face of Man—of any of us human beings—which is the True Buddha."[5]

Another kind of metaphor is paradox; it combines opposites in such a way that a new insight appears. Paradoxical metaphors insist that the sacred is simultaneously revealed and concealed. They reverse and upend the world as we know it. Jesus of Nazareth, for example, used such language: "Those who believe in me, even though they die, will live, and everyone who lives and believes in me will never die" (Jn 11:25-26). He tells a parable that describes the Kingdom of God, the social arrangement implied in the gospels, as a place in which reversal is routine; late coming workers receive the same pay as those who showed up at daybreak the same day (Mt 20:1-16).

Religious language also describes what mystery is not. Because we can speak about the sacred only indirectly, we gain some knowledge of the sacred by learning what it is not. Ancient Egyptian (1290-1224 B.C.E.) hymns of praise to the Sun god Amon-Re deny that this god is like other gods and challenge any claims that humans can know him. Some Islamic thinkers from the ninth century C.E. insisted that they could only make negative assertions about Allah:

> [Allah] is one; there is no thing like him ... he is not a body, not a form, not flesh and blood, not an individual, no substance nor attribute ... no movement, rest, or division ... he is not comparable with men and does not resemble creatures in any respect ... he is unlike whatever occurs to the mind or is pictured in the imagination.[6]

These statements from two different traditions represent the intuition that the sacred is truly mysterious, too dense for humans to grasp. Negative language is the most accurate way to describe it.

Religious language indicates that while the human may resemble the sacred, it also may not. Analogy underscores similarity; negation emphasizes difference; paradox simultaneously affirms the "is" and the "is-not" aspect of any comparison.

RELIGIOUS METAPHORS

Each religious tradition has its own purchase on one or more aspects of mystery or life: Allah, Krishna, Buddha, God, Great Spirit, the LORD, Adonai, Goddess, Gaia, Tao. This sacred is forever unfamiliar. We make it familiar by constructing metaphors that describe how our relationship to the sacred is like and not-like ordinary, everyday relations. The metaphor is the lens through which we view mystery; it may sharpen or distort what we see.

For example, "God the father" is a metaphor that affirms that our experience of the sacred resembles our relationship to a male parent. It may create a safe, ordered world in which we are dependent upon a kind provider for our needs. It may also create a cold, chaotic world in which we must rely on a distant, harsh task-master. How we read the metaphor depends, in part, on our own experience of father. This metaphor does not, however, exhaust all potential ways for constructing the relationship between the sacred and the human worlds. We can insist that our experience of relating to God is like the experience of relating to a mother or companion or lover or healer or liberator or friend. These are mutually enriching models or metaphors which we use to describe our experience of the holy.

Culturally Conditioned Metaphors

Metaphors we use about the holy are culturally and politically conditioned. For example, for centuries in Christian Europe the metaphor of Christ as king was very popular. Christ the divine king governed the world and the universe; the secular rulers governed their empires. Christians were expected to be loyal subjects to both kings and to serve them completely. They honored Christ as king, affirming their belief that Christ was in sure control of world events, even if the powers of evil seemed to be winning, and that one day he would arrive to reveal his kingdom and reward his faithful followers. As political systems changed and monarchies disappeared, this metaphor of Christ as king gradually lost its power to mediate the Holy.

In fact, the ethicist Gloria Albrecht questions whether such an image of Christ is faithful to the gospel message. In *The Character of Our Communities: Toward an Ethic of Liberation for the Church* (Nashville: Abingdon, 1995) she describes the challenge her Baltimore church community found in its relationship with Santa María Madre de los Pobres, a parish of refugees in El Salvador who defied the efforts of the Salvadoran government to silence their resistance. She writes:

> We sing all the time about a God who is an almighty king with kingly power. Is it any wonder that we expect God to act like one, or that we think we see God in such expressions of power? ... We wanted to identify God with the power to control, the power to win, not with another peasant crucified.... We had to go back and read the story again: a poor prophet ... [who] proclaimed good news to the poor and insisted that the best perspective on the quality of social relationships, even on the whereabouts of the sacred, comes from the underside of society. (163)

In place of this Christ-as-king-of-the-universe metaphor, Albrecht offers a metaphor developed by Rita Nakashima Brock: the power of God as the power of heart, the power of relationship, our capacity to know our world by heart, to experience and respond to the needs and the terrors of the oppressed (*Journeys by Heart: A Christology of Erotic Power* [New York: Crossroad, 1988]). This metaphor is, of course, as culturally conditioned, value-laden, and, in a sense, biased, as the Christ as king metaphor. Despite its appeal, it has its limits. It reminds us, however, that all metaphor, all language bears the values and perspectives of its creators and receivers as well as the cultures in which it flourishes.

The metaphor God the father is also rooted in a worldview that no longer dominates much of Western European society, including the United States. One place it originated was the patriarchal society of the ancient Near East, in the second millennium B.C.E. The metaphor grew out of the experience of being cared for. It expressed the belief that the gods provided for their worshipers just as a human father provided for his own household, including his wife, children, extended family, and slaves. Today, in some geographic and cultural areas, people point out the inadequacy of that metaphor for describing their relationships with the sacred. In numerous communities throughout the United States, for example, women head households, supporting and raising their children by themselves. Fathers are often absent and unable or unwilling to support their children. In such situations, the metaphor "God as mother," "God as mother and father," or "God as parent and provider" may offer a more accurate and honest model for relating to God. Others, however, insist that Christian religious traditions retain this metaphor, so adults and children who have been abandoned or abused by their birth fathers can turn to God to experience a father's healing and unconditional love. Still others draw comfort from this metaphor because their own fathers were a warm and loving presence in their lives. God the father is a powerful metaphor that can reconcile or alienate, as we shall see in chapter 11.

In the past many Native American peoples in the United States drew their metaphors for mystery or power from their lives as farmers and hunters. For example, such animals as the bear, the deer, and the eagle represent encounters with power and wisdom in individual visions. In a story from the Lenape people of Delaware, a deer was such a representation. The people originally lived in darkness beneath a lake; the animal guided the Lenape leader to a point of escape and then instructed the leader to kill it and give its flesh to the people. By eating the deer's flesh, the Lenape acquired the knowledge they needed to live in the forests. Many Native American people also revere the earth under the title "mother." In some native stories of origin, the people emerge from the earth as from a womb. And like a mother, the earth nourishes her children, providing good crops for harvest and large herds for hunting. The farming and hunting contexts of these metaphors for mystery give them their power and meaning.

The metaphor Mother Earth can be attractive to people who live in other cultural contexts. In these contexts, however, it may not be a helpful model for relating to the creativity of the sacred. The metaphor may, however, be reinterpreted as a symbol for related concerns. Pan-American leaders are trying to unite Native Americans in a common spirituality centered on Mother Earth. Members of ecological movements use the metaphor of Mother Earth to suggest that pollution of air and water, along with destruction of wetlands and endangered species, destroys a sacred balance of nature. In a similar fashion, some feminist theologians identify physical violence acted out on women's bodies and industrial pollution of the "body" of Mother Earth as related symptoms of a patriarchal society that knows too little about intimacy and collaboration and too much about domination and control. Metaphors and their interpretations are culturally conditioned; they draw their power as much from their context as they do from the reality they mediate.

Jesus the Mother

The impulse to use feminine language and imagery to describe the sacred has been part of religions from the very beginning. Human beings have

MARYKNOLL PHOTO LIBRARY/E. WHEATER

To call God mother is to evoke the frustration of love in its fierce fight against death. To call God mother is to wait through death for the stirrings of life.

generally peopled the realm of power with goddesses and female spirits. In much ancient mythology, goddesses possess cultural knowledge and teach human beings how to farm and weave, how to make music and pottery; they act as midwives for kings and heroes, and they control fertility. Many scholars point out that in the Jewish and Christian traditions, God often does what would have been regarded as "woman's work" in the ancient world. He sews clothes (Gen 3:21) and mothers Israel (Hos 11:3-4) whom he loves more than a human mother loves her child (Is 49:14-15). In fact, Moses suggests that God has conceived and given birth to his people (Nm 11:10-15), while Isaiah declares that God comforts Israel like a mother comforts her son (Is 66:13). We can find similar imagery in the Christian New Testament. Jesus likens himself to a mother hen in his desire to protect Jerusalem (Lk 13:34). One of his parables—the image of a woman losing money, searching for it energetically, and throwing a party for her friends and neighbors when she finds it— describes God's delight at the return of a sinner (Lk 15:8-11).

The use of feminine imagery to describe one's relationship with God also appears throughout Christian tradition. An early Christian writer, Clement of Alexandria (ca. 150-220) spoke of "the Father's loving breasts" and "the milk of the Father." In the twelfth century, some writers used "Mother Jesus" as a symbol of tenderness and supportive love. The English mystic Julian of Norwich (1342-ca. 1423) often mentioned the "motherhood of Jesus" in her writings.

Julian of Norwich lived a secluded life with her maid and, some say, her cat, in a tiny room attached to the village church in Norwich, England, during the late fourteenth and the early fifteenth centuries. She often prayed for the grace of a serious illness in order to imitate the crucified Christ more closely. During such an illness, she claimed that the crucified Christ visited her many times. During these visions she learned through experience about God's great love for each person and about the delight Christ takes in each human being. She first wrote down the content of these visions in a short collection. Later, after she had thought more about these teachings, Julian wrote a second, longer version of the manuscript, which now bears the name *Showings*. In the following passage, she describes the motherhood of Jesus.

> Our Mother in nature, our Mother in grace, because he [Jesus] wanted altogether to become our Mother in all things, made the foundation of his work most humbly and most mildly in the maiden's womb.... The mother's service is nearest, readiest and surest: nearest and surest because it is truest. No one ever might or could perform this office fully, except only him. We know that all our mothers bear us for pain and death. O, what is that? But our true Mother Jesus, he alone bears us for joy and for endless life, blessed may he be. So he carries us within him in love and travail, until the full time when he wanted to suffer the sharpest thorns and cruel pains that ever were or will be, and at the last he died. The mother can give her child to suck of her milk, but our precious Mother Jesus can feed us with himself, and does, most courteously and most tenderly with the blessed sacrament, which is the precious food of true life; ... The mother can lay her child tenderly to her breast, but our tender Mother Jesus can lead us easily into his blessed breast through his sweet open side, and show us there a part of the godhead and of the joys of heaven with inner certainty of endless bliss.[7]

Thinking with Religious Metaphors

1. What is your reaction to Julian's use of maternal language about Christ? How does Julian justify calling Christ mother? Throughout her writings Julian celebrates the great love Christ has for individuals. She seldom mentions sin or punishment for sin. How does this text reflect that attitude?
2. Julian's image of motherhood was influenced by her own experience of having been mothered and by her culture's understanding of mothering. What images of mothering exist in your culture? Who mothers you? In what ways? Whom do you mother? In what ways?
3. Rewrite the passage to reflect your own understanding and experience of mother.

PARABLE

A **parable** is an extended metaphor, often with plot and characters, and is part of the literature of many religious traditions. It involves imagination and intuition, belief and revelation and is probably about the sacred even when it occurs in literature and cinema. Unlike other stories, a parable is an interactive narrative, much like an electronic game. It works only if the reader works with it, for "it leaves us in such doubt about its precise meaning that we are challenged into active thought."[8]

The writers of the Christian gospels in the New Testament show Jesus of Nazareth using parables to teach about the central theme in his preaching, the realm of God. These stories are not about abstract concepts or ideas; they are models which describe life within God's domain. They are not allegories which make sense only if the reader can figure out the equivalents of the parable's important elements. Rather they draw their audiences into the action of the story and, perhaps, into a new experience of what it means to live within the domain of God. Parables demand a careful analysis of all their parts since these parts are its meaning. They are generally very ordinary; they do not draw attention away from this world to a more pleasant or exciting one. They invite us to see in new ways, to experience the sacred in unconventional ways as part of the world we inhabit.

Consider this parable from the Gospel of Matthew.

Once more Jesus spoke to them in parables, saying: "The kingdom of heaven may be compared to a king who gave a wedding banquet for his son. He sent his slaves to call those who had been invited to the wedding banquet, but they would not come. Again he sent other slaves saying, 'Tell those who are invited: "Look, I have prepared my dinner, my oxen, and my fat calves have been slaughtered, and everything is ready; come to the wedding banquet."' But they made light of it and went away, one to his farm, another to his business, while the rest seized his slaves, mistreated them, and killed them. The king was enraged. He sent his troops, destroyed those murderers and burned their city. Then he said to his slaves, 'The wedding is ready, but those invited were not worthy. Go therefore into the streets, and invite everyone you find to the wedding banquet.' Those slaves went out into the streets and gathered all whom they found, both bad and good, so the wedding hall was filled with guests." (Mt 22:1-10; compare Lk 1:16-20)

Interpreting a Parable

First, read the parable several times; let it move inside your imagination as you move into the world it evokes. Pay attention to the dynamics of that world. Do unexpected events happen? Does anyone get special treatment?

In Matthew's parable, the social setting is significant. A king invites influential subjects to his son's wedding banquet. No surprises yet; we expect this. Yet the guests refuse to honor the invitation once they hear that the party is ready to begin. What kind of guests are these who take back their word? What kind of king is this that his subjects ignore his invitation? The king persists, hoping his elaborate menu will make them reconsider. Why does he appeal to their stomachs and not to the relationship they share? Why does he beg for their attendance? After all, he is king! His guests answer his second summons by murdering his slaves. Now pushed to his limit, the angry king orders their deaths; for a moment, he meets our expectation of a "real" ruler. Then he quickly reverts to old behavior. Still eager to gather guests for his son's celebration, he sends his slaves out to the streets and highways to collect whomever they find, good and bad, stranger or subject, prepared or not; it doesn't matter.

This story is purposefully open-ended. Who finally accepts the invitation to come to the king's feast? What is the nature of this invitation? Who deserves it? What kind of ruler is this? There are many insightful answers to these questions. Each reader deals with the questions for herself. We may read the parable as an allegory, identifying the king as God, the son as Jesus, the slaves as the prophets, the first round of guests as first-century Jews who reject Jesus as the Messiah, and the second round as those Jews and Gentiles who accept him. But we miss the parable's power if we do not explore other meanings and accept its challenge to participate in the realm of God from new and unsettling perspectives.

Think about parable as a paradigm, a model, of reality placed in a new context, like playing football on a baseball diamond. What new insights might you get into both the game of football and baseball's playing field? Parables invite us into a situation taken from ordinary life, a situation about to be revolutionized before our very eyes by insight. We approach parables best with imagination and wonder, roving freely through time past, present, and future as our world quakes and re-forms. The language of parable is often the language of paradox; it confuses and scrambles the sense we usually make of our worlds.

A Buddhist Parable

Buddhism also uses parables to explain the Buddha's teachings. The following parable is from the *Lotus Sutra*, or *The Lotus of the True Law*, one of the sacred writings of Mahayana Buddhists. The parable explains why the Buddha did not begin his preaching with the way of Mahayana Buddhism, which teaches that all human beings are children of Buddha, called to the same enlightenment that he experienced, that is, called to become Buddhas themselves. As you read it, consider the figurative language of the parable and how that language influences the way you think about the story. You may also wish to discuss or write about this parable in relationship to the selection from Julian of Norwich's *Showings* above.

THE UNEXPECTED TREASURE

[At the beginning of the parable, four old men have heard the Buddha lay out this new teaching. They approach the Buddha and tell him how they have been faithful to their duties, thinking they had achieved nirvana, when suddenly they hear that they are predestined to perfect enlightenment. To explain its impact on them, they recount this parable:]

It is a case, O Lord, it is as if a certain man went away from his father to some other place. He lives there for many years. In the meantime, his father becomes a great man. The son is poor; seeking employment, he goes off to another place. His father also moves to another country. He takes with him his great wealth, his servants, his elephants and livestock. He has his money invested in great territories and does great things in business, money-lending, agriculture, and commerce.

Eventually, the poor man reaches the place where his wealthy father is living. Now the poor man's father had always and ever been thinking of the son he has lost fifty years ago, but he never mentioned his thoughts to anyone, thinking: "I am old, aged, advanced in years, and have more than I need of gold, corn, treasures and granaries, but have no son. If death overtakes me, all this will perish unused. Oh how happy should I be, were my son to enjoy this mass of wealth!"

Meanwhile, the poor man, searching for food and clothing, is gradually approaching the house of the rich man. His father happened to sit at the door of his house, surrounded by all kinds of holy teachers. He was sitting on a magnificent throne, hundreds of thousands of gold pieces passing through his hands, under an awning decorated with pearls and flowers. The poor man is overcome with great shame. He thinks: "Unexpectedly have I come upon a king or a noble. People like me have nothing to do here; let me go. In the street of the poor, I am more likely to find what I am looking for. If I stay here, I may be forced into labor with no pay."

The rich man has recognized his son; he is content and in high spirits, filled with joy and cheerfulness. He thinks: "The one who will enjoy all these riches has been found. The one of whom I have been thinking is here now." The father sends runners after his son. However, the poor man faints from fear as he nears the house. The father is dismayed and releases the poor man. Then the father has a better idea. He hires two men to find his son and hire him to work for them in the father's own house. The poor man returns and performs such menial tasks as moving a large pile of dirt. The rich man exchanges his wealthy robes for the

COURTESY OF THE NATIONAL GALLERY OF ART

Both Buddha and Jesus of Nazareth found in the metaphor "father" rich compassion and respectful freedom. In "The Return of the Prodigal Son," seventeenth century Dutch painter Jan Steen depicts the father's eagerness to welcome his son home in the detail of the father's hand reaching across the space between to grasp his son's arm.

soiled clothes of a worker and talks briefly with the poor man. He tells him, "Remain here in my service; I will give you extra pay and whatever else you need. . . . Look upon me as if I were your father for I am older and you are younger. In the time you have been working for me, I have seen no wickedness or malice in you. From now on, you are like my own son." So for twenty years, the old man calls him his son, and the poor man calls him his father and no longer fears going in and out of the great house.

After a while, the old man falls sick. He summons the poor man: "Come here. I possess abundant gold, money, and grain, treasures and granaries. I am very sick, and wish to have someone upon whom to bestow my wealth." The poor man accepts this great bequest, but he is quite indifferent to it. He keeps on living in his little straw hut, and he considers himself as poor as he was before.

The rich man realizes that his son is mature and mentally developed. Therefore, he feels ashamed and disgusted when he thinks of his son's former poverty. He sends for the poor man and presents him to a gathering of his relatives, before the king, and in the presence of all the citizens of the country. This is what he says: "Hear, gentlemen! This is my own son, I am his father. Fifty years ago he disappeared from such and such a town. He is called so and so, and my self I am called so and so. In searching after him, I have from that town come here. He is my son, I am his father. To him I leave all my revenues, and all my personal wealth shall he have as well."

The poor man, hearing this speech was astonished and amazed; he thought to himself: "Unexpectedly have I obtained this gold and money, treasures and granaries."

[The four old men interpret the parable for the Buddha, pointing out how exactly they are like the poor man.][9]

MYTH

Parables are one type of story, one way of talking about the sacred in narrative. Myth is another category. While parables deal with the unpredictability of the sacred and often challenge or subvert a particular worldview or moral understanding, myth offers perspectives on such ultimate questions as the origins of the universe, the meaning of being human, the beginnings of evil, the destiny of the world and its inhabitants. Parables and myth exist side by side in the same religious traditions. Myth describes the interrelationships between men, women, nature, and the sacred that constitute social order or disorder; parables remind us that such order is far from permanent.

Sometimes we may think of myth as something false, something that facts can dispute. This is a popular understanding of myth. However, the field of religious studies has its own definition of myth that challenges that popular understanding. Within a religious tradition, myth is a narrative that builds a worldview. We are not always able to express through factual statements what is trustworthy or genuine about the ordering of our world. While myth is not factual in the same way that news reports or personal memories are factual, myth does embody helpful insights into the network of relationships that make up our world. It constructs the world or the universe in a certain way and offers this model as "the ways things really are" or "should be." Myth also shows us how to live in that world; it creates the structures we need to negotiate social relationships.

Thus, it portrays gender in such a way that women and men can learn how their culture expects them to be feminine or masculine. It demonstrates the relationship between the human and the nonhuman worlds, between different occupations or economic classes. Myth suggests that this configuration is necessary to maintain order and relationships. Such configurations are not universal norms; they promote specific value systems. They often establish power relationships that privilege the groups who had a part in their creation and disadvantage groups who are cut off from such privilege.

Functions of Myth

Scholars continue to debate the function of myth for religious groups. In chapter 1 we saw evidence for this in the different ways Mircea Eliade and J.Z. Smith describe that function. Eliade found myth, especially myths of origin or creation, to be a reference to an original condition outside time, a paradise for which we all yearn. Smith, on the other hand, argues that myth relates how a community goes about organizing its present life together. Within myths of origin, creation of the universe may be a metaphor for the structure of current social arrangements and does not necessarily point toward a past unique event.

For anthropologist Bronislaw Malinowski, myth satisfies our desire to know our place in the universe, to know what to believe and how to act; it relieves feelings of apprehension about misfortune and doom by attributing the origins of what we most fear, death for example, to human choice or error rather than divine whim or edict. A part of universal human experience, death is often the result of human curiosity or desire.[10]

While Malinowski analyzed myth in terms of the religious group, psychologist Carl Jung studied the role of myth in the maturation or individuation of the human person. He was impressed with the universality of human experience and the similarities among myths from different cultures. Jung theorized that myths express the collective unconscious, the spiritual heritage of the human community which all individuals share. He developed the idea of archetypes, images arising from the unconscious that contribute insight and awareness to the maturation process and that appear as themes in the religious literature of most cultures. Jung himself examined the themes of the divine child, Mother Earth, the hero, the self, and the shadow self. In the hero myth, for example, an individual, completely human or partially divine, frees people from all forms of evil, including death. Through a particular hero myth—the story of the death and resurrection of Jesus Christ, for example—individuals may identify with the hero and integrate this archetypal representation into their conscious selves, finding in it a pattern for their own experiences of death and rebirth. Jung insists that the loss of cultural myth has both psychological and moral implications: alienation from self, the loss of a sense of community, insensitivity to violence and brutality.[11]

For Joseph Campbell, myths express cultural attitudes toward life, death, and the universe. Although his tendency to ignore differences in myths in favor of a universal "mono-myth" underlying all cultures has won him criticism, Campbell's categorization of the functions or roles of myth in the lives of individuals and religious communities is helpful. First, myths play a spiritual or mystical function; they evoke the same feelings of awe and gratitude, fascination and dread as does Rudolph Otto's *numinous*, described in chapter 3. They elicit experiences of mystery and address significant questions: Why are we here? What are our responsibilities? How can we maintain hope in the face of death? Second, myths present an ordered universe and clearly locate us within that universe; they diminish the threat of chaos and reduce anxiety. Third, myths integrate individuals into the group, teaching us how to negotiate relationships and achieve our goals as constructive group members; they also provide patterns of behavior to imitate in times of crises when we cannot think or plan logically. Fourth, myths contribute to psychological development and enrichment, guiding us through life stages from childhood through death. For Campbell, mythic figures are aspects of the divine within each person.[12]

Types of Myth

Many different kinds of myth exist in religious traditions and cultural groups. The most universal kind of myth is the myth of origin. On Christmas Eve in homes around the world, Christians retell the story of the birth of Jesus of Nazareth, a myth which annually renews the ritual cycle which leads to the death and resurrection of this same Jesus. Some cultures have myths of separation, which explain such issues as why human beings are at odds with each other, with themselves, and with the gods. The Bantu people of Mozambique, for example, tell a story in which the god Mulungu has Spider spin a rope so that Mulungu and his court can climb up to the sky, because humans have violated the sacred harmony of the earth. Through hunting, killing, and making fires to control and develop their environment, men and women have driven the gods away. Many myths recount a hero's life, patterning the way a culture thinks about life and providing a paradigm through which people can interpret their own experiences. We can think about the Christian gospels in this way or about the stories of Muhammad preserved in the *Hadith*, narratives which demonstrate the Prophet's virtue and dedication to the Qur'an. Other myths concern quests on which the hero embarks to discover her identity or his life-task; these myths sometimes pattern the life stages through which we pass in the work of creating our identity. Some myths struggle with questions of evil, undeserved suffering, and the inevitability of death. Others push beyond the boundaries of death, suggesting that our lives continue. We will consider several of these myths from different religious traditions in the second part of this chapter.

Myths of Origin

Myths dealing with the creation of the universe are the most universal type of myth. As we have already noted, they often address ongoing issues of order rather than establish an eternal or sacred order. They represent the drive to discover meaning in or to impose meaning on the worlds of cosmos, polis, family, and self.

The Making of the Dogon World

The creation myth of the Dogon people, an agricultural tribe in the Sudan, shows complex correspondences among these levels. The individual, for example, while only part of the group on the level of community, represents the whole group on another level. Individual actions affect the same universal order which the individual represents; the individual life is sacred on many levels.

The wise man Ogotemmeli recounted this story to the French anthropologist Marcel Griaule.

> In the Dogon world creation happens in three stages, each stage ending in a word or revelation. Once the god Amma has created the sun, moon, and stars out of earth mixed with water, he throws another lump of clay, which spreads out into the form of a female body, whose "sex organ is an anthill, and its clitoris a termite hill." Lonely, Amma tries to have intercourse with the earth, but cannot. The engorged termite hill, "displaying its masculinity," bars his entry. In anger and frustration, Amma excises the offending clitoris and has sex with the earth, conceiving the jackal, a single birth and the "symbol of the difficulties of god." Later the earth bears Amma divine twins, the Nummo, present throughout the universe as water and light. With plant fibers they have brought from heaven, they weave speech into grass garments to cover the earth's nakedness. This speech, the first word, is the sound of wind moving through the grasses; "Its syntax was elementary, its verbs few, and its vocabulary without elegance."
>
> While speech was supposed to provide order, from the beginning it let loose disorder. Desiring speech, the jackal rapes its mother the earth as she burrows deep inside her own womb. The jackal wins the gift of speech and is now able to reveal divine schemes to fortunetellers. The rape wounds the earth and she bleeds; her menstrual flow dirties her covering of grasses. As a result Amma rejects the earth as the partner with whom he will generate people and creates a human couple out of lumps of clay to fulfill that plan.
>
> The Nummo twins intervene, reminding Amma that the jackal had acted so badly because he "was alone from birth." Amma then draws two outlines on the ground, one on top of the other, one male and one

female. The newly created man stretches himself over these shadows of himself and takes them both for his own. Amma does the same for the woman. Thus each person is endowed with two souls corresponding to two distinct persons. The prepuce, or foreskin of the penis, houses the man's female soul; the clitoris, the woman's male soul. Because one individual cannot live as two people, the man undergoes circumcision to remove the female soul, the foreskin. The humans have intercourse, and the woman gives birth to the first of eight children, the ancestors of the Dogon people. All the pain of giving birth is concentrated in the clitoris, which an unseen hand cuts off. The discarded clitoris becomes the scorpion; the pain and blood of birth, its venom. Children born to these eight ancestors were given dual souls at birth. The Nummo trace soul outlines on the ground next to women in childbirth. The baby is held over the outline, with its hands and feet touching it, to receive the dual souls. Later the extra soul is removed by circumcision or excision.

Meanwhile the Nummo go about the task of regenerating and purifying the earth. They return to live in the anthill from which they emerged at birth. Over time the ancestors are attracted to the anthill; in exploring it, one by one the ancestors slip through the anthill and into the earth's womb, each leaving behind its human body and nature in the fingerprints on the food bowl it carried with it to the anthill. Each ancestor returns to the water that had been its origin; perfected by the words the Nummo spirits kept repeating inside the earth's womb, the ancestor-spirit leaves the earth and goes to heaven.

Something unusual happens with the ancestor seven, a number representing perfection, the combination of the female number four and male number three. This ancestor receives a second word, so that everyone could make progress in the world. This new word has a powerful effect on ancestor seven. Once inside the earth, the ancestor takes possession of it; the opening to the anthill widens and becomes the ancestor's mouth, lined with eighty pointed teeth, representing future Dogon families. Then the seventh ancestor-spirit spits out eighty cotton threads and distributes them among his teeth. By opening and closing his jaws, the threads are woven together. The tips of the spirit's forked tongue push the threads back and forth, and the web takes shape in the breath of the second revealed word. The spirit speaks during the whole process, demonstrating the need for cooperation between material actions and spiritual forces. The spirit's words are woven in the threads. They were the cloth and the cloth is the word. The Dogons call cloth *soy* which means, "It is the spoken word"; *soy* also means "seven" because it was the seventh ancestor who spoke while he wove.

While the weaving is going on, the ant hears and remembers the spirit's words. She passes these words on to the others who followed the transformation of the sex of the earth. First they lived in holes they dug in the earth, a parallel to earth's womb, which each eventually enters for revelation and transformation. Then, when they notice the ancestors' food bowls littering the ground around the anthills, they copy the shape of the anthills, constructing rooms and passageways as shelter for themselves and their harvested crops. They also imitate the teeth ringing the anthill, setting great clay teeth around their dwellings for protection against wild animals. The human anthills are crude images of the marvelous granary that would later come down to them from heaven.

Following the ant's example, the men repeat the words it taught them as they imitate its weaving activity. These instructions are passed down from generation to generation of weavers to the accompaniment of the clapping of the shuttle and the creaking of the block, sounds they call the "creaking of the word."

After the eighth ancestor is transformed into Nummo, for some reason discord breaks out in the heavenly world. The eight ancestors return to earth bringing with them a new cosmic system and a final definitive word, necessary for the working of the modern world. The system, shaped like an up-ended basket, provides the pattern for Dogon granaries. Each part of the granary participates in several levels of meaning. Eight interior compartments hold the eight grains the ancestors received in heaven; they also represent the organs of the Nummo water spirit. In the center of the eight compartments stands a jar enclosing a smaller jar, representing a full womb. The walls and inner partitions hold everything together like a skeleton. The granary resembles two things: a woman reclining on her back, arms and legs outstretched and open, and a model of the universe. This new system of order works like a human body, taking in nourishment, processing it, circulating it throughout the organism as blood, and generating breath, air moist with the water that creates and maintains life.[13]

This retelling of the Dogon creation story contains many references to issues we have already discussed. First, there is the gradual acquisition of different kinds of words, which make possible different forms of order. Language seems to knit together the spirit world and the human world. As we suggested earlier, language can be a bridge on which we encounter mystery and power. Second, in this myth there are correspondences and interactions among cosmic, communal, and personal levels. No clear boundaries separate the different levels of existence. Harmony on one level reinforces harmony on another. Third, patterns of social organization are also patterns of gender representation. While women may struggle against men, they are, in the end, defenseless against them; they are impregnated with the water of the male semen; the earth fills with rain and bears crops; the granaries are filled; cosmic order continues. This myth also has connections with the rituals of circumcision and excision discussed in chapter 4. The rituals remove the unused soul once the child has settled into a clear identity.

Hindu Creation Myths from the Chandogya Upanishad

Upanishads, meaning "sessions with" or "sitting next to," record monologues of and debates among wise Hindu teachers about issues raised in Vedic scriptures. They generally emphasize self-denial, the way of asceticism, as a means to find religious truth and illumine the One, the absolute spiritual reality in and behind all the visible elements and beings of the physical world. Hindus also refer to them as Vendata (end of the Veda) because they form the conclusion to the Vedic scriptures. Many Upanishads have survived; however, the most important date from 800–400 B.C.E. The Chandogya Upanishad is one of the earliest.

This myth begins at a more distant point than the Dogon myth. Like a movie director, the storyteller focuses on a faraway point on the horizon. The universe originates with nonbeing which goes on to generate the universe and its occupants.

> In the beginning, this universe was non-existent. It became existent. It grew. It turned into an egg. The egg lay for the period of a year. Then it broke open. Of the two halves of the eggshell, one half was of silver, the other of gold. That which was of silver became the earth; that which was of gold, heaven. What was the thick membrane of the white became the mountains; the thin membrane of the yolk, the mist and the clouds. The veins became the rivers; the fluid in the bladder, the ocean. And what was born of it was younger Aditya, the sun. When it was born shouts of "Hurrah" arose, together with all beings and all objects of desire.[14]

From this account we learn how some Hindus think about the universe. The power of creativity is present within nonbeing. The egg hatching, present in myths from Greece, China, and South America, is the metaphor used for the unfolding of the universe; the metaphor evokes associations with fertility and life and omits the dualism and violence sometimes found in creation myths, like the Dogon myth, which feature a male sky god and a female earth. In the Hindu myth, the universe develops from one reality into a plurality of forms. After the sun appears, human beings and the objects of their desire come into being. In Hindu religious traditions, this desire is the root of all suffering; the goal of Hindu religious practices is release from desire and reunion with that One which undergirds the universe. Desire is the metaphor that names the restless, hard-to-satisfy aspects of the human condition, those aspects which make it difficult to seek the One beneath or within the many and thus impede release from suffering and, ultimately, the attainment of nirvana and union with nonexistence.

This Hindu story uses language on two levels. It first offers a hatching egg as a metaphor for the self-directed, systematic emergence of the universe. At the same time, it constructs, from the very beginning, the dualism of the one and the many which Hinduism seeks to overcome. Present, too, is desire which lures men and women to confuse the many for the One. Creation of the universe, then, becomes the backdrop for the story's main purpose, the construction of a Hindu model for being in the world and an explanation for the difficulties Hindus face in their life journey.

A second myth from the same *Upanishad* takes an opposite view. Mocking the idea that nonbeing can produce being, the storyteller argues that being was in place before the universe and that being, desiring to reproduce itself, creates fire and water. This myth also places more positive value on plurality.

> It [being] thought to itself: "Would that I were many! Let me procreate myself!" It emitted heat. Heat thought to itself: "Would that I were many! Let me procreate myself." It emitted water. Therefore, whenever

peoples grieve or perspire from the heat, then water is produced. Water thought to itself: "Would that I were many! Let me reproduce myself." It emitted food. Therefore when it rains, then there is plenty of food. So food for eating is produced from water.[15]

Like other creation myths, this one contains etiological elements, that is, it connects the origins of biological, meteorological, and geographic phenomena with order or its breakdown in the universe. Here, for example, human tears and perspiration are the result of heat's desire to reproduce.

Many religions have more than one creation myth. In chapter 7, we will read two very different creation myths important in both the Jewish and the Christian traditions; the myths offer conflicting commentaries on the human situation.

Thinking with Myth

1. Describe the stories that surround the origin of your family, as far back as you can. Are there stories about your ancestors connected with particular places? Did your ancestors make important journeys? Have they always lived in one location? How did your parents meet? What story surrounds your birth? Do you have a special naming story? All these stories constitute your myth of origin. They order your world and contribute to your identity.

2. Compose a myth that accounts for your present world. What relationships and rituals govern this world? What contributions do the relationships make to re-creating order within your world on a regular basis? What is your role within this world? How do you maintain it?

3. Comment on this observation: "Myths are maps and myth is symbolism, and for this reason myths are not to be taken literally. It is rather that when the dust falls from our eyes, human beings are themselves the gods and demons, acting out, not the piddling business of worldly life, but the great archetypal situations and dramas of the myths. The gods are the archetypes but they exist as perpetually incarnate in ourselves" (Alan Watts).[16]

4. What similarities and differences can you point out between the myths of origin in this chapter and those we read in chapter 1? Describe the customs, beliefs, and values that constitute the social worlds these myths create.

Myths of Alienation

Many religious traditions also contain myths which introduce elements of alienation into the relationship between the divine world and the human world. A story, called "The Fall" in most Christian Bibles, is a good example of this type of myth.

Now the serpent was more crafty than any other wild animal that the LORD God had made. He said to the woman, "Did God say, 'You shall not eat from any tree in the garden'?" The woman said to the serpent, "We may eat of the fruit of the trees in the garden; but God said, 'You shall not eat of the fruit of the tree that is in the middle of the garden, nor shall you touch it, or you shall die.'" But the serpent said to the woman, "You will not die; for God knows that when you eat of it your eyes will be opened, and you will be like God, knowing good and evil." So when the woman saw that the tree was good for food, and that it was a delight to the eyes, and that the tree was to be desired to make one wise, she took of its fruit and ate; and she also gave some to her husband, who was with her, and he ate. Then the eyes of both were opened, and they knew that they were naked; and they sewed fig leaves together and made loincloths for themselves.

They heard the sound of the LORD God walking in the garden at the time of the evening breeze, and the man and his wife hid themselves from the presence of the LORD God among the trees of the garden. But the LORD God called to the man, and said to him "Where are you?" He said, "I heard the sound of you in the garden, and I was afraid, because I was naked; and I hid myself." He said, "Who told you that you were naked? Have you eaten from the tree of which I commanded you not to eat?" The man said, "The woman whom you gave to be with me, she gave me fruit from the tree, and I ate." Then the LORD God said to the woman, "What is this that you have done?" The woman said, "The serpent tricked me, and I ate." The LORD God said to the serpent,

"Because you have done this,
　　cursed are you among all animals
　　and among all wild creatures;
upon your belly you shall go,
　　and dust you shall eat
　　all the days of your life.
I will put enmity between you and the woman,
　　and between your offspring and hers;
he will strike your head,
　　and you will strike his heel."
To the woman he said,
"I will greatly increase your pangs in childbearing;
　　in pain you shall bring forth children,
yet your desire shall be for your husband,
　　and he shall rule over you."
And to the man he said,
"Because you have listened to the voice of your wife,
　　and have eaten of the tree,
about which I commanded you,
　　'You shall not eat of it,'
cursed is the ground because of you;
　　in toil you shall eat of it all the days of your life;
thorns and thistles it shall bring forth for you;
　　and you shall eat the plants of the field.
By the sweat of your face
　　you shall eat bread
until you return to the ground,

for out of it you were taken;
you are dust,
    and to dust you shall return."
The man named his wife Eve, bcause she was the mother of all living.
And the LORD God made garments of skins for the man and for his wife,
and clothed them.

Then the LORD God said, "See, the man has become like one of us,
knowing good and evil; and now, he might reach out his hand and take
also from the tree of life, and eat, and live forever"—therefore the LORD
God sent him forth from the garden of Eden, to till the ground from
which he was taken. He drove out the man; and at the east of the garden of Eden he placed the cherubim, and a sword flaming and turning
to guard the way to the tree of life. (Gn 3:1-24)

Notice the role of animals here. In many cultures the serpent is associated with life or wisdom. Although Christian and Jewish interpreters
later identify this serpent as the devil, nothing in the text suggests that
the serpent is evil. It is simply part of God's creation. The serpent only
asks the question which shakes Eden's harmony; it sparks the woman's
curiosity and fuels her desire. In her response, the woman reveals that she
herself is already an interpreter of texts; she has expanded the divine

MARYKNOLL PHOTO LIBRARY

*"Knowledge of good and evil" represents "all knowledge," the power to transform
oppressive situations. The first step toward liberation is learning to use language
well in order to discover when the gods are lying.*

command about the tree of the knowledge of good and evil in the center of the Garden, adding "nor shall you touch it" (Gen 3:3).

Why does the woman desire the fruit? Curiosity? Rebellion? How we assess her action may reflect our own socio-economic living situation. In *Thinking about God* theologian Dorothee Sölle recounts one experience of teaching this story using traditional categories of disobedience and rebellion. Suddenly

> a black woman pastor interrupted me and said: "But it's quite clear. Adam and Eve wanted to have more than others and so they ate the apple, and that is covetousness. Sin is the immeasurable greed of people who want to possess something, and everything else follows from this desire to possess."[17]

Sölle concludes that "the poor read the Bible and the tradition with different eyes than ours." In a socio-economic system where a few people possess everything because they have exploited the rest of the population, it may be more natural to read Genesis 3 as a story about the impact of individual greed on others rather than as a story about breaking a divine command. The story has many interpretations.

Eating the fruit, of course, breaks one of the deity's commands, a command which sought to deny the couple access to knowledge. Once the first couple eat the fruit, "Their eyes were opened," and they become like gods, "knowing all things." The serpent's assertion is proved true; they do not die. Instead they use their knowledge to make clothing to protect their new consciousness of self; at the end of the narrative, the deity follows their example, making more durable clothing and acknowledging their move toward culture already within the garden. The myth itself, not the action of Eve and Adam, may generate some alienation between its readers and God. The serpent suggests that God has lied about the tree of knowledge, an uncomfortable thought. If so, what is the motivation? Are there details in the story to support such an interpretation?

Painful or troublesome elements in human experience are the background for the judgments the deity pronounces on the three characters. Long before Israelites told this story, snakes crawled on their bellies and women suffered pain giving birth to their children. The judgments are etiological; they acknowledge the givenness and unchangeability of certain aspects of life which accompany living in the world as we know it.

Myths of Destiny

Unlike stories of origin, stories of destiny are about the future. They do not seek to explain human existence or to mirror it accurately. They look for a restoration of unity, the disappearance of all forms of alienation and hostility toward the target audience; they reflect the human hope that the deity will someday make things right for the faithful within the religious tradition. They are, however, very similar to stories of origin in that they share much of the same language and imagery; often, they expect a re-establishment of an original, blessed condition. Here we see connections with Mircea Eliade's understanding of myth as a way to satisfy the yearning for an imagined wholeness that existed before the creation of time.

Some of the strongest images of future restoration are in the prophetic literature in the Bible. There are several types of these stories. In each one the people of Israel are granted a secure, peaceful place. They enjoy agricultural and economic security. In this future age, God will be with the people, and his presence will protect and bless believers. Israel and Jerusalem will want for nothing.

The other nations surrounding Israel suffer various fates as one writer or another modifies the plot. Sometimes they begin to worship the God of Israel and become Israelites, traveling to Jerusalem in order to learn the Torah.

> Peoples shall stream to it,
>   and many nations shall come and say:
> "Come, let us go up to the mountain of the LORD,
>   to the house of the God of Jacob;
> that he may teach us his ways
>   and that we may walk in his paths."
>   (Mi 4:1-2; see also Is 2:1-3; 25:6-8)

Sometimes foreign nations are completely destroyed: their armies, their populations, their very lands.

> Egypt shall become a desolation
>   and Edom a desolate wilderness,
> because of the violence done to the people of Judah
>   in whose land they have shed innocent blood.
>   (Jl 3:19-21)

Sometimes, the foreign nations rebuild Jerusalem and serve the people of Israel as slaves (Is 60:10-12). This restoration is not other-worldly; it takes place in history. A new human leader will occupy David's throne in Jerusalem; the people will live faithfully in covenant with each other and with Israel's God, protected from agricultural disasters and military invasions.

Stories about the fate of faithful Israelites who died before they could experience the benefits of their religious devotion developed in the face of Jews being persecuted and murdered for following the covenant. Instead of reaping the material blessings of a long life, many children, and economic prosperity—rewards for living according to God's law—Palestinian Jews who defied laws banning circumcision and Sabbath observance were tortured and killed. Some storytellers re-interpreted the covenant blessing as a resurrection faithful Jews would receive after death.

> Many of those who sleep
> > in the dust of the earth shall awake;
> Some shall live forever,
> > others shall be an everlasting horror and disgrace.
> But the wise shall shine brightly
> > like the splendor of the firmament,
> And those who lead the many to justice
> > shall be like the stars forever.   (Dn 12:2-3, NAB)

This story relocates the blessings of the faithful from this life to the other side of death. Israel's God will raise those wise enough to remain within the covenant to a place in heaven. This new image allows the faithful to maintain their hope in God's faithfulness and probably reflects the evolution of the community's own belief and its dissatisfaction with its former model of religion (fidelity leads to blessings and life in the here and now).

Some stories of destiny describe a divine hero returning to claim his faithful followers and destroy his opponents. Mark 14:61-62 is a miniature of this story. The passage is part of a scene in the passion story where the Jewish chief priest is interrogating Jesus of Nazareth. The official has just challenged Jesus to answer the witnesses who have testified against him.

> But he [Jesus] was silent and did not answer. Again the high priest asked him, "Are you the Messiah, the Son of the Blessed One?" Jesus said, "I am; and
> > 'you will see the Son of Man
> > seated at the right hand of Power,'
> > and 'coming with the clouds of heaven.'"

In Matthew's gospel, the triumphal return of Jesus as the **Son of Man** is associated with an elaborate judgment scene. When the Lord returns, he will hold court, separating people "as a shepherd separates the sheep from the goats." The blessed, the sheep on his right, inherit the kingdom of heaven and eternal life; they are blessed because they cared for the most disadvantaged of the Lord's family and, in doing so, ministered to the Lord. The accursed, the goats on his left, enter eternal, fiery punishment; they ignored the disadvantaged and, in so doing, ignored the Lord.

Some stories of destiny involve the abandonment or destruction of this world. Many Christians read the book of Revelation in the New Testament in this way. The world as they know it is under the rule of Satan. Famine, wars, and disease mark its last days. Some believers cannot distinguish between Christ and the anti-Christ. This final time ends with a catastrophic battle between the forces of good, led by Christ, and the forces of evil, led by Satan. The good triumphs. Satan, the anti-Christ, and their followers burn in a lake of fire. The earth is destroyed and replaced by the New Jerusalem, where the good live joyfully in God's presence. Later Christian theologians drew on this imagery to describe heaven and hell.

Christian and Islamic mythologies offer different stories of destiny about heaven. Both view the heavens as the dwelling place of God and Allah; both agree that only those who have lived according to the divine will can gain entry. Christian mythology, however, places God at the center of heaven. In an atmosphere of harmony and order, individuals dwell in the presence of God, participating fully in divine life. A good illustration of this comes from Dante's *Paradiso*. A white rose stands in the center of a garden to which Beatrice guides him; the saints are part of this rose, their eyes fixed on God. At the same time, their bodies are visible, their identity finding its wholeness in the rose. There is movement from the many to the one and from the one to the many. At the center of Dante's vision is a still point, the love which is the center of the universe.

> Instinct and intellect balanced equally;
> As in a wheel whose motion nothing jars;
> by the love that moves the sun and other stars.
> (*Paradiso*)

Islamic mythology presents another picture. Unlike the Christian story which emphasizes union and intimacy with the deity, the Qur'an's description of heaven is notable for its silence about Allah's presence in heaven or Allah's activities in relationship to the blessed. Muslims look forward to a series of heavens, each one more elaborate than the next and created with men in mind. They are all filled with the sensual delights most appealing to masculine tastes; the Qu'ran gives very little details about the kind of heaven Muslim women can expect. Faithful Muslims who have lived in total submission to Allah dwell in a magnificent oasis, surrounded by an abundance of silk robes, fruit, and wine.

In the Name of God, the Compassionate, the Merciful: Does there not pass over man a space of time when his life is a blank [life in the womb before birth]?

We have created man from the union of the two sexes, so that We may put him to the proof. We have endowed him with hearing and sight and, be he thankful or oblivious of Our favors, We have shown him the right path.

For the unbelievers We have prepared chains and fetters, and a blazing Fire. But the righteous shall drink of a cup tempered at the Camphor Fountain, a gushing spring at which the servants of God will refresh themselves: they who keep their vows and dread the far-spread terrors of Judgement Day; who, though they hold it dear, give sustenance to the poor, the orphan, and the captive, saying: "We feed you for God's sake only; we seek of you neither recompense nor thanks. We fear from our Lord a day of anguish and of woe."

God will deliver them from the evil of that day and make

their faces shine with joy. He will reward them for their stead-fastness with robes of silk and the delights of Paradise. Reclining there upon soft couches, they shall feel neither the scorching heat nor the biting cold. Trees will spread their shade around them, and fruits will hang in clusters over them.

They shall be served with silver dishes, and beakers as large as goblets; silver goblets which they themselves will measure; and cups brim-full with ginger-flavored water from a fount called Salsabil [Arabic for "ginger"]. They shall be attended by boys graced with eternal youth, who to the beholder's eye will seem like sprinkled pears. When you gaze upon that scene, you will behold a kingdom blissful and glorious.

They shall be arrayed in garments of fine green silk and rich brocade, and adorned with bracelets of silver. Their Lord will give them pure nectar to drink. Thus shall you be rewarded; your high endeavors are gratifying to God.   (Surah 76:1-22)

In another passage (Surah 56:1-39), the faithful recline on jeweled couches, drinking wine "that will neither pain their heads nor take away their reason"; they enjoy gushing waters and abundant fruits, "unforbidden and never ending." For their pleasure and companionship, Allah creates the *houris*, perfectly beautiful, dark-eyed virgins.

Some Native American traditions also have stories of destiny which tell of a new age and the restoration of past tribal glories. In the late nineteenth century, Jack Wovoka, a Nevada Paiute, told a story based on a vision the Great Spirit had shown him. The story and the dance that accompanied it quickly spread through the native population in the western Plains states. In the story Wovoka described a place he had seen in his vision where all Indians who had died were young and happy again. The land was theirs; there were plenty of buffalo. They eagerly followed the old ways of life. To transform the present world into this vision world, Wovoka urged other Indians to learn and perform what he called the "Ghost Dance"; their performance would restore the dead to earthly life and spark a revival of Native American culture. Wovoka's story revived the hopes of many; some came to believe that the dance would drive white settlers off Indian lands and protect Indians from bullets. While severe losses at Wounded Knee, South Dakota, in 1890, destroyed these immediate expectations, the Ghost Dance and its promise of a new flourishing for Native American cultures remain an important part of the native imagination; many Indians continue to search for signs that it is time to begin the Ghost Dance again and restore past glories.

Asian religions such as Hinduism and Buddhism do not have myths expressing their hopes for restoration or a new creation. Their stories about human destiny are more internal and abstract. In Hinduism, the soul (*atman*) is Brahman, eternal perfect Being. Human beings live in the changing world of appearances and in the immutable Brahman. The souls of individuals captivated by love of life and ignorance of true being migrate from one body to another in an endless cycle of reincarnation. Liberation from such reincarnation is the goal of Hinduism, accomplished through a surrender of individuality in union with Brahman. The natural world is not part of this union. While Buddhism rejects the existence of a permanent self, it does affirm a connection between the several lives a person may endure. Thus a life in this world is connected to other lives in the many worlds that Buddhists accept. Buddhists recognize desire as the root of all suffering. Their goal, achievable in this life, is nirvana, an indescribable void, a way of being characterized by the absence of desire.

Prophets and Their Stories

Not all myths within a community are created equal. Because they create order and structure power relationships, myths carry with them the potential for life or death. Each community must, therefore, determine the adequacy of its underlying myths through critical reflection on a regular basis. If the community ignores or refuses this task, there are often men and women within it who will challenge the community's predominant story. Dietrich Bonhoeffer, who lived in Germany during the rise of the Third Reich, was one such person. A pastor of a Lutheran church, he spoke out against the Reich's normative story, a story of Aryan superiority and Jewish inferiority. The alternate story of the dignity and value of each human person, the center of both Judaism and Christianity, held such power for him that he gathered together others who supported his views; this group worked together to unmask the fallacies of the myth of Aryan superiority. Because of his allegiance to Christianity's core story, he left the woman he was about to marry and continued to fight the Nazi government, until the SS arrested and executed him for participating in a plot to assassinate Adolf Hitler. Bonhoeffer lived a prophetic life; through his words and actions he sought to dismantle a myth which sought to establish order on the broken bodies of the men, women, and children it judged substandard.

Rosa Parks also opposed one of the prevailing cultural myths in Montgomery, Alabama, in 1955. According to that myth, she should have surrendered her bus seat to a white man as she was returning home from a long day of cleaning other people's houses. Parks was an African-American woman, viewed by some residents of Montgomery as marginally human. Nevertheless, she spoke out of her belief in her own humanity and personhood when she said: "I believe I'll keep my seat. I'm tired." Her quiet act of rebellion lead to her arrest. However, it also sparked the Montgomery Bus Boycott, a formative event in the African-American community's fight for civil rights, headed by Dr. Martin Luther King, Jr., and other African-American leaders. Her belief in her human dignity challenged Montgomery's racism. Like Bonhoeffer, she unmasked the inadequacy of a myth whose power depended upon the dehumanization and exclusion of certain groups of people of color.

The Old Testament contains many stories of individuals who challenged the controlling stories of their societies. The prophet Amos in the eighth century B.C.E. contested Israel's dominant story of that time. That story went something like this. The nation was enjoying prosperity and domestic security. Its political and religious leaders interpreted this as evidence that their God was blessing the people, that their relationship with him was whole and operative. They congratulated themselves on their ability to please God with elaborate sacrifices on all the days of festival. They looked forward eagerly to the "Day of the Lord," when they expected the Lord to destroy all their national enemies and reward them with greater economic and political power. Amos, however, disagreed with that assessment. He looked at the situation and told another story. He paid attention to the silent voices. He told the story of a God concerned for the people who were suffering because of the prosperity of the upper classes: small farmers who had been forced to sell their land, others who had sold themselves into slavery to pay their debts.

> For three transgressions of Israel,
>   and for four, I will not revoke the punishment;
> because they sell the righteous for silver,
>   and the needy for a pair of sandals—
> they who trample the head of the poor into the
>   dust of the earth,
> and push the afflicted out of the way. (Am 2:6-7)

The prosperous had forgotten that Israel was one family, that the quality of their relationship with God was determined by their concern for the poor and homeless in their land. Amos maintained that the blessing the upper classes were enjoying had nothing to do with God's blessing; rather it was a lightning rod that would soon attract their destruction. The Day of the Lord would soon blast them; it would bring destruction, not glory. Amos holds out little hope that God will change his mind and be gracious, even if they "seek good, not evil" (Am 5:14). Their excessive worship is a poor substitute for what their God desires:

> Let justice roll down like the waters,
>   and righteousness like an everflowing stream.
>   (Am 5:24)

MANY FORMS OF RELIGIOUS LANGUAGE

In our discussion of religious language thus far, we have mostly considered words, words spoken, words written. While words are one important aspect of talk about the sacred, we acknowledge that many other ways of talking about mystery also exist. Feet pounding the earth in rhythmic pat-

بِسۡمِ اللّٰهِ الرَّحۡمٰنِ الرَّحِیۡمِ ۞

الۡحَمۡدُ لِلّٰهِ رَبِّ الۡعٰلَمِیۡنَ ۞
الرَّحۡمٰنِ الرَّحِیۡمِ ۞
مٰلِكِ یَوۡمِ الدِّیۡنِ ۞
اِیَّاكَ نَعۡبُدُ وَاِیَّاكَ نَسۡتَعِیۡنُ ۞
اِهۡدِنَا الصِّرَاطَ الۡمُسۡتَقِیۡمَ ۞
صِرَاطَ الَّذِیۡنَ اَنۡعَمۡتَ عَلَیۡهِمۡ غَیۡرِ الۡمَغۡضُوۡبِ
عَلَیۡهِمۡ وَلَا الضَّآلِّیۡنَ ۞

The Prologue of the Qur'an in Arabic. The Islamic philosopher Sa'in al-Din ibn Turkah writes that letters and words descend into the physical with an inner spiritual substance. Thus, each letter in the Qur'an has three forms: the spoken form for the ear, the written form for the eye, and the spiritual form for the heart. Arabic calligraphy joins with the spoken word to unlock inner meanings for Qur'anic texts within the heart.

terns; heavy drumming, sometimes loud, sometimes soft; bodies swaying to the movements of spirits; arms raised in glad salute to the sun; space ordered with flowers and incense; quiet breathing in harmony with a beating heart; soaring cathedral spires and golden icons—gestures, art, dance, music, and architecture are also words in human language about the sacred. In this final section we consider two such words: the word of Arabic calligraphy in the Islamic tradition and the word of basket weaving of the Yekuana tribe in the South American rain forest.

Islamic Calligraphy

Islam has long prohibited representational statues, pictures, and other images of the deity. Throughout Egypt, Syria, and Jordan, for example, intricate geometric patterns of inlaid wood and mosaics decorate mosque ceilings and floors. As they catch the sun, lattice-worked window shutters create shadows and designs on bare walls. Editions of the Qur'an in Arabic script contain no illustrations; instead intricate calligraphy, or decorative handwriting, draws the reader's intellect and imagination into the recitation of the text. It is not unusual to find framed verses of the Qur'an, in elaborate script highlighted with gold, for sale in tourist gift shops; a popular subject is the divine name Allah, which begins with *alif*, the first letter of the Arabic alphabet. Nor is it unusual to find, in museum displays in Aleppo or Amman, pen boxes and dinner plates from the twelfth or fourteenth century decorated with calligraphy. This writing transforms these articles, once part of someone's daily life, into reminders of the God whom Muslims seek to remember throughout their day.

For centuries Muslims have practiced calligraphy, not only to cultivate good handwriting, a sign of traditional culture, but also to discipline
their souls. As they draw a line from right to left, the direction of Arabic
writing, they move from the edge of themselves to their heart; through
concentrating on writing words in beautiful forms, they gather together
fragments of their souls. Meditation on the beauty of these forms leads
them to the divine word flowing from beauty's source:

> for every *alif* cannot help but remind us that only the *alif* Allah
> should occupy our heart and mind while every point brings
> about the recollection ... "God was and there was nothing with
> Him," and that furthermore "He is even as He was."[18]

Allah created cosmic order and natural space as divine models for this
written language as well as for the space of Islamic architecture and the
other arts. Islamic calligraphy, then, makes visual and visible the inner reality of Islamic revelation. For Muslims, divine presence resides in the Qur'an.
Through calligraphy, the visual embodiment of Allah's word, Muslims can
experience this presence and "taste the reality of the spiritual world."

Basket Weaving and the Yekuana Tribe

In calligraphy, Muslims may detect the invisible, discover the order Allah
has written into the cosmos, and re-establish order within themselves. In
a similar fashion, the baskets the Yekuana basket makers weave for their
villages recreate their world, imbuing it with light and order. The
Yekuana, or "Canoe People" located alongside two rivers in the South
American rain forest, are hunters and farmers, living in self-contained
autonomous villages.

The myths associated with the origins and designs of their baskets
depict a deeply divided world filled with negativity and darkness; terrible
monsters prey on the people. In the myths not only must they drive
death away, they must somehow incorporate it into their world and control it. For the Yekuana, weaving is the symbolic way they accomplish
this. Weaving incorporates the wild cane into ordered, useful patterns;
thus the basket makers, all men, are custodians of order in their villages.
They produce new baskets, whose patterns embody myths in which
ancestors gain control of hostile forces. The completion of each new basket asserts that these forces are still tamed, held fast in the woven cane.

The Yekuana world is also a complex dual reality. It has an invisible
double, both independent of it and eternal. Rituals negotiate between
these worlds, weaving spirit world and visible world together into a
coherent pattern and neutralizing the powers of the spirit world for the
Yekuana. Just as new baskets are prepared for each ritual, rituals accompany each aspect of basket weaving, from collecting the raw cane, to
preparing dye, to cleansing the completed baskets and inviting the spirits

MARY N. MACDONALD

Weaving is a powerful symbol of our ability to create order out of chaos. The Hopi Spider Woman weaves a world; the Yekuana men weave cosmic order into their baskets; the Dogon storyteller weaves the ancestors into the life of each generation. This woman in Mararoka, Papua New Guinea, weaves string bags out of colorful yarn. The people of Papua New Guinea use them to carry what they need for each day. In the Kewa language, the word for "string bag" is also the word for "womb."

of the material it will hold to come fill it. At each stage of the process invisible spirits are met and disarmed, their powers incorporated into the basket.

Different kinds of baskets play significant roles in rituals of puberty, marriage, and fasting. Like the rituals, the weave and design of the baskets represent a successful resolution of opposites and the creation of integration. The baskets promise resolution at the ritual's beginning, assist in it, and then witness that it has occurred.

In addition to languages of myth and song, the Yekuana weave a language of baskets. The baskets assert that hostile powers are trapped in their weave and in their design; they assure the people that their world is secure and meaningful.[19]

CONCLUSION

In this chapter we have considered different ways we use to talk about the sacred. We started with language and discovered that we use it in many ways. We most commonly use language figuratively, that is, so that it means something different from what it says. The language we use to talk about the sacred, which may be a dimension of human experience but not one we can access directly, is the language of metaphor. The metaphors we use about the sacred are the products of our culture and our relationships. No one metaphor exhausts the ways we can describe the holy. No one metaphor defines mystery.

In the second part of the chapter, we looked at myth. Myth is a story which embodies a community's value systems and power structures. Although myths talk about the origins of the universe, they are generally about the relationships which must be in place for the present community to function. Myths of alienation account for the presence of aspects of human living which we cannot change. Myths of destiny motivate religious people to remain faithful to their traditions in the hope of later experiencing harmony and fulfillment. Prophetic myths judge the accuracy of a community's myth in terms of a competing story whose order it supplants. Finally we looked at two types of religious language whose words are neither spoken nor written. Arabic calligraphy and Yekuana basket weaving speak words of order and protection to their respective communities; like myths, they too symbolize the order they create.

In chapter 7 we will continue to look at religious stories. Our categories, however, change. Many religious traditions have their own scriptures. We will study how scriptures are collected, what criteria are used to decide the material to include, and what different attitudes these traditions have toward their scriptures. We will also have the opportunity to read selections from different traditions. These scriptures are often the basis for the creation of doctrine, the normative beliefs of a community. Both doctrines and creeds, statements in which doctrines are sometimes expressed, are other versions of the community story. Like myth, their language is figurative, not literal. Like myth, they are metaphors that order our relationship with the sacred.

RESOURCES

Activities

1. Ask several people from different age, ethnic, and social groups what metaphors they use to describe their relationship with the sacred? Where do they find these metaphors: scripture, ritual, personal reading, personal experiences or relationships, their imaginations? Are there metaphors which they no longer use? Why? What metaphors do you or someone you know use to describe a relationship with the sacred? What associations do you make with each metaphor? Where did you find these metaphors? Combine your data with other students who worked on this activity and present your findings to the class.
2. Consult a good translation of the New Testament (New Revised Standard Version [NRSV] or New American Bible [NAB]) and read as many parables as you can find. Analyze the figurative language each uses to describe the Kingdom of God/Heaven. Rewrite several of the parables using contemporary figurative language. Share your analysis of language and your rewrites with your group, with the whole class, or post this information on your class bulletin board.

3. Read the book of Jonah in an edition of the Bible that provides an introduction and notes to the text. When you have finished, construct a map of your world. Place a symbol of yourself at the center of the map. Then draw four concentric circles; the first circle has your symbol in the center. Label the circles, moving from the center out: Myself, Family, Friends, Acquaintances. Outside the fourth circle, write "Strangers." Fill each circle, including the space outside the fourth circle, with language you use, both positive and negative, about the individuals you associate with each circle. Study your use of language: Is it inclusive? personal? dehumanizing? What kind of a world does it create? What value systems does it represent? Pretend that you are Jonah and study your map in terms of the question God poses at the end of the book. Are there groups or individuals on your map that you think should be excluded from the "good things" of life, for example, quality medical care or housing, the right to marry or raise children? Are they also excluded from your God's care and concern? Why? Who is the one person or group whom you cannot imagine God loving? Why? How does the book of Jonah relate to these questions?

4. Find Quentin Tarentino's 1995 film *Pulp Fiction* in a library video collection or in a video store. Watch it several times to catch its nuances. How is the film a parable? What surprises does it offer? What doubts does it raise? What thoughts does it provoke?

5. Interview the leader of a church, synagogue, or mosque in your neighborhood and find out how that religious tradition understands its prophetic identity. How does that identity direct its involvement in the neighborhood or city? What social problems does it target? If one of the individuals discussed in the section on prophets were to accompany you on the interview, what questions would she/he ask? How would he/she respond to the minister/priest, rabbi, or imam?

6. Create your own anthology of sacred stories from several religious traditions. Use the categories in this chapter or create your own. Provide commentary for the stories you select, and give information about the religious traditions in which they are found. Share your work with your group. You can find collections of religious myths in the library or online on the WWW.

7. Joseph Campbell has argued that movies like the *Star Wars* trilogy are the best examples of contemporary mythologies. Along with your group, use these films or others (e.g., *2001*) to identify their mythic structure: the views of humanity, the world, and the sacred that are its themes. This would make a good class presentation, especially with film clips to illustrate the themes.

Readings

Marcel Griaule. *Conversations with Ogotemmeli: An Introduction to Dogon Religious Ideas.* London: Oxford University Press, 1970. The record of a thirty-day conversation between a French ethnographer and a wise man of the Dogon tribe of the Sudan. Connections are shown between Dogon cosmology and the gestures and objects of their daily life.

David M. Guss. *To Weave and Sing: Art, Symbol, and Narrative in the South American Rain Forest.* Berkeley: University of California Press, 1989. Describes a culture in which weaving is a metaphor for order-producing activities.

Archibald MacLeish. *J.B.* A 1950's adaption of the biblical book of Job in which
J.B., the main character, struggles to maintain faith and hope in the aftermath
of terrible loss.

Barbara C. Sproul. *Primal Myths: Creation Myths Around the World.* 2nd. edition.
San Francisco: Harper, 1979. A collection of myths of origin, organized
according to geographic area, with an extensive introductory essay on myth
and background and with commentary on each entry.

For additional examples of parables see: Plato, "The Cave," in *The Republic*;
Franz Kafka, *Metamorphosis, The Trial.*

Audiovisuals

Popol Vuh. A PBS presentation of the Mayan creation myth, with animated
images based on figures carved on Mayan architecture.

The Power of Myth. A series of six videos. Available from Films for the
Humanities and Sciences, P.O. Box 2053, Princeton, NJ 08543-2053. 1-800-257-
5126; custserv@films.com; http://www.films.com. Conversations between Joseph
Campbell and PBS journalist Bill Moyers. Illustrated with images and myths from
many religions and cultures.

Pulp Fiction. 1995 Quentin Tarentino film. The title is a reference to the inexpen-
sive and sensational "dime" novels printed on cheap paper at the beginning of
the twentieth century. Healing, forgiveness, and grace run through the film.

Storytellers of the Pacific. Available from Films for the Humanities and Sciences,
P.O. Box 2053, Princeton, NJ 08543-2053. 1-800-257-5126; custserv@films.com;
http://www.films.com. A two-part PBS series examining the identity and self-
determination of the native people of the Pacific Rim. In the second program of
the series, storytellers share their people's spirituality, histories, cultures, and
ability to survive in the face of colonizers' policies and customs. Each program
one hour.

"When Faith Meets Physics." Part II in the *Religion and Culture* series. Available
from Films for the Humanities and Sciences, P.O. Box 2053, Princeton, NJ 08543-
2053. 1-800-257-5126; custserv@films.com; http://www.films.com. This twenty-
eight-minute conversation among philosophers, scientists, and theologians
explores the possibility of resolving tensions between scientific theory and religious belief about creation and evolution.

NOTES

1. Cited in Sally McFague TeSelle, *Speaking in Parables: A Study in Metaphor and Theology* (Philadelphia: Fortress, 1975) 24.

2. Stanley Fish, "Rhetoric," in Frank Lentricchia and Thomas McLaughlin, eds., *Critical Terms for Literary Study* (Chicago: University of Chicago Press, 1990), 209.

3. Stewart Guthrie, *Faces in the Clouds: A New Theory of Religion* (New York: Oxford University Press, 1993), 117.

4 Paul van Buren, *The Edges of Language,* cited in James C. Livingston, *The Anatomy of the Sacred* (New York: Macmillan, 1989), 96.

5. Shin'ichi Hisamatsu, "Zen: Its Meaning for Modern Civilization," R. DeMartino and Gishin Tokina, trans., *The Eastern Buddhist* (I:1, 9/65): 32.

6. W. M. Watt, *Islamic Philosophy and Theology* (Edinburgh: Edinburgh University Press, 1962), 246-47.

7. Julian of Norwich, *Showings: Revelations of Divine Love*, trans. with introduction by Edmund Colledge and James Walsh (New York: Classics of Western Spirituality, Paulist Press, 1978), chap. 60.

8. C. H. Dodd, *The Parables of the Kingdom* (Rev. ed.; New York: Scribners, 1961), 16.

9. Lucien Stryke, ed., *The World of the Buddha: A Reader* (Garden City, NY: Doubleday/Anchor, 1969), 95-101.

10. Bronislaw Malinowski, *Myth in Primitive Psychology* (New York: Norton, 1926); reprinted in *Matic, Science, and Religion* (Garden City, NY: Doubleday, 1954).

11. C. G. Jung, *Man and His Symbols* (Garden City, NY: Doubleday, 1964); Wallace Clift, *Jung and Christianity* (New York: Crossroads, 1982).

12. Joseph Campbell, *Myths to Live By* (New York: Bantam/Viking, 1972); with Bill Moyers, *The Power of Myth* (New York: Doubleday, 1988).

13. Marcel Griaule, *Conversations with Ogotemmeli: An Introduction to Dogon Religious Ideas* (London: Oxford University Press, 1970), 11-40.

14. Adapted from Barbara C. Sproul, *Primal Myths: Creation Myths Around the World*, 2d ed. (San Francisco: Harper, 1991), 186.

15. Adapted from Sproul, *Primal Myths*, 187.

16. Cited in Leonard J. Biallas, *Myths: Gods, Heroes, and Saviors* (Mystic, CT: Twenty-Third Publications, 1989), 37.

17. Dorothee Sölle, *Thinking about God: An Introduction to Theology* (Philadelphia: Trinity Press International, 1990), 61.

18. Seyyed Hussein Nasr, *Islamic Art and Spirituality* (Albany: State University of New York Press, 1987), 34. This section is based on the book's second chapter, "The Spiritual Message of Islamic Calligraphy," 17-34.

19. This discussion of Yekuana basket weaving depends heavily on David M. Guss, *To Weave and Sing: Art, Symbol, and Narrative in the South American Rain Forest* (Berkeley: University of California Press, 1989).

Chapter 7

Scriptures, Canons, and Creeds

INTRODUCTION

Each religious tradition has a collection of stories, prayers, songs, curses and blessings, lists, incantations, and laws that it considers powerful and authoritative. These collections shape the lives of its members in many ways. In the United States, for example, some Christians use their scriptures to condemn the death penalty and to oppose enhancement of the military budget. Others appeal to the same scriptures to support their opposition to legalized abortion and to demand the execution of violent criminals. Some citizens think a copy of the Ten Commandments belongs on courtroom walls, while others are content to display a family Bible in their homes as a repository for birth announcements and obituaries. In Israel some groups oppose the establishment of a Palestinian state because, in their eyes, God promised Abraham, Sarah, and their descendants the territory from the Sinai Peninsula to the Euphrates River (Gen 15:18-21). Muslim leaders use the Qur'an to place constraints on the behavior, movement, and dress of Islamic women around the world; yet the degree of restriction differs from group to group.

In this chapter we will consider the role and function of scripture in religious traditions. We will also examine doctrine and creed, symbolic statements interpreting the central story of a religious tradition; history, culture, and language influence these formulations that convey a range of normative beliefs for individual religions.

SCRIPTURE

Scripture, from the Latin verb *scriptura*, means "that which has been written down," whether on a Torah scroll or in a gospel **codex**, on a **Jain** palmleaf manuscript or in a contemporary edition of Buddhist texts. In addition, the word "scripture" is generally reserved for writings or books considered sacred or holy. In chapter 6 we saw that a favorite mode of talking about the sacred was the form of story or narrative. Are scriptures holy because they contain important, foundational stories?

Many scriptures are, in fact, made up largely of narrative. A central narrative woven together from many disparate stories governs the Tanak, for example. The Israelite God acts in history to free a people from Egyptian slavery, make a covenant with them, and lead them into the land of Canaan. Once there, this God helps the Israelites dispossess the indigenous populations and incorporate them into the Israelite nation. Under David and Solomon, the Israelites establish a monarchy and centralize their worship in the Jerusalem Temple. However, kingship, temple, and economic prosperity so interfere with fidelity to the covenant that their God weakens the people through a series of military disasters, destruction of the temple, and capture of Jerusalem; he commissions the Babylonians to relocate them as prisoners of war, with little hope of return, until the Persian hero Cyrus appears. The prophet Isaiah of Babylon names the non-Israelite Cyrus *mashiakh adonai*, the Lord's anointed/messiah.[1]

The material in the Tanak is scripture not only for the Jewish community, but also for Christianity. Whatever doctrinal differences they may have, most Christian denominations interpret the Tanak as the first volume of or introduction to their own scriptures, the New Testament, the new covenant which God inaugurated in the person of Jesus of Nazareth. By rearranging the order of books in the Tanak so that the book of the prophet Malachi immediately precedes the Gospel of Matthew, Christianity's narrative declares that Jesus of Nazareth is the reference point for many of Israel's hopes and expectations. In Malachi, Israel's God is ready to send a messenger to prepare for him. Not too far into the Gospel of Matthew, the reader realizes that the author is presenting John the Baptizer as that messenger, and Jesus of Nazareth as Israel's Lord.

A large part of the New Testament is narrative. The four gospels of Matthew, Mark, Luke, and John interpret the life, ministry, death, and resurrection of Jesus. The **Acts of the Apostles** tells how, despite persecution and hardship, the fledgling Christian community, alive with the spirit of the resurrected Christ, spread from Jerusalem through Asia Minor and the Mediterranean basin to Rome. The narrative embedded in the book of Revelation, discussed briefly in chapter 6, encourages Roman Christians to remain faithful, because Christ has already won a definitive victory over evil.

Not all scriptures are centered so dramatically on a continuous story. As we saw in chapter 6, the Hindu *Upanishads* generally deal with metaphysical philosophy; for example, they wonder how being and nonbeing may be related to the beginning of the cosmos. Moral or ethical philosophy dominates the *Analects* of Confucianism. The Hindu *Vedas* are full of directions and songs for sacrifice.

This illuminated page from the two-volume Urbino Bible depicts the story told in the book of Revelation (Apocalypse). An ornate vine connects its author John, exiled on the island of Patmos, with the world of God and his court. The symbol for the Christ in Revelation is the lamb, the image in the upper left-hand corner of the page.

Even those scriptures which are largely narrative contain other kinds of literature. Native Americans and indigenous groups around the world look to their oral texts for sacred stories, customs, and guides to direct their lives in the ways of their ancestors. Embedded within Genesis through 2 Kings of the Tanak are law codes, hymns, speeches, prophetic oracles, erotic love poetry, and administrative records; like the creative interplay of light and shadow in a well-made film, they add depth and challenge to a richly textured plot. Half of the New Testament is made up of letters written to individual communities on matters of discipline, behavior, and doctrine. Woven into this material are early Christian hymns and prayers, household codes, fragments of baptismal rituals and celebrations of the Lord's supper, and suggestions for church discipline; from them, scholars learn how the earliest communities interpreted the gospels.

RELIGIOUS TRADITIONS AND THEIR SCRIPTURES

No one **genre** or literary form, then, is common to all scriptures; nor does any one genre confer sacredness or holiness on scripture. In fact, scriptures, in and of themselves, are not naturally or essentially holy. Rather they become sacred within the lives of communities that respond to them as sacred and holy realities; the communities' response bestows holiness on them. The power of scripture, then, is relational, dependent upon its place within a community. Just as it transforms the community into a holy people, so each community transforms its scripture into a holy book.[2]

The scriptures in each religious tradition bear a special relationship to the members of that tradition; sometimes there are stories embedded in the scripture itself about that relationship. The Qur'an recounts how the angel Gabriel taught Muhammad to recite the contents of the heavenly Qur'an, which remains with Allah in the heavens. Muslims believe that the written Qur'an is literally the divine word for them. The Jewish God is the source of revelation transcribed in the Tanak, especially the Torah; this God revealed it to the earliest founder of Judaism, the prophet and liberator Moses. Moses, in turn, received it on behalf of the Israelites assembled at the foot of Mount Sinai. Each generation of Jews understands itself at Sinai, accepting that same revelation.

Traditions also acknowledge, in ways other than story, that their scriptures are authoritative for them. Through careful study of and reflection on the New Testament, Christians learn how a faith relationship with Jesus the Christ empowers them to live a holy life as they work together to build a more just and loving society. The Qur'an contains Islam's Five Pillars, the will of Allah for observant Muslims. Orthodox Jews shape their lives around the 613 laws given by their God, recorded in the Torah, and later interpreted in the **Talmud**. Buddhists maintain that the essence of Buddhism is the practice of *dharma*, the way of moderate living out-

MARY N. MACDONALD

A prayer group at Mararoko in the Southern Highlands of Papua New Guinea begins its service with the Bible covered with fragrant flowers to emphasize the fresh sweeetness the word of God brings to their gathering. In a similar fashion, when a young Muslim boy has successfully memorized and recited his first Qur'an passage, his teacher dissolves honey in a glass of water for him to drink so that he connects sweetness with the Qur'an throughout his life.

lined by the Buddha, and found in Buddhist writings. Buddhist scriptures and the Buddha himself are secondary to *dharma* because "*dharma*, not the Buddha, saves."

SCRIPTURES AND THE SACRED

Religious communities understand that scriptures are one of the modes in which the sacred is revealed and made present for them. The community invests these writings with authority; it names the writings as a revelation to the community and, in some cases, to the entire world (Mt 28:16-20; Acts 1:6-8). Thus, each community uses its scriptures to evaluate what ultimately matters. Such usage indicates that a religion considers its scriptures canonical, that is, normative for belief and practice. For example, according to the Hindu Code of Manu, those teachings that differ from the *Veda*, the eternal word from which the world originates, "are worthless and false," since the Veda is "infallible regarding all that is imperceptible." Some Christians label attitudes as gospel-oriented (justice, compassion, inclusiveness) or as secular (excessive concern for self, disregard for the poor, getting ahead at any cost) and try to live close to the gospel because it is the "Word of God." Practitioners measure scientific discoveries and medical procedures against the ultimate meaning they attribute to their scriptures. In the seventeenth century, for example, church leaders, afraid they would be committing **blasphemy,** refused to look into Galileo's telescope to see the evidence that verified his theory of the earth's rotation around the sun. Some traditions condemn medical developments like contraceptives, meant to curtail human fertility, as solutions to overpopulation and famine, arguing that these procedures challenge divine control over life and death.

Religious traditions treat their scriptures with respect, especially when they use them in ritual. Jews decorate Torah scrolls with ornate coverings, breastplates, and crowns. When they remove them from the **Ark of the Covenant**, they are careful to touch them only with their hands wrapped in prayer shawls. Members of the synagogue often kiss their prayer shawls and touch them to the scroll. Sometimes the scroll is carried in procession throughout the synagogue. Occasionally the rabbi, carrying the scroll, leads his synagogue in dance. Readers during the Sabbath service in the synagogue use a Torah marker in the shape of a tiny hand or finger to keep their place to avoid touching the sacred scroll with their bare hands.

In many Christian churches, people stand during the reading of the gospel and affirm afterwards that they have heard the Word of the Lord. Orthodox Christians decorate their **lectionaries** with embroidered covers set with beads and semiprecious stones. While Hindus seldom see or venerate the *Veda* book, its words and their sounds, like those of the Qur'an, are the center of the worship that actualizes its power.

SCRIPTURE AND CANON

In our discussion so far, we have described scripture as writing accepted and used by a religious tradition which regards it as especially powerful and authoritative, or **canonical**. Today, along with the canons of **Zoroastrianism** and **Sikhism**, the canons of Judaism, Christianity, and Islam are closed. Long ago their religious leaders officially identified the canonical scriptures of these religions; from that point on, writings can neither be added nor deleted from this list. Christianity, for example, claims that God's public revelation ceased with the death of John, the last apostle (ca. 100 C.E.); anyone claiming to speak a new divine word after that becomes suspect.

On the other hand, the Church of Jesus Christ of Latter Day Saints, the Mormons, has a different view. Mormons believe that God has spoken in the past, continues to speak in the present and will speak in the future. The Mormon sacred books include 1) the Bible; 2) the Book of Mormon, the translation of an ancient text which the angel Moroni gave to Joseph Smith, the group's founder; and 3) *Doctrines and Covenants* and *The Pearl of Great Price*, additional revelations Smith received from God before his death. The Mormon canon is open; Mormons expect and are ready to accommodate new revelations. Other religious traditions also have open canons. Although their practitioners may not use this terminology, the scriptures of Hinduism, Buddhism, Jainism, Confucianism, and Taoism all represent vast bodies of religious literature which remain open, that is, they continue to develop.

MARYKNOLL PHOTO LIBRARY/HOOSIER

Even though the sounds and shape of the Arabic letters of the Qur'an are valued more than the printed book itself, Muslims ritually wash their hands before reciting from the Qur'an. These Islamic women in Bangladesh follow the custom of resting the Qur'an on a small book stand so it does not touch the floor.

The process through which religious texts become scripture and scripture becomes canon is complicated. Scholars hypothesize about the earliest stages of the process since none of the decision makers left notes explaining the selection process. Often regional politics, history, economics, and personal preferences, as well as a concern for orthodoxy, played a role. In the Tanak, however, there is a short narrative which describes how a scroll found during renovations of the Jerusalem Temple became canonical. The priest Hilkiah takes the scroll to the prophet Huldah to determine whether it is God's word. She replies that it is and that it will serve as the norm against which Judah and Jerusalem will be judged.

Hilkiah takes the scroll back to Josiah the King. Josiah, in turn, makes the scroll the center of political and religious reform (2 Kgs 22:14-20). Today scholars agree that the scroll which Huldah examined makes up a large part of the Book of Deuteronomy.

The Formation of the Gospels

To illustrate this process, we consider how the canon of the Christian New Testament developed. Much of what follows is a highly speculative reconstruction, something like trying to solve a complicated mystery with few clues. Most New Testament scholars describe three broad stages in the formation of the gospels. The first stage is the life of the historical Jesus of Nazareth. Nothing written survives from the time of Jesus' public preaching, either from Jesus or from his disciples. As was probably the custom in first-century Palestine, some of these followers, representing a cross-section of Judean life, preserved his teachings orally. Thus we have no direct access to Jesus' preaching or to Jesus himself.

The second stage is the teaching and preaching ministry of the early Jewish Christians in Palestine after Jesus' death. During this time, individuals gathered together collections of the sayings of Jesus. Scholars today call one such collection of sayings **Q** (from the German word **Quelle,** "source"). They claim they can reconstruct the contents of Q from the Gospels of Matthew and Luke. These scholars identify as Q the material that Matthew and Luke have in common but which does not appear in the Gospel of Mark. At the same time, others gathered together the parables of Jesus, along with other types of stories about Jesus: for example, miracle stories, healing stories, stories of confrontation and controversy with Jewish religious leaders.

Preachers and teachers also generated new material, drawing on the Tanak to support their assertions that this Jesus was God's anointed, the messiah. This would not have been immediately evident to a first-century Jew, since Jesus had died a criminal's death on the cross and had been rejected by the religious leaders in Jerusalem. It is not surprising, then, that the first continuous narrative about Jesus, created during this phase, puts his passion and death in the context of a divine plan. This hypothetical narrative may identify Jesus as the Son of Man, an eschatalogical figure charged with executing God's justice. Such a **passion narrative** may have formed the core of the Gospel of Mark, sometimes described as "a passion narrative with a long introduction." Teachers and preachers in the early community used all this material to introduce others to the story of Jesus of Nazareth. Many collections were probably in use, some written, some oral; the sayings and the stories were modified or expanded to emphasize different points of view and to accommodate individual audiences.

The third stage is the actual writing of the **gospel,** a literary form developed by early Christian writers. Each canonical gospel represents a new level in this phase. Working from early passion narratives, collections of sayings and stories, and from their own private sources, individual authors wrote these narratives which celebrated the victory of Jesus over the powers of darkness, especially death and evil. The writers filtered their sources through the lens of their own theological programs, their opposition to existing gospels, their allegiance to philosophical movements. Even though the four gospels in the present New Testament are traditionally linked with individuals who were or had close connections with one of the twelve apostles,[3] their authors probably had no first-hand knowledge of Jesus. Their acquaintance with Jesus came through preachers and teachers who used second-stage material.

Gospels are stories of victory, "good news," presented to the believing community. Neither biography nor history, they are interpretations of the life and ministry, the death and resurrection of Jesus from particular points of view; written for believers, they elaborate and strengthen the faith already present in the community. Of the four gospels, the Gospel of John is distinctive in language, style, and content; in fact, it bears little resemblance to the other three gospels. The Gospels of Matthew, Mark, and Luke share a good deal of material in common; for that reason, they are called the **synoptic** gospels. The relationship among them, that is, who borrowed what from whom, is so complex that scholars have characterized it as the **synoptic problem**.[4]

Thinking with the Gospels

Read this material from the New Testament: Matthew 1-3, Mark 1, Luke 1-4, and John 1-2. Keep in mind that these texts do not recount "what really happened." They are symbolic texts which express what each writer believes about Jesus of Nazareth, how he interprets this Jesus. For the most part, each author is depending upon individual sources in this material. The variations among the accounts are important; they convey different understandings about Jesus of Nazareth and demonstrate how these understandings developed as people reflected on his teachings.

1. What differences do you notice about how these gospels introduce Jesus of Nazareth?

2. How do these variations reveal the different ways in which Christians, then as now, have understood Jesus?

3. Think about the way in which chapter 1 suggested we understand the virginity of Mary. What other details in these texts could we view as symbolic statements, e.g., God as Jesus' father?

4. Beginning with Mark and ending with John, compare the different accounts of the baptism of Jesus. Baptism here is not Christian baptism; it does not remove sin; rather, it is a symbolic gesture. The people whom John baptized were people who wanted to live as good Jews; their baptism proclaimed their desire to renew their commitment to God and their intention to live more observant lives. In the narratives, the same is true for Jesus of Nazareth. What different statements do these symbolic narratives make about Jesus?

These four canonical gospels were not the only gospels to be written in the early days of Christianity. Other writings also called gospels appeared; sometimes these gospels filled in parts of the life of Jesus of Nazareth that were ignored by the other gospels.[5] The childhood of Jesus was a favorite topic of such narratives, some of which border on legend. One gospel, for example, shows Jesus as a boy modeling birds out of clay, breathing on them, and letting them fly away. Another recounts a story of Jesus and his friends playing; one boy knocks Jesus down. In retaliation, Jesus strikes his playmate dead; only when their mothers call them into supper does Jesus return the boy to life. As problematic as we may find such material, it helps us see that gospel narratives are symbolic stories. Because we may be so used to viewing the canonical gospels as "what really happened," we lose sight of the fact that they are interpretation in narrative form; they express insight and belief, not fact.

An important noncanonical gospel is the Gospel of Thomas.[6] Originally written in Greek, it claims to be a compilation of one hundred fourteen sayings, proverbs, parables, and prophecies which Jesus secretly taught to a small inner circle of followers. While some of the teachings have a **gnostic** flavor, many sayings parallel those found in the canonical gospels. The Gospel of Thomas may preserve an older form of Jesus' words along with authentic sayings not included in Matthew, Mark, Luke, and John. Compare, for example, "Let the little children come to me; do not stop them; for it is to such as these that the kingdom of God belongs. Whoever does not receive the kingdom of God as a little child will never enter it" (Mk 10:14-15) and "Jesus saw infants being suckled. He said to His disciples, 'These infants being suckled are like those who enter the Kingdom'" (Thomas 22a).

Other New Testament Genres

Even though the gospels occur first in the New Testament, its earliest material is Paul's correspondence to the Christian community at Thessalonica (ca. 38). Paul wrote letters to many of the Christian communities he established, often to settle disputes or to answer questions about order or belief that developed once he had moved on to another area. He also wrote at least one letter to an individual, Philemon, urging him to welcome back his runaway slave Onesimus. Of the twenty-one letters in the New Testament, Paul himself wrote nine. Others are the work of Paul's companions (Timothy and Titus) or later writers who had adopted Paul's theology as their own. The rest are attributed to apostles or leaders in the early church, for example, Peter and James, Jude, and John; one (the letter to the Hebrews) is anonymous.[7]

Most church historians agree that the four-gospel canon that we have now developed in response to several crises. The most noteworthy of these crises was publication of the **Diatessaron**, a harmony of the four gospels, which **Tatian** produced in Syria in 165. Tatian had edited the four gospel texts into one continuous biography of Jesus of Nazareth, thus creating a synchronized story that removed the gospels' inconsistencies and contradictions. His work raised questions about the nature of gospel. Was it a historical document or a faith statement? What did the lack of harmony between the gospels on some issues mean? Did Christianity need four gospels?

By the fourth century we have the first documentation for the canon of four gospels in Eusebius's *Church History* and in the *Muratorian Fragment*.[8] In response to the proliferation of gospels that had sprung up, church leaders accepted only the four gospels of Matthew, Mark, Luke, and John, in that order, because they seemed to conform to accepted criteria: 1) they eliminated **heresy**, an opinion about central issues in Christianity that differed from a standard range of beliefs; 2) they encouraged martyrdom in response to the gospel mandate, "Take up your cross and follow me" (Mk 8:34); 3) Christian communities had traditionally linked these canonical gospels, directly or indirectly, to individual apostles; and 4) most important, they had also been adopted by local Christian communities as sources for teaching, preaching, and right living. In other words, they had stood the test of faith; people found them helpful and challenging. In canonizing these four gospels, leaders ratified the insight of many local churches that these gospels conveyed the message of Jesus in a way that the others did not.

The **Council of Chalcedon** (451) established the current New Testament canon, with twenty-seven books. Some books in the list had been assigned apostolic authorship, for example, the book of Revelation was attributed to the apostle John, the Letter to the Hebrews to Paul, even though these individuals had not written them.

In the sixteenth century the most recent statement about the Christian canon attempted to resolve a controversy about the content of the Roman Catholic canon in opposition to the canon of Martin Luther and the Reformers. As part of his program to repudiate ecclesial **tradition** and return to the roots of Christianity (**sola Scriptura**), Luther rejected those Old Testament books not found in the Tanak, books which the Roman church claimed as part of its scripture.[9] In reaction, the **Council of Trent** officially defined the Roman Catholic scriptures to include, as the inspired word of God, both the books of the Tanak, and all the material Luther had excluded. In Catholic editions of the Bible today, for example, the New American Bible, this **deuterocanonical** material is located throughout the Old Testament; in other editions, for example, the New Revised Standard Version, the same material is printed in a supplementary section placed between the Old and the New Testaments, where much of it belongs chronologically, or in an appendix following the New Testament.

INTERPRETING SCRIPTURE FROM WITHIN A TRADITION

We have seen how religious traditions revere their scriptures and find in them a connection with power and life. Buddhist monks meditate on the teachings of the Buddha, hoping to look through the words on the page to the meaning behind them. During the Middle Ages, Benedictine monks began the practice of group *lectio divino*, one monk reading aloud a single gospel passage over and over again while the rest tried to take in its message by concentrating on the words. In the Appalachian mountains of Kentucky, Tennessee, and West Virginia, women and men hold snakes at arm's length above their heads to demonstrate their trust in the power of faith. These actions represent the conviction that the meaning and truth of each scripture is hidden within text; believers can access it through meditation, reading, or practice.

These examples also demonstrate scripture's need for interpretation. Because scripture uses figurative language, it means more than it says; it has many meanings. For example, in the parable of the Good Samaritan in the Gospel of Luke (10:29-37), meanings are layered one on top of another. The passage is a story of a life-saving chance encounter between a mugging victim and a kind-hearted traveler; it is also a story about being a neighbor and about the identity of neighbor. The story also reverses "the way things are," for it is the Samaritan, a code word here for "despised and Godless," whom Jesus uses to teach his Jewish audience about right behavior. The reversal continues when Jesus indirectly equates worship of God with caring for a neighbor in need.

A scripture passage may yield obvious meanings; it may only hint at or imply others. The parable of the Good Samaritan may yield an understanding of neighbor as local (a friend living with AIDS, the clients at a nearby soup kitchen) or as global (starving peoples in Asia and Africa, political prisoners in Central America). The meaning of other passages may make no literal sense. The Gospel of John uses metaphors of Christ as Lamb of God, Bread of Life, the Way, the Word; in the Tanak Israel's God is rock, eagle, rain, husband, parent. These figures of speech depend upon similarity rather than identity. The reader must struggle with this figurative language, against its background in the text, to understand the text.

Individuals in different religious traditions may disagree with the idea that the language of scripture is figurative language. Such literalists claim that the meaning of scripture is obvious; they mean exactly what they say, and what they say is clear. They swear allegiance to the letter of the text. If Jesus said, "Call no man 'Father'," they find other titles for their religious leaders. If Buddha told his monks to avoid silver and gold, that is exactly what he meant. If God criticized the extravagance and ceremony of Israel's sacrifices, then God clearly must prefer simplicity and economy (Is 1:10-17). In a small southern town, a Baptist minister recently closed his church's day care center because its existence encouraged women in his church to sin against God by working outside the home. In his view God intended for the home to be the center of a woman's world; this, he maintained, is clear from Titus 2:5, where women are instructed to be "self-controlled, chaste, good managers of the household, kind and submissive to their husbands so that the word of God may not be discredited." Literalists are divided about what to do if scripture does not cover particular situations. Can Buddhist monks use paper money? If scripture is silent on the matter, can someone use a computer, train to be an astronaut, or play professional football? Some literalists would answer positively, while others would argue that these activities are forbidden because they are not sanctioned by scripture.

Those religious practitioners across traditions who recognize that the language of scripture is figurative language developed alternative ways to interpret scripture. One such approach is scripture as **allegory**. Some early Christian commentators on the dietary laws in the Torah found a moral dimension to them; in addition to distinguishing between clean and unclean foods, these laws condemned gluttony. Some biblical texts, taken literally, seemed to compromise the belief that the biblical God is spirit; thus, God walking in the garden of Eden (Gen 3:8) or Moses' view of God's back are figurative, symbolic statements about divine presence. In a similar fashion, the duration of the flood in Genesis 6-9 is forty days, and the duration of Israel's wanderings in the desert is forty years. In both cases the "forty" is a figurative, not literal, expression. They are the equivalent of "as long as it took to achieve a purpose": the destruction of the world in one case, the death of the rebellious first generation of Israelites in the second.

This distinction between literal and figurative language exists in many cultures. When the French anthropologist Marcel Griaule asked Ogotemmeli how so many animals could stand together on the steps of the heavenly granary, he replied, "All this has to be said in words, but everything on the step is a symbol, symbolic antelopes, symbolic vultures, symbolic hyenas.... Any number of symbols can find room on a one-cubit step."[10]

While this interpretive method generally avoids the ingenuous assertions of literalism, it easily leads to **eisegesis**, that is, reading into the text meanings that are not present in it. For example, in Isaiah 7:12-16, the prophet Isaiah describes to King Ahaz of Jerusalem a sign that his God is giving him: "The young woman is with child and shall bear a son, and shall name him Immanuel."

In interpreting this passage figuratively, such early Christian writers as the evangelist Matthew turned the young woman into a virgin, identified her as Mary of Nazareth and her son as Jesus. Thus, they could claim that their Jewish scriptures pointed toward the birth of Jesus of Nazareth and that he realized the promises it contained. Later theologians took the interpretation an unlikely step further, maintaining that when Isaiah was preaching, he actually had Jesus of Nazareth in mind.

Another example of eisegesis is Augustine of Hippo's allegorical interpretation of the parable of the Good Samaritan mentioned above. Augustine finds God's plan of salvation hidden in the parable. The traveler is Adam, whom the devil (in the person of thieves) robs of his immortality. The Law of Moses cannot save him (the priest and the Levite who pass the wounded traveler by). Christ is the Samaritan who heals Adam's wounds (sin) and delivers him safely to the church (the inn). Augustine dealt with the figurative nature of the New Testament's language by tying it to the Christian theology he was constructing. His interpretation, however, is itself symbolic and multivalent. It reveals more about Augustine's theology than it does about the parable.

So far we have been dealing with Jewish and Christian scriptures. The question of authoritative interpretation of scripture is also an important concern in Islam. The Qur'an is the "rule of thumb" or principal text that governs rules of conduct about what is required, desirable, allowed, undesirable, and forbidden. All of Islamic life is ideally governed by its divinely ordained patterns. Muslims argue that what is consistent with or paralleled in the Qur'an is true, and what is at odds with it is false. When this principle is applied to Allah's revelation to prophet Moses and prophet Jesus, the passages in the Torah and the New Testament that are in accord with the Qur'an are true, and those not in accord with it are false. These deviations, however, result from mistranslations, misinterpretations, and other forms of human frailty, not from defects in divine revelation.

In Buddhism, the primary problem is how to deal with conflicting representations of what the Buddha taught. Buddha's primary goal was the liberation of others. Buddhists point out that he adapted his teachings on how to achieve this liberation to his students, emphasizing as needed good words, knowledge, devotion to Buddha. This observation accounts for some inconsistencies. To account for others, Buddhists use "four reliances" as guides for the correct interpretation of scripture:

1. The *dharma* (the truth in the text) is more important than the teacher,

2. The meaning of the text is more important than the literal letter of text,

3. The definitive teaching, the interpretation that conveys ultimate realities, is superior to the interpretable teaching, the interpretation that conveys superficial realities,

4. Scripture enables the individual to move beyond rational thought to a direct, intuitive knowledge of reality and one's own mind. Scripture is an instrument of enlightenment, not an end in itself.[11]

Once Buddhists have achieved enlightenment, they have no further use for their scriptures. In a sense, then, discrepancies and interpretations are of no real concern if the scriptures achieve their purpose.

INTERPRETING SCRIPTURE FROM OUTSIDE A TRADITION

Scholars have also developed methodologies to deal with the figurative, symbolic nature of religious languages and texts. These methodologies treat religious texts as cultural and literary artifacts, not as divine revelation, since that is a category beyond the scope of academic analysis. Two important analytical methods in use today are historical analysis (or the historical-critical method) and narrative analysis. In addition, other interpretive methods can be associated with each of these. Historical analysis, for example, has links to archaeology, source analysis, and redaction analysis. Narrative analysis has connections with **feminist hermeneutics** and gender analysis; it is also helpful in uncovering classist and racist agendas in the reading of texts. In the following discussion, we use examples from the Jewish and the Christian scriptures.

Historical Analysis

Historical analysis began during the Enlightenment. Scholars removed the Jewish and the Christian scriptures from their natural habitats, Jewish and Christian rituals, to study them as cultural and historical artifacts. Historical criticism asks questions about the origins of the text and tries to establish, when it can, the original version or versions. Many stories in the Bible were first told orally. Several versions developed, each with different details. Recall the discussion about the Warlpiri story and the Haudenosaunee creation story in chapter 1. If we read the story of the flood in Genesis 6-9, we may notice some inconsistencies. Historical analysis explains these inconsistencies as the result of an editor combining two separate versions of a flood story that may have already existed in written form; these versions may have themselves been based on non-Israelite material.[12] In a similar fashion, the two creation stories in Genesis 1-2 are assigned to two different literary traditions on the basis of vocabulary and structure; for example, the deity has the name God (*elohim*) in Genesis 1 and the name LORD God (*adonai elohim*) in Genesis 2-3.

This type of analysis also tries to establish the historical situation in which the oral text was composed or written down and the text's relationship to other nonbiblical material of the same period. Many scholars, for example, suggest that Genesis 2:4b-3:25 may have been written in the Jerusalem court of King Solomon, near the last half of the tenth century B.C.E. The writer may have been a court scribe, a royal employee charged with writing a national epic. Some elements in the narrative do suggest a royal setting. For example, the garden, set in Eden, is probably a royal enclosure which the human creature farms. The divine command carries a death penalty if broken just as a royal command would. In Genesis 3 (the sequel to Genesis 2), the LORD God says, presumably to a divine court, "See, the man has become like one of us, knowing good and evil" (v 22). Throughout this story, then, the author uses the highest political authority he knows, the royal court, as a metaphor for organizing both the divine world and the human world.

By the same token, the first story in Genesis (1:1-2:4a) may have been written five hundred years later, perhaps in Babylon. The writer may have been a prisoner of war, one of the educated upper class deported by the Babylonians during their siege against Jerusalem, 598-586 B.C.E. Perhaps he was a priest, concerned about boundaries and classifications, the separation of dissimilar things, the careful distinction between the human and the divine. Some scholars suggest that this narrative with its repetition of the antiphon, "And God saw that it was very good," may have also been used in Israel's worship, perhaps during the New Year's celebration which re-established the triumph of order over chaos. The narrative may also have been intended to mock such Babylonian gods as the moon or the sun because, in the Genesis myth, they are created by Israel's god and are under his control.[13]

Historical analysis, then, tries to determine what the original audience heard and understood, and it seeks the original meaning of the text. It contributes interesting and important information about the text. However, the claims it makes, such as the original meaning or even the date of the text, are often hypothetical; further, it sometimes assumes that the biblical texts, whether Old or New Testament, can function as sources of historical information about the development of ancient Israel or the life of Jesus of Nazareth. Its greatest failure is that it does not deal directly with the text itself; its interpretations are, at best, paraphrases. Like the human creature in Genesis 2, historical criticism requires a partner.

Literary Analysis

A complementary type of biblical interpretation is literary analysis. This interpretive method reads the text like a contemporary short story or novel, paying attention to character and plot, language and description. The individual text has a life of its own, separate from its author. The reader or interpreter plays a part in creating the meaning of a text. Thus, literary analysis argues that the text's original meaning, even if it could be recovered, should not be preferred to later readings. Texts can, in fact, have many meanings, as many meanings as there are readers.

The text represents a model of a world, a representation of value systems. In the process of unfolding, the story emphasizes some elements and disregards others. Some characters are present; others are invisible.

Some speak; others are silent. Some look; others are looked at. Through narrative analysis, we may explore these disparities of power; we uncover what has been hidden and speak what has been left unsaid. Because the narrative represents a value system, our task as readers and interpreters is to identify its elements and, if we wish, to relate them to the questions of values, doubts, beliefs, and apathy that make up our own worlds. In understanding the text, we see ourselves and our own world more clearly; in understanding our own world and ourselves, we see the text more clearly. Narrative analysis tries to reveal what texts may mean now. It acknowledges that the reading of texts is active and creative.

Reading Critically: A Case Study

You may be familiar with the creation myths that Judaism and Christianity share. You can find them in your Bible in Genesis 1:1-2:4a and Genesis 2:4b-25. These are two ancient and distinct narratives. While these myths were originally part of the Israelite religion, they have influenced the way mainline Jewish and Christian traditions view humanity, sexuality, gender, and ecology. This story is so familiar that to question its popular interpretation is to suggest that the "givens" of reality are untrue.

We are going to use narrative analysis to interpret these creation stories. Take some time to read the two texts. Write down differences between these texts, surface differences and thematic differences. What do you think is the most important thing created in each narrative? (Often in Hebrew narrative, the major episode of the plot appears near the conclusion of the story.) Also, how does each narrative create a world? In other words, what values and beliefs dominate, what power relations exist, what hierarchies structure society, how are the feminine and the masculine constructed? Do the two narratives create the same world? What elements are absent from these worlds? What roles do gender and sex play? What doubts does each story raise? What is the relationship between humanity and nature? What are the predominant images of God? What does it mean to be human in these worlds? There are many "right" answers to these questions; they are hidden in the details of the two stories. Reading a text is often like doing archaeology; hidden beneath the surface are new ideas, new ways of seeing. Each reading yields surprising results.

Genesis 2:4b-25

First, Genesis 2:4b-25. This story has been used to justify the subordination of women in Christian practice. Woman, after all, is created second and out of the earth creature's rib; later she leads her man to break the divine command because of her desire for the fruit of the tree of the knowledge of good and evil. Reading in a different direction, feminist interpreters, both women and men, point out that the woman's taking of this fruit is the first act of human independence and that it puts humans on a more equal footing with the divine.

At the beginning of the story, the universe is already in place, so the narrative focuses on human and animal life. God first shapes a clay figurine out of mud from a riverbank. This activity recalls the work of a potter. The deity gets dirty hands forming the clay figure. To give this figure life, God breathes his own breath into it. God then plants a garden, giving this new creature the task of cultivating and caring for it. The image of the deity shifts; God is a (wealthy?) landowner who provides the human creature, now a tenant farmer, with food in return for its labor. The command, which sets apart the tree of the knowledge of good and evil and carries with it a death penalty, suggests an imbalance of power. The privileged—whether deity, king, or landowner—control resources, including knowledge. Knowledge separates the "haves" from the "have-nots." It is also a key to power; armed with knowledge, tenant farmers may question, grow dissatisfied, protest. The narrative warns, however, that such knowledge is a double-edged sword; it brings power and hardship. Man and woman are forced out of the garden, away from security and sustenance; yet they now possess the knowledge to acquire such things for themselves. From this reading, Genesis 2:4b-25 creates a world of privilege in which the poor have a place as long as they obey their masters; the narrative only half-heartedly encourages resistance. It legitimates a social organization that privileges the powerful who control others through fear; a cherubim, flaming sword in hand, guards the way to the tree of life.

We can also read the narrative from the perspective of gender. God realizes something is wrong; the creature is alone. This "it is not good" contrasts with the litany of "and God saw how good it was" in the Genesis 1 story which we will look at in a moment. To remedy the situation, God creates again, out of the same clay that he had used for the human creature. This project, however, fails to find a suitable companion for the creature, even though it produces the animals of the earth. The creature apparently witnesses their creation and claims ownership of them by giving them appropriate names, thus demonstrating ownership and control. How does God know that being alone is not good for the creature? What does the creature think? Why does the creature and not God name the animals? Is God graciously sharing power with the creature? Does the creature have more affinity with the animal world than it does with the divine world? Such questions draw us into the narrative and guide our exploration.

The creation of humanity is only completed in the final scene of Genesis 2. The deity finally realizes that any suitable companion must be made of the same substance as the creature he first created. Thus, he puts the creature into a trance so he does not witness the mystery of this creation; he builds a companion for the creature out of its own bone. Now humanity is complete. The character who awakens is man; human sexuality has entered creation. He knows himself as man only when he recognizes the newly created human as woman. His cry of recognition—"This, at last, is bone of my bone and flesh of my flesh"—establishes identity and kinship with her. He recognizes sameness and correspondence in the woman. But what about the woman? What does she recognize in the man? Where is her voice? What is her cry?

The woman is a suitable, appropriate helper for the man; in light of the discussion above, "helper" does not mean "servant." It is a positive term, pointing to equality, not subordination. "Therefore a man leaves his father and his mother and clings to his wife, and they become one flesh" (Gen 2:24). This sexual-social relationship between woman and man re-creates the unity that the deity destroyed in his earlier search for a partner for the creature and overcomes the aloneness that God had noticed in 2:18. Other interpreters think the text is hopelessly androcentric. The description of woman as helper is put in God's mouth; he creates a partner with whom man can reproduce and create yet more workers to cultivate the soil. The word "helper" does not indicate woman's superiority, equality, or partnership with man, only her reproductive role.

However one understands "woman as helper," this story of creation ends with an affirmation of unity. The couple experience no shame in each other's presence, even though they are naked, because they know only their alikeness; they do not yet know that they are also different. We can argue that they experience this unity because each has accepted her/his place in the world. They do not ask troublesome questions; they accept everything as given. While this attitude benefits those in power, it numbs the imagination. The couple needs a question to shake off stupor, a nudge toward doubt. As we have already seen in our discussion of Genesis 3, the serpent provides both.

Genesis 1:1-2:4a

According to Genesis 1, we live in an ordered universe. There are carefully determined boundaries. Dry is separated from wet, light from darkness. As long as boundaries are maintained, there is order. The universe, however, is secular; it is not sacred. God created the universe; however, God is not part of the universe. He has taken himself out of it. The elements of the universe—sun, moon, and stars, for example—are exactly what they are; they are not manifestations of particular gods. In Genesis 1, humanity plays an important role. The second-to-last thing to be created, humanity alone, male and female, is created in the image of God. Male and female alone represent the deity in the universe and together receive the tasks of governance and ordering. They are empowered to continue creation by procreating and filling the earth. Male and female share this task equally.

Their creation, however, is not the final task God accomplishes. On the seventh day, this deity rests. In the logic of the narrative he can do that and expect order to continue, because he has set up male and female as his active representatives in the universe. Notice that creation here is good and delights the creator: God saw how good it was (Gen 1:4, 12, 18, 21, 24, 31). There is no mention of evil or sin, no suggestion that materiality, the human body, or human sexuality is in any way opposed to God, even though they are not God.

The orderly universe acts as a metaphor for ordered social living. Division and separation are ways of controlling disorder and turmoil. For members of the Jewish tradition, whose myth this is, this motif of separation and division governs many aspects of their lives: the foods they eat and their combinations, the way they arrange their kitchens, the rhythms of their week and their annual festivals. The myth also confers on them part of their identity as Jews; as images of their God in the world, they are charged with maintaining order in the world by observing the Sabbath in imitation of God who also rests on that day.

This narrative invites us to affirm the beauty of order, the goodness of the creation, the value of body and matter, the equality of male and female. It suggests that in managing and governing our own worlds we may hear echoes of mystery's creative word.

THINKING WITH SCRIPTURES

For many pages we have read about how different religious traditions interpret their scriptures. We have also looked at ways in which scholars of religion interpret texts. We saw that interpretation is necessary because the language of texts is figurative language. It is also necessary because the scriptures of individual traditions often contain contradictory texts or texts that challenge the presuppositions of the religion itself. Now would be a good time to apply some of the methods we have looked at.

Religious traditions often contain stories that challenge the main beliefs of the tradition. For example, the major storyline of the Tanak is presented in the book of Deuteronomy. In its simplest form, that storyline is "Obey the LORD and you will prosper [that is, you will enjoy a long prosperous life in the land with many blessings]." The opposite is also true: "Disregard the LORD and you will suffer the loss of the land along with every possible misfortune." The authors of Deuteronomy insist that Israel's God selected Israel as his own special people, promising to protect them from misfortune if they are faithful to him. Thus, if they suffer loss individually or collectively, they only have themselves to blame. One story challenges this view; the story is about the good man Job who keeps the Lord's commands faithfully.

The book is unsettling, for it presents a God who seems to care no more for his human creatures than he does for the animals who roam the wild. It challenges Deuteronomy's simplistic formula and suggests that there is little correlation between one's behavior and what happens in one's life. It is also challenging, for it models a commitment to God and to right living that expects no reward or blessing except the relationship itself.

Through history, people have sought explanations and understanding to resolve the paradox. Like Archibald MacLeish's modern J.B., they bellow, "What I can't bear is the blindness. If I only knew why!"[14] Others, like Kurt Vonnegut in his novel *Cat's Cradle*, wonder whether suffering has any meaning or purpose.

Man blinked. "What is the purpose of this?" he asked politely. "Everything must have a purpose?" asked God. "Certainly," said man. "Then I leave it to you to think of one for all this," said God. And he went away.[15]

Thinking with Job

1. Read the first two chapters of the book of Job in the Tanak. What kind of a person is Job? According to Deuteronomy, what can Job expect in his life? What does the Satan (a member of God's court, charged with prosecuting God's causes; not the devil) have against Job? Why does God cooperate with the Satan?

2. How does Job respond to the losses he experiences? What advice does his wife give him? Why? What notion/s about woman might be at work here? Where is Job at the end of chapter 2?

3. Friends arrive to comfort Job. Like him, they are well educated in their religious tradition; these are teachers of wisdom. They are so overwhelmed with horror when they see him, they keep silent for a week. Why do they react this way?

4. Read through chapters 3-37, a series of speeches. How does Job describe his situation? What advice do his friends give him? How do they rationalize what has happened to him? What do you think of their responses? Whose interests do they serve? How does Job respond to his friends? What emotions does he experience? What does he demand?

5. God does eventually address Job in chapters 38-42. What is his speech about? What challenges does he lay down for Job? Does he do what Job has demanded?

6. How does God explain Job's losses? What is his opinion of Job's friends? What has happened to Job's wife? Now that you have read the whole book, re-evaluate her advice, independent of Job's response. What would have happened to Job had he followed her advice?

7. Think of a time of loss or grief in your life. What, if anything, helped you make sense of it? In a reflective essay, poem, or short story, articulate your understanding of suffering in life.

8. The psychologist Carl Jung wrote *Answer to Job*,[16] in which he argues that the God of Job is, in fact, God's shadow self. Thus God acts out his own doubts about himself and Job's loyalty to him by making Job suffer. Using poetry, song, or art, compose your own "answer" to Job's question about why he is suffering.

DOCTRINES AND CREEDS

By this time, the following statement should not come as a surprise. Religion is story, story acted in ritual, lived in ethical action, proclaimed in figurative language; a story with the potential as much for alienation as for reconciliation, renewing itself and being renewed in conversation with

MARYKNOLL PHOTO ARCHIVES

If I speak, my pain does not lessen; if I keep silent, how much of it disappears? God has worn me out, ... rushing at me like a warrior. My face glistens with my tears, shadows weight down my eyelids (Job 16:6-17; K. Nash, trans.).

history and culture. There are two final dialects of religious language to consider: doctrines and creeds. Both grow out of a community's reflection upon its story.

Doctrine

Doctrines (literally, teachings) are formal and authoritative statements which articulate a religion's beliefs. For example, the central Christian **kerygma** or teaching is the death and resurrection of Jesus the Christ (1 Cor 15:3-4); acceptance of this teaching marks a person Christian. In our discussion of scripture and canon, we saw that already in the first century, Christians were struggling to understand and interpret this central belief for their communities. Out of that struggle came the gospels and the letters, as well as numerous treatises and letters written by the earliest theologians. All these works, along with their interpretations, are part of the doctrine of the Christian church; they represent efforts to assist the church in remaining faithful to its central teaching. In the Roman Catholic church, this body of teaching and interpretation is called tradition.

Doctrines are rooted in history as well as in mystery; for Christians that mystery is Jesus the Christ, his words and deeds. Each doctrine articulates truth and meaning, but no doctrine exhausts either truth or meaning; thus new doctrines, in response to the recurring questions, may be formulated again and again. In each historical age, the community has the privilege and the responsibility to participate in the development of doctrine by bringing it into conversation with the experiences of individuals and with the insights of philosophy, psychology, literary theory, and science. Moreover, the language, thought patterns, and concerns of a particular community or historical era shape the language of doctrine.

This language is figurative language; it, too, requires interpretation and reformulation. Over the last two centuries, Christian theologians have reformulated doctrines on such topics as the sacraments of baptism and eucharist, the nature of the church, the role of the Spirit, grace. While one function of doctrine is to promote right thinking, a far more important function is the creation of a religious worldview. Christian doctrine, for example, establishes a world in which Christians may understand themselves in their relationship to the God of Jesus Christ and to each other.[17]

Creeds

The word "creed" derives from Latin *credo*, "to believe." However, the action of believing is more than an intellectual exercise. *Credo* also has the sense of committing one's heart or self to someone or something. A creed is a statement in verbal form of the faith of an individual or a community. By means of its creed, a religion both defines and teaches the beliefs its members must accept.

Miriam, a young Jewish woman, is studying with a rabbi to learn how to live a properly Jewish life. She describes some of the practices she has learned:

> In these small boxes are parts of the Torah. Two of them [Ex 13:1-10, 11-16) remind me about the Passover of the messenger of Death and the Exodus from Egypt and how the first born of animals and humans are consecrated to God. The other parts of the Torah (Dt 6:4-9; 11:13-21) make up the Shema. This states that our God is one and that we must obey his commands to receive blessings. My rabbi tells me that the Shema is Judaism's creed, its core; I recite it every morning. The tefillin that I put on my head and on my arm help me remember these events and these teachings which are so important to my people. They are slowly becoming important to me, too.

The recitation of the Shema, which articulates their belief that their God is one and is the only God, unites Jews throughout the world.

In a similar fashion Muslims also recite their creed, the *shahadah*,

"There is no God but Allah, and Muhammad is Allah's prophet," when they pray. The one ritual required of anyone who wishes to enter the Umma, the Islamic community, is the recitation of this creed. Buddhists identify the Four Noble Truths and the Eightfold Path as essential to the teachings of the Buddha; this material fits easily into the category of creed. As mentioned above, belief in the death and resurrection of Jesus the Christ is essential for Christians.

The earliest Christian creed was the simple affirmation, "Jesus Christ is Lord" (Phil 2:11). The questioning of candidates at baptism about Jesus, Father, and Spirit led to the development of a Trinitarian creed, with separate sections describing the saving work of Creator, Redeemer, and Sanctifier. These creeds sprang up all over the Christian world; the Apostles' Creed was based on one of the oldest such creeds used by the community in Rome.

A second important Christian creed is the Nicene Creed, adopted by the Council of Constantinople (381) and promulgated by the Council of Chalcedon (451). This creed is used by Catholics, Orthodox, and many Protestant denominations.

Thinking with Creeds

The Apostles' Creed

I believe in God, the Father almighty, creator of heaven and earth.

I believe in Jesus Christ, his only Son, our Lord. He was conceived by the power of the Holy Spirit and born of the Virgin Mary. He suffered under Pontius Pilate, was crucified, died, and was buried. He descended to the dead. On the third day he rose again. He ascended into heaven, and is seated at the right hand of the Father. He will come again to judge the living and the dead.

I believe in the Holy Spirit, the holy catholic Church, the communion of saints, the forgiveness of sins, the resurrection of the body, and the life everlasting. Amen.

The Nicene Creed

We believe in one God, the Father, the Almighty, maker of heaven and earth, of all that is, seen and unseen.

We believe in one Lord, Jesus Christ, the only Son of God, eternally begotten of the Father, God from God, Light from Light, true God from true God, begotten, not made, of one Being with the Father. Through him all things were made. For us and for our salvation he came down from heaven: by the power of the Holy Spirit he became incarnate from the Virgin Mary, and was made man. For our sake he was crucified under Pontius Pilate; he suffered death and was buried. On the third day he rose again in accordance with the Scriptures; he ascended into heaven and is seated at the right hand of the Father. He will come again in glory to judge the living and the dead, and his kingdom will have no end.

We believe in the Holy Spirit, the Lord, the giver of life, who proceeds from the Father and the Son. With the Father and the Son he is worshiped and glorified. He has spoken through the Prophets. We believe in one holy, catholic and apostolic Church. We acknowledge one baptism for the forgiveness of sins. We look for the resurrection of the dead, and the life of the world to come. Amen.

1. Along with your group, write a creed or faith statement to which you all can subscribe. Your creed does not have to be religious. You could construct a creed of basic beliefs which someone would have to affirm in order to become part of your learning group or your social group.
2. Go through each creed statement by statement. How does the Nicene Creed expand on statements in the Apostles' Creed?
3. Compare the statements in each creed with what we learn about Christian belief from the Gospel of Mark. What are the differences? How do you account for them?

CONCLUSION

In this section, we have grappled with the complexity and ambiguity of language. In the world of language, things are never as they appear. Most language, including language that we think is most objective and factual, is figurative; it is the model through which we experience ourselves and others. In many ways, language is like a computer simulation program. Students in an archaeology class may work through *Adventures in Fugawiland*[18]—constructing hypotheses, "excavating" sites, analyzing data, modifying assumptions, formulating a final report—without leaving their computer terminals. In an analogous fashion, we rely on language and its propensity for hyperbole, paradox, and ambiguity to build and inhabit worlds where we negotiate relationships and devise meanings.

Out of such language religious traditions create their own models for interaction with mystery. In myths of origin and destiny, parables, and stories of challenge, we experience both the ordering and the disordering aspects of power. Religious traditions also use art and architecture to order their worlds. Calligraphy and basket weaving are only two of the many artifacts that speak to us about the holy and assure us that order endures from one day to the next.

Narratives about the sacred are generally canonical, normative for belief and behavior. They are, however, holy only in relationship to a believing community. As we saw, there are many scriptures, many articulations of truth and meaning. No one formulation is intrinsically absolute or more accurate than the next. Every sacred story is "true." Its truth does not reside within the story, but within the lived experience of practitioners of the religious tradition. Its truth derives from personal experiences of the holy, from the manner in which we hear them. Paul Ricoeur has observed that "forgetfulness and restoration" characterize our relationship with scripture and symbol. We distance ourselves from sacred narratives when they do not resonate with our expectations or provide adequate answers to wrenching questions; we return to them with the humble realization that they are our best tools for re-creating order and remembering the holy.[19]

> When the great Rabbi Israel Baal-Shem-Tov saw misfortune threatening the Jews, it was his custom to go into a certain part of the forest to meditate. There he would light a fire, say a special prayer, and the miracle would be accomplished and the misfortune averted. Later, when his disciple, the celebrated Magid of Mezritch, had occasion for the same reason, to intercede with heaven, he would go to the same place in the forest and say: "Master of the Universe, listen! I do not know how to light the fire, but I am still able to say the prayer," and again the miracle would be accomplished. Still later, Rabbi Moshe-Leib of Sasov, in order to save his people once more, would go into the forest and say: "I do not know how to light the fire, I do not know the prayer, but I know the place and this must be sufficient." It was sufficient and the miracle was accomplished. Then it fell to Rabbi Israel of Rizhyn to overcome misfortune. Sitting in his armchair, his head in his hands, he spoke to God: "I am unable to light the fire and I do not know the prayer; I cannot even find the place in the forest. All I can do is to tell the story, and this must be sufficient." And it was sufficient.[20]

Religious traditions look within their sacred stories and scriptures to rediscover the path to the forest place and to remember the words that kindle holy fire. In this way, they re-create and maintain order.

The following part introduces the concept of religious change and development within the lives of individuals and communities. This change may sometimes occur as a dramatic reversal; it may also appear as the natural progression and development of one's life. Within religious communities changes herald renewed creativity and angry division. However, change occurs; whatever its consequences, it alters existing order and reinterprets foundational stories.

RESOURCES

Activities

1. Many contemporary theologians are using the life experiences of women as well as the customary practices and scriptures of their religious traditions to retell their communities' stories. Find examples of this in the work of African-American, Latina, Native American, U.S., and Asian theologians. Share your findings with your group or class; lead a discussion on how these interpretations may influence how different traditions understand the sacred and relate to it. Summarize the discussion in a short paper or post the summary in the class bulletin board and invite additional comments.

2. The scripture of a tradition often becomes the source of a group's prayers and hymns, even when that scripture is the scripture of the oppressor. Bereft of their indigenous African religions, slaves found comfort and hope in stories from the scriptures of their white owners. They claimed the stories that mirrored their own experiences of suffering and death, that nurtured their desires for freedom and release. Such stories became the basis for the spirituals. Find texts and recordings of these songs. How do they use the language of Christian scripture to interpret the slave experience? How does the slave experience interpret the scripture? Present your findings to the class, using multimedia if possible.

3. In the New Testament gospels there are four different accounts of the suffering and death of Jesus of Nazareth. Using a synopsis, list the differences in events and in details. Since each gospel presents its own unique interpretation of Jesus, what do the differences among the passion narratives contribute to each gospel's understanding of Jesus? You may wish to consult a good introductory text on the New Testament for an overview of the four differing presentations of Jesus.

4. Watch one of the segments of Bill Moyers's *Genesis: A Living Conversation.* Describe the participants' attitudes toward the book of Genesis. With your group, plan a similar discussion on some text in Genesis or another book of the Bible. Provide time for your classmates to react to your group's discussion and to add their own insights.

5. Select passages from the Qur'an , for example, Surah 15:16-48, 16:1-17 (Creation); Surah 2:28-27 (Adam, his Wife, and the Fall); Surah 4:1-10 (Women and Orphans). Read them carefully. What do you learn about the values of Islam from these few passages? Compose a letter to a Muslim friend in which you share what you have learned about Islam.

6. Read through the Gospel of Mark in the New Testament. Select a passage that interests you. Find three commentaries on the gospel. How do the authors of these commentaries discuss the passage? What method/s of interpretation do they use? What understandings and beliefs do they bring to the text? Which interpretation do you like best? Why?

7. Describe the creeds of Judaism, Islam, and Buddhism, the beliefs central to each tradition. You may need to consult some introductory texts to these religions. Then describe your understanding of creed in Christianity. You may wish to formulate your own creed. Compare it with the Apostles' Creed and the Nicene Creed. Explain the symbolic language of these creeds to a Buddhist friend.

Readings

Frederick M. Denny and Rodney L. Taylor. *The Holy Book in Comparative Perspective* (Columbia, SC: University of South Carolina Press, 1985). Critical essays on the scriptures of Judaism, Christianity, Latter Day Saints, Islam, Zoroastrianism, Hinduism, Buddhism, Confucianism, Taoism, and indigenous oral traditions (Sam Gill on Native American traditions).

David M. Gunn and Danna N. Fewell. *Narrative in the Hebrew Bible* (New York: Oxford University Press, 1993). In this literary analysis of Genesis–2 Kings of the Tanak, the authors discuss literary theory, character, and plot, as well as the construction of meaning and responsible reading. Extensive bibliography for each section of the text.

Stephen L. Harris. *Understanding the Bible* (Mountain View, CA: Mayfield Publishing, 1997). A substantive introduction to the Bible, historical-critical and theological in scope. Well illustrated; comprehensive glossary.

Carol A. Newsom and Sharon H. Ringe, eds. *The Women's Bible Commentary* (Louisville, KY: Westminster/John Knox, 1992). Contributors discuss texts and issues that touch women's lives within each biblical book. Also includes essays on women's lives in biblical times and on feminist hermeneutics (interpretation).

B. Stowasser. *Women in the Qur'an, Traditions, and Commentaries* (New York: Oxford Press, 1994). Excellent treatment of the status and role of women in the different levels of Islamic literature.

Robert E. Van Vorst. *Anthology of World Scriptures* (Belmont, CA: Wadsworth Publishing, 1997, 2nd ed.). Good introductory material on major world traditions and excerpts from most scriptures in the categories of teachings, ethics, ritual and worship, and organization.

Serenity Young. *An Anthology of Sacred Texts by and about Women* (New York: Crossroad, 1993). Wide-ranging selections of scriptures and other significant writings from Judaism, Christianity, Islam, Hinduism, Buddhism, Confucianism, Taoism, ancient European and Near Eastern religions, shamanism and indigenous religions, new religions of modern times.

Audiovisuals

Three Faces of Protestantism. Part of the *Long Search* series, this film, although dated, provides a good portrait of how a mainline Christian church in the suburbs, a fundamentalist Christian church in the Bible Belt, and a store-front African-American Pentecostalist church in the inner city interpret the same gospel.

The following videos are available from Films for the Humanities and Sciences, P. O. Box 2053, Princeton, NJ 08543-2053. 1-800-257-5126; custserv@films.com; http://www.films.com.

Genesis: A Living Conversation with PBS journalist Bill Moyers. A ten-part series. In each one-hour segment Moyers speaks with religious scholars, psychologists, theologians, academics, and performers about major themes in the book of Genesis; such as, God's image, temptation, the first murder, call and promise, deception, God wrestling, exile.

Testament: The Bible and History. A seven-part historical-critical approach to the Old and New Testaments from a Christian perspective. Provides a good view of the relationship between archaeology and the biblical text.

The Gospels on CD-ROM: The Scriptures in Art, Music and Text. This interactive program features textual comparisons, maps, music, and works of art related to the Christian gospels.

The Old Testament in Art. This seventy-five-minute video illustrates the narratives in the Old Testament and clarifies their metaphoric range.

Too Close to Heaven: The History of Gospel Music. This three-part series traces the two-hundred-year history of gospel music from black churches to the Civil Rights movement, to its influence on modern music.

NOTES

1. Another narrative (1 Chronicles through Nehemiah) offers a more idealized and hopeful reading of Israel's history. This narrative retells Israel's history up to the rebuilding of the Jerusalem Temple after the Babylonian exile and continues Israel's story under Persian (Ezra-Nehemiah) and then Greek rule (Daniel).

2. Robert E. Van Voorst, *Anthology of World Scriptures* (Belmont, CA: Wadsworth, 1994), 5. The discussion of scripture in the present chapter depends heavily on Van Voorst's book.

3. According to Eusebius, a fourth-century church historian, Papias (second century), identified the authors of canonical gospels in this way: Matthew the tax collector and one of the twelve apostles; John Mark, a companion of Paul for a time and a confidant of Peter; Luke, Paul's traveling companion in Acts of the Apostles; John, the beloved disciple and close associate of Jesus. Thus Mark and Luke, while not apostles, had authoritative sources in Peter and Paul.

4. For a clear, well-organized discussion of the synoptic problem, see Christopher M. Tuckett, "Synoptic Problem," in David Noel Freedman, ed., *The Anchor Bible Dictionary* (New York: Doubleday, 1992), 6:263-70.

5. Among these texts are the *Infancy Gospel of Thomas* (mid-second century) and *The Protoevangelium of James*. Supposedly authored by James, the brother of Jesus, *The Protoevangelium* is the source for legendary material about Mary, the mother of Jesus. It recounts, for example, that from the age of three she was raised by priests in the Jerusalem Temple until she was engaged to a much older Joseph, a widower with children, who acted as her guardian and respected her virginity. Texts of these and other noncanonical gospels are available on the WWW. See also Robert J. Miller, ed., *The Complete Gospels* (Annotated Scholars Version. Sonoma, CA: Polebridge Press, 1992).

6. This document is part of the "Nag Hammadi library," named for the Egyptian village near where it was found. It was attributed to "Didymos [the twin] Judas Thomas," sometimes identified as Jesus' twin brother. It now survives only in a Coptic translation. See Elaine Pagels, *The Gnostic Gospels* (New York: Randon House, 1979) and James M. Robinson, ed., *The Nag Hammadi Library* (San Francisco: Harper & Row, 1988).

7. Not all New Testament letters are addressed to local communities. The pastoral letters (1-2 Timothy and Titus) are about church structure and order; their audience was church leaders. The letters of James, 1-2 Peter, 1-3 John, and Jude are called catholic epistles; that is, they were intended for public reading in many different communities. The intended audience of the anonymous Letter to the Hebrews is unknown.

8. In 1740 Lodovico Antonio Muratori discovered this fragment, which bears his name, in Milan's Ambrosian library in a codex dating to the seventh or eighth century. The fragment contains only eighty-five lines and begins in midsentence.

9. This material includes the entirety of the books of Tobit, Judith, the Wisdom of Solomon, Sirach, Baruch, 1 and 2 Maccabees; additions to biblical books: the letter of Jeremiah; additions to the Greek version of Esther; Azariah's prayer and the Song of the Three Jews, Susanna, Bel and the Dragon (additions to the Greek version of the Book of Daniel).

10. Griaule, *Conversations with Ogotemmeli*, 37.

11. Roger Schmidt, *Exploring Religion* (Belmont, CA: Wadsworth Publishing, 1988), 220-22.

12. Archaeological excavations in Israel at Megiddo, a tenth century B.C.E. Israelite administrative center, recovered clay tablets containing a flood story very similar to the narrative in Genesis 6-9. Two other ancient non-Israelite versions of the story are also extant. See Stephen L. Harris, *Understanding the Bible* (Mountain View, CA: Mayfield, 1997), 84-85.

13. There are thematic and structural similarities between Genesis 1:1-2:4a and the Babylonian creation myth *Enuma Elish*. See Lawrence Boadt, *Reading the Old Testament* (New York: Paulist, 1984), 114–118.

14. Archibald MacLeish, *J.B.* (Boston: Houghton Mifflin, 1958), 108.

15. Kurt Vonnegut, Jr., *Cat's Cradle* (New York: Dell, 1965), 177.

16. Carl Jung, *Answer to Job* (Princeton, NJ: Princeton University Press, 1973).

17. This discussion depends heavily on Nancy C. Ring, "Doctrine" in Joseph A. Komonchak *et al.*, eds., *The New Dictionary of Theology* (Wilmington, DE: Michael Glazier, 1987), 291-293.

18. *Adventures in Fugawiland* (Mountain View, CA: Mayfield Publishing, 1996).

19. This discussion is based in part on Roger Schmidt, *Exploring Religion,* 2d edition (Belmont, CA: Wadsworth, 1988), 224-25.

20. Elie Wiesel, *The Gates of the Forest* (New York: Holt, Rinehart & Winston, 1966), preface.

PART IV

RELIGIOUS CHANGE

Through their symbolic processes, religions bring order to our lives, both personal and communal. They help us establish and maintain relationships. We often decide how to conduct our lives on the basis of religious teachings. Religious myths help us to understand our roles in our families, our communities, the natural environment, even the unfolding of history. Through ritual and storytelling we pass on our religious traditions to another generation. When we think about religion in these terms, we are describing it as a symbol system: a system, that is, of symbolic actions and symbolic narratives that help to maintain a particular worldview. To describe a religion in these terms is like looking at a snapshot; we can describe everything in the picture and how all the pictorial elements relate to one another at a particular moment. Scholars of religion label this approach to the study of patterns of religious thought and action *synchronic* (see pages 16-17).

A snapshot, however, is static; it does not allow us to see how time alters the individual elements of a snapshot or their relations to one another. If we imagine the study of religion as watching a movie, we will understand better that religion is not only a system, it is also a process. Since religions are embedded in human culture they are embedded in history; to omit this element is to ignore an important part of what it means to be human. Therefore, along with our synchronic study of religion we also want to include *diachronic* study of religion—study of the ways that patterns of religious thought and action change over time. This approach is important in the study of religious biography as well as in the study of religious communities.

Perhaps you have had the experience of returning to your hometown after an extended absence. Although friends and relatives who remain there have assured you over the years that nothing is changing, when you go back you find everything changed: your favorite stores gone, abandoned houses boarded up, apartment complexes under construction, even new highways leading out of town. For those who still live there, these changes have been so gradual that they were barely noticed, but for you the changes appear dramatic.

Or maybe you have returned to your elementary school years after graduation. Although the structure is physically the same, the building seems smaller and shabbier, the playground equipment is barely adequate, and the playing fields no longer stretch on forever as they once seemed to do. Because you have changed and matured, you see this environment with new eyes.

We live in a world that is constantly changing. As we move through this world, we both instigate change and are affected by change. In this uncertain world people frequently cling to their religious traditions as insurance against instability. Christians, for example, who call on God as "the one who was, and is, and is to come" expect their religious communities and practices to endure without appreciable change throughout their lives and beyond. Religion, however, is a human institution, subject to the same forces of change as other human institutions.

In chapter 8 we will consider the process of change in the lives of individuals. Some persons undergo personal crises and leave the practices and beliefs of their youth for new modes of religious action and knowledge. A person who has been an indifferent practitioner of the faith of his or her youth may become a fervent and influential promoter of the faith. In other cases, religious change may happen more slowly, as a matter of development over a lifetime.

Chapter 9 investigates the process of religious change in communities. Thinking about religion (particularly our *own* religions) in terms of process may provoke feelings of insecurity and uncertainty. Indeed, as we will see, living through a period of religious change can be challenging, confusing, or even alienating. Often religious change occurs so subtly that members of a community are barely aware of the process of change. In other cases communities deliberately decide to adopt new beliefs or practices. Such changes in the structure of religious thought and habit often accompany shifting social, political, and economic contexts.

Finally, we will focus on the effects of religious change. Does such change inhibit or promote human flourishing? The answer, of course, is that depending on the circumstances, change can be harmful or beneficial. However, even when a community experiences change as a breath of fresh air, some individuals within that community may resist it. An experience of change that enables a community to function more fully in the world may nonetheless alienate members within that community.

Chapter 8

Personal Religious Change

Christians remember the words of the apostle Paul to the first-century Christians in Corinth, "When I was a child, I spoke like a child, I thought like a child, I reasoned like a child; when I became an adult, I put an end to childish ways" (1 Cor 13:11). He implies that the present knowledge of mature Christians is childlike when compared to the knowledge God will reveal at the end of time. "For now we see in a mirror, dimly, but then we will see face to face. Now I know only in part; then I will know fully, even as I have been fully known" (1 Cor 13:12). These words evoke the spectrum of change that is possible in the lives of religiously observant persons. In the life of an individual, religious change may occur almost as a natural process, part of maturing from infancy through childhood to young adulthood; the process of religious change continues in adulthood as an individual moves through various life crises and stages of maturity. For Christians, however, the notion of religious change is not confined to an organic process, but holds the potential for ultimate transformation at the finale of all things—"in a moment, in the twinkling of an eye, at the last trumpet. For the trumpet will sound, and the dead will be raised imperishable, and we will all be changed" (1 Cor 15:52). Thus, for Christians, the notion of religious change has theological importance, for it implies God's ongoing work of bringing creation to fulfillment.

As we consider religious change in the lives of individuals, we will encounter examples both of gradual maturation and of sudden conversion and drastic changes in life. We can see these as two patterns of religious change (growth and conversion), yet each person's biography offers a unique story of change. A woman may have an experience of enlightenment or conversion whose significance she understands more deeply as the years pass; a man may live a life of quiet unfolding of faithfulness, yet welcome moments of keener awareness of God's presence.

Furthermore, not all personal religious change tends toward heightened faith or closer observance. A man whose ties to family and childhood community diminish over time may find that his faith is also gradually eroding in the absence of external structures to support it. A woman may confront catastrophic personal loss or illness only to realize that she can no longer believe that this chaotic and frightening world is in the hands of a loving God.

PERSONAL RELIGIOUS CHANGE AS DEVELOPMENT

For some religious traditions, the notion of a lifelong maturing into one's tradition is valued far more than the experience of a conversion that causes a break with a personal or communal past. In the Confucian tradition which has historically been important in China, the notion of the good life includes an education in virtue that begins in the cradle and extends to the grave. Confucius (551-479 B.C.E.), remembered as the founder of the Confucian tradition, passed on to his many students his understanding of the principles of the good life. The goal of the Confucian life is to learn to be fully human, a goal that is always just beyond the grasp of the wise man. According to the Confucian idea of selfhood, a person is not a free-standing individual; a person, a self, represents the intersection of relationships. Most classical Confucian texts focus on the roles of men. A man sees himself as a son, a brother, a friend, and a loyal subject of the state. As Confucius humbly said:

> There are four things in the Way of the profound person, none of which I have been able to do. To serve my father as I would expect my son to serve me; that I have not been able to do. To serve my ruler as I would expect my ministers to serve me; that I have not been able to do. To serve my elder brother as I would expect my younger brother to serve me; that I have not been able to do. To be the first to treat friends as I would expect them to treat me; that I have not been able to do.[1]

An emphasis on conversion is foreign to the Confucian tradition. An intense experience that might cause a person to re-evaluate or even to renounce former ties to family and community would betray the Confucian ideal of *jen*. *Jen* is the highest Confucian virtue; no single English word offers a satisfactory translation. We could translate *jen* as love, or as human-heartedness; it implies both empathy and self-respect, an appreciation for the dignity of humanity. A man does not achieve *jen* by shedding his earlier ways; rather, personal religious change in the Confucian tradition involves a painstaking education and detailed attention to ritual from youth. One Confucian tradition invites the eldest grandson to take the most honored seat, even when he is a young boy. This is the seat of the deceased ancestors. When the boy is thus seated, the older men of the family bow before him because he represents their departed fathers and grandfathers. The boy learns what it is like to receive honor and respect, and so he finds it easier to show due honor and respect toward others. In this and other ways, he cultivates *jen*. As an old man, a Confucian would not want to describe his life as a series of new beginnings and fresh starts. Rather, the Confucian views his life as a careful cultivation of an original virtue, a virtue that encompasses his dutiful attention to others in his personal network of relationships and his equally dutiful acceptance of the respect and honor due to him. Development, not conversion, is the model for personal religious change in the Confucian tradition.

Although the notions of conversion and repentance are central to many Christian biographies, other Christians live lives that are marked more by continuity than by discontinuity. Religious change occurs along with other kinds of emotional, moral, and intellectual development. For example, a Christian child who grows up in a stable home situation may have little reason to struggle with the question of how to reconcile the reality of human suffering with belief in a loving and powerful deity. As the child grows to adulthood, however, she will surely confront some of the evils of the world: lives lost to warfare and random violence, the untimely death of a parent, the injustices suffered by children living in poverty, the random assaults of cancer or AIDS. She learns that belief in God and faithfulness to religious demands will not protect her or those she loves from pain or loss. If she is open to growth in her faith life, she may still pray the prayers of her youth, but she will pray them in a new way. As a child she may have heard the words of the twenty-third psalm as a promise of safety from all harm: "Even though I walk through the darkest valley,/I fear no evil;/for you are with me" (v 4). As an adult who has walked through the dark valleys of job loss, death of loved ones, and human cruelty, she will understand that the promise of these verses is not that God will protect her from all harm, but rather that God will be with her in moments of crisis. In such a life religious change does not take place through moments of dramatic conversion; rather, religious change is manifest in gradual insights, deepening faith, and eventually a mature religious vision.

The life of St. Catherine of Siena (1347-1380) is a story of one woman's intellectual, moral, and spiritual development. Although Catherine had visions and other intense religious experiences, she never underwent a major conversion experience in which she dramatically renounced her earlier ways to follow a new path. Rather, her mature spiritual writings represent the culmination of her lifelong faith. As a young girl she had her first vision in which a radiant Jesus smiled at her. On another occasion she prayed to the Virgin Mary that she might enter into a mystical marriage with Jesus. She then had a vision in which Mary and Jesus appeared to her, and she received a ring from Jesus marking

MARY N. MACDONALD

Statue of Catherine of Siena with the Vatican in background.

her as his bride. Catherine's family did not approve of her religiosity; they wanted her to marry, and they exerted pressure on her to do so. However, she persisted in her personal ascetic practices, denying herself both luxuries and what others would think of as necessities; she was finally accepted as a Dominican tertiary. That is, she affiliated herself with the Dominican order although she did not formally become a nun. Only then did she have the opportunity to learn to read. She came to believe that God wanted her to take an active public role that included preaching. As a woman assuming such an unusual role, she became a controversial figure. Her personal prayer life included a variety of mystical experiences; in her public role she even influenced Pope Gregory XI in his decision to return from Avignon to Rome.

Although she spent her young life secluded in her parents' home, she ultimately traveled to Rome where she recorded her visions and served as an advisor to Pope Urban VI. Catherine was one of the most influential women in medieval Europe, and her story includes her dramatic rise from conventional beginnings into the confidence of the pope. Although she died at the young age of thirty-three, her writings are marked by rare spiritual maturity. In Catherine's story, religious change appears not as renunciation of former ways accompanying a dramatic conversion, but as a deepening of an intense personal faith she already enjoyed in her childhood.

PERSONAL RELIGIOUS CHANGE AS CONVERSION

In the lives of individuals religious change can follow a developmental model, or it can redirect the course of a person's life. At the turn of the century, the pioneering psychologist William James wrote a book called *Varieties of Religious Experience.* This volume was one of the first scholarly treatments to break away from theological concerns and to examine religion as a human institution. James's treatment of the experience of conversion has been especially influential:

To be converted, to be regenerated, to receive grace, to experience religion, to gain an assurance, are so many phrases which denote the process, gradual or sudden, by which a self hitherto divided, and consciously wrong, inferior and unhappy, becomes unified and consciously right, superior and happy, in consequence of its firmer hold upon religious realities. This at least is what conversion signifies in general terms, whether or not we believe that a direct divine operation is needed to bring such a moral change about.[2]

James's insights into the character of religious conversion remain important in the contemporary study of religion. We will rely on his framework as we analyze a variety of stories of conversion. Many cases of conversion experiences substantiate his claims, although there are certainly exceptions. For example, people who undergo a conversion experience often live first through a period of difficulty or even despair, a period of an "unhappy self"; however, as we will see, such unhappiness does not seem to be a necessary first step in the conversion process. While we may notice typical features in every story of conversion, each story is ultimately unique.

The Latin author Apuleius offers a fanciful but insightful look at the process of conversion in his novel *The Golden Ass*. Apuleius was born in northern Africa, probably around 123 C.E. The protagonist of his novel is a character named Lucius, whose misfortune leads him into a series of minor comic mishaps—and then he is transformed into a donkey. As a donkey he endures beatings, a variety of indignities, and brushes with death. Just when he is in greatest despair, he has a vision of the goddess Isis, who tells him the simple steps that he must take to be restored to human form. Scholars believe that Apuleius's novel, based on an already popular tale, vividly symbolizes his own experience of conversion to the Isis cult. Such experiences of conversion to the Isis cult seem to have been common in the Roman empire. Originally an Egyptian goddess, Isis and her cult became wildly popular during the imperial period of Roman history.

Apuleius's novel illustrates several of William James's key points about conversion. First, a man who turns into a donkey aptly symbolizes a divided and unhappy self in desperate search of unification. Second, the conversion can be understood as both gradual and sudden. Although there is an obvious moment of conversion when Lucius is finally restored to human form and gratefully acknowledges Isis's role in his healing, he has been seeking a means out of his predicament for some time. Furthermore, even after he comes to believe in Isis's power, he spends a prolonged period of initiation into various levels of the cult, achieving a greater understanding of the goddess and a feeling of great intimacy with her.

Apuleius's description of the restoration of Lucius to human form symbolizes the feeling of regeneration that is typical of conversion. In this excerpt, the donkey Lucius is following Isis's instructions to join the high priest in a religious procession, and to eat the garland of roses he is carrying.

My bestial features faded away, the rough hair fell from my body, my sagging paunch tightened, my hind hooves separated into feet and toes, my fore hooves now no longer served only for walking upon, but were restored, as hands, to my human uses. Then my neck shrank, my face and head rounded, my great hard teeth shrank to their proper size, my long ears shortened, and my tail which had been my worst shame vanished altogether.

A gasp of wonder went up and the priests, aware that the miracle corresponded with the High Priest's vision of the Great Goddess, lifted their hands to Heaven and with one voice applauded the blessing which she had vouchsafed me: this swift restoration to my proper shape.

When I saw what had happened to me I stood rooted to the ground with astonishment and could not speak for a long while, my mind unable to cope with so great and sudden a joy. I could find no words good enough to thank the Goddess for her extraordinary loving-kindness. But the High Priest, who had been informed by her of all my miseries, though himself taken aback by the weird sight, gave orders in dumb-show that I should be lent a linen garment to cover me; for as soon as I regained my human shape, I had naturally done what any naked man would do—pressed my knees closely together and put both my hands down to screen my private parts. Someone quickly took off his upper robe and covered me with it, after which the High Priest gazed benignly at me, still wondering at my perfectly human appearance.

The divided self is thus unified; the unhappy soul rejoices at its redeemer. A new life begins for Lucius. He desires only to serve the goddess who has rescued him from his dismal fate. Although Lucius's conversion was sudden, he continues to grow gradually in his understanding and appreciation of Isis. He fasts in preparation for his official initiation into the cult, which we could view as a time of ritual conversion to following Isis. In this excerpt Lucius hints at the drama of the ritual:

However, not wishing to leave you, if you are religiously inclined, in a state of tortured suspense, I will record as much as I may lawfully record for the uninitiated, but only on condition that you believe it. *I approached the very gates of death and set one foot on Proserpine's threshold, yet was permitted to return, rapt through all the elements. At midnight I saw the sun shining as if it were noon; I entered the presence of the gods of the underworld and the gods of the upper-world, stood near and worshipped them.*

Well, now you have heard what happened, but I fear you are still none the wiser.

The solemn rites ended at dawn and I emerged from the sanctuary wearing twelve different stoles, certainly a most sacred costume but one that there can be no harm in mentioning. . . .

The curtains were pulled aside and I was suddenly exposed to the gaze of the crowd, as when a statue is unveiled, dressed like the sun. That day was the happiest of my initiation, and I celebrated it as my birthday with a cheerful banquet at which all my friends were present."[3]

The story of the apostle Paul is an archetype for later Christian stories of conversion. Saul (whose name was later changed to Paul) was a **Pharisee,** a Jew committed to strict observance of the law of Moses. He was also an archenemy of the earliest Christian community. According to the Acts of the Apostles, he was present at and approved of the stoning of the first Christian martyr, Stephen. We read in Paul's letter to the Galatian Christian community his own recollections of those days: "You have heard, no doubt, of my earlier life in Judaism. I was violently persecuting the church of God and was trying to destroy it" (Gal 1:13). Acts of the Apostles supplies the famous story of his moment of conversion (Acts 9:1-19; 22:6-16; 26:12-18). Saul was traveling to Damascus with some companions on a mission against members of the church who resided there. A bright heavenly light unexpectedly came over him, knocking him to the ground: "[He] heard a voice saying to him, 'Saul, Saul, why do you persecute me?' He asked, 'Who are you, Lord?' The reply came, 'I am Jesus, whom you are persecuting'" (Acts 9:4b-5). Under the direction of the voice a temporarily blinded Saul continued to Damascus, where a Christian disciple named Ananias healed him of his blindness. Saul was baptized and became the greatest of the early Christian missionaries to the Gentiles. In his own writings Paul does not offer anything like this vivid story of conversion. He writes simply that "God, who had set me apart before I was born and called me through his grace, was pleased to reveal his son to me, so that I might proclaim him among the Gentiles" (Gal 1:15-16).

What is particularly important to later Christians in Paul's call is its suddenness and completeness. The Pharisees had a special commitment to observance of the Torah, or Jewish law. As a Pharisaic Jew, Paul perceived himself as completely in the right by trying to destroy the new religious movement of Christianity. Paul turns (or is turned) 180 degrees to promote this very church. He writes to the Philippians words that express a sense of loss over the end of his former way of life, a loss that is more than compensated by the riches of his new way of life:

> Yet whatever gains I had, these I have come to regard as loss because of Christ. More than that, I regard everything as loss because of the surpassing value of knowing Christ Jesus my Lord. For his sake I have suffered the loss of all things, and I regard them as rubbish, in order that I may gain Christ.... (Phil 3:7-8)

These words have influenced subsequent generations of new Christians, strengthening them to leave behind their "old lives" for "new lives" in Christ. In the words of a popular hymn,

> Amazing grace, how sweet the sound
> that saved a wretch like me.
> I once was lost, but now am found,
> was blind, but now I see.

In Paul's generation all Christians were in fact converts, since Christianity had not existed in the previous generation. Centuries would pass before infant baptism was commonly accepted. Paul did not view conversion to Christianity as an individualistic, solitary experience. In his understanding, being a Christian meant belonging to the community, the body of Christ. Therefore, conversion was not only cognitive, coming to hold a new set of beliefs; conversion also entailed a new identity as a member of the Christian community. He links the conversion experience to baptism into the community: "As many of you as were baptized into Christ have clothed yourselves with Christ. There is no longer Jew or Greek, there is no longer slave or free, there is no longer male and female; for all of you are one in Christ Jesus" (Gal 3:27-28).

Thinking about Personal Religious Change

These questions ask you to think about the process of change in the religious faith and practice of individuals. You might address these questions to someone you know who is comfortable talking about his or her religious autobiography, or you might prefer to think through these questions with respect to your own life.

Questions to address to the person being interviewed, or to answer yourself:

In what ways have your religious *beliefs* changed in the past ten years? in the past twenty years? since childhood?

In what ways have your religious *practices* changed in the past ten years? in the past twenty years? since childhood?

Did these changes occur gradually or rapidly?

Would you describe these changes as major or minor?

What kinds of continuities link your religious beliefs and practices as a child and as an adult?

Would you categorize your religious autobiography as a story of growth, a story of conversion, or a story of growth *and* conversion? Or is your religious autobiography a story of erosion or sudden loss of faith?

An early Christian legend tells the story of a young woman named Thecla whom Paul converts to Christianity. Thecla is engaged to be married, but when she hears Paul preach she decides to give up her marriage plans so that she may fully live out a Christian calling. Her fiancé and her mother denounce her publicly. Despite opposition, she persists in her newly found path and is sentenced to the gladiatorial arena. In the full sight of the crowd, she baptizes herself in a ditch of water. Miraculously, the beasts fight on her side rather than against her; she is finally saved thanks to the intervention of a wealthy woman named Tryphaena who has befriended her. Thecla converts Tryphaena and the majority of her female slaves to Christianity, but she wants to rejoin Paul. She dresses herself in men's clothing and finds Paul, who at last blesses her teaching mission. Although most (if not all) elements of Thecla's story are legendary, we can see several aspects of Paul's influence on the tale. When Thecla chooses to wear men's clothing she is living in the sphere defined by Paul in Galatians: for those who are in Christ, there is no division between male and female. New clothing also symbolizes the new life on which she has embarked. (Note that in Apuleius's fable Lucius's initiation into the Isis cult culminates in his appearance in special clothing, the twelve stoles.) Furthermore, Thecla's conversion is linked with the conversion of a number of other women, notably Tryphaena and her slaves. Although her conversion means the loss of her family, particularly her mother, she gains a new family: Tryphaena, Paul, and the other Christians.

Another important story of conversion in Christian antiquity comes to us from the *Confessions* of Augustine. Augustine (354-430) spent his youth seeking meaning and truth. In his various searches he exemplified what we recognize from William James as the divided consciousness, the unhappy soul. He sought consolation in sexual relationships and in philosophy—"Being in love with love I looked for something to love" (III.1). He established a long-term relationship with a woman, whose name he does not record, who bore him a son; he fell under the intellectual sway of a dualistic philosophy called Manichaeism. However, none of this satisfied him. In his *Confessions* he records his struggles as he tries simultaneously to hold on to his old ways and to begin anew as a Christian: "I hesitated to die to death and to live to life; inveterate evil had more power over me than the novelty of good, and as that very moment of time in which I was to become something else drew nearer and nearer, it struck me with more and more horror" (VIII.12). However, the moment finally came in which he was "to become something else." In a moment of anguish he heard a child's voice singing to him, "Take it and read it." He picked up the Bible and began to read, chancing upon a passage that convinced him that he would have the strength to follow through in his new way of life: "[I]t was as though my heart was filled with a light of confidence and all the shadows of my doubt were swept away" (VIII.12). A lifetime of searching had culminated in a conversion that at last brought him clarity, security, and peace.

In the *Confessions* Augustine provides a classic example of William James's tortured soul seeking relief.

> This was just what I longed for myself, but I was held back, and I was held back not by fetters put on me by someone else, but by the iron bondage of my own will. The enemy held my will and made a chain out of it and bound me with it. From a perverse will came lust, and slavery to lust became a habit, and the

habit, being constantly yielded to, became a necessity. These were like links, hanging each to each (which is why I called it a chain), and they held me fast in a hard slavery. And the new will which I was beginning to have and which urged me to worship you in freedom and to enjoy you, God, the only certain joy, was not yet strong enough to overpower the old will which by its oldness had grown hard in me. So my two wills, one old, one new, one carnal, one spiritual, were in conflict, and they wasted my soul by their discord (VIII.5).

Francis of Assisi (1182-1226), the son of a prosperous businessman, experienced a conversion that led him into a life of service to the poor and the founding of major religious orders for men and women. As a youth Francis led a carefree life, spending his father's money and running with a fast crowd. Even before the dramatic moment of his conversion, however, he had begun to search for greater meaning in his life. After a serious illness he began to show signs of what William James would call a "divided and unhappy self." He sought solitude for prayer and had visions he did not yet understand. Once when he was praying in a decaying old church he heard a voice say from the cross, "Francis, repair my house which is falling into ruin." Francis assumed that the voice was referring to the physical decay of the small church in which he was praying. Only after his conversion did he come to believe that God was calling him to the work of healing the corruption and spiritual ruin that characterized the excesses of the medieval church. He began to dress in the clothes of the poor, and donated the proceeds of his father's business to the poor. According to legend, this behavior led to the dramatic scene of his conversion. His father summoned him to court in the presence of the bishop of Assisi to account for the money he had transferred from the family business to the poor. Francis responded by renouncing his family ties, stripping himself and returning his clothes to his father in a symbolic severance of his connections. From that day forward, Francis was committed to forming a community who would

St. Francis, from a plaque based on the Giotto frescoes in Assisi.

live together in poverty to witness to the gospel through service to the poor. Although this famous moment of regeneration may have seemed sudden to Francis's father and the bishop of Assisi, in fact Francis's conversion had been a gradual one, as he sought various ways to ease his troubled soul.

Augustine and Francis provide us with stories of two men with misspent youths whose dramatic conversions led to lives of devotion to God's will. We find a more contemporary example of such a conversion in *The Autobiography of Malcolm X* (as told to Alex Haley). In Malcolm X's own words, as a young man he lived "like a predatory animal," supporting himself with a habit of robbery, and living for a nightlife that centered on drugs. The police apprehended him when he took a stolen watch for repair. Reflecting on his life story years later, Malcolm said:

> I want to say before I go on that I have never previously told anyone my sordid past in detail. I haven't done it now to sound as though I might be proud of how bad, how evil, I was. . . .
>
> [T]he full story is the best way that I know to have it seen, and understood, that I had sunk to the very bottom of the American white man's society when—soon now, in prison—I found Allah and the religion of Islam and it completely transformed my life.

While in prison Malcolm began to receive letters from family members who had joined Elijah Muhammad's Nation of Islam, a Black American branch of Islam. Although he at first resisted their message, prison afforded him much time both to educate himself and to contemplate the direction of his life. At the urging of his family, he wrote to Elijah Muhammad, whose prompt and warm response encouraged him to go forward. He began praying to Allah. Still in prison, he became a Muslim; when he left prison, his family helped him become still further involved with the Nation of Islam, until he became a leader in the movement.

The dramatic conversion from savvy criminal to devout Muslim was not the only transformation of Malcolm's life. Tension between Elijah Muhammad and Malcolm developed over the years, and eventually Elijah Muhammad ousted him from the Nation of Islam movement. At the same time, Malcolm had a yearning to become more involved with Islam worldwide. The Nation of Islam taught that the white man was the devil, not to be trusted under any circumstances. Malcolm's prominence (or notoriety) had brought him into contact with some white people who were supportive of him, and who did not seem to embody the devil. He also had begun to realize that the religious practices of the Nation of Islam were out of step with the practices of other Muslims:

> At one or another college or university, usually in the informal gatherings after I had spoken, perhaps a dozen generally white-complexioned people would come up to me, identifying them-

Malcolm X, a poster for a rally in Harlem.

selves as Arabian, Middle Eastern or North African Muslims. . . .
They had said to me that, my white-indicting statements not
withstanding, they felt that I was sincere in considering myself a
Muslim—and they felt if I was exposed to what they always
called "true Islam," I would "understand it, and embrace it."

When he finally turned to the world of orthodox Islam for instruction, he
found that the Muslim community was eager to welcome him as one of
their own.

He decided to make the *hajj,* one of the Five Pillars of Islam, the pilgrimage to Mecca that all Muslims are required to make at least once in
their lives. His experience was transformative. He found himself in the
company of Muslims from around the world, of every racial and ethnic
background, whom he discovered to be brothers and sisters in their submission to Allah. Prominent Muslims heard that he was on the *hajj* and
offered him hospitality and support. On the *hajj* he found himself treated
with the honor and respect long denied him in his native land; what
was even more important to him was the recognition that all who were
on the *hajj* accorded one another such honor and respect. From that time
forward, he endeavored to live as a Muslim according to the classical
traditions. Furthermore, although he was still damning in his indictment
of white America, he no longer subscribed to the notion that "the white
man is the devil." He came to believe that it was not the complexion or
genetic make-up of white people that was problematic, but their attitudes
and actions toward African-American and other people not of European
descent.

On February 21, 1965, less than a year after returning from the *hajj* a changed man, Malcolm X arrived at the Audubon Ballroom in Harlem to speak. He was assassinated there. Malcolm X did not survive long enough to build on the momentum of the *hajj*. However, his story exemplifies the power of conversion in the individual life.

Actually, Islam teaches that the experience we have been calling "conversion" is better identified as a kind of homecoming. According to Islam, everyone is born Muslim: each baby submits to Allah. However, as our personalities develop, the stubbornness of the human person emerges; we find ways to resist Allah's will for us, which is to acknowledge and submit ourselves to him. When adults turn in submission to Allah, they are really coming home, returning to the state into which all are born. The transition that Malcolm X began on the *hajj* was an intensification of his existing faith, part of a long journey of Islamic "homecoming" that dominated his adult life.

DEVELOPMENT AND CONVERSION IN AN INDIVIDUAL LIFE

Although we are trying to distinguish personal religious change as *development* from personal religious change as *conversion*, this is often a difficult distinction to maintain. The life of the martyred archbishop Oscar Romero of El Salvador has often been narrated as the story of a mature and public conversion, yet Romero himself resisted this version of his life. Romero was a native of El Salvador, a man of humble origins whose piety had directed him early in life to the priesthood. He was best known as a traditionalist who was resistant to the winds of change in the Latin American church when he was ordained bishop in 1970, a few years after **Vatican II** (a Roman Catholic church council that encouraged large-scale liberalization in Catholic teaching and practice). It was a vibrant and exciting time for the Latin American church. New ministries for lay people, religious women and men, and clergy brought the church into closer contact with the daily struggles and longings of the poorest sectors of society. Romero was, at most, lukewarm toward these innovative ministries. As editor of the archdiocesan newspaper, Romero published attacks on progressive efforts of the church. He helped oust the Jesuits from the archdiocesan seminary, on the grounds that they were moving too radically from traditional ways; he took over as rector of the seminary. When confronted with human rights atrocities, including the brutal murder of members of his diocese by members of national security forces, he was unwilling to hold national leaders accountable for the actions of their own forces. When Romero was installed as archbishop of San Salvador in early 1977, his appointment was applauded by the most conservative sectors of the Salvadoran church, government, and society.

Within weeks of becoming archbishop, a number of incidents forced Romero to begin to rethink his earlier assumptions. After the murder of a

MARYKNOLL PHOTO LIBRARY/O. DURAN

Archbishop Oscar Romero, El Salvador.

Jesuit, Rutilio Grande, Romero asked the president of El Salvador, Arturo Molina, to investigate the murder. Molina promised to do so; however, he never followed through on his promise. Grande had worked in a very poor parish, where he encouraged his parishioners to recognize and resist injustice and economic exploitation, a message considered subversive by those who held power in El Salvador. Molina's refusal to investigate the circumstances of Grande's death was one of the early clues that suggested to Romero that the Salvadoran government was working against the legitimate interests of the people.

When Romero became archbishop in 1977, he was associated with traditional and conservative elements in church and society; when he was murdered while celebrating Mass on March 24, 1980, he was known worldwide for his passionate preaching of the gospel as good news to the poor and oppressed. Romero called on the Catholic church to become more Christlike by associating itself with those who were marginalized, oppressed, and persecuted, and to share in the sufferings of the poor as Christ had shared in all the sufferings of the world. He wrote:

> The church is persecuted because it wants to be truly the church of Christ. As long as the church preaches an eternal salvation without involving itself in the real problems of our world, the church is respected and praised and is even given privileges. But if it is faithful to its mission of pointing out the sin that puts many in misery, and if it proclaims the hope of a more just and human world, then it is persecuted and slandered and called subversive and communist.

Supporters celebrated and opponents condemned what they saw as Romero's conversion. However, Romero insisted that what looked like a conversion was merely another step in his lifelong journey of following Christ; his new situation as archbishop had convinced him that Christ was calling the church to a more profound identification with the poor. He stated: "What happened in my priestly life, I have tried to explain for myself as an evolution of the same desire that I have always had to be faithful to what God asks of me."

Until the end of his life Romero continued his observance of such traditional Catholic practices as devotions to Mary. In a sense he remained a very conservative Catholic, but he recognized that change could mean new life for the church. Although we have focused on Romero as an exemplar of personal religious change, his story is part of the larger story of religious renewal in Latin America, and his story thus exemplifies the necessary interconnections between individual and communal religious change. In his own words:

> To keep oneself anchored, out of ignorance or selfish interest, in a traditionalism without evolution is to lose even the notion of the true Christian tradition. The tradition that Christ confided to his church is not a museum of souvenirs to preserve. It comes, indeed, from the past and is to be loved and preserved faithfully, but always with a look to the future. It is a tradition that makes the church fresh, up-to-date, and effective in each epoch of history. It is a tradition that nourishes the church's hope and its faith so that it can keep on proclaiming and inviting all toward the "new heaven and new earth" that God has promised (Rev 21:1; Is. 65:17).[4]

PERSONAL CONVERSION AND NEW RELIGIONS

A story of personal conversion often introduces the story of the birth of a world religion. A Jewish legend suggests that as a boy Abraham was the son of a pagan idol maker. However, he became convinced that the idols were worthless, and he smashed all the idols in his father's shop. According to Genesis, God calls Abraham to be the father of the people we come to know as the Israelites. The story of the enlightenment of Siddhartha Gautama of the Sakyas—the Buddha—provides a more elaborate example of a personal religious conversion that led to the founding of a new religious movement.

Siddhartha was born in India in the sixth century B.C.E. He was the favorite son of a wealthy and aristocratic family. According to tradition, an oracle at his birth predicted that he would either become a political leader who could unite all India, or a man whose renunciation of the world would lead to the world's redemption. Because his father had political ambitions, he raised Siddhartha in a way that would promote his attachments to the world, to wealth, and to power. He surrounded him with every possible beauty and luxury, creating an environment in which Siddhartha would never encounter ugliness, pain, destitution, or death. Despite his father's efforts, however, Siddhartha did see such sights as he went riding in the countryside. On one ride, Siddhartha saw an aged man;

on another ride, he saw a disease-ridden person at the side of the road; on another ride, he saw a corpse. Perhaps, the story hints, these visions were incarnations of the gods who were committed to Siddhartha's ultimate enlightenment. In a final vision, Siddhartha saw a monk in simple robes carrying his bowl for begging, and he became aware of the possible path of world renunciation.

Although this particular version of Siddhartha's early life may not be historically accurate, we do know that as a young man Siddhartha grew dissatisfied with his life of luxury and comfort. He left his beautiful wife and young son and set out to discover a meaning in life that could satisfy him. Dressed now in rags, he first apprenticed himself to two Hindu masters who instructed him in the way of *raja yoga*, a mental, physical, and spiritual discipline central to advanced Hindu piety. He appreciated the instruction, but it did not satisfy him. He then joined with some ascetics and spent years engaged in fasting and other austere practices. From these lessons he also learned, yet the way of asceticism did not satisfy him either. (In fact, one of the principles that he would later articulate is the idea of the "Middle Way"—that one should follow a path between indulgence and denial of the body.)

Finally, Siddhartha tried the way of mystical contemplation. He sat under a tree—later known as the Bo Tree—and decided that he would remain there until he was enlightened. Demonic powers tried to tempt him away from his course, but he had already reached a stage of enlightenment that made him immune to their attacks. Finally, in the deepness of his meditation, the enlightenment dawned. According to Siddhartha, he "woke up." Siddhartha had become the Buddha, the enlightened one.

Siddhartha's story exemplifies the way of conversion outlined by William James. People who are seeking truth and wholeness, who find themselves unhappy because such wisdom is always just beyond their grasp, find themselves blessed with that wisdom and the unification of their own selves. The aftermath of the Buddha's conversion follows the path that we have seen in other conversion experiences: the Buddha gathers around himself a community to share his way of life and his vision for the world. He founded an order of monks and preached to those who were not able to join the monastic movement. The convert thus finds his experience reinforced by acting in concert with others. From these beginnings the new religion known as Buddhism emerged.

FROM PERSONAL TO COMMUNAL
RELIGIOUS DEVELOPMENT

We have been considering religious change as it develops in individual lives; however, we cannot ultimately separate models of individual and communal religious change. For example, as we hinted in our discussion of Archbishop Romero, the direction of his personal religious growth was influenced by changes within the Latin American Roman Catholic church. Or, as we have seen with figures from the Buddha to Francis of Assisi, individuals who undergo profound personal conversions often reinforce these conversions by founding a religious community or joining with like-minded individuals in communal religious life.

In the eighteenth and nineteenth centuries several waves of Christian renewal swept over the Protestants of the American colonies and early Republic. Known as the First and Second Great Awakenings (1730-1760 and 1800-1830), these moments of societal religious change continue to have an important impact on the shape of American religious experience. What is of special interest to us here is the intertwining of personal and communal religious change. In a sense, the Great Awakenings were the collection of a large number of individual conversion stories; in another sense, it seems unlikely that individuals would have had those conversion experiences without the excitement generated by living in communities where new styles of preaching and personal piety were emerging.

The Puritan settlers of the earliest New England colonies attempted to establish a religiously based society in the new world, and at first they seemed to succeed. Power in the social structure was originally linked to church membership, and church membership was restricted to those who were perceived to be chosen by God for salvation. However, the availability of land allowed many colonists to gain wealth and power apart from publicly acknowledged sanctity. The spiritual intensity of the early years gave way to a routinized and bureaucratic church life by the early 1700s. Then a wave of spiritual regeneration crested across the Eastern colonies. Known as the First Great Awakening, the movement was based on a new style of powerful personal preaching and a new experience of intense personal conversion among those who heard such preaching. We could choose any one individual affected by the Great Awakening and study her or his biography as a story of profound personal religious change. However, it is important to understand that the social climate promoted and even induced these conversion experiences.

Some of the preachers involved in the Great Awakening were itinerant; that is, they traveled from town to town spreading their message. George Whitefield is the best known of these figures; he had already had a successful preaching career in England before arriving and electrifying the colonies from Nova Scotia to Georgia. Not all preachers were itinerant; some managed to build their reputations while working from a base of a particular congregation. Jonathan Edwards of Northampton, Massachusetts, remains the best known of all the preachers of the Great Awakening. His sermons prompted those who heard him to experience the softening of their hearts by God's power; interestingly, he also made many references to the larger cultural phenomenon of religious conversions, and he urged other congregations not to miss out on sharing this experience.

Edwards's theology can sound harsh to contemporary ears unused to the Puritan doctrine of election. According to this tradition, humanity tends toward depravity. Because God is just, all humanity should fear the fires of hell. But God is also merciful and has called a certain number to salvation. In one famous sermon, "Sinners in the Hands of an Angry God," Edwards wrote:

> The God that holds you over the pit of hell, much as one holds a spider, or some loathsome insect over the fire, abhors you, and is dreadfully provoked. . . . You have offended him infinitely more than ever a stubborn rebel did his prince; and yet it is nothing but his hand that holds you from falling into the fire every moment. . . . And there is no other reason to be given, why you have not dropped into hell since you arose in the morning, but that God's hand has held you up.

Edwards urges individuals to repent and experience God's transforming love in an intense experience of personal regeneration and conversion. However, as he urges individuals to open themselves up to this experience, he deliberately evokes the movement of renewal that is sweeping the colonies:

> And now you have an extraordinary opportunity, a day wherein Christ has thrown the door of mercy wide open, and stands in calling and crying with a loud voice to poor sinners; a day wherein many are flocking to him, and pressing into the kingdom of God. Many are daily coming from the east, west, north and south; many that were very lately in the same miserable condition that you are in, are now in a happy state, with their hearts filled with love to him who has loved them, and washed them from their sins in his own blood, and rejoicing in hope of the glory of God. How awful is it to be left behind at such a day! Are not your souls as precious as the souls of the people at Suffield [a nearby town], where they are flocking from day to day to Christ?

Edwards thus instigated the personal crises that led to moments of highly individual renewal, but he did so by urging people to be part of a much larger cultural phenomenon, a societal awakening. As he needled a congregation, "Will you be content to be the children of the devil when so many other children in the land are converted, and are become the holy and happy children of the King of kings?"

Thinking about Being "Born Again"

Are you born again?

Have you been saved?

Have you worked, studied, or socialized with individuals who posed those questions to you?

Are you comfortable or uncomfortable with these questions? Why or why not?

The phrasing of these questions, with their emphasis on profound individual conversion as essential to personal salvation, is part of the legacy of the Second Great Awakening. Protestants of the Reformed traditions who comprised the majority of Northern European colonists who settled these shores believed that God had chosen an "elect" group for salvation. One could not choose to be in that number; one had to be invited and singled out by God for salvation. During the Second Great Awakening (1800-1830) preachers began to tell their congregations that they could choose to be saved, marking a major break with earlier Reformed theology. The hallmark of someone who was saved was a personal conversion, often highly emotional, in which an individual claimed Jesus as her or his personal savior. The Second Great Awakening left other important legacies to the young Republic; for example, the heightened social consciousness which emerged at this time helped promote emerging antislavery sentiment.

The next time someone asks you if you have been saved—or you reflect on a personal experience of being saved—you might recall the ways that a larger social movement shaped this uniquely personal mode of spiritual expression.

As a final example of the interdependence between personal spiritual conversion and social context, let us consider the twentieth-century emergence of Alcoholics Anonymous and other twelve-step programs modeled on AA. Many people not involved with AA know it simply as an organization that helps alcoholics to achieve sobriety. However, members of AA acknowledge that the movement has helped them give birth to themselves as they begin new lives—not just sober but spiritually awake. The first step of the program encourages alcoholics to recognize that they are powerless over alcohol. The remaining steps invite alcoholics to rely on a Higher Power (God, however one understands God); to make an inventory of how one has wronged others, and to make reparations; to seek to know and to follow God's will in all ways; and to share this healing word with other alcoholics. Those who find strength in the program experience tremendous spiritual growth and conversion of heart, along with an unexpected and rewarding closeness to the God of their understanding.

AA literature is full of the conversion stories of individuals—alcoholics who finally realize that they cannot "fix" their lives on their own.

According to the practice of AA, they tell their stories anonymously, or using only their first names: an executive who destroys her marriage through her drinking; a student whose consumption of alcohol ends his academic career; a father estranged from his teenage children. William James's description of the unhappy or divided self seeking unification would apply to many of these individuals. Through reliance on a higher power, they find peace and a purpose in life. For the first time, they see themselves at one with themselves, living honestly in the world. However, these dramatic individual conversions occur as part of a larger movement, the fellowship of AA. Without the movement, which began in the 1930s, many alcoholics would not acknowledge their problem or begin to call on a Higher Power for help. According to those whose lives have been changed by the program, they would not have had the strength to continue on paths of sobriety and spiritual growth without AA. Each individual's story is unique, yet without AA these stories would not emerge. AA is a good example of a larger social movement that fosters, promotes, and sustains highly personal experiences of religious growth and conversion. Without the individuals who live the twelve steps, there would be no AA; but without AA, very few of these individuals think they would have spiritual awakenings to narrate.

RESOURCES

Activities

1. We have relied on a classic work by William James, *The Varieties of Religious Experience*, in our discussion of conversion. James's work has been influential in defining categories in the secular study of religion. Read the volume, and summarize the main topics for the class. Such a summary could serve as a catalyst for a class discussion on the psychology of individual religious experience.

2. Make a scrapbook of your family's religious history. You could include a genealogy highlighting the religious affiliations (or lack of such affiliations) of family members, photos of family members involved in religious rituals, a list of religious artifacts in your home and/or dorm room (noting if those artifacts have been passed down through generations), and other relevant memorabilia. Then analyze the trends that have arisen in the course of several generations in light of discussions in this chapter.

3. Two recommended films, *Dead Man Walking* and *The Rapture*, tell very different stories of religious conversion. View one of these films, and write an analysis of the process of conversion in the film.

4. Assign various class members to read Augustine's *Confessions*, *The Autobiography of Malcolm X*, Apuleius's *The Golden Ass*, and *The Book of Margery Kempe*. Organize a presentation highlighting aspects of conversion that are common to these four accounts and that are unique to each narrative.

5. Research the life of Archbishop Oscar Romero. Organize a class presentation connecting changes in his personal theology with larger social shifts in El Salvador and the Roman Catholic church. (Perhaps you could include film clips from the film *Romero* in your presentation.)

Readings

Apuleius. *The Golden Ass* (available in a variety of translations). This Latin novel of the second century C.E. relates the comical adventures of Lucius, a well-born young man who falls into a series of mishaps, is accidentally transformed into an ass, and ultimately finds redemption through conversion to the Isis cult.

Augustine. *Confessions* (available in a variety of translations). Augustine's spiritual autobiography is a classic of Western spirituality.

The sermons of Jonathan Edwards (available in a variety of editions and anthologies). Vivid imagery accompanies Edwards's message of human depravity and divine sovereignty. Considered by many to be a highlight of early American literature.

James W. Fowler. *Stages of Faith: The Psychology of Human Development and the Quest for Meaning.* San Francisco: Harper & Row, 1981. A scholarly discussion of the intersection between spirituality and developmental psychology.

William James. *The Varieties of Religious Experience* (available in a variety of editions). James's work was a pioneering attempt in the field of psychology and remains essential for the study of individual experience of religion.

Margery Kempe. *The Book of Margery Kempe* (available in a variety of editions and anthologies). A late medieval woman's tumultuous spiritual autobiography.

Malcolm X, *The Autobiography of Malcolm X,* with the assistance of Alex Haley. New York: Ballantine Books, 1992. The dramatic tale of Malcolm X's disadvantaged childhood, troubled youth, discovery of Islam, and development as a major international figure.

William McLoughlin. *Revivals, Awakenings, and Reform: An Essay on Religion and Social Change in America.* Chicago: University of Chicago Press, 1978. A scholarly account that situates a variety of American religious reform movements in their social and political contexts.

Audiovisuals

Dead Man Walking. Based on a true story of a man on Death Row, *Dead Man Walking* tells a unique story of repentance and conversion.

The Rapture. A challenging drama of personal conversion and theological disenchantment.

NOTES

1. Huston Smith, *The World's Religions: Our Greatest Wisdom Traditions* (New York: HarperCollins, 1991), 157.

2. William James, *Varieties of Religious Experience* (New York: Modern Library, 1902/1929), 186.

3. *The Golden Ass,* Robert Graves, trans. (New York: Farrar, Straus and Giroux, 1951), 271-272 and 279-280.

4. Quotations from James R. Brockman, *Romero: A Life* (Maryknoll, NY: Orbis Books, 1990).

Chapter 9

Communal Religious Change

NEW RELIGIONS

As we have seen, religious change in the life of an individual can be incremental, marked by a gradual deepening (or erosion) of faith; or it can be dramatic, marked by a sudden and life-changing conversion experience. Similarly, religious change in the life of a community can occur incrementally, almost imperceptibly, over the lifetimes of its practitioners; or it can occur dramatically, so that the face of a religion changes in a single generation or less. We will begin our consideration of communal religious change with a discussion of the origins of several "new religions": Islam and Christianity.

Muhammad was born in 570 in Mecca, a city that is now located in Saudi Arabia. Arabia was a tribal society where rival family groups were constantly fighting each other, not only for political power but also for economic gain. When Muslims recall this period prior to Islam, they label it ignorant. Arabia was a **polytheistic** society; people lived in fear of the demons who were said to inhabit the vast, sandy reaches of the desert. Mecca itself was a religious attraction, home to hundreds of shrines to the vast pantheon of Arabian deities. Mecca's role as a pilgrimage center helped solidify its place as a regional economic power.

Muhammad, an orphan, was adopted by his uncle. The young Muhammad shared both love and hard economic times with his new family. When he was twenty-five he married his first wife, Khadija, a forty-year-old widow. After her death Muhammad married multiple wives; however, while she lived Muhammad had no other wife. Muhammad spent years engaged in the caravan business, years that were also a time of spiritual searching. A small number of people who lived around Mecca worshiped one god exclusively, a god known as Allah, meaning, "*the* God." Muhammad was among this number, and he spent many long nights in prayer and contemplation of Allah. Sometime around 610, he had an experience in which he heard a voice speaking to him from heaven, calling him to the service of Allah. After a long night of wrestling with the call, Muhammad returned to Khadija and told her about the experience. She became the first convert to Islam.

In the years that followed, Muhammad preached the message of Allah around Mecca. At first he was the object only of mockery; however, as he began to win converts, he was the object of hostility and violence. His message of one God named Allah threatened the economic livelihood of the city, which relied on its situation as a center of polytheistic pilgrimage for economic health. Furthermore, his strongly moral message threatened the hedonism and corruption of the city.

A turning point came in 622, when the city of Medina invited Muhammad to bring the message of Islam there. Medina, like the rest of Arabia, was in severe turmoil because of tribal and other rivalries. A number of residents of Medina who had traveled to Mecca returned to their city speaking of Muhammad and his unifying and righteous message. They decided to invite Muhammad to take up residence. He agreed to do so when they accepted an uncompromising version of the message he bore: a message of complete submission to the one God, Allah. Muhammad proved himself an exceptional administrator. Although he continued to live a humble life, he united the city of Medina under his rule, and the message of Islam took hold.

Ten years after Muhammad arrived in Medina, he died. In those ten years Medina and Mecca engaged in a series of battles. First, Islamic Medina won; then, power reverted to the larger and better equipped Mecca. However, Medina won the next round, and eventually Muhammad returned in triumph to the city that had rejected him. At his death Islam had spread not only from Medina to Mecca but to virtually all Arabia. Within a century, the Islamic empire spread still further, as far as Spain.

To a Muslim, there is only one explanation necessary for the unprecedented spread of Islam: God was with Muhammad, who was truly the greatest prophet of Allah. Scholars of religion must be careful to respect the belief systems they are studying; however, they often go beyond those belief systems to offer a variety of other explanations for religious phenomena. Islam was born in a chaotic and violent world, and it brought a great measure of order and morality to that world. It served an important political function and helped people make sense of their difficult lives. The spiritual success of Islam is perhaps inseparable from its political success. Furthermore, like many new religious movements, Islam built on elements of earlier traditions. For example, Islam builds on insights of Judaism and Christianity, which Islam respects as flawed attempts to articulate a monotheistic faith. After the birth of Islam Mecca was no longer the home of hundreds of shrines dedicated to minor deities. However, it became a greater pilgrimage site than could have been imagined by its earlier residents; all Muslims are bound (if it is possible) to make at least one pilgrimage to Mecca to retrace some of the steps of Muhammad's route of revelation. We have noted the importance of this pilgrimage, the *hajj*, to one Muslim, Malcolm X.

Like Islam, the story of Christianity originates in the story of one man, Jesus of Nazareth. What we can confirm historically about Jesus is slight. He was born in Palestine, probably about 4 B.C.E., and he grew up in Nazareth. In adulthood he came into contact with John the Baptist, who was leading a movement of repentance and renewal within Judaism. Following this encounter, Jesus began his own ministry: preaching the imminence of God's reign, reaching out to heal those who were ill, extending a welcome to those who were marginalized by first-century social structures. He gathered about himself a core group of followers, including not only the group of men known as "the twelve" but others, including women such as Mary Magdalene. As his ministry began to attract greater attention, political and religious leaders in Jerusalem sought to eliminate his influence. They executed Jesus by death on the cross, a disgraceful death generally reserved for slaves.

Although Jesus gathered around himself a number of followers, or disciples, during his lifetime, we do not speak about "the church" until after Jesus' death, when his followers begin to proclaim the resurrection. (Contrast this with the foundation of Islam, which clearly develops *within* Muhammad's lifetime.) Acts of the Apostles tells the story of the emergence of the church under the power of God's spirit after Jesus' death and resurrection. Jesus' followers began to proclaim that the Crucified One had been raised, and that God had therefore vindicated his beloved son and anointed one: Jesus is the Messiah.

It can be difficult for us today to realize that this declaration that Jesus was the Messiah did not mean that Peter and other early members of the Christian church ceased to be Jews. In fact, the New Testament document known as Acts of the Apostles indicates that they continued to gather for prayer at the Jerusalem Temple, the center of Jewish ritual practice (Acts 2:46, 3:1). Yet today, we certainly think of Judaism and Christianity as distinct religious movements. How Judaism and Christianity come to define themselves in mutually exclusive terms is an important study in religious change.

One partial and misleading insight is that when Peter and the others called Jesus "Messiah," they marked themselves as Christian. We have to remember that they did not stop being Jews when they made this declaration; they were simply Jews who believed that the messiah had come. First-century Jews entertained a variety of ideas of who the messiah—the anointed one—would be: a political leader who would restore Israel as a sovereign nation, perhaps, or a priest who would purify the corrupt leadership of the temple cult. However, the ideas and terminology of messianism were distinctively Jewish.

In the course of Jewish history, other Jews have been declared messiah, yet their followers did not cease to be Jews. In the seventeenth century more than half the Jews in Europe declared that Sabbatai Zevi was the messiah. Jews who disagreed did not think those who identified Sabbatai Zevi as the messiah had severed their ties to Judaism. (This messianic movement came to an abrupt end when Sabbatai Zevi converted to Islam in 1666.) More recently, a small group of Hasidic Jews claim that the messiah has come in the person of the late Rebbe Menachenem Schneerson. While the vast majority of Jews scoff at this claim, they do not declare that those who view Schneerson as the messiah are no longer Jews. Thus, we should not assume that Jesus' followers destroyed their Jewish identities by acknowledging him as Messiah.

Thinking about the Historical Jesus

Regardless of their religious affiliation, scholars agree on certain historical claims about Jesus. However, from the perspective of faith, Christians affirm many additional things about Jesus of Nazareth. For many Christians, it is important to note that tradition claims that Jesus' mother Mary was a virgin at the time of his conception and birth. The gospels suggest that during Jesus' ministry God acknowledged Jesus as his own son. An important foundation of later Christian faith is the belief that after Jesus died on the cross, God vindicated him by raising him from the dead. Christian tradition includes the further claim that the resurrected Jesus ascended to heaven and sits at God's right hand until the end of the world, when he will come again in judgment. All these claims are matters of faith, shared only by Christian believers. An agnostic historian who recognizes that Jesus of Nazareth suffered capital punishment in Roman-occupied Jerusalem does not accept as a necessary corollary that God raised this Jesus from the dead.

Survey some people you know about their beliefs about Jesus. After you compile a list of commonly held beliefs (you may include your own beliefs if you like), categorize those beliefs as matters of historical fact or items of faith.

Is it always possible to separate what we consider to be "historical fact" and what we consider to be an item of faith?

What, then, prompted the separation of the early Christians from their parent religion of Judaism? We can identify three major factors that led to this significant religious change. First, the Jewish War of 67-70 was a political event that caused Judaism to look at itself more critically and to draw clearer lines to demarcate the boundaries of Judaism. Second, increasing numbers of Gentiles entering the church, accompanied by increasing indifference to the Jewish law, caused a marked lessening in the Jewish identity of the church as a whole. Third, the development of the idea that Jesus was not only Messiah but God challenged the limits of Jewish monotheistic faith. Each of these factors deserves further comment.

The church emerged in Roman-occupied Jerusalem at a time when Judaism was highly factionalized. A small group of Jews who proclaimed that the Messiah had come was easily incorporated into the pluralistic picture. The political context changed in 67-70 with the outbreak of the Jewish War, a bloody war for liberation from Rome that the Jews lost. Apparently many Christians refused to fight, perhaps on the basis of pacifist principles, a position that seems to have alienated them from many compatriot Jews. Perhaps more importantly, the Romans demolished the Jerusalem Temple, causing Judaism to undergo one of its most significant periods of self-examination. Political circumstances forced the Jewish community to articulate more carefully what it meant to be a Jew; this process of self-definition resulted in the demise of various sects that had existed before the war. In such a political climate, early Christianity's demise as a messianic Jewish sect may have been inevitable.

A second factor in the separation of Christianity from Judaism was the increasingly large number of Gentiles entering the Christian community, along with a marked indifference to Jewish law observance among the Christians. Some early Christian missionaries who preached to the Gentiles insisted that conversion to the Jewish covenant must accompany conversion to a belief in Jesus as Messiah. However, the church eventually decided to baptize Gentiles without insisting on circumcision and the observance of food laws. This decision was important in the history of the separation of Judaism and Christianity for two reasons. First, as greater numbers of Gentiles entered the community, the church ceased to be an ethnically and culturally Jewish movement. Second, from a Jewish perspective, when Christians decided not to insist on Torah observance, they ultimately defined themselves as outside the boundaries of Judaism.

We have seen that Jews who proclaimed Jesus as Messiah did not thereby end their ties to Judaism. However, as Christians began to proclaim that Jesus was God, they made a theological claim that almost all Jews would recognize as incompatible with a Jewish interpretation of monotheism. Centuries of Christians have acknowledged Jesus both as Messiah and as God, so it may be hard to recognize that before the Christian movement Jews did not expect their messiah to be divine. However, there is little if any precedent in Judaism for the notion of a messianic figure who is himself God. While the claim that Jesus was the Messiah was not theologically problematic, an emerging Christian belief that Jesus was the incarnation or embodiment of God proved impossible for Judaism to accept.

The emergence of Christianity as a religion separate from its parent religion of Judaism is a dramatic example of communal religious change. We could see this development as the culmination of a large number of individual conversion stories, as Jews who acknowledged Jesus as the Messiah began to act and believe in ways that were incompatible with their Jewish heritage. We have seen that it is also the result of a political context, which forced Judaism to re-examine and redefine itself in new ways. What is perhaps most important is that Christianity did not simply emerge overnight as a distinct religious tradition, but that over the course of several generations a number of factors precipitated a division between the synagogue and the church. The shame of this situation is that Christians over the centuries have forgotten the enormous debt they owe to Judaism, the religious movement that gave them birth.

RENEWAL AND REFORM WITHIN A RELIGION

At what point do we say that a new religion is born? At what point did Christianity cease to be a reform movement within Judaism and become a distinct religion? Certainly, religions can sustain major reform movements and still retain their identities. The Protestant Reformation is an important example of a movement that greatly altered the contours of a religion without effecting a split into a new religion. (Although some confusion prevails on this point, Roman Catholicism, Protestantism, and Orthodoxy are all branches of a single religion, Christianity.)

At the end of the European Middle Ages, the Roman church wielded broad cultural influence and great political power. The popes were important patrons of the arts: Julius II, for example, who was pope in the early 1500s, commissioned such great Vatican art works as the Sistine Chapel. Julius II was also a warrior-pope, leading troops into battle to claim northern Italian lands for the papacy. Because of its sometimes self-interested involvement with secular matters, the church had begun to attract criticism from a number of quarters, both political and theological. Although there were a number of minor attempts at reform, not until Martin Luther (b. 1483) did the process of reform really grip Europe.

Luther was a German monk, steeped in the theological world of the late Middle Ages. He came to public attention in 1517 when he posted a list of criticisms on a church door in the German city of Wittenberg where he resided. Luther intended the list to spark discussion; in university towns such as Wittenberg, posting such lists was a relatively common practice. (Think of the use of bulletin boards for public announcements in colleges and universities today.) The criticisms focused on the sale of indulgences. An indulgence was essentially a reprieve from penitential time in purgatory, where Catholics believed that the souls of those who were forgiven but not entirely purified went after death. In the "ninety-five theses" posted in Wittenberg, Luther emphasized the corruption of selling such indulgences, a practice which would imply that God would release the souls of the rich sooner than the souls of the poor. Luther thought that the church preyed on people's vulnerabilities, in its teaching that one could buy relief for loved ones who had died and were suffering in purgatory. In his words, "There is no divine authority for preaching that the soul flies out of purgatory immediately [as] the money clinks in the bottom of the chest."

Luther was certainly not the first Catholic to make such criticisms; however, for a variety of political and social reasons his articulation of theological concerns triggered an unusually strong response from ecclesiastical authorities. Leaders of the church asked Luther to take back his criticisms. He considered this. He did not want to see division in the church, which he loved. However, the more he thought about the situation the more disturbed he was. Pushed to his limits, he dug in his heels and argued his position even more strongly than he had at first. His meditations on church teachings about purgatory and indulgences led him to articulate his understanding of "justification by faith." Luther, influenced by the letters of the apostle Paul to the Romans and the Galatians, came to believe that human beings would not be rectified before God because of their own deeds, and particularly not by participating in the ritual system of the church. Rather, Luther believed that salvation was a free gift of God, freely given to those of faith. He stood his ground against the church on grounds of conscience, always hoping that the breach between him and the hierarchy would be mended. It was not. By the end of his life, Luther was aware that his words had initiated a process of both reform and division that resulted in the existence of the Protestant churches alongside the Catholic church, headed by the bishop of Rome.

A number of factors contributed to the growth of the Lutheran Reformation, as well as other branches of the Protestant Reformation. Luther appeared on the scene at a time of growing nationalism, when the various nation-states of Europe had begun to resist the political control of the papacy. His writings offered some theological rationale for ending one's allegiance to the pope. At least initially the Protestant churches seemed to be free from the overtly corrupt practices of the late medieval church, such as the sale of church offices and the propensity of certain priests to live openly with women to whom they were not married. Ministers in Protestant churches were allowed to marry. Luther promoted popular reading of the Bible, translating it himself into a lucid German edition; he wrote hymns that people loved, that taught aspects of their faith. Perhaps most importantly, though, the interpretation he offered of the gospel, the teaching of Jesus, convinced many Christians throughout Europe that they were hearing the good news for the first time.

Other religious traditions have gone through significant moments of reform that redefine the tradition without marking a definitive break from it. Native American tradition provides another example of this phenomenon. From 1799 to 1815 a Seneca prophet named Handsome Lake preached to the people of the Six Nations of the Haudenosaunee. At this time the westward expansion of people of European descent threatened the ways and the existence of the Six Nations. Threats to their well-being were both overt and insidious. Not only were there political threats to their sovereignty; internal problems had arisen as contact with outsiders introduced new problems into their communities. Alcoholism, for example, was rampant. Many women chose to have abortions, because they did not believe that the world was hospitable to new life. Handsome Lake's message recalled older traditions but also included a number of directives necessary for sustaining the health of the communities. Avoid alcohol; remain faithful and loving to your spouse; don't be afraid to bring children into this world; care for the elderly—these are among the messages Handsome Lake delivered to his people, conveying messages from the Creator.

The message of Handsome Lake was pivotal in the development of the thought and practice of the Six Nations. Every fall the nations still gather in their longhouses to recite his prophecies. At the time of his death, however, Handsome Lake does not seem to have been held in great honor. One tradition even reports that he had been expelled from the reservation where he was living because he seduced a young woman who had come to him to heal her illness. How does one move from the tarnished reputation of a dying man to the commemoration of a significant moment of religious renewal? Political and social circumstances are certainly factors; the Iroquois nations needed Handsome Lake's message of spirituality and caring for one another in order to sustain the life of their people. Nonetheless, acceptance of his message was not automatic; it took the hard work of his followers to keep his prophecies alive in the years and decades after his death. Approximately a decade after Handsome Lake's death, around 1825, women who remembered his message despaired as they viewed the problems which still beset the Six Nations. Furthermore, they realized that those who remembered his prophecies vividly were declining in number. They therefore invited a descendant of Handsome Lake to publicly recall Handsome Lake's words. Thus began the annual recitation of Handsome Lake's prophecies. It seems that at first the recitation of the prophecies took place at only a few longhouses, but as time passed the practice spread throughout the confederacy. Strangely, we can say that the Handsome Lake revival among the Six Nations of the Iroquois confederacy dates not to the lifetime of Handsome Lake, but to the preaching of his grandson a decade after his death.[1]

SOCIAL CHANGE AS A CATALYST FOR RELIGIOUS CHANGE

Social change often accompanies religious change; indeed, distinguishing the two is often impossible. In the nineteenth century, when scholars began to study religion as a system or an institution, they offered a variety of explanations for the relationship between religious and other social phenomena. Karl Marx, for example, saw religious beliefs and actions primarily as symptoms or manifestations of underlying social conditions. According to this view, religious change would always follow fundamental social change; religious change could not cause a reordering of the larger relations of society. Max Weber, on the other hand, believed that

MARYKNOLL PHOTO LIBRARY/E. WHEATER

A Marian procession in Chile. The large statue of Mary (behind and to the left of the cross) is being carried by a group of men.

religious thought and practice play more complex roles in the structuring of society. Weber referred to "elective affinity" between religious and other social change. That is, he noted that religious change often accompanied social change, and that social change often accompanied religious change. However, he thought that it was overly simplistic to separate religious change from other kinds of social change and to identify one set of changes as "causes" and the other set of changes as "effects."

In some cases alterations in social and political circumstances prompt changes in patterns of religious thought, practice, and community life. In many agricultural areas, for example, festivals of planting and harvesting dominate the ritual calendar. When factories replace farms, some communities abandon their rituals, others reinterpret them, and still others continue to preserve seasonal rituals, but no longer as the organizing aspects of community life. As changing circumstances alter the totality of a community's worldview, religious beliefs and practices are also likely to evolve.

When Roman Catholics arrived in large numbers on American shores in the late nineteenth century, they often settled in ethnic neighborhoods where they maintained traditions familiar to them from the old country. Polish families brought baskets of paschal bread and eggs to church to be blessed on Holy Saturday (the day before Easter), and Italian immigrants organized large festivals in honor of the Virgin Mary and other saints. As the decades passed, immigrants increasingly integrated themselves into American culture, often marrying members of other eth-

nic groups and otherwise reducing their exclusive reliance on ethnic networks of support. By the 1960s and 1970s, large numbers of Catholics
had moved from ethnic urban clusters to live in suburban communities.
The slow process of cultural change included diminishing attachment to
older religious practices. At no point did ethnic communities consciously
decide to alter their practices. Because customs were abandoned one at a
time as family members moved away from one another, or as upwardly
mobile generations began to feel at home in suburban parishes, there was
no definitive break with the past. Nonetheless, American Catholicism had
assumed a new face.

Thinking about Ethnicity and Religion

Do you or your immediate family have traditions associated with
your ethnic heritage(s)? Do you consider these traditions religious?

Do your parents or grandparents remember participating as children
in religious traditions associated with their ethnic heritages that they
have not passed on to your generation?

When and why did your family abandon these traditional practices?

If your family retains significant aspects of an ethnic religious heritage, what do you think accounts for this attachment?

What does this suggest about the process of change in the religious
heritage(s) of your family?

Trying to grasp the moment when religious change happens is often
impossible. Change is a process. At times we may single out a moment as
crucial in the unfolding of change. However, as we look more deeply we
will realize that a variety of circumstances have led to the symbolically
important moment, and that a variety of consequences result from it.
One key moment in the recent development of American Christian history was the controversial ordination of fifteen women to the priesthood
of the Episcopal church in Philadelphia on July 29, 1974. We can pinpoint
the moment at which the ordination occurred, but to understand its significance we need to understand the historical context in which it took
place. The women and their supporters were involved in the Women's
Liberation movement, which in turn had been largely influenced by the
Civil Rights movement. The preacher at the ordination was Dr. Charles
Willie, a professor at Harvard, African-American leader, and Episcopal
layman (that is, not a member of the clergy). Dr. Willie's sermon explicitly linked the women's ordination to these two movements: "There are
parallels between the Civil Rights Movement and the Women's Movement and this is what we are witnessing today.... As blacks refused to
participate in their own oppression by going to the back of the bus in

1955 in Montgomery, women are refusing to cooperate in their own oppression by remaining on the periphery of full participation in the Church in 1974 in Philadelphia."[2]

Dr. Willie, the women priests, and the bishops who broke ranks with their brother Episcopal bishops to participate in the ordination were aware that developments in American society over the previous twenty years had created a social climate in which the ordination of women was conceivable. Nor were the ordinations the end of the story. Since then, the Episcopal church has been trying to understand what it means to have women in addition to men as priests and even bishops. To those involved in the ordinations, the action was a way of honoring more fully several biblical insights: that both women and men are formed in God's image, and that in Christ there is neither male nor female. While we can focus on key scenes in various dramas of religious change, to understand their significance we will need to examine the larger settings in which they are enacted.

In 1979, America was shocked when Islamic militants overthrew the Shah of Iran, who had been a staunch American ally. This event, which symbolizes the explosive growth of Islamic fundamentalism in the 1970s and 1980s, appears much less surprising when viewed against the backdrop of the changing political and social circumstances of Islam in the twentieth century. As the century began, the Turkish Empire still survived as a testament to the potential of Islamic political power. Although considerably diminished from the height of its power—in 1683 the Turkish Empire had come close to annexing Vienna—other Islamic nations considered the Empire's persistence as evidence of Islam's ultimate dominance of the world. Turkey allied itself with Germany during World War I; Germany's loss in that war meant the end of the Turkish Empire in 1918. This was a traumatic blow to the worldview of the Islamic world, especially when Mustafa Kemal began to rebuild Turkey's power as an entirely secular nation, excluding Islamic law and tradition from the nation's political and social structure.

In succeeding decades technological differences exacerbated the gap between the largely Christian countries of Europe and North America and the Islamic nations of East Asia and North Africa in the areas of living conditions, economic influence, military might, and international political sway. In order to close the gap, a number of Islamic nations began to adopt a variety of Western ways. In Iran the ruling Pahlevi family tried especially hard to "modernize" the nation. Although the real goal of the effort was to help Iran catch up to Europe and the United States in economic, military, and political strength, the Pahlevi family also focused on other symbolic aspects of Iranian Muslim practice as targets for change. In 1935 the shah (king) forbade woman to wear the *chador*, the traditional heavy black cloak, which to him was a visible expression of his country's "backwardness." This decree was painful to Iranian women, most of whom had never left their houses without this clothing which they felt protected them from male eyes. Even the shah's wife wept when

MARYKNOLL PHOTO ARCHIVES/UNESCO

A Muslim woman in Bombay examining a film-strip through her veil.

she left home without the *chador*. In 1941, the shah decreed that it was again legal to wear the *chador*, although he continued in a variety of ways to discourage it.

The Pahlevis' position on the *chador* serves as a symbol of their plan for Iran's restoration to a position of political and economic power, a plan that largely relied on adaptation to Western ways. Many Muslims in Iran and other nations rejected this response to Islam's diminished role in world affairs. They believed that Islam would again rise in world-historical importance not by rejecting traditional ways but by following them more closely than ever, not by emulating the West but by distancing themselves from it.

The rise of fundamentalist Islam took a particular course in Iran. Iran has a distinctive religious tradition in which a particular form of Islam known as Shi'ism is dominant. In Shi'ite Islam clergy mediate between believers and Allah. In the 1979 revolution against the last of the Pahlevi shahs, the Ayatollah Khomeini achieved an international reputation first as a critic of the Pahlevi regime and then as a leader in the new Islamic republic. (An ayatollah is an honored jurist, a legal scholar and judge.) Predictably, early legislation mandated that women wear modest dress (loose clothing and a head scarf), and a national campaign emerged to encourage (or coerce) women to wear the *chador* that successive Pahlevi shahs had tried to eliminate from the nation's wardrobe. The revolutionary government responded to the various crises of the country not by adapting Western ways but by reinterpreting the shari'ah, the traditional Islamic code of law, to fit the complex realities of late-twentieth-century life. The existence of an Islamic Republic in Iran since 1979 has been a constant reminder that certain social, economic, and political conditions can be fertile ground for the growth of a religious sensibility that seeks its own way of ordering the world.

What we are calling Islamic fundamentalism takes a variety of forms, depending on the particular economic and political situations of various nations. In Egypt, for example, as the Westernizing policies of a succession of leaders accompanied a growing gap between the wealthy and the poor, a fundamentalist group known as the Muslim Brotherhood worked to enact laws that conformed with their interpretation of the duties of Islam. As Americans applauded official Egyptian efforts to work for peace with Israel, members of the Muslim Brotherhood interpreted these efforts as capitulation to decadent foes of Islam. Perceptions of political and economic vulnerability thus fostered growth in one form of Islamic fundamentalism.

CULTURAL CONTACT AND RELIGIOUS CHANGE

Contact between two or more cultures is a social circumstance that often catalyzes religious change. When two worldviews collide, individuals and communities may begin to challenge one or another aspect of their traditional ways of seeing and acting in the world. The history of European exploration in Asia, Africa, and the Americas affords many examples of such encounters.

Economic advantage was a goal in European exploration, perhaps the major goal. Missionaries often followed and sometimes even accompanied the traders. At times, missionary efforts offered a justification for the aggressive actions of the explorers. Bartolomé de Las Casas (1484-1566), a Spaniard who was the first priest ordained in the Americas, was an early critic of the practices of Europeans in the lands they had newly encountered. After many years in the recently established colonies, Las Casas returned to Spain where he published a blistering attack on what he saw as the savagery of the Christians. Las Casas identified gold as the motivation for his fellow Europeans to travel to the Americas, despite the claims of many that they were attempting to convert the natives. He described one such attempt: as a band of explorers approached a local village, they read—in a language the villagers could not comprehend—statements demanding conversion to Christianity. Naturally, no villagers came forward to convert. Their supposed resistance to the gospel was the alleged reason for destroying their village, killing many inhabitants, and capturing others to sell as slaves. In fact, Las Casas suggests, the real goal was not to convert the inhabitants, but to eliminate them so their gold could be stolen. Las Casas tells of an indigenous leader who was about to be executed. His captors told him that if he would convert to Christianity he was assured of going to heaven after death, but if he resisted he would go straight to hell, which they described in terrifying terms. The leader asked whether all Christians went to heaven, and those about to execute him said yes. Then, said the man, he would prefer to go to hell. In the words of Las Casas, "Such is the fame and honor that God and our Faith have earned through the Christians who have gone out to the Indies."

A portrayal of the encounter between Bartolomé de Las Casas and Cortés in a portion of a mural by Diego Rivera.

Alliances between traders and missionaries have continued to be common not only in the Americas, but also in Africa and the Pacific. Las Casas demonstrates the ambiguity of such alliances. Himself a missionary, he was a vehement critic of missionary practices, raising the awareness of Europeans about the activities of compatriots in the Americas. His grounds for criticism were religious. He expected God's eternal condemnation of those Christians who exploited and killed native peoples. Conversion was a high priority for Las Casas. He worked peacefully to teach the gospel to the peoples of the Americas, insisting that such a method was far more efficacious than forceful baptisms leading to enslavement. We could also say that he worked and prayed for the conversion of Christian Europe to an attitude of compassion and love.

If we focus only on the horror stories narrated by Las Casas, we will be surprised to learn that Christian missionaries ever succeeded in winning the hearts of people they encountered. Of course, most missionaries have been far from the cynical opportunists Las Casas portrayed. In Papua New Guinea, a large island northeast of Australia, missionaries followed traders in the late nineteenth century. At first the inhabitants of New Guinea were suspicious of the missionaries and indeed killed some of them. In time, however, many islanders came to accept the missionaries. Islanders offered a variety of reasons to explain their acceptance of the Christian message. Some believed that the hymns the missionaries taught were powerful. Others said that, unlike the traders, the missionaries "walked softly." According to one story, a missionary intervened in a risky situation to save a woman's life; other island women were amazed. In their worldview, one typically acted on behalf of family members, and the missionary obviously was not kin to the woman. The incident led local people to think about the possible benefits of the message they were hearing. Whether the teachings are ultimately embraced or rejected, however, those who have had contact with outsiders never see the world precisely as they did prior to the encounter.

In 1965 the Kenyan writer Ngugi wa Thiong'o published a novel entitled *The River Between* that dramatizes the pain inherent in cultural struggles between Christianity and indigenous traditions. Waiyaki is the protagonist of the novel. His father, who is committed to the tribal ways, reveals to him that ancient prophecies foretell a role for Waiyaki in saving his people. However, European Christians have come to the area, and the father understands that the people cannot ignore these new influences. He orders Waiyaki: "Arise. Heed the prophecy. Go to the Mission place. Learn all the wisdom and all the secrets of the white man. But do not follow his vices. Be true to your people and the ancient rites." Waiyaki struggles to follow his father's advice. He goes to the Christian school, and then returns to his village. He starts a school that will teach the children reading, writing, and other skills he thinks are necessary to cope in the modern world. However, the school does not teach Christianity; it teaches tribal traditions. Waiyaki's larger goal is to organize the people so they will be able to resist the political and economic compromises that accompany their expanded interactions with the white man.

Even as Waiyaki's mission gains momentum, he falls in love with Nyambura, the daughter of a local Christian preacher. Because her father has rejected the ancestral ways, Nyambura is not circumcised. (Female circumcision has been discussed in chapter 4; it involves the removal of all or part of the female genitalia. Rites of female and male circumcision are important coming-of-age rituals in much of Africa. The uncircumcised are unable to participate fully in the life of their people.) Waiyaki exemplifies the contradictions of traditional religions after contact with the West. Educated at a Christian school, Waiyaki longs to be a teacher of traditional ways. An adherent of ancestral practices, his attachment to an uncircumcised woman renders him suspect in the eyes of his peers. Ngugi expands on Waiyaki's dilemma:

> For Waiyaki knew that not all the ways of the white man were bad. Even his religion was not essentially bad. Some good, some truth shone through it. But the religion, the faith, needed washing, cleaning away all the dirt, leaving only the eternal. And that eternal that was the truth had to be reconciled to the traditions of the people. A people's traditions could not be swept away overnight. That way lay disintegration. Such a tribe would have no roots, for a people's roots were in their traditions going back to the past, the very beginning.[3]

Waiyaki understands that his people will lose themselves if they lose their ancestral ways, but that their life after contact with the Christian missionaries will never be what it was before.

Study of the contact between two or more cultures dramatically reveals what is true of all religions: human institutions are not static, but dynamic. We cannot capture the essence of a religion with a snapshot; we need the metaphor of the movie to help us understand how religious life changes as communities move, disintegrate, regroup, absorb foreign influences, or otherwise confront altered circumstances. In this context we consider the situation of enslaved Africans who arrived on American shores. Since we have considered the ways that social and political changes trigger religious evolution, we are in a position to appreciate the religious changes that followed the upheaval and involuntary relocation of hundreds of thousands of Africans.

The enormity of the dislocation experienced by the enslaved Africans is hard to imagine. They were forcibly removed from their own shores to travel to a land of whose existence they were probably unaware, to speak a language they had never heard until their adulthood, never to see family or familiar places again—long before the internet, faxes, or phone service helped people keep in touch. One newly arrived slave said: "As every object was new to me, every thing I saw filled me with surprise."[4] Once on American shores the experiences of the enslaved varied considerably. Until about 1800 slavery was legal throughout the English-speaking colonies/states, even in the North. Some slave-traders sold African slaves in northern ports, although in most northern areas concentrations of African-Americans remained small. Smaller communities of African slaves meant greater contact between slaves and Americans of European heritage, and more rapid acculturation into the larger society. Phillis Wheatley offers an extreme example of such adjustment. She arrived in Boston as a child and learned not only English but also Greek and Latin; she published a learned book of poetry in 1773, at the age of only eighteen. Although Phillis Wheatley seems to have assimilated into the dominant culture with unusual rapidity—and one may wonder what memories of her African childhood she nurtured without committing them to the language of her captors—her story points to wide opportunities for contact between black and white residents of Boston in the late eighteenth century. Such contact extended to Christian education and worship. By the end of the eighteenth century, a number of important Northern congregations were integrated, and other autonomous black churches had developed, whose worship styles closely resembled those of neighboring white institutions.

Africans sold onto Southern shores had a very different experience. Particularly in the coastal areas of the Carolinas, many slaves continued to live in communities that were predominantly African. Living in enclaves of other Africans and their descendants, slaves continued to draw on traditional African medicine, agricultural and fishing techniques, and crafts styles. In many ways these communities continued to transmit an African religious heritage, emphasizing belief in a world of good and bad spirits who influence the course of the world and of human events. However, African traditions suggested that spirits permeated *particular* places and objects, and that after death the ancestors returned to the people and territories they had known in life. The "middle passage" across the Atlantic in the holds of the slaveships had twisted and broken many of the slaves' connections to the world of spirits and ancestors. Their removal to American shores in itself necessitated some measure of religious change.

Only slowly did slaveowners begin to instruct the slaves in Christianity. Their reluctance stemmed from their belief that baptism into Christianity would cause slaves to become arrogant and perhaps to demand their freedom. When the slaveowners did begin Christian instruction, the gospel they taught was this: Obey your master and your mistress if you want a reward in heaven after death. Understandably, this message was not especially appealing in slave quarters. However, other Christian messengers got through to many slaves, and the Christian message was sufficiently multilayered that the slaves were able to develop their own interpretations of the gospel. We have already discussed the First and Second Great Awakenings of the eighteenth and early nineteenth centuries, which emphasized spirited preaching and intense personal conversion experiences. Missionaries of these periods sought opportunities to preach to slaves, who often responded fervently to the message of God's love and renewal of life.

The Christianity the slaves came to practice was different in many respects from the Christianity practiced by their white neighbors. When two cultures come into contact with each other, it is unlikely that either culture will remain unaffected by that contact. When African slaves came to these shores, their traditional patterns of belief and habit altered; when they embraced Christianity, the scope of Christian thought and action also altered. The slaves became Christian, but Christianity in turn became Africanized. One way that slaves were able to connect to Christian thought was to find areas of similarity between their old ways and the new message they were hearing. So, for example, the benevolent and loving God of the Protestant missionaries might remind them of the benevolent and loving high God of West African religions. Evangelical Christian preaching emphasized that God was taking possession of the body and spirit of the convert; this experience resonated with West African understandings of spirit possession. Visitors (including African-American visitors from staid Northern congregations) commented on many African elements that remained in the Christian worship of Southern blacks, such as a communal circle dance. The development of unique forms of Christianity among the slaves, incorporating remnants of African thought and practice along with missionary influences, is evidence of the tremendous power of religious traditions to adapt as they conform to new circumstances.

RELIGION AS A CATALYST FOR SOCIAL CHANGE

Social change triggers religious change; contacts among various cultures spark new religious configurations. If we stop our analysis here, religious worldviews will appear merely as by-products of the material arrangements of people's lives. While social and political circumstances certainly affect the development of worldviews, the religious imagination also shapes visions of the kinds of life people want to lead. As a result, shifting religious perspectives can alter social and political landscapes.

As previously noted, the Second Great Awakening (1800-1830) was a period in American religious history when waves of renewal swept through the new Republic. This time of religious regeneration precipitated the movement for the abolition of slavery. A shifting theological perspective thus engendered change in the social and political arrangements of the nation. Understanding the theological innovations of the Second Great Awakening will help us see how those involved extended their concerns to encompass the situation of American slaves.

American Protestantism had strong Calvinist roots. (John Calvin was an early Protestant reformer, working only a few years after Luther's actions instigated the Protestant Reformation.) Many colonial churches (especially in New England, New York, and New Jersey) followed Calvin's teaching that God had predestined certain people for salvation and others for damnation. Those predestined for salvation were known as "the elect," those for whom Jesus had died. This scheme leaves little scope for the operation of free will, since it implies that human beings cannot choose to act in a way that will gain salvation. During the eighteenth century another view of human nature became popular among intellectuals in Europe and America. The Enlightenment was a philosophical movement which emphasized the rationality of human nature and the importance of free will in the ethical decision-making process. Enlightenment teachings about human power to define and shape the world formed the intellectual background for the American and French Revolutions.

This re-evaluation of human nature eventually began to affect the ways religious people saw the world. In the early nineteenth century, evangelical preachers began to minimize or omit the role of predestination in salvation. The excitement of living in a new nation fostered a climate where many came to believe that human nature could bring itself to perfection, freely vanquishing the powers of sin. According to the theology which swept the nation, human beings have the capacity to will a conversion to new life in the gospel. This teaching offered a markedly more optimistic view of human nature than the older Calvinist view. Around 1830 two evangelical preachers, Charles Grandison Finney and Theodore Weld, began organizing church-based abolitionist societies that called for an immediate end to slavery. Finney in particular believed that this goal could be reached by preaching conversion to slaveowners, who would on their own reject the sin of slaveowning. Finney, of course, was wrong; the nation went through a long and bloody struggle before the abolition of slavery. However, in the decades leading to the Civil War leaders of the abolition movement continued to arise from the ranks of evangelical Christians influenced by the Second Great Awakening.

Churches provided not only a theological but also an institutional base for the abolition movement. Black churches in particular were often the location for anti-slavery societies and activities. In Boston, for example, both black and white abolitionists assembled in black churches to hear prominent antislavery speakers. Pastors preached against slavery from the pulpits, and congregations worked together to give safe refuge to runaway slaves, an increasingly dangerous ministry. African-American churches even developed rituals to commemorate key moments in the struggle against slavery: the abolition of the trans-Atlantic slave trade, for example, and the end of slavery in Britain and its territories.

The black church has remained a force in shaping black communities and hence the national fabric. In particular, during the Civil Rights era black churches offered an institutional base and religious inspiration in the struggle for human dignity. Martin Luther King, Jr.'s dream for America was based on a biblical vision of peace and justice. Countless preachers proclaimed from their pulpits that God was on the side of those working for justice. White America was slow to comprehend the power of the church in shaping political opinion in the black community. An incident from the Montgomery, Alabama, bus boycott (1955-1956) illustrates both the influence of the black church and the lack of white comprehension. The boycott began when a respected woman named Rosa Parks refused to move to the back of the bus, as the law required. The subsequent refusal of blacks to ride segregated buses—instead walking miles upon miles and organizing elaborate car pools—was an economic blow to the city of Montgomery. One weekend, the leaders of the city hatched a plan to restore black ridership. They wrote an article to appear in Sunday's paper saying that black leaders had negotiated an end to the boycott. Somehow, the story was leaked to King on Saturday night, and he organized all the black ministers in Montgomery to denounce the story in their sermons. When Monday morning arrived, white Montgomery was stunned as empty buses continued to roll by; they had underestimated the efficacy of the black church network and the degree to which the black church was a factor in shaping black opinion and community life.

A final example of the influence of religious factors on social and political structures is the role that Christianization has played in the emergence of new nation-states in the postcolonial era (roughly since World War II). Papua New Guinea, for example, achieved independence from nearby Australia in 1975. The constitution of the new nation acknowledges both "our noble traditions" (local religions) and "Christian principles." This dual recognition encapsulates the past century of local history and the intertwining of ancestral ways with the new Christian religion. Papua New Guinea is a relatively small country in which more than 800 languages are spoken; the various communities have sustained separate identities both through warfare and exchange alliances. Christianity has forged a new understanding of neighboring peoples as "brothers" and "sisters" in Christ, helping to create an ideological configuration in which national loyalties can emerge. In Africa as well the spread of Christianity and Islam created the common languages, educational opportunities, and wider loyalties necessary for the apparatus of statehood in the countries which won independence from colonial powers in the 1960s. Even as social and political circumstances help shape a people's religious vision, the religious imagination is a powerful instrument in shaping people's understanding of the potential for social and political growth.

RESISTANCE TO CHANGE

Change is not always easy to accept. Even if we choose to move to a new town or to enroll in a new school, we may be unsettled by unanticipated circumstances; we may find ourselves lonely as we lose touch with people we were convinced were friends for life. When change is involuntary, we are often still more overwhelmed by it. When parents announce that a family is relocating, for example, children and teenagers may be angry and resentful. It can be difficult to imagine that one will find another soccer team quite as supportive as one's current team, or that a current boyfriend or girlfriend will be easily forgotten in new romance. Societal change can also be as slow, painful, and uneven. Decades ago, American government and industry began to discuss switching over to the metric system of measurement used by most of the rest of the world. Although Americans often buy beverages by the liter rather than the quart, a mile is still the standard measure of distance, and weights are reported in pounds rather than kilograms.

Thinking about the Difficulty of Change

Take a minute to think about two major changes you have made in your lifetime. Choose one major change that was voluntary and another that was involuntary.

For the voluntary change: Were there problems with it that you had not anticipated? What were your expectations when you made the change? Did it live up to your expectations? Were you happy with your decision?

For the involuntary change: Did you have fears? Were they justified? Were there unexpected benefits that came with the change? In the end, did you come to accept the change, or do you still wish things could be as they were?

Have these experiences encouraged you to seek change in your life, or have you become more resistant to it?

Because religious issues are so central to people's worldviews and self-definitions, religious change can be especially painful. Both individuals and communities resist innovations that are accepted by others as healthy. Not all change promotes human well-being, of course, nor do all people agree on the nature of human flourishing. Fear of change itself, however, or at least a strong attachment to what is familiar can lead religious individuals and communities to cling tenaciously to the past. Congregations that introduce a new hymnal, for example, find that many members at first are critical of both words and music. They miss those hymns that have been dropped, and they belittle hymns recently introduced. After a period of use, however, such criticisms are often forgotten. In the 1950s, the release of the Revised Standard Version (RSV), an important translation of the Bible, attracted much negative publicity. Pastors condemned it, and religious writers found fault with its theological tendencies. (Every translation involves some measure of interpretation.) What was most disturbing to many about the RSV, though, was that it replaced a translation that was much closer to the King James version, familiar in the English-speaking Protestant world since the 1600s. The RSV was problematic to many simply because it was unfamiliar.

Resistance to religious and cultural change in the early twentieth century was a major factor in the rise of Protestant fundamentalism. Fundamentalists accept the Bible as the literal Word of God and resist many aspects of modern value systems. Contemporary fundamentalism is a complex phenomenon, and there is not a single profile that adequately describes all Protestant fundamentalists, nor is there even complete agreement on the question of who qualifies as a fundamentalist. We will make better sense of the rise of fundamentalism by discussing its wider historical context.

A number of cultural factors affected the religious landscape in the late nineteenth and early twentieth centuries. The writings of Charles Darwin on evolution were influential. Many liberal church leaders accepted the scientific theory of evolution and suggested that the creation accounts in Genesis should be read as metaphor rather than as scientific or historical reporting. Intellectuals in Europe and the United States gave serious consideration to communism and other forms of socialism; many watched hopefully to see the direction the newly established Communist government in Russia would take after the Bolshevik Revolution of 1917. Again, many liberal church leaders were receptive to socialist ideas, which they believed were in keeping with Jesus' declaration that he had come to proclaim good news to the poor. While this was a period of excitement for many, the fundamentalists were among those who saw these new teachings as threats to the values with which they had been raised.

World War I (1914-1918) was unsettling to all who lived through it. The introduction of weapons of mass destruction, such as chemical agents, shocked and frightened much of the world. As the 1920s began, many believed that the world had been irrevocably changed by the bloody conflict. In 1921 the Irish poet William B. Yeats published a poem called "The Second Coming," which invoked the climate of the postwar era: "Things fall apart; the centre cannot hold;/Mere anarchy is loosed upon the world." A year later, the American-born poet T.S. Eliot published a long poem called "The Waste Land" that reflected his sense of the disarray of European culture in the aftermath of the war. Throughout the poem he includes fragments of earlier literary works, and toward the end of the poem he declares, "These fragments I have shored against my ruins." Nostalgia for the past was not confined to the fundamentalist movement.

While others greeted the future with a mixture of hopeful anticipation and mourning for a world that seemed to have died, fundamentalists refused to accept change as inevitable. They responded to cultural and religious change by resisting it. In doing so they constructed a worldview in which those who disagreed with them were seen as evil influences. One issue that particularly vexed them was the teaching of evolution. This involved them in arguments with both secular intellectuals and liberal Christians. Their disagreement with other Christians was interpretive in nature. A prevailing question was, how shall we interpret the opening chapters of Genesis? Fundamentalists insisted that Genesis proved that God had created the world in seven days. Liberal Christians not only embraced the idea of evolution; they also advocated scientific methods of Bible study. So, for example, liberal scholars focused on differences between the two versions of the Genesis creation accounts, while fundamentalists refused to acknowledge that discrepancies between the two accounts existed. More broadly, fundamentalists started with the words of the Bible, on the basis of which they evaluated modern thought and practice. Liberal Christians often started with insights and methods derived from secular criticism and then applied them to the Bible. There was little common ground.

The conflict between fundamentalists and liberal forces within church and society came to a symbolic climax in the 1925 "Monkey Trial" of John Scopes. Scopes was a biology teacher in a small town in Tennessee who angered local fundamentalists when he taught his students about evolution. Fundamentalists had worked for the passage of a Tennessee law which forbade the teaching of evolution, which they saw as blasphemous contradiction of God's words in Genesis. The trial became a symbol for those on both sides in a debate that still resonates in the current political landscape. For Scopes's supporters, major issues included the credibility of modern science and the separation of church and state. For fundamentalists, the overriding concern was to resist any accommodation with the corrosive forces of the modern world.

As we evaluate fundamentalists and their resistance to cultural and religious change, we should consider not only what they stand for but also what they stand against. Fundamentalism develops as resistance to aspects of the modern world that are often confusing and even alienating. The twentieth century has brought changes that sometimes seem beyond individual control. Because of economic demands, people move more than they used to. Families are likely to live hundreds of miles apart. Shifting employment patterns and "downsizing" make people worry that their futures are not secure. Rising costs of health care restrict the options of young families. In such an uncertain climate, people crave security and constancy. The rock-solid claims of fundamentalism can be very appealing to those who seek stability in a rapidly changing world.

EVALUATING RELIGIOUS CHANGE

On both an individual and a communal level, religious change can either enhance or diminish human lives. The next and final part will discuss the ways that religious experience can be either alienating or reconciling. We close this chapter with a brief discussion of alienating and reconciling elements of religious change.

Joining a religious movement can bring painful breaks with one's past. The first Christians, for example, often found themselves alienated from families and communities when they joined the church. No wonder they treasured Jesus' saying that anyone who left father and mother, sister and brother, would receive a hundredfold. From the perspective of their peers, the early Christians probably seemed to be members of a strange cult that encouraged giving away possessions to the poor and leaving familiar surroundings to live in a community of other cult members. Jerusalem officials saw the movement as dangerous and tried to suppress it. One rabbi named Gamaliel argued that the authorities should leave the cult alone. He said that if the Christian community was not of God, then it would not survive. On the other hand, he said, if this movement is of God, you do not want to interfere with it. Later generations of Christians have always believed that the first followers of Jesus had found an authentic way of reconciling themselves to God, the world, and themselves. However, from the perspective of their contemporaries, they seemed to have chosen a strange way.

New religious movements are particularly likely to be seen by outsiders as evidence of alienation from the larger society, which may in fact be true. Nonetheless, many of those who join what are often called "cults" believe that they have found peace in a community setting. In the decades since World War II, Japan has witnessed the development of many new religious movements. A number of factors contribute to the popularity of these sects. For example, young people who must continue to live at home because land and housing stock are in chronically short supply can find a community of like-minded peers an important outlet. Some sects require great devotion; others require only casual, nonexclusive allegiance. The vast majority of Japanese who experiment with membership in a new religious sect find the experience either temporarily or permanently beneficial, or else they leave. However, the experience of one religious group, Aum Shinrikyo, illustrates the dynamic by which an entire community can become alienated from the larger society in a destructive manner.

Aum Shinrikyo means "the true teaching of Om." (**Om** is considered to be a sacred syllable in Hinduism and Buddhism.) Shoko Asahara, the founder of the movement, based his teachings largely on Buddhism, although he also included Christian and Jewish elements. His followers typically gave their property to Aum Shinrikyo and lived with other members of the religious community. Cult members usually severed ties with their families. They sought spiritual insight through practices ranging from meditation to drugs. Although many who joined found what they wanted, others tried to leave the cult. Asahara tried to coerce them into staying; he may even have ordered the murders of some who tried to leave. Most Aum Shinrikyo members did not realize that Asahara was using the money they brought the movement to finance the production of sarin, a nerve-gas so deadly that the greatest challenge in its manufacture is to prevent killing those who synthesize it. In March 1995, Asahara ordered his followers to release sarin gas in the crowded Tokyo subway system at rush hour. Eleven people died; thousands were hospitalized.

The Aum Shinrikyo experience exemplifies one tragic dynamic that can unfold as a religious group that perceives itself to be misunderstood cuts itself off from society. Because personal conversion experiences are so powerful, those who undergo them are often unquestioning of the movement to which they have converted. The members of Aum Shinrikyo surrendered themselves so thoroughly to a new and powerful experience that they were unable to assess the terrible power they were giving their leader.

On the other hand, religious change can be life-giving to those who brave it. Vatican II was such an adventure in religious change. Pope John XXIII called Vatican II, a global council of the Roman Catholic church that met from 1962 to 1965. Church councils are an ancient tradition of the Catholic church; the decisions of a council are binding even on the pope. To this council John XXIII invited not only Roman Catholics but also observers from a variety of faith traditions, a move typical of the openness of the council. For many Roman Catholics, Vatican II was a fresh breeze blowing through open windows; it marked a new openness to engagement with the world.

The council declared, "The joys and the hopes, the griefs and the anxieties of the men of this age, especially those who are poor or in any way afflicted, these too are the joys and hopes, the griefs and anxieties of the followers of Christ. Indeed, nothing genuinely human fails to raise an echo in their hearts." With these words the Roman Catholic church announced its willingness to align itself in closer solidarity with all the peoples of the world than it had previously been perceived to do. The council reminded the world that "the Church has always had the duty of scrutinizing the signs of the times and of interpreting them in the light of

MARY N. MACDONALD

The contemporary architecture of a Baptist church contrasts with the traditional architecture of a Methodist church on a city street.

the gospel." By emphasizing the church's duty to respond to the "signs of the times," Vatican II cleared the way for lasting reform of church teachings and practices.

The legacy of Vatican II is rich. The council emphasized the biblical insight that the church is the people of God, thus empowering the entire membership of the church to share in the ministries of the gospel. In order to guarantee full understanding of the **Mass**, the central Catholic rite, Vatican II ended the centuries-long practice of conducting Mass in Latin and introduced the use of local languages for the celebration of the Mass. Even church architecture and music changed after Vatican II. Most Roman Catholic churches constructed since then tend to be modern, light, and airy; older churches tend to be darker and more inward-looking. Different kinds of worship spaces have different benefits; many people prefer to pray or meditate in old, quiet, churches. However, the new style of architecture seemed to embody the spirit of change. After Vatican II, many congregations began to substitute guitars for organs, folk-style hymns for more traditional service music. (Remember the great popularity of acoustic guitars and folk music in the 1960s.) Because the church had begun to understand itself as the people, its life grew closer to the daily rhythms of ordinary life.

Few complex human experiences can be simply categorized in positive or negative terms. Even many of those who welcomed and promoted the changes of Vatican II had some nostalgia for older ways, some of which have been re-introduced. Elderly people who had worshiped in

Latin their entire lives were denied the consolation of hearing that language again in communal prayer. Change, even healthy change, can be painful. Developments that help many reconcile themselves to God, community, and world may leave others feeling alone and alienated. We now turn to a more thorough examination of reconciliation, alienation, and the search for authenticity in religious experience.

RESOURCES

Activities

1. Organize a multimedia class presentation on the impact of the Reformation on art, architecture, and music.
2. Research "fundamentalist" movements in contemporary Islam, Protestantism, Catholicism, and Judaism. What are the common elements of these movements? How is each movement unique? Do you think that "fundamentalism" is a useful or adequate term for describing these movements?
3. Religions affect (and even effect) political change. Organize a debate on the merits and liabilities of religious influence on the political sphere.
4. Research the impact of the Holocaust on the development of Jewish thought and life, both religious and secular.
5. Analyze the dynamics of cultural contact represented in one of the following: the film *The Mission*, Ngugi wa Thiong'o's novel *The River Between*, or Bharati Mukherjee's novel *Jasmine*.
6. Organize a panel discussion on the impact of shifting cultural and religious patterns on women's roles. (You may want to include reports on Mary Gordon's *Final Payments* or Anzia Yezierska's *The Bread Givers*.)

Readings

The Acts of the Apostles. The New Testament book that records the history of the new religious movement that came to be called Christianity.

Roland Bainton. *The Reformation of the Sixteenth Century*. Boston: Beacon Press, 1952. Still a useful scholarly treatment of the Protestant Reformation.

Mary Gordon. *Final Payments*. New York: Random House, 1978. A novel of a young Catholic woman caught between family obligations and a changing world.

Bartolomé de Las Casas. *The Devastation of the Indies: A Brief Account*, trans. Herma Briffault. Baltimore: Johns Hopkins University Press, 1992. A brutal account of the actions of Europeans in colonizing the Americas.

Bharati Mukherjee. *Jasmine*. New York: Grove Weidenfeld, 1989. A contemporary novel, *Jasmine* tells the story of a young woman named Jyoti who is born in a village in India. She travels to the United States and makes a new life for herself on an Iowa farm.

Ngugi wa Thiong'o. *The River Between*. London: Heinemann, 1978. This powerful novel follows a young man from a traditional African family who attempts to mediate between the ways of the Christian missionaries and his people's customs.

Max Weber. *The Protestant Ethic and the Spirit of Capitalism,* trans. Talcott Parsons. New York: Scribner, 1958. A classic work in the sociology of religion.

Anzia Yezierska. *The Bread Givers.* New York: Persea Books, 1975. A novel of Jewish life in New York in the early twentieth century and the conflicts faced by a young Jewish woman who wants to study.

Audiovisuals

The Mission. Dramatizes two styles of cultural contact and change in the encounter of European Christian missionaries with indigenous people in the Americas.

NOTES

1. Elisabeth Tooker, "On the Development of the Handsome Lake Religion," *Proceedings of the American Philosophical Society* 133 (1989): 35-50.

2. Quoted in Alla Bozarth-Campbell, *Womanpriest: A Personal Odyssey* (New York: Paulist Press, 1978), 134-136.

3. Ngugi wa Thiong'o, *The River Between* (London: Heinemann, 1978), 141.

4. William E. Montgomery, *Under Their Own Vine and Fig Tree: The African-American Church in the South, 1865-1900* (Baton Rouge: Lousiana State University Press, 1993), 14.

PART V

LIVING AUTHENTICALLY

In the previous chapters we have suggested that religion is one way in which we structure our lives. Religions are systems that help us to organize our experiences meaningfully. One way in which religions assist us in organizing our lives is through ritual activity. Rituals set apart certain times and spaces as special or sacred. These rituals help us to find a meaningful place in our cosmos, one which relates us to ourselves, to others, and to the ultimate principle(s) in our lives. Rituals such as Sabbath observances help us to maintain our place in the community. Other rituals such as marriage ceremonies announce that our place within the community has changed. Rituals also embody norms of behavior that assist a person to live well.

Religious texts orient us to issues larger than ourselves and connect us to others whose lives have also been shaped by these same texts. Together, rituals and texts combine to situate us in the world, to provide us with a position from which we make decisions and order our lives. We have seen that even those religions considered to be most traditional change due to the influences of history and the changing demands and customs of the society in which the religion is practiced.

From our study of religion, then, it would seem that participating in a religion would contribute to our happiness and well-being. Many times it does. Sometimes, though, the practice of religion tends to alienate or distance us from ourselves and the world around us. When we talk about the effect that institutional religion has on a particular person, we speak of religion as "reconciling" or as "alienating."

When we say that religion is reconciling we mean that practicing a religion helps us to grow and develop into responsible and free persons and to contribute to the society in which we live. It means that we find our place within a particular religion's worldview or cosmology, and that this adds meaning and purpose to our lives. In religions such as Islam, Christianity, and Judaism, it means that we live in harmonious relation to a personal God who is the source of all that is good and life-giving. People who experience religion as reconciling say that their religion contributes greatly to their feeling at ease with themselves and the world. This feeling of being at home with oneself usually results in an openness to others and a concern for their welfare. Many of the world's social activists are motivated by religious traditions that consider every person who lives as a brother or sister.

Religion, however, sometimes has a very alienating effect on people. When we say that religion is alienating it means that we perceive that religious traditions require us to abdicate responsible decision making, that they impede our freedom to think freely, and that they may contribute very little to the society in which we live. Rather than nourishing our imaginations and offering us challenges, they seem to require unthinking observance of outdated practices. Their ritualism keeps us from coming into contact with the deepest parts of ourselves. The practices of alienating religion leave us feeling out of kilter with ourselves. We soon feel adrift in the world. When we experience religion as alienating, we find little meaning in the religion's cosmology, and we find its rituals suffocating and its God either oppressive or meaningless. Often, people experience religion as ambiguous, at times reconciling and at times alienating.

Although the reconciling and alienating dimensions of religion nearly always coexist, chapter 10 will emphasize the reconciling features of religion. In this chapter, we will discuss both personal and social forms of reconciliation as well as practices that various religious traditions provide to aid us in maintaining interior peace and harmony in our world.

In chapter 11 we will investigate the reasons that contribute to the alienating qualities of religion. Part I treated the interrelation that exists between religion and culture. Chapter 11 will develop this point further by showing that many cultural norms, such as patriarchy, contribute to the religious alienation we experience. In this chapter we will also discuss the correlation that exists between religious and psychological maturity. Finally, we will discuss cults as one response to alienating religion.

Although we can conceptualize and discuss religion as either reconciling or alienating, in most people's experience religion is neither completely reconciling nor totally alienating. This should not surprise us, because in real life we seldom experience anything as completely good or completely bad. For example, we are glad we live in the United States or Canada or wherever we live. But for some reason or another we hesitate to give that country our total allegiance. We are not prepared to overlook its weaknesses; neither do we want to deny its strengths. In such a case, we say that our attitude toward our country is equivocal or ambiguous. In the same way, most people are ambivalent toward institutional religion. They see its strengths but cannot deny its weaknesses. If we have been raised to think of religion as totally good, we may hesitate to under-

NANCY RING

Symbols are ambiguous because their interpretation depends on the context of the person relating to the symbol. The flag of the United States is perceived by some as a symbol of reconciliation; by others as a symbol of alienation. What feelings does this image evoke in you?

score its limitations. On the other hand, unless we are aware of the limitations and weaknesses of an institution, including the institutions of religion, there is no incentive to improve it. More importantly, we will not be able to discriminate between reconciling and alienating religious practices and understandings of religion. Consequently, we will be unable to appropriate those aspects which help us to live meaningful, authentic lives, from those aspects which are insignificant and even detrimental to our flourishing. Now, we will discuss in more detail religion as reconciling, as alienating, and as ambiguous.

Chapter 10

Reconciling Religion

PERSONAL RECONCILIATION WITHIN THE COMMUNITY

We need some degree of order in our lives. This order is at least partially realized by virtue of being born into a culture that has been handed on to us from our parents and grandparents, a cultural worldview which was passed on to them from their parents and grandparents. To a great extent, then, we are raised in a world that has already been ordered for us by our ancestors. With broad strokes, their cultural and religious stories tell us what is important and direct us to order our personal lives with these values as guidelines. In this way we are taught how to order our lives according to cultural and religious values. A worldview is not static, however. As it was passed on from generation to generation, it was modified, even if unconsciously, to accommodate new insights, attitudes, and discoveries. We, in our turn, are also adjusting this worldview to our particular circumstances. Nevertheless, being born in societies characterized by industry and technology shapes people differently from being born in societies that are less industrialized. The former generally appreciate values associated with individualism more than those associated with community. The latter seem to value the good of the community more highly than individual achievement.

The values embedded in worldviews are usually transmitted through the literary genre of myth. Initially, these myths are transmitted orally. At a later time, some of them may be committed to writing. Relying on the cultural and religious myths within which we live, we find our place in relation to one another, to nature, and to God or the source of life that we consider to be ultimate. So, living in accordance with a particular cosmology (worldview, myth) provides a person with a sense of being connected with the world, rather than being a cosmic orphan, unrelated even to one's self, in free-fall, totally at the whim of chaotic forces.

Two Examples of Living within a Worldview

Two people whose religion motivated them to seek peace and justice for marginalized peoples were Martin Luther King, Jr. (1929-1968), and Mohandas Gandhi (1869-1948). Gandhi, an Indian Hindu, is remembered for his struggle for the civil rights of Indians living in South Africa, for leading the Indian struggle for independence from Great Britain, and for advocating the elimination of the caste system from Hindu life. Raised in a deeply religious family, Gandhi's spirit was nurtured by the Bhagavad-Gita, a text of his religious tradition.

Gandhi studied law in England and was sent by his Indian firm to represent them in South Africa. The twenty years Gandhi spent in South Africa influenced him greatly. He experienced an appalling degree of discrimination toward Indians, which served to sensitize him to the plight of the politically powerless. Through the Russian writer Tolstoy, he came to know Christianity and was inspired by the figure of Jesus, especially as he was portrayed delivering his **Sermon on the Mount** (Mt 5-7). The spirit of one of the beatitudes from that Sermon, "Blessed are the peacemakers, for they shall see God," resonated with and strengthened his Hindu affinity for nonviolence. From a Hindu worldview, reinforced by his reading of another tradition, Gandhi conducted his liberation movements in a nonviolent manner. His Indian countrymen and women gave him the name "Mahatma" which means Great Soul.

Martin Luther King, Jr., born in Georgia, was a Baptist minister, the son of a Baptist minister. He discovered within his Christian tradition the resources to lead his fellow African-Americans in their struggles for civil rights during the 1960s. In his studies and travels, King became deeply affected by the peaceful, nonviolent revolution brought about by the leadership of Gandhi. Today, we remember King for his belief that to achieve positive change, violence must be met with nonviolence. Both Gandhi and King are examples of persons whose fundamental religious orientation served both to anchor their lives and to open them to respond to others' needs. Further, each person was attuned to finding wisdom in traditions other than his own.

Thinking about Reconciliation

Recall a time when you felt at peace with yourself, in harmony with your environment, and in kinship with others. Such an experience is akin to reconciliation. Can you identify a tradition or practices which help you maintain this feeling of being reconciled and in harmony with life? Did this experience of reconciliation make you more attentive to the lives of others?

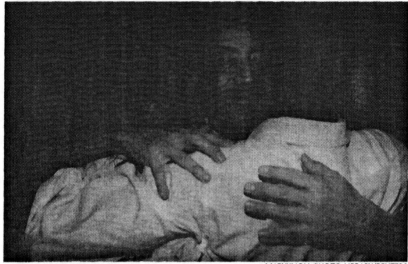

People who reconcile with one another often express this in a bodily manner. Here three men embrace to show their solidarity.

Since we are born into an already existing culture and religious worldview, it may seem that we have no choice in how we situate ourselves in relation to others. Although this may be true initially, in the very earliest years of our life we begin testing this worldview as soon as we learn to say, "No!" As early as the "terrible twos" we test boundaries. This continues in various ways until we are satisfied (or dissatisfied) that living the values of our received worldview, for the most part, results in an interesting, meaningful, and fulfilling way of life, one that is humanly satisfying. We may also experience that living outside these patterns causes feelings of dislocation. Although we may choose to live within the general contours of an inherited worldview, we continue to explore various ways of living within it, exploring its boundaries, learning whether the boundaries as they were transmitted to us are pliable or rigid. This type of exploration and interpretation is the reason why Jews, Christians, and Muslims can share the creation narratives and the stories of the ancestors (such as that of Abraham and Sarah), which we find in the Book of Genesis. Because they share these sacred texts, the three religions embrace a worldview in which God is the fundamental reality, and human beings live in a world of God's making. Yet, further interpretation of these same texts results in religions that differ greatly from each other. Adding to the complexity of this situation is the fact that there are persons within each of these religions who interpret these Genesis myths literally and those who interpret them symbolically.

Regardless of how individuals interpret the religious worldview within which they live, they will at times violate the value and belief system which they have embraced. Perhaps a religious orientation places a great deal of emphasis on living in harmony with nature and observing good ecological practices. Although the person has willingly embraced this value and finds it meaningful, it is conceivable that he or she may be lured by a business deal to ignore sound ecological practices for the sake of profit. Or, those whose worldview demands that justice and a regard for the dignity of each person structure relationships may act in a mean-spirited or demeaning manner toward people whom they find irritating. St. Paul knew this experience of struggling with opposing tendencies and inclinations. In Romans 7:15 he says, "I do the things I do not want to do, and I don't do those things I want to do." St. Augustine was even more expressive when he cried out to God, "Lord, make me chaste, but not today." How often we have experienced this state of affairs. "I want to stop smoking, but I'll finish this pack first." "I want to spend more time studying, but tonight I want to go out with my friends."

CONFLICTING WORLDVIEWS

At times, it is not only our personal values and actions that are in conflict with our religious or cultural worldview, but the cultural and religious values we have embraced come into conflict with each other and, consequently, put us in conflict. Consider these two cases. During World War II, the German cultural myth was that of Aryan supremacy. The cultural myth of Aryan supremacy shaped the consciousness of the German people to believe that they were racially superior to others, especially Jews. Of course, many Germans were also Christian. The Christian story teaches people to value all people as if they were other Christs. You can easily see that the values of these two worldviews were in conflict. Some German Protestant groups tried to accommodate themselves to National Socialism, Hitler's party. Other Protestants found they could not accommodate themselves, and they formed the Confessing Church, which resisted Hitler's effort to enlist the churches in his totalitarian endeavors. The Confessing Church supported the Barmen Declaration, issued in 1934 by church people from various traditions, which defined Christian opposition to National Socialism. Dietrich Bonhoeffer, an influential Lutheran pastor, was imprisoned and eventually executed for resisting Hitler and his views. As we learned in chapter 2, worldviews do have consequences.

The practice of burning witches, which swept Europe between the fourteenth and sixteenth centuries, is another example of the conflict between personal and religious values. In medieval Europe, cultural and religious worldviews coincided, for the most part. This is the phenomenon often referred to as Christendom. During this period church officials often classified as witches those women who did not conform to the usual cultural norms. Among such women were those who chose neither to marry nor to enter a convent, or those who practiced traditional forms of healing. From one point of view, we can say that these women were put to death because they did not conform to the worldview of Christendom. From another point of view, we can say that the horror of this witch hunt led to a new understanding of the Christian message. The beloved French saint, Joan of Arc (1412-1431) is a symbol for such women. As a young girl, Joan believed she received messages from heavenly voices that urged her to lead France in battle against the English. She donned armor and led the French army to a decisive victory. In a later battle, however, she was captured. In a church trial, Joan was convicted of witchcraft for wearing masculine clothes and of heresy for claiming that she was compelled to follow her "voices" even when doing so put her at odds with the Roman Catholic church. At the age of nineteen, Joan, also known as the Maid of Orleans, was burned at the stake. Twenty-five years after her death, she was cleared of all charges of **sorcery** and heresy. Religious worldviews, although in one sense normative, are always in the process of reformation.

THE CONFESSION OF TRANSGRESSIONS

When we have disconnected ourselves from meaningful patterns of relationship, participation in public rituals can help us to re-establish and maintain these connections. Such rites and rituals are reconciling. They have the effect of healing dislocation and of revitalizing individuals and communities. We will investigate some of these practices of reconciliation. Ritual practices which include the confession or acknowledgment of sins, transgressions, defilements, or the breaking of taboos are practiced in many religions. Most Christian denominations include within their order of public worship a rite of confession in which the community participates. This rite is an acknowledgment that relationships have been broken and need to be repaired. It is the belief of these religions that such acknowledgment, if entered into sincerely, reconciles one to the community.

Religions recognize that all personal transgressions affect the community by weakening the bonds that unite its members. This social aspect of personal reconciliation can be seen very graphically in the early practices of the Christian church. At that time the norm for reconciliation was public confession. People seeking reconciliation confessed their sins in the midst of the assembly. The presiding minister, usually a bishop, imposed a penance in the name of the community. Often the penance was also public, such as the wearing of a distinctive garb, the performance of good deeds, or even exclusion from the community for a certain period of time. Today this seems very harsh, and we may wonder if people would submit to this discipline. Still, the traces of this understanding of the social nature of even our most private acts are found in the contemporary rites of various religions. Let us consider some of these public rites.

Jews gathered for evening prayer on Yom Kippur. An illustration from a seventeenth-century Jewish prayer book, Frankfurt, Germany.

In Judaism, the notion of reconciliation plays a major role. Yom Kippur, the holiest day of the year for Jews, is a Day of Atonement, a day when individuals align themselves anew with the community *and* with the community's worldview. Between Rosh Hashana, the day observed by Jews as New Year's and Yom Kippur, which occurs ten days later, observant Jews reflect on how they have lived during the previous year. If they admit to themselves that they have held a grudge against someone or have acted unjustly, they make amends to the persons involved. On Yom Kippur itself, Jews fast from sunset to sunset. They gather in their synagogues or temples and spend the day in prayer. This attitude toward reconciliation is a development of the prophetic insight that the quality of people's relationship with others mirrors the quality of their relationship to God. At the conclusion of Yom Kippur, observant Jews participate in a celebratory meal. Reconciliation engenders joy and good comradeship, and this demands social expression. The sharing of food is among the most deeply symbolic and reconciling rituals known to humankind. We don't eat with our enemies, and if we do, they usually do not remain enemies.

FROM *THE JEWISH PRAYER BOOK FOR THE DAYS OF AWE*

Our God and God of our fathers, forgive our sins on this Yom Kippur. Blot out and pass over our transgressions, as Isaiah declared in Your name: "I alone blot out your transgressions, for My sake; your sins I shall not recall. I have swept away your transgressions like a cloud, your sins like mist. Return to Me, for I have redeemed you." And the Torah promises: "For on this day atonement shall be made for you, to cleanse you; of all your sins before the Lord shall be cleansed."

Rites of reconciliation reflect the cosmology, culture, and geographical context of a particular community. The Navajo are a Native American tribe who live in the arid lands of the Southwest where there is an abundance of sand. Within the Navajo cosmology, physical illness is understood to be a symptom of spiritual dislocation from the community. Therefore, the restoration of health is a function of becoming reconciled with the community. In order to achieve this restoration, the Navajo singer, who is the traditional healer, calls upon the mythic ancestors or holy people and mediates their healing power to the sick person. On the floor of the ceremonial **hogan**, in the sand, the singer draws mythic figures who bear some relation to the type of illness from which the person is suffering. When the sand painting is completed, corn pollen is sprinkled on both the painting and the afflicted person. The sprinkling of the pollen creates a connection between the mythic figures and the one who seeks healing. Then, the one seeking healing sits in the middle of the painting. The singer, hands moistened with medicine, transfers sand from the faces of the various figures to the face of the suffering one. Next, the healer transfers sand from the feet of the figures to the feet of the one for whom the ritual is being performed. This pattern continues until the person, through the transfer of sand, has become totally identified with the holy persons represented in the sand painting. By this means, the spiritual power of the ancestors has been mediated to the sick person. Through this rite, the person is reconciled with the community and thus healed.

The realization that one's physical well-being is in some way tied to one's spiritual well-being is not limited to the Navajo conceptualization of the world. This understanding is widespread in both religious and secular settings. Modern medicine, as deeply embedded in science as it is, acknowledges that headaches and stomachaches, in fact aches of all kinds, are often signs of something askew in the spiritual or psychological dimension of our lives. Even cancer, which is certainly an organic disease, appears to sometimes be triggered by stress.

The use of substances such as sand, spittle, and oils to anoint the sick person's body is also a widespread practice. The New Testament recounts the story of Jesus applying spittle to the eyes of a blind man in order that he be healed (Jn 9:6). Among the Highlanders of Papua New Guinea, various oils obtained from trees are often used in healing rites.

In Christianity as well as in Judaism and among the Navajo, the ordinary place of personal reconciliation is within the context of public worship or of community. Each Eucharist in the Roman Catholic church begins with a rite of reconciliation. The Presbyterian order of worship, *The Service for the Lord's Day*, includes the *Call to Confession* and the *Confession of Sin*. The directives for the Presbyterian service offer several options for this rite of reconciliation, but each minister is also at liberty to call the congregation to repentance in his or her own words. It is significant that after the congregation has acknowledged its sinfulness, the members are invited to extend a greeting of peace to one another.

CALL TO CONFESSION

If we say we have no sin,
we deceive ourselves, and the truth is not in us.
But if we confess our sins,
God who is faithful and just
will forgive us our sins
and cleanse us from all unrighteousness.
In humility and faith
let us confess our sin to God.

CONFESSION OF SIN

Merciful God,
you pardon all who truly repent and turn to you.
We humbly confess our sins and ask your mercy.
We have not loved you with a pure heart,
nor have we loved our neighbor as ourselves.
We have not done justice, loved kindness,
or walked humbly with you, our God.
Have mercy on us, O God, in your loving kindness.
In your great compassion, cleanse us from our sin.
Create in us a clean heart, O God,
and renew a right spirit within us.
Do not cast us from your presence, or take your Holy Spirit from us.
Restore to us the joy of your salvation
and sustain us with your bountiful Spirit.
From the Presbyterian Order of Worship

Many people never participate in a formal ritual of reconciliation such as those just described. Everyone, however, has experienced the need to acknowledge failures and weaknesses. This need appears to be rooted in the human situation and to express a universal need to live in proper relationship. Recall a time, for example, when a friend offended you. Connections were broken. The next time you saw your friend, there was tension or unease between you. It was impossible for the two of you to proceed with your relationship as if nothing had happened. One of you had to break the ice. Either you had to acknowledge that you had been hurt, or your friend had to acknowledge that he or she had disrupted your relationship. Recall with what relief you resumed your friendship. Sometimes people describe this experience as having had a load lifted from their shoulders. Religious practices of confession are, basically, a ritualization of this felt human need to live a life reconciled to one's environment and all that is included within it.

Religions teach that there is no such thing as a purely private offense which affects only the transgressor. If a person tells a lie, it has the social effect of lowering the level of trust among the members of the community. If a person steals, others become very cautious to ensure that they are not victimized. Dorm directors counsel students to lock the doors to their rooms even if they are simply going to get a soda from the vending machine. College cafeterias check the card of each person who enters. This level of caution has developed gradually over the span of a few generations. Among other reasons, this distrust developed because an increasing number of individuals became dislocated from the community and initiated an avalanche of distrust. In the next chapter, we will examine possible reasons for this dislocation or alienation from the community. The purpose of these examples, though, is to understand that the personal and the social effects of transgressions are always intertwined.

Because every transgression has social consequences, the ordinary place for rites of confession or of reconciliation is within the context of social or public worship. Acting upon this understanding, we have seen that Jews celebrate Yom Kippur in the synagogue, the Navajo enacts the sand painting ceremony in the ceremonial hogan, and the Christian confesses in a house of worship.

There are some Christian denominations, such as Anglican and Roman Catholic, whose practice of reconciliation includes private confession. In such a case, the individual acknowledges personal transgressions to a minister or priest, who gives verbal assurance that the person has, indeed, been reconciled. However, even this practice of individual confession emphasizes the social consequences of transgression, because the priest or minister reconciles the penitent in the name of the community.

> God the Father of Mercies, through the death and resurrection of Jesus His Son, has reconciled the world to Himself and has sent the Holy Spirit among us for the forgiveness of our sins. Through the ministry of the church may God grant you pardon and peace and I absolve you in the Name of the Father, the Son, and the Holy Spirit.

RECONCILIATION BETWEEN RELIGIOUS GROUPS

Thus far, the emphasis in our discussion has been on the dynamics of personal reconciliation to the community. Intimately related to this, however, is the necessity for religious communities to acknowledge or confess publicly their transgressions. An example of such a corporate transgression would be a community's complicity in dehumanizing individuals either within or outside their religious group so that those devalued feel worthless or insignificant. In such cases, the community needs to confess publicly its wrongdoing for two reasons. The group needs to remain connected to its own worldview, and it needs to maintain connections with other religious bodies.

Whereas religious traditions generally include prescribed rites and ceremonies for the reconciliation of the individual to the community, communal gestures of reconciliation are usually initiated and expressed in the name of the community by the community's leadership. Such corporate confessions of repentance occur much more rarely than personal expressions of transgressions. There are many reasons for this, but the principal reason is that Western modernity seems to lack an adequate understanding of the many and intricate ways that groups of human beings are connected with one another. Another reason that leaders are reluctant to voice the shortcomings and sins of their religious groups is the fear that such admissions will lower the level of confidence members have in the religious community. Still, there are such admissions of corporate guilt, and we need to pay attention to their significance. Instances of such gestures of communal or corporate attempts at reconciliation are illustrated by the following examples.

Pope John XXIII, who was pope from 1958 to 1963, was referred to by Catholics and non-Catholics alike as "Good Pope John." He brought to the papacy an openness to new ideas, a trust in ecumenical and interfaith dialogue, and confidence in the goodness of the world. Because he wanted to bring the Roman Catholic church into conversation with the contemporary world, he convened the Second Vatican Council (Vatican II) which met from 1962 to 1965. This council is considered to be one of the most important religious events of the twentieth century. It was important for non-Catholics as well as for Catholics because it brought to an end a period of isolation, defensiveness, and triumphalism in the Catholic church.

Pope John XXIII seemed to understand more than any previous pope the deep bonds which unite Judaism and Christianity. While he was pope, he was visited by a delegation of Jewish leaders. He greeted them thus: "I am your brother, Joseph." Pope John knew there were several levels of meaning present in his simple greeting. First, Joseph (Giuseppe) was his given name. Immediately, by this greeting, he showed that their common humanity bound them together as equals. Then, of course, brothers have a common ancestry. Pope John thus acknowledged the ancestral history shared by Jews and Christians. Finally, within this greeting was an allusion to the story of reconciliation between Joseph, the son of the ancestor Jacob, and his brothers (Gen 45). To these leaders of Judaism, immersed in the common ancestral history of Judaism and Christianity, this simple phrase had profound resonance and was heard as an acknowledgment of the desire of Christians to be reconciled with their Jewish brothers and sisters.

Although that encounter was only a quasi-official acknowledgment of kinship, the same pope was responsible for the revision by Vatican

Council II of the Good Friday liturgy of the Roman Catholic church. In the Liturgy for Good Friday, the church prays for many groups of people. Among those groups are the Catholic church, the pope, those in government and the Jews. In the pre-Vatican II liturgy, the Jews, because they did not accept Catholic teachings concerning Jesus, were described as having a veil over their hearts, a veil that needed to be removed. After they were described in that manner, this prayer was made for them:

> Almighty and everlasting God, You drive not *even* the Jews from your mercy; hear our prayers which we offer for the blindness of that people, that, acknowledging the light of your truth, which is Christ, they may be rescued from their darkness.

Vatican II, in the liturgical renewal which took place under the auspices of Good Pope John XXIII, replaced that Good Friday prayer with this one.

> Almighty and eternal God, you made the promises to Abraham and his descendants. In your goodness, hear the prayers of your church so that the people whom from of old you made your own may come to the fullness of redemption.

In changing the public rite of the entire Roman Catholic church, its leadership acknowledged it had wrongly and insensitively understood its relationship to the Jews and had attributed bad faith to them. Consequently, the Christian-Jewish relationship had become marked by an alienation so extreme that the Holocaust could be tolerated by Christian people.

Expressions of reconciliation and alienation have results within our everyday world. As we saw in Part III, words are effective in shaping our imaginations. The imaginations of countless generations of Christians had been formed so as to interpret Jewish motivations, actions, desires, and worship as "blind." The untold suffering and persecution of Jews over the centuries at the hands of Christians were partly the result of such alienating language. Although the persecution of the Jews by Christians cannot be reduced solely to the use of language, this example does show us how large a part language actually plays in shaping imaginations and effecting action.

The change in the prayers of the Roman Catholic liturgy is akin to an official acknowledgment that throughout the centuries, untold harm has been done to Jews by Christians. The new language, although relatively recent, has been effective in furthering the process of reconciliation between Roman Catholics and Jews.

From the viewpoint of an observer outside the Roman Catholic tradition, and even for some within that tradition, the change of language in the Good Friday ritual did not go far enough. That may be. Yet, it remains significant that the language no longer is that of hostility and alienation.

A second example of the corporate acknowledgment of wrongdoing and repentance is that of the **Southern Baptist Convention**'s admission of racism. This admission of guilt is even more striking when we consider that Southern Baptists came into existence because they seceded from the American Baptist church, which opposed slavery. In June 1995, more than a century after they were founded to legitimate the owning of slaves, the convention issued a "Resolution on Racial Reconciliation." The Resolution states:

[W]e apologize to all African-Americans for condoning and/or perpetuating individual and systemic racism in our lifetime; and we genuinely repent of racism of which we have been guilty, whether consciously or unconsciously.

This acknowledgment by the Southern Baptist Convention of its complicity in supporting the institution of slavery in the United States provides another instance in which a religious community seeks reconciliation with those whom its practices have harmed. It is also an example of the necessity every institution has to continually interpret its worldview in the light of personal, corporate, and historical developments. As the resolution so correctly points out, some of the alienating attitudes and beliefs which we hold may be unconsciously held. Yet, we are bound to consciously reflect upon our religious worldviews and to reinterpret them as we ourselves become more mature and as knowledge in all fields, not only religion, is advanced.

RECONCILIATION TO ONESELF

Understanding ourselves within the context of worldviews, religious and nonreligious, and living in harmony with the values proposed by these worldviews would be easier if the connections between ourselves, institutions, nature, and other people were more neatly drawn. Neat and exact distinctions, however, can exist only in our minds. Although it is important to be able to think conceptually and theoretically about reconciliation and alienation, we must never forget that life blurs these theoretical distinctions. In everyday living, nothing is as clear cut and precise as it may appear to be in our thoughts.

For example, conscious participation in public rites of reconciliation, such as Yom Kippur or in Navajo sand painting, often helps a person re-establish inner harmony. But there is nothing automatic about it. Some people attend these rituals, and they either feel no greater peace than before they attended, or they feel even more ill at ease. However, these same people may experience that the closeness with nature that occurs in activities as simple as gardening or hiking can result in a more genuine concern for neighbor or a more receptive attitude to oneself. Sometimes, the starting point of the reconciliation process begins with the attempt to realign or evaluate one's priorities in respect to how one is actually living. At other times, achieving harmony and balance within ourselves may mean re-evaluating the merits of our currently held viewpoints to determine if they continue to be meaningful.

People who continue to find their religious worldview meaningful frequently appeal to the spiritual traditions within their religion to nourish their religious development. Through these spiritual practices, they re-establish harmony or meaning within their lives, keep in touch with who they really are, who they want to become, and what they value. In contrast to the rites which reconcile us with the community, however, the exercises which foster personal reconciliation tend to be practiced privately rather than publicly. Examples of private rituals are personal prayer, meditation, retreats, fasting, and works of charity. Although these particular practices differ depending on whether they are shaped by Hindu, Christian, Muslim, or Native American traditions, they are similar in this respect: those who engage in these practices over a period of time report that they are quite effective in fostering in them an authentic way of living.

Personal Prayer and Meditation

Personal prayer has many shades and hues. It can take the form of the simple repetition of a phrase or sound such as, "Jesus, Lord, have mercy upon me," or the "Om" of the Hindus and Buddhist monks. The "Jesus prayer" has traditionally been more widely practiced by members of the Greek and Russian Orthodox churches than by other Christian denominations. Because people have become more open to investigating religious traditions other than their own, this is now changing. People of other traditions practice this chant and discover its value for them. It has often been referred to as a centering prayer, since its purpose is to gather and focus on God the energies of heart and mind. For Hindus, the chanting of the Sanskrit word "Om" is somewhat similar. For the Hindu, "Om" is the most sacred of sounds. It contains the whole meaning and power of the universe. As we learned in chapter 9, the person who chants it with full realization will contemplate the ultimate reality and will be freed from the karmic effect of previous lives. "Om" may be recited privately or in communal prayer.

Prayer can also take the form of a heartfelt outpouring of our deepest emotions and feelings to the mystery that surrounds us. Those who practice this type of prayer report that this manner of praying opens them to possibilities they have not imagined, and that it often transforms the way they look at the circumstances of their lives. They also report that it takes courage to engage in this type of prayer, because when we allow our deepest feelings to emerge, feelings that we may have covered over for a long period of time, this may initially disconcert us. What if we discover we have feelings of hatred toward our spouse or our children? If we are caregivers for aging parents, our feelings may reveal that there are times when we wish they were dead. Perhaps we feel that God is absolutely of no help in our lives. If or when this occurs, we are likely to experience discomfort. After all, we have been raised since infancy to believe that good people love their children unconditionally, that we should want our parents to live forever, and that we should never wander from loving God, trusting that God has a purpose for everything.

The **suppression** or **repression** of such feelings, however, results in blocks to intimacy with divine mystery. When we want to be intimate with another, whether that other be our spouse or divinity, it is necessary for the two parties to reveal themselves to one another. At times, communication is blocked by unexpressed feelings, usually negative feelings of anger, inadequacy, or rebellion. Communicating these feelings both dissipates the power they have over us and establishes communication with the source of our being.

People who practice this model of prayer make the claim that prayer, by putting them in touch with their feelings which are often suppressed during the course of daily activities, keeps them in touch with their center. In other words, prayer is effective in discovering or rediscovering within themselves that which is most meaningful. That is why the expression of feeling is so important. Feelings are an indicator of who we really are at a particular moment, rather than who we think we should be or who we may want to be. Remember Augustine's heartfelt prayer: "Lord, make me chaste, but not now"! That prayer reveals the complexity and confusion of his feelings at that particular moment. But it is an honest prayer wherein he reveals himself to the other.

Because prayer is understood as communication with a holy one, we can also expect some sort of response. People report that this response takes many forms. Sometimes it is a change in feelings. A particular situation may not have changed, but we are more at peace with it. We experience an increase of energy or creativity. We become clearer about what we really value. We begin to see God in a different way, to express ourselves more openly to our spouses, and to acknowledge our own lovableness. The **Psalms** of the Hebrew Bible are moving illustrations of this type of prayer. Listen to the Israelite psalmist. Notice the range and depth of emotion he pours out to Israel's God.

PSALM 137

By the rivers of Babylon—
   there we sat down and there we wept
   when we remembered Zion.
On the willows there
   we hung up our harps.
For there our captors
   asked us for songs,

and our tormentors asked for Mirth, saying,
  "Sing us one of the songs of Zion!"

How could we sing the LORD's song
  in a foreign land?
If I forget you, O Jerusalem,
  let my right hand wither!
Let my tongue cling to the roof of my mouth,
  if I do not remember you,
if I do not set Jerusalem
  above my highest joy.

Remember, O LORD, against the Edomites
  the day of Jerusalem's fall,
how they said, "Tear it down! Tear it down!
  Down to its foundations!"
O Daughter Babylon, you Devastator!
  Happy shall they be who pay you back
  what you have done to us!
Happy shall they be who take your little ones
  and dash them against the rock!

Not all prayer, though, takes the form of words. If you think about your relationships with your closest friends or your spouse, you will remember times when it was enough simply to be in the presence of the person whom you cherish. It seemed inappropriate to disturb your togetherness with words. So, you remained silent in one another's presence. Some people remark that simple presence in the company of a loved one is not a lack of communication, but it is, in reality, the deepest kind of communication. Prayer, also, has its wordless form of expression. Although the prayer itself is wordless, those who reflect on this experience describe it in lyrical language.

Jalal al-Din Rumi, who lived from 604 to 672 A.H. (1207 to 1273 C.E.), was a renowned spiritual teacher of Islam. In the following selection, this holy person of Islam describes living in the presence of Allah.

When I start from the beginning, He is my leader; when I seek my heart, He is its ravisher.
When I strive for peace, He intercedes for me; when I go to war, He is my dagger.
When I go down to the mine, He is the ruby and carnelian; when I dive into the sea, He is the pearl.
When I cross the desert, He is the oasis; when I ascend the spheres, He is the star.

***

When I awaken, He is my new awareness; when
I go to bed, He enters my dreams.

When I seek a rhyme for my poetry, he eases
the way for my mind.

He stands above whatever form you can picture,
like painter and pen.

No matter how much higher you look, He is still higher
than that "higher" of yours.

Go, abandon speaking and books—much better
it is to let Him be your book.

Be silent! For all six directions are His Light;
and when you pass beyond the directions, He Himself is the
Ruler.[1]

Mysticism

Many of the world's religions include mystical traditions of prayer. People who follow the mystical path of prayer seek experiential union with the source of life and power in their religions. Nevertheless, people who adopt this way of prayer tell us that the mystic advances through various stages of purification until at last, union is achieved. The "Om" of Hindus, the Jesus prayer of Christians, and the Vision Quest of Native Americans, as well as the wordless prayer of many other traditions, foster this experience of union.

William James in *Varieties of Religious Experience* states that mystical prayer has these four characteristics: It is noetic (gives new knowledge or

MARYKNOLL PHOTO LIBRARY/ D. DUNLEAVY

Prayer takes many forms. Here, women take time from their work to share with one another in the presence of mystery.

insight), ineffable (cannot be put into words), transitory, and passive. Because what is considered ultimate differs from religion to religion, there are differences in how this union is perceived. Consequently, all four characteristics are not always present in experiences of mystical union. Yet, at least two always seem to be present, regardless of the religious tradition of the mystic.

Some persons who attain mystical union state that they arrive at a new knowledge or understanding of divinity (noetic). They describe the knowledge as similar to the knowledge parents have of their children or spouses have of one another. It is a knowledge born of love. Often, spousal language is used to image the reality they have experienced. The mystic experience is described as ineffable; there are no words that can adequately describe this prayerful experience. It is transitory; it comes and goes. This sort of prayerful union is sustained only for short periods of time. Finally, such prayer is passive. Individuals can prepare themselves for this experience by practicing the Jesus prayer, **yoga**, or impassioned dancing such as the **Sufis** do (practices which foster self-forgetfulness). Mystics report, however, that the experience of intimacy is given to them. They are recipients of a gift.

Whatever form of prayer persons practice or whatever spiritual tradition gives shape to the prayer, people who pray generally share a common assumption. Antoine de Saint-Exupery, a twentieth-century French author, expresses this quite well through the principal character in *The Little Prince*: "What is essential is invisible to the eye." People who practice personal prayer and meditation feel the need to focus their attention on the essentials of life, to clarify their needs and desires, to live life deeply rather than to move superficially from day to day. They feel there is more to life and reality than what they presently experience, and they want to explore this more deeply. It is true that not all people who experience this need to touch more deeply the sources of life do so by prayer and meditation. But people who live within a religious worldview often employ these means.

Retreats

People who have had profound experiences often feel compelled to spend time reflecting upon the experience or attempting to make some sense of it. Notable religious figures who exemplify this basic human tendency are Siddhartha Gautama (the Buddha), Muhammad, and Jesus. Accounts of their lives record that a profound spiritual experience was followed by a period of silence and reflection, or retreat. When these religious figures emerged from their period of reflection, they seemed confirmed in the direction they wanted to take with their lives.

We know about the stories of these men because their lives and teachings influenced subsequent generations of people. Yet, for as long as history has been recorded even until today, there are accounts of ordinary women and men who regularly take time to get in touch with themselves by spending shorter or longer periods in silent reflection. Retreats are simply extended periods of personal prayer.

College students sometimes put aside their studies and ordinary social activities, and physically separate themselves from the places associated with their day-to-day activities. They reflect on their lives and often find it useful to share their insights with one another. Dialogue is frequently an important part of a retreat, because the retreatants value the community that dialogue engenders and profit from the support that the community provides. One college junior described what a retreat experience meant to her:

> I can hardly express what a gift these retreat weekends have been to me. They offer a time for reflection in addition to a break from busy campus life. I have come from the retreats with an enhanced and unbreakable relationship with God, and a community of faith that provides fellowship and support. We meet throughout the year to pray and share with each other, celebrate the liturgy and welcome new members to the retreat community. The retreat program truly offers more than just a weekend of peace and quiet, but a community that fosters faith and an experience that will change your life.

Why is silence important to self-discovery? All of us have good days and bad, times when our spirits are high, and times when we feel low. We also have periods when life is going well, and we don't want to be bothered with ethical questions, such as those with which we dealt in chapter 2. We can sometimes keep the "demons" at bay, or ethical and other personal questions at arm's length, if we keep ourselves involved and active. It is the silence of night we fear when we have only ourselves to keep us company. Retreats provoke reflection by removing us from the busyness of everyday life. Like the Buddha, people emerge from such periods of reflection with new insight into or deeper commitment to that which gives their lives meaning. A very moving story, which although probably only partially factual, nevertheless captures the dynamics of silence and retreats, was written in the fourth century by Saint Athanasius, the spiritual biographer of Saint Antony.

When he was a young man, Antony was inspired to remove himself from his usual concerns and from the company of his friends. He went outside the town and lived in a cave where he fought with the "demons," those conscious and unconscious worries and self-doubts that rob us of peace. From time to time his friends would leave him some bread or other types of food. After twenty years, Antony left the cave and rejoined his friends and entered a daily routine. According to Athanasius, when Antony emerged from the cave he had the appearance of a strong young man, vigorous, energetic, and very much alive!

Fasting

Fasting is the practice of reducing our intake of food in order to make us more focused or more alert to what is going on in our lives. Fundamentally, its purpose is the same as surrounding ourselves by silence. Siddhartha (the Buddha) found that a too-restrictive fast, however, defeated his purpose of self-knowledge. Fasting became an end in itself rather than a means to an end. It was only after he had moderated his fast that he had his profound and transformative experience of enlightenment. Still, fasting remains an important spiritual discipline fostered in many religions.

Islam, like some other religions, prescribes periods of public fasting. In Islam, during the month of Ramadan, the ninth lunar month, Muslims for whom it would not be too great a burden abstain from eating, drinking, tobacco, and sexual activity from sunup until sundown. Muslims fast to remind them of two elements of religion which we have already discussed: 1) the idea of transcendence and 2) the notion of community.

Human beings are very capable of making themselves the center of their lives, in which case they focus on satisfying their physical needs and desires. Muslims believe that material desires are quite valid, but that the desire for God should dominate all other desires. The fast reminds the Muslim that humans need to order their desires so that bodily satisfactions do not eclipse the desire for God. Abstaining, temporarily, from fulfilling bodily desires is an aid to achieving this attitude. As an eleventh-century Islamic theologian and mystic named Al-Ghazzali observed, unless the fast results in a positive interior focus on the Lord and the hereafter, people are left with only hunger and thirst for their pains.

Besides emphasizing the highest dimension of life, fasting reminds the Muslim of the plight of the countless humans living in destitution who have no choice about fasting. Their fasting is extreme, involuntary, and seldom interrupted. Experiencing the pangs of hunger and thirst, even in a mitigated way, reminds Muslims of the suffering of others. This experience of hunger and thirst may motivate Muslims to relieve the suffering of their fellows. Fasting is thought to promote inner or personal reconciliation for those who fast. If those who fast become more conscious of other people and reach out to them, it could also enable the poor and disenfranchised to become less alienated from the community. Thus, fasting reminds Muslims of two central tenets of Islam: the transcendence of Allah and their bond with all other people.

Works of Charity

Since biblical times, hospitality, particularly the sharing of food, has been a fundamental value for Jews. In particular, the stranger was to receive hospitality. The Hebrew scriptures contain many stories about hospitality and the significance of sharing food, but one particularly moving story is that of the prophet Elijah who was fed by a widow during the time of drought and famine.

As the story is narrated (1 Kgs 17:8-16), a drought came over the land. Elijah, instructed by Yahweh, went to the land east of the Jordan River, where he drank from the stream and ate food which the ravens brought. Eventually, however, the water dried up, and Yahweh instructed him to go to Sidon where he would be fed by a widow. And in fact, when he reached the city gate, he met a widow who was gathering firewood. Elijah asked her to bring him water and a bit of baked bread. The widow replied: "As Yahweh your God lives, I have no baked bread, but only a handful of meal in a jar and a little oil in a jug; I am just gathering a stick or two to go and prepare this for myself and my son to eat, and then we shall die." However, Elijah insisted and told the widow not to be afraid because neither her supply of flour nor her oil would diminish. In that way, the widow, who from her meager supply fed a stranger, was rewarded by having a permanent supply of meal and oil during the time when there was no rain to water vineyards or wheat fields.

The Jewish attitude toward hospitality is a particular instance of the view that the world belongs to everyone, and that everyone is entitled to enough of its goods to live with some degree of dignity. Jewish prophets such as Amos and **Micah** who lived in the eighth century B.C.E. reminded the people that the quality of their relationship with God was determined by the quality of their relationship with the least and poorest among them. Listen to the intense and powerful words of Micah:

> With what shall I come before the LORD,
>   and bow myself before God on high?
> shall I come before him with burnt offerings,
>   with calves a year old?
> Will the LORD be pleased with thousands of rams,
>   with ten thousands of rivers of oil?
> Shall I give my first-born for my transgression,
>   the fruit of my body for the sin of my soul?

He has told you, O mortal, what is good:
and what does the LORD require of you
but to do justice, and to love kindness,
and to walk humbly with your God? (Mi 6:6-8)

Christians recognize that their understanding of justice comes from the prophetic insights of Judaism. They also emphasize the reconciling value of sharing material, intellectual, or spiritual goods with others. The Gospel of Matthew expresses this perspective in a striking manner.

In his gospel, Matthew includes a moving scene of the Final Judgment. Jesus has come again to judge who will enter into the presence of his Father and who will be banished from the Divine Presence into everlasting fire. Jesus' criterion for deciding this is neither arbitrary nor obscure. It arises from the prophetic tradition of the Hebrew scriptures, such as the one from Micah you just read, and it would have been well known to Matthew's audience. In the Last Judgment scene which follows, the king (Jesus) suggests that righteous people practice works of mercy toward all those with whom they come in contact. They do not differentiate between the deserving and the undeserving; everyone, in fact, is deserving of food and shelter. These are the words Matthew attributes to Jesus:

Then the King will say to those at his right hand, "Come, you that are blessed by my Father, inherit the kingdom prepared for you from the foundation of the world; for I was hungry and you gave me food, I was thirsty and you gave me something to drink, I was a stranger and you welcomed me, I was naked and you gave me clothing, I was sick and you took care of me, I was in prison and you visited me." Then the righteous will answer him, "Lord, when was it that we saw you hungry and gave you food, or thirsty and gave you something to drink? And when was it that we saw you a stranger and welcomed you, or naked and gave you clothing? And when was it that we saw you sick or in prison and visited you?" And the King will answer them, "Truly I tell you, just as you did it to one of the least of these who are members of my family, you did it to me." (Mt 25:34-40)

The story of Zaccheus recorded in Luke's gospel (19:1-10) is among the most appealing and engaging stories found in the Christian scriptures. It, too, illustrates the covenental requirements of justice and community. As the story goes, Zaccheus was a tax collector who collected taxes for the occupying Roman government from his fellow Jews. That occupation in itself was enough to distance him from most faithful Jews. Additionally, however, tax collectors usually defrauded the people from whom they collected taxes. One day, Jesus came to the neighborhood in which Zaccheus lived and began to teach. Zaccheus was curious and, being short, climbed up a sycamore tree to get a better view of the itiner-

MARYKNOLL PHOTO LIBRARY/BISCEGLIE

Maryknoll Sister Mary Annel, M.D., visits a prisoner in El Salvador.

ant teacher about whom he had heard many tales. The scriptures are silent concerning the words Jesus spoke that day. Whatever they were, Zaccheus was moved to reconcile himself with his community and the worldview of Judaism. He responded to Jesus with an exuberance that belied his former greedy ways. He invited Jesus to dinner and vowed to repay four-fold whomever he had cheated and to give half of his possessions to the poor. Jesus affirmed Zaccheus's decision by assuring him that salvation had come to him that day. Indeed, Zaccheus had not only fulfilled the demands of justice, but had far exceeded them.

The fourth of the Five Pillars of Islam is the obligation to share material goods with others. With Muslims as with Jews, the fundamental reason for sharing material goods is the belief that the world belongs to all, and that there are many gratuitous and arbitrary reasons why some women and men prosper and others do not. One gives, therefore, not because one is more virtuous than other people, but because those who lack necessary material goods have a right to them. As stated in the Qur'an:

> They will question thee concerning
> what they should expend (for charity).
> Say: "Whatsoever good you expend is for
> parents and kinsmen, orphans, the needy,
> and the traveler; and whatever good you
> may do, God has knowledge of it." (2:211)

In reply to the question, How much is enough?, the Qur'an suggests that the question itself betrays a mindset at variance with the intention of the command and with the Islamic worldview. The injunction demands the development of an attitude of sharing the world's goods. A legalistic mentality, one that asks, "What is my strict obligation?" tends to inhibit the cultivation of a generous spirit that the practice of almsgiving is intended to foster.

At the beginning of this chapter, we observed that our actions always have social effects. Personal sins, such as lying, lessen the bonds of trust within the community. Now, when we consider some of the spiritual practices and disciplines found useful by various religions to promote reconciliation, we notice the same phenomenon. When we pray, meditate, fast, or perform good works in order to live in right relation to ourselves and to our worldview, there are social effects. Although we can talk about public and personal reconciliation as if they were distinct realities, they are not. In real, day-to-day life, they occur in a relationship of reciprocity; when we practice one, we are also practicing the other. One aspect of reconciliation—personal or communal—may be the one emphasized in a particular action, but both aspects of reconciliation are always present. Personal and communal reconciliation are not exactly the same thing; there are distinctions between them that can be made. Neither are they totally unrelated to or entirely separate from each other.

Judaism, Christianity, and Islam, the three religions we have considered in our discussion of good works, are often referred to as Religions of the Book. In each case, written scriptures play a very prominent role in the adherent's imagination. Also, each of the holy books shares certain stories, such as those of creation and the call of Abraham, that appeared first in the Tanak. Consequently, there is a family resemblance among the worldviews of these religions. This is evident in regard to their understanding of personal reconciliation, especially through the performance of good works.

BUDDHISM AND INNER PEACE

In places where the Religions of the Book flourish, many people are less familiar with the worldviews of religions which originated in India or the Far East, religions such as Hinduism and Buddhism. Since their worldviews differ, so do their practices of reconciliation. Buddhists believe that reconciliation is the acknowledgment that unmoderated desire is the cause of all of our suffering. The four Noble Truths of Buddhism reflect this worldview. They are:

1) All life is suffering

2) Suffering is caused by desire

3) Suffering can be ended by the termination of desire

4) The way to terminate desire is through the practice of the Eightfold Path.

The Eightfold Path is a path of moderation which involves right intention, right action, and right contemplation. This path emphasizes the teaching of the Buddha that extremes give rise to excessive concern about oneself. It includes practices that enable the Buddhist to achieve interior peace and harmony. Thus, the Eightfold Path encourages Buddhists to adopt the viewpoint of the Buddha, to relate to others and earn their living in a nonviolent and peaceful manner, and to practice meditation that leads to enlightenment. In describing the Buddhist way of life, we have continued to use the term "reconciliation." This is not entirely inappropriate, but Buddhists themselves would probably not use this term in describing themselves. In relation to Buddhists, it is probably more accurate to say that by living in accordance with the Buddha's teachings and by practicing the Eightfold Path, Buddhists believe they will achieve enlightenment or arrive at the state of nirvana. Nirvana is the *experience* that results in release from desire. The account of the Buddha's enlightenment will help us understand the experience of nirvana. This will give us some idea of what "reconciliation" or living in harmony with their worldview means for Buddhists. The Indian poet Asvaghosa wrote this account at the end of the first or at the beginning of the second century C.E., approximately six hundred years after Siddartha Gautama, the historical person who became the Buddha, lived (563-483 B.C.E.).

MARYKNOLL PHOTO ARCHIVES

Ho Tai, the Laughing Buddha. There are many depictions of the Buddha. This one shows the joy he experienced when he reached Enlightenment.

THE BUDDHA'S ENLIGHTENMENT

He had conquered the hosts of Evil
    with his firmness: with his peace
    he wished to know the highest reality: & he meditated (the
    master of meditation)

he mastered all the ways of meditation and in the first watch of the night
he remembered all his former lives.

    (in such a place I had such a name I passed away from there
    & I came here): he remembered a thousand lives as if

experiencing each one he remembered his birth:
his death in each destiny & the compassionate one felt compassion for
all living creatures

& the conviction arose in him as he remembered (the
controlled one):
this world is insubstantial as a hollow reed

And in the second watch of the night he attained (he of unequaled
might) the divine eye: the supreme eye (he who is the best of those with
eyes to see)
& with that pure divine eye he saw the entire world as in a clear mirror

saw beings appear & pass away according to their deeds

& grew in compassion: for surely those of evil deeds
go to evil destiny (& those of virtuous deeds set forth for heaven) &
some are born in hell
in terror. . . .

& some are born among men in the filthy hellish pool they call a
womb (vermin fit for suffering)
weak: they scream seized by rough hands as if chopped by sharp
swords.

and they play: enjoy themselves with kinsmen
gather possessions with love
are tortured by diverse sorrows
and all by their own deeds.

& some go to heaven
who have done good deeds
and burn in the flames of lust as in a blazing fire
unsatisfied. . . .

And in the third watch of the night
he sought to know the truth of the world: & he meditated
(the best of meditators)
abiding in courage: unseized by ignorance
nowhere do creatures find peace or stability
they are born: they grow old: they die again & again
surely the vision of the world is covered over
with lust and delusion
for they cannot see how to set out on the true path
because of their suffering

and what is it that through its mere existence
is the cause of the suffering of old age & death?
and he thought: & he understood why this state exists

(the best of those who know)
for old age and death exist only when there is birth

...

but old age & death will cease when birth is done
and birth will be destroyed
with the destruction of becoming
and the coming to be of deeds will cease
when clinging is cast aside

(& thus he meditated his inner enlightenment
increased)

clinging ends when thirst is over and there is no thirst
when feelings are destroyed
feelings cease when contact is no more
and contact vanishes when the senses & their objects
are destroyed
the senses end when name-and-form are finished
and name-and-form will cease
when there is no more awareness

and surely awareness ceases when one yearns
no more for existence
(& the sage knew the causes one by one)
for there is no more yearning for existence
when ignorance vanishes

And he knew what was to be known: he became a Buddha
awake from his meditation and saw a self
nowhere in the world
gained the highest peace by the eightfold noble path

I have attained this path: I have fulfilled this path
which the great seers followed
(who knew the true & the false)
for the benefit of others

And in the fourth watch, when dawn appeared
and the whole world was tranquil
he gained omniscience: the imperishable state

& the earth trembled like a drunken maiden
when he was enlightened
the heavens shown with his success
and kettledrums sounded in the sky

(From Stephen Beyer, *The Buddhist Experience:*
Sources and Interpretations
[Encino: Dickinson, 1974], 191-197.)

THE CONCEPT OF RECONCILIATION IN REVIEW

We have spoken of our human need to feel at home with ourselves and others. We have discussed the fact that our imaginations are shaped by religious and cultural stories and histories, and that these stories cause us to see the world in a particular way. For example, the Religions of the Book teach us to desire the good things of this earth. Buddhism and some other Eastern religions, however, tell us that desire is the source of all of our misery. Should we cultivate desire or seek to eliminate it? From our own experiences, we can gather data to support either view. The worldview we favor and accept as our own, however, often has to do with the circumstances of our birth and how we were socialized.

In any case, worldviews, to a large extent, reflect our values and contribute to our feelings of belonging or of dislocation, of being either at home or at odds with ourselves and the world. It is true that our stories shape us; it is also true that our stories are always in flux, subject to new interpretations as personal and historical conditions change. This phenomenon of change was the subject of Part IV. Although we can achieve a "comfort level" within our religious stories, many people find it detrimental to identify themselves completely with the prevailing worldview of their religious institution for several reasons: 1) Our personal stories are subject to continual interpretation and reinterpretation; since our personal stories change more easily and more quickly than institutional or cultural stories, there will most often be some degree of incompatibility between individuals and their religious institutions; 2) When we continue our dialogue with our stories, we discover which parts of the story help us to become who we want to be, and which do not; 3) If we become totally identified with a particular set of values, there is no longer a vantage point from which to judge either the values of the religious tradition or ourselves in relation to it. We could compare our relation to religious traditions to the relation of parent to infant. As children grow to maturity, they choose their place in the world. Even when their choice coincides with parental values, the choice is their own. They no longer depend on their parents to tell them what to do. We could also say that our worldviews provide us with the chapter headings for the stories of our lives, but that we ourselves fill in the content of the chapters to create our personal stories.

When we accept the values of our religious stories because they make sense to us, when living by them gives our lives a sense of meaning, we sometimes feel dislocated and ill at ease when we violate these values. All religions have rites, rituals, and practices—both personal and social— to reconcile us to the community, to holy mystery, to ourselves. Practices of reconciliation differ depending on the worldview with which we are attempting to live in harmony.

RESOURCES

Activities

1. Select one of the practices that religions suggest are reconciling. Practice it for one week. Describe your reactions to this in a journal that you share with your class or discussion group.
2. The depth psychologist Carl Jung once stated that if his Catholic patients were still believers, he would suggest that they receive the sacrament of penance (confession). Often, Jung said, this relieved their neuroses and helped their recovery. Choose the work of one psychologist, and research the place that self-revelation holds in that system.
3. Dietrich Bonhoeffer, the Lutheran theologian who was mentioned in the introduction to this chapter, said that Christianity was not an easy religion to follow; he thought that many people practiced it superficially, or simply went through the motions. (This could possibly describe various religious traditions.) Apply this idea to the concept of reconciliation. How can an attempt at reconciliation be superficial? Write a short story or create a skit which depicts reconciliation that is only apparent and cosmetic.
4. Prepare a report for your class or for your discussion group on the similarities and dissimilarities that exist between religious and nonreligious practices of reconciliation.
5. Interview three persons, such as a minister or rabbi, who are the religious leaders of three different communities or congregations. Ask them to describe the place that the concept of reconciliation holds in their weekly services.
6. Select one of the spiritual disciplines described in this chapter, and research both its history and its contemporary practice.

Readings

Gregory Baum. *Religion and Alienation.* New York: Paulist Press, 1975. A theology of religious alienation which employs sociological categories in its critique. It is a very good and reliable introduction to the topic.

Victor Frankl. *From Death-camp to Existentialism.* Boston: Beacon, 1959. Often found under the title, *Man's Search for Meaning.* This is a moving, biographical account of one Jewish man's search for meaning amid the horrors of a Nazi concentration camp.

Trudy Griffin-Pierce. *Earth Is My Mother, Sky Is My Father: Space, Time and Astronomy in Navajo Sandpainting.* Albuquerque, NM: University of New Mexico Press, 1992. This book portrays the world view and symbolism of the Navajo sandpainting ritual.

Dag Hammarskjold. *Markings.* New York: Knopf, 1964, translated by Leif Sjoberg and W.H. Auden. The diary of the former Swedish Secretary-General of the United Nations. Its entries reveal this diplomat's experience of the sacred.

Patricia Hampl. *Virgin Time.* New York: Farrar, Straus and Giroux, 1992. An autobiographical account of the religious development of a contemporary

woman whose questions led her to Assisi, Lourdes, and a Trappist monastery
in the Pacific Northwest.

Thomas Merton. *The Seven Storey Mountain*. New York: Harcourt and Brace,
1948. The autobiographical account of a man whose spiritual journey took
him from Quakerism and Communism to Roman Catholicism and the
Trappist Monastery of Gethsemani, Kentucky. This is the first of his more
than eighty works on spirituality.

H. Richard Neibuhr. *Christ and Culture*. New York: Harper & Row, 1956. A theological classic which cogently and incisively shows how cultures and religious
traditions influence our understanding of who is Christ. The categories are
easily applicable to the question of God images.

Chaim Potok. *The Chosen*. New York: Simon & Schuster, 1967. A fictional
account of a young Jewish boy's interaction with his father. Within the dynamics of this interaction, the boy finds his place in the Jewish worldview.

Maulana Jalal Al-Din Rumi. *The Sufi Path of Love*. Translated by William Chittuk.
Albany: State University of New York Press, 1983. The poetry of a thirteenth-
century Islamic mystic who followed the Sufi path.

Paul Tillich. *Systematic Theology, Vol. 1-3*. Chicago: University of Chicago Press,
1951-63. A comprehensive theological analysis of Christianity. Throughout,
Tillich, a theologian from the Lutheran tradition, refers to the modes of
human alienation and reconciliation.

Audiovisuals

The Shawshank Redemption. This film relates the alienation that occurs in prison
and the power of friendship which may be redemptive.

The Great Religions and the Poor. Available from Films for the Humanities, P.O.
Box 2053, Princeton, NJ 08543. 1995. This video explores the religious and social
aspects of poverty from the perspectives of Christianity, Islam, and Judaism. It
also shows how these religions use modern means to alleviate poverty.

Principles and Practices of Zen. Available from Films for the Humanities, P.O. Box
2053, Princeton, NJ 08543. 1992. This video follow the path of a student priest of
Zen Buddhism. It explores the physical and mental disciplines demanded by this
way of life.

The Sufi Way. Cos Cob, CT: The Hartley Foundation. Presents the ritual, dance,
art, music, and philosophy of Sufism, the heart of Islam.

Taizé, the Little Springtime. Mount Vernon, VA: Journey Communications, 1985.
This film portrays the life style and prayer style of the Protestant ecumenical
monastic community of Taizé, France.

NOTE

1. William C. Chittuck, ed., *The Sufi Path of Love* (Albany: State University of New York
Press, 1983), 234.

Chapter 11

Alienation

Recall that in Part I we differentiated between the search for meaning, the religious impulse, and institutional religion. The religious impulse is not always supported by the rules and practices of institutionalized religions. Often, we discover a contradiction or discrepancy between the ideals proposed by a religion and our own religious impulse. Even when we accept the values of a particular worldview, we are at times disconcerted that so few people, including their designated religious leaders, live according to the proposed ideals. We become aware of priests who drink too much in public, of rabbis who eat nonkosher foods, of ministers who are unfaithful spouses. We meet people who scrupulously observe the laws of their religion but who are racists or who are intolerant of the differences among various religions.

These realizations about religious institutions often come during adolescence. Sometimes, during this period of our lives, it seems that our minds are flooded by new information. Further, we not only observe that religious leaders have failings, but we recognize that our parents are not perfect. For that matter, other authority figures such as teachers, policemen, and lawmakers have their shortcomings—some of them grave.

These realizations about the weaknesses of religious leaders and parents often cause us to question the value of some of the religious beliefs and practices they have taught us. It is not unusual for parents to tell their sons and daughters that, if they follow the rules of the family and of their religion, God will bless them and look after them. Perhaps we believe that God answers our prayers or that if we have enough faith we can move mountains. Then, disaster strikes: a parent or much-loved relative dies a dreadful and painful death. Prayer seems to make no difference. We discover that people who manipulate and cheat are often the students or workers who reap rewards and get ahead in life. We have done all the right things, but our lives don't seem much different from the lives of those who seem to live with no regard for the well-being of other people. Additionally, adolescence is generally a time when, developmentally, **idealism** unfolds. Idealism, the conviction that the ambiguities of life are not to be tolerated, is often very pronounced during adolescence. This may compound the discomfort we experience because the more idealistic we are, the more clearly we see hypocrisy and the other inconsistencies between what religious people say and what they do.

These experiences of discomfort, doubt, and disillusionment frequently result in alienation. Although such experiences may disconcert us, they may also help us to sort out what we really believe. They may prompt us to rethink on a more mature level the meaning of such values as honesty and compassion and the meaningfulness of prayer. Even when these experiences of estrangement or disorientation prove to be catalysts for growth, they nevertheless cause us pain. The distress may be occasional and brief or constant and lasting. Whatever the degree of dislocation we experience, it often has several causes that occur singly or in combination. Some of the more common causes of alienation are 1) Religion, as an institution, very often legitimates cultural biases that are themselves sources of alienation to certain groups within the religion; 2) Images of God are proposed and passed down that have no connection with contemporary cultural or historical development; 3) Religious authorities may use their power to control the lives of members; and 4) In the face of evil or of profound suffering, religion too often provides facile or glib reassurances such as, "It is God's will," or, "Only have faith and everything will be all right," instead of remaining silent before the inexplicable.

Even when these institutional sources of alienation are not present to a great extent in people's lives, some people may still have ambivalent feelings toward religious institutions. This may not be due to the imperfections of the institutions, but because these persons have not yet attained psychological, social, or religious maturity. Consequently, they are incapable of relating in an appropriate way to religious or other types of institutions. Some of these personal sources of ambivalence may be 1) fear of personal freedom and responsibility; 2) a legalistic mentality; and 3) fixation at a particular stage of psychological development. Usually not one, but several institutional and personal factors combine to precipitate and determine the degree of alienation someone experiences.

THE RELIGIOUS LEGITIMATION OF CULTURAL BIASES

Hierarchy

Look around your classroom or church, the shopping mall or your place of employment. Notice how things are ordered. Where is your attention

THE CATHOLIC SUN, SYRACUSE/MATTHEW COULTER

Hierarchy and androcentrism pictured. In this image, sacred ritual is enacted by an all-male group of priests. Attention is focused on their actions.

directed? Where are the best stores or offices? In most cases, the people and stores considered the most important are situated so that they are the center of attention. In the traditional classroom, the teacher's desk is located in front of the classroom, sometimes even on a platform. In the malls, the most important stores have the best locations. In church and synagogue, our attention is focused on the priest or cantor. These are common everyday examples of a way of ordering called hierarchy. Some people would argue that hierarchy is natural, that it is rooted in nature, and is therefore the order established by the deity. After all, we observe hierarchy in the animal kingdom. There are dominant and submissive animals; the dominant animals direct the hunt, take the best food, and, in some cases, determine which females will be impregnated. By analogy, many societies are structured so that certain people, either because of some natural characteristic or because of the position they hold in the community, possess rights and privileges that others in the community do not share. They not only lead and instruct others, but they make decisions about what is to be learned, what is to be believed, and how things are to be organized. Hierarchy is a mode of authority very compatible with autocratic or monarchical forms of government. It is akin to the medieval concept of the divine right of kings.

Not all religious groups acknowledge that hierarchal administration reflects a sacred order. Anglican, Roman Catholic, Episcopalian, Russian and Greek Orthodox, Methodist, and Lutheran churches, though, are among those denominations with the most formally articulated hierarchical structures. Notice that these churches also have the most elaborate and highly organized public worship services. In a hierarchical understanding of reality, only some members possess the God-given power to administer sacraments. According to this manner of thinking, if a person who did not have the power to execute the sacraments did, nevertheless, perform a sacramental ritual, there would be no sacrament, because that person did not have the intrinsic power to bring it about.

Baptist and Pentecostal churches, on the other hand, have governing bodies, but they are not hierarchical. There are leadership positions within the community, but no one person has more intrinsic power than another. The authority lies within each congregation. Usually, these churches have less formal public worship and fewer nonbiblical dogmas which believers are expected to accept.

In religions which have their origins in Asia, hierarchy is evident more in the rights of groups than of individuals. In Hinduism, there are four castes: the Brahmin, from whom the priests come; the Kshatriya, the warrior and governing class; the Vaishya, the class of merchants and farmers; and finally, Sudras, the peasants and serfs. This way of understanding the world was derived from the *Purusa*, the creation account of the first man, which we read in chapter 1. There are also those who belong to no caste. They are the "untouchables." Only the highest class, the Brahmins, can be religious leaders. Gandhi, among others, tried to eradicate this system, but it is deeply rooted in the Indian approach to order, and it prevails in spite of legislation.

Throughout the world, hierarchy is often linked to patriarchy and androcentrism, two cultural patterns that various religions legitimate, and that we will discuss next. When this is the case, males are dominant within each caste or group, and the dominant group becomes even more elitist.

Many members of the hierarchy are leaders in service to others and are exemplary models of religious authority. The Dalai Lama, the leader of Tibetan Buddhism, is universally admired by religious people. Many people throughout the world, however, consider hierarchy to be intrinsically unfair, because people acquire position or dominance either by birth or by office. Those who object to hierarchy do so on the basis that possession of the qualities necessary to govern well is a secondary concern. Prayerful and talented people who are well-educated in their religious traditions often occupy a subservient position to members of the hierarchy who are less well-developed religiously and psychologically. This is often a source of deep alienation, especially when combined with androcentrism or patriarchy.

Androcentrism

Androcentrism is a cultural pattern which attributes normativity to the male of the species. The most accomplished males provide the standard by which everyone is measured.

Let us begin our discussion of this cultural attitude with an everyday example. In most sports, gymnastics and figure skating being notable exceptions, the men's events are considered to be more interesting and more skillfully played than the women's events in the same sport. "March Madness" focuses on male teams. If you asked sports enthusiasts which teams had won the NCAA championship for the last five years, nearly everyone could quickly list the men's teams that had won. Yet, women's teams play in the NCAA tournament, also. Could the same people who named the winning men's teams also name the winning women's teams? Can you?

Let us now consider how androcentrism plays a role in the way we read, view movies, or enjoy art. Many times, when we read a book, watch a movie, or go to a museum, we spontaneously "read" or "see" from the point of view of the male. We do this automatically and spontaneously because this attitude permeates our cultural environment.

When you think of the portrayal in sculpture or art of the perfect human body, what comes to mind? Is it Michelangelo's David? Perhaps it is the figure of Adam receiving life from God as this is portrayed, again, by Michelangelo, on the ceiling of the Sistine Chapel in the Vatican. For some of you, it may be the Venus de Milo. But even if the Venus de Milo comes to mind, we must remember it represents the male vision of the perfect female body.

If none of these classic examples leap to mind, perhaps more contemporary examples of the ideal body, like that of Arnold Schwarzenegger or Cindy Crawford, do. If so, we can draw the same conclusions. In our contemporary, Western society, the ideal of the human body is either male or the male notion of the ideal female figure. Why else would so many young women starve themselves nearly to death? Why else would those trying to alter their eating habits describes their successes and lapses in moral terms? I've been "good"; I've been "bad"?

Androcentrism pervades literature, also. In Shakespeare's *Macbeth*, our sympathies are usually with Macbeth. If only Lady Macbeth were not so ambitious. A closer reading of the text shows that Macbeth is equally responsible for their heinous act of murdering Duncan while he slept in their castle. It is true that Shakespeare depicts Macbeth as the weaker member of the couple; perhaps that in itself is why we so despise Lady Macbeth. As she herself says, she is unwomanly. She is not supposed to be the strong partner. If only the woman had not led her man into harm's way!

Thinking with Movies and Novels

Call to mind one of your favorite movies, novels, or short stories. Reflect on these questions: With which character do I identify? What are the character traits I attribute to the male character? To the female character? To which character am I willing to extend forgiveness (if such is necessary)? Would the predicament posed by the plot be resolved if only the female character would change her attitude or approach to the male character? Finally, with which character do your sympathies lie? Now, compare your responses with those of other members of your class or reading group. What conclusions do you draw?

What is noteworthy about these examples of androcentrism is that we are usually seeing or reading from the viewpoint of male normativity because our imaginations have been formed to see and read in this manner. It is not a conscious choice. The unquestioned and spontaneous nature of this pattern of thinking gives us a clue to its cultural pervasiveness. The conclusion that androcentrism is deeply rooted in cultures and the collective unconscious is well documented. People are born into this milieu of androcentrism and are affected by it. We must ask ourselves questions if we want to determine the shape of our own imagination: When I read, do I spontaneously adopt a masculine perspective? From where do I derive the norms by which I judge the excellence and beauty of the human body? If we never consciously reflect on such questions, we contribute to the perpetuation of this cultural attitude. Both females and males are responsible for this.

When we recall that religions are always practiced within a particular culture, and that all cultures are to some degree androcentric, it is easy to understand why religions themselves have developed and promoted androcentric attitudes.

Let us consider the alienating effects androcentrism has in various religions. A study of androcentrism enables the reader to more easily understand the connection between the manner in which *Macbeth* and Genesis 2-3 are traditionally read. Reread the section in chapters 6 and 7 concerning the interpretation of Genesis 2-3. You will see that the biblical text does not support the traditional androcentric reading. Many of the traditional interpretations of Genesis 2-3 have more to do with the androcentric imagination reading the text than with the text itself. We are so used to reading the text through an androcentric lens, that it is very difficult for us to arrive at an interpretation in which Eve is not the culprit and Adam the victim of so-called feminine wiles.

Some Christian religions honor Mary, the Mother of Jesus, in a special way. In these religions, Mary is proposed as a model for all Christian women. The image of Mary that is proposed for emulation, though, is often an image of a woman who is the ideal of an androcentric culture:

MARYKNOLL PHOTO LIBRARY/J. TOWLE, M.M.

Two Peruvian girls celebrate Mary's feast by dancing at a fiesta. For them, Mary is a reason to celebrate life.

subservient, without passion, tending to household duties. The Mary about whom we read in the New Testament does not fit this description at all. It is no wonder that strong, articulate, decisive women feel alienated by this androcentrically shaped image of womanhood.

PATRIARCHY

Another cultural phenomenon that influences our patterns of relationship is patriarchy. Patriarchy is a social arrangement which legitimates the concept that in a family unit, or any social unit analogous to the family such as a business or nation-state, the dominant male has authority over those males who have no power and over all females and children. In the Western world this tradition comes to us through the Roman Empire and is known as *pater familias*. We see how this idea of *pater familias* is enacted in mosques, synagogues, and churches. Although culture is in transition, and all institutions have been affected by the women's movement, most religious institutions are still headed by dominant males. The fact that we use the expression "woman rabbi" or "woman minister" shows us the novelty of that reality. We never hear the expressions "male priest" or "male rabbi." Indeed, in Islam and Roman Catholicism, patriarchy is viewed as divinely legitimated by either the Qur'an or the New Testament.

New religious organizations, such as the Promise Keepers, reassert that the husband should be head of the household. He is to be a loving head, but nevertheless the head. The woman is to be the heart. In a patriarchal culture, the head possesses rationality and intelligence; the heart is the source of emotion. The head is the one who leads and makes decisions. Recall the examples given in chapter 8 where, often, holy women experienced metamorphosis into a male form. This suggests how powerful an influence these cultural structures exert on the psyche.

Thinking about Patriarchy

To satisfy your curiosity about the extent of patriarchy, investigate and/or discuss these areas. In your school, business, or place of worship, is the power structure patriarchal? If a woman occupies the dominant position, do people think of her as a man? Do they say she is as aggressive as or as hard-working as any male CEO? What words are used to describe her? What is the meaning of the expression "glass ceiling"? How many women hold office in the legislature of the United States? When the Constitution was written, who qualified as a voter?

These attitudes of androcentrism and patriarchy have subtle but nonetheless profound effects on how both women and men relate to themselves, to one another, to religious institutions, and to divine mystery. Although what you have just read concerning androcentrism and patriarchy may appear to be solely a women's issue, this is certainly not the case. Rather, it is a human issue. It is true that men and women experience androcentrism and patriarchy differently, but both genders are alienated by these cultural phenomena.

Having explored the pervasiveness of androcentrism and patriarchy generally, let us now see how these attitudes permeate institutional religions and the effects they often have on people who are affiliated with these institutions.

Several important distinctions must be kept in mind. First, if you, the reader, are female, you may not consciously consider that you are less than a male simply because divine mystery is nearly universally referred to in male images. Images do work, however, on our psyches at a less-than-conscious level. It is a fact that a higher percentage of women seek treatment for depression than men do. Certainly, this phenomenon cannot be reduced to a single cause. However, women in androcentric religions often become alienated or separated from their deepest desires. This is because they have been taught not to overreach themselves by desiring positions in church, synagogue, or mosque that are more suitable for men, because women lack the qualities that leadership demands; or because divine mystery mandates their exclusion. Karl Marx once made the statement that at times we are so alienated from ourselves that we don't realize we are alienated. He named this situation falsification of consciousness. By this he meant that the shape of our imaginations coincides with dominant cultural expressions like androcentrism and patriarchy. We have become so adapted to our culture that it is impossible to perceive that things could be otherwise. That is one reason we may have come to believe that God is *actually* a male, not simply imaged as one.

Many women in androcentric and patriarchal religions declare that they have never desired to be ordained into the ranks of the clergy. They add that they are very grateful for this because they can't imagine the frustration a Roman Catholic woman would experience who wanted to be ordained but for whom it was considered to be against divine mandate. Then, they sometimes acknowledge that—as a defense mechanism —perhaps they will simply not allow into consciousness a desire that would result in such frustration. When vocational choices are denied to women by religions that legitimate androcentrism and patriarchy they may never know what they truly desire. To be separated from our deepest desires, especially those involving religious orientation, can be profoundly alienating and result in chronic malaise.

We must not forget, moreover, that males can be alienated by religiously legitimated androcentrism. All of us have various public personae, the faces we show publicly. Teachers, for example, assume the persona of a teacher when in a classroom or meeting with students in the role of a teacher. This is fitting. But if they were to become totally identified with that persona or role, they would no longer know who they were other than teachers. They could relate to themselves and others only as teachers. Consequently, their capacity for intimacy would be greatly hindered.

Now, think of the male who has been burdened with being the image *par excellence* of the divine. Think further of the male clergy in androcentric religions such as Christianity, Islam, orthodox Judaism, and Confucianism. They, more than other men, are burdened by andro-

centrism and with symbolizing the divine. Many such men become so
identified with the normative role they play in religion—even to being
assimilated to the divine—that they become alienated, unable to relate to
themselves or others as people with desires, hopes, failings, yearnings,
faults.

Religions that legitimate patriarchy confer power on the dominant
male (minister, pope, imam, tribal leader) to regulate the lives of less
powerful men and all women and children in the particular religion.
Often, this way of organizing the religious polity is viewed as a reflection
of the way things occur in nature and, therefore, as the way affairs are
most properly organized. Hierarchy is also frequently viewed as divinely
ordained. People, clerical or not, are usually reluctant to give up power
voluntarily. If we are in a position of power or dominance, we instinc-
tively seek to legitimate that authority by an appeal to cultural or religious theories. Some persons who hold positions of power become
identified with that power. When this occurs, self-worth depends on
retaining dominance. The result comes close to being a vicious circle.
Theoretically, only those who hold office can change the rules. But why
would a person want to change the rules when one believes—even mistakenly—that his position is legitimated by the status quo?

Now we can begin to appreciate how alienating religious patriarchy
can be for those who do not occupy positions of dominance. Women and
men without power are excluded from governance, even when they have
a better understanding of the ways in which the church, synagogue, or
mosque could be organized to assure greater participation of adherents.
These persons are excluded from the decision-making process even when
the decisions made are ordinances about how they are expected to live
their lives. Once the patriarch or religious head has spoken, neither
recourse to reason nor to a variant interpretations of a religion's story
makes any difference. To those who lack participation in the power of the
father or patriarch, the system appears to enact laws and interpret religious texts that ensure the continuation of the patriarchal system.

For some people, patriarchy is alienating at so fundamental a level of
their being that they choose to align themselves with another religious
institution. They make this choice in order to remain authentic to themselves, to remain in harmony and reconciliation with themselves, and to
feel at peace. Mary Daly (b. 1928) was a former Roman Catholic and
among the first to bring to light the alienating effects of patriarchy in two
of her earlier books, *The Church and the Second Sex* (1968), and *Beyond
God the Father: Toward a Philosophy of Women's Liberation* (1973). She
received the highest degree that is granted by Roman Catholic schools of
theology, the Doctor of Sacred Theology (S.T.D.). Eventually, however,
she decided that patriarchy was so central to the biblical message as well
as to the governance of Christian denominations, that she extricated herself completely from Christianity in order to maintain a sense of her own
integrity.

Thinking with Mary Daly

Mary Daly left the United States to study Roman Catholic theology in
Europe. It was necessary for her to leave the United States because at
that time there was no place in the United States where women were
allowed to study for advanced degrees in theology. Mary Daly received
her doctorate and returned to the United States where she was quite
coldly received by male clerics. Her alienation was profound. In 1971,
she preached at Harvard Memorial Church; she was the first woman to
preach there in its 336-year history. This excerpt from that sermon
shows that her profound and scholarly acquaintance with the Jewish
and Christian scriptures allowed her to critique the patriarchy within
the churches.

Sisters and Other Esteemed Members of the Congregation: There is
a problem. It is this: There exists a world-wide phenomenon of sexual
caste, which is to be found not only in Saudi Arabia but also in Sweden.
This planetary sexual caste system involves birth-ascribed, hierarchically
ordered groups whose members have unequal access to goods, services,
prestige, and physical and mental well-being. . . .

Theology which is overtly and explicitly oppressive to women is by
no means a thing of the past. Exclusively masculine symbolism for
God, for the notion of divine "incarnation" in human nature, and for
the human relationship to God reinforces sexual hierarchy. Tremendous
damage is done, particularly in ethics, when theologians construct one-
dimensional arguments that fail to take women's experience into
account. . . . The entire conceptual apparatus of theology, developed
under the conditions of patriarchy, has been the product of males and
serves the interests of sexist society. . . .

Sisterhood is also functioning as church, proclaiming . . . for the first
time in history, the liberation of women—first. . . . The sisterhood of
man cannot happen without a real exodus. We have to go out from the
land of our fathers into an unknown place. (From Mary Daly, "The
Women's Movement: An Exodus Community," *Religious Education* 67
[September/October 1972]): 327-333.)

Others also feel alienated but at not so profound a level. Many men
and women decide that patriarchal religions, in spite of the alienating
aspects of governance, provide worldviews and traditions of spirituality
that are life giving and reconciling. Rosemary Radford Ruether, who is
another outstanding feminist theologian of this century, stated that a lifetime of studying and living the Christian message provided her not only
with the resources to show how patriarchy corrupts the Christian message but also with the tools to see that the tradition, although at times
alienating, nevertheless offers valuable insights into living in a meaningful

way. Authenticity is a value for both Mary Daly and Rosemary Ruether. This does not mean, though, that they are compelled to make identical choices in order to remain faithful to their insights.

The majority of religious feminists are women who have had the advantages that education offers. Their education has sensitized them to the social construction of knowledge, which we studied in Part I. When these women applied this concept to religious institutions, they realized that hierarchy, androcentrism, and patriarchy are social concepts that privilege the male of the species. Religions had simply assumed that male privilege was due to nature. Initially, religious feminists were Caucasian Jewish and Christian women who called into question the religious legitimation of androcentrism and patriarchy. Soon, however, African-American women and Latin American Christians, whose issues were somewhat different, entered the ranks of those seeking to separate religious worldviews from outdated social constructs. Now, there is a nascent feminist movement among Muslim women.

Not only women, but men as well have espoused the cause of women's religious liberation. Among them are the North American theologian David Tracy, the Dutch theologian Edward Schillebeeckx, and the Sri Lankan theologian Tissa Balasuriya. Such men join their sisters in seeking to lessen the alienation engendered by hierarchy, androcentrism, and patriarchy.

ALIENATING IMAGES OF GOD

As we have tried to understand how hierarchy, androcentrism, and patriarchy function in religious institutions, we have mentioned in passing how these cultural features influence our idea or concept of God. Androcentrism and patriarchy are so ingrained in our culture that we often come to think that maleness and fatherhood are actual attributes of God rather than metaphors that point in the direction of God. For example, we talk and act as if God *were* a male; as if God *were*, literally, a father. Imaging God in this way can alienate us from the whole notion of God. It does this by limiting our idea of God, by creating, really, a false god. If, as the various religions propose, the word "God" refers to whatever one conceives to be ultimate in the cosmos, for oneself, for the community; if it refers to whatever makes us believe that life is at some level trustworthy; if it refers to the depth and the height of our life, then we need as many metaphors as possible to point us in the direction of this mystery. We learned in chapter 3 that language influences action. Now we are going to consider how images, specifically images of God, can also be effective in alienating us from our centers. We need to examine how some images of God function to alienate us from divine mystery, nature, our brothers and sisters, and ourselves.

Thinking with God Images

Write down the first words that spontaneously come to mind when you hear the word "God." If words such as "all powerful" or "judge" are among the first that come to mind, try to imagine what you mean by that term. Is "God" like a judge? How does "he" use power? If words such as "spirit" or "life" come to mind, try to image what that spirit or life is like. What are its characteristics? Now, refer to your own experience. What effect does your image of God exert on the way you think and act; on how you view your job or career; on how you view your relationship to the earth and to your brothers and sisters? Would you say your image of God is reconciling, alienating, or neutral? What conclusions do you draw from this exercise?

Many years ago, St. Thomas Aquinas (1225-1274), who was among the most influential theologians of Christianity, made the statement, "Everything is received according to the mode of the receiver." Let us examine what this means using contemporary concepts. Throughout this book, the authors have shown how we read and understand contextually. The geographical space which we inhabit influences our choice of religious symbols. We saw this in the first chapter in the discussion of how fish are portrayed in the cultures of New England fishing villages and in the Solomon Islands. We've seen how historical circumstances, as well as our personal and collective development, influence our reading of a text. All of these circumstances and conditions shape the "receiver," our psyches. When we read a religious text like the Muslim Qur'an, the Hindu Vedas or the Christian scriptures, or when we hear an exhortation from a religious source, we read and understand it according to the "the mode of the receiver," that is, according to how our understanding or our psyches have been shaped.

Imagine mixing a cake batter. Until we put the batter into a particular cake pan, it is a shapeless, amorphous mass. When we pour the batter into a pan, it takes the shape of the pan. It can be formed into the shape of a rectangle, a square, an angel, a heart, or an automobile. In the same way, our psyches have been shaped by our cultural patterns. In this example, our psyches are analogous to cake pans. New perceptual and sensory data that we experience are received by our psyches and take their shape. That is why it is so very difficult to read the story of Adam and Eve except through the lens of patriarchy.

Of course, it is not quite so simple because the boundaries of our psyches change also. Imaginations, though, have varying degrees of elasticity. Some people's imaginations have rigid boundaries with very little flexibility; such people find change very difficult and usually change very little. When change does occur, it is often dramatic, like some of the conversions about which you read in chapter 8. Other people's imaginations are more flexible; for such people, change usually occurs more continuously, and the changes in their ways of thinking are seldom dramatic. Now, let us apply this concept to various alienating images of God.

God as Superman

Throughout the chapters in this book, we have repeatedly explored the nature and function of myth, metaphor, image, and imagination. We have seen that religious language is closely allied with poetry, that it seeks to denote realities that can only be described metaphorically. People who think seriously about religious questions understand that the realities they are trying to describe can only be hinted at. That is, we know "mystery" in a different way than we know "book." Our metaphors point us in a direction, but they are not that reality itself.

When we forget that the deity is not a human being, even when imaged as one, the deity often becomes *Superman*. Then, when this deity does not act in our lives in the same way as *Superman*, when he does not rush in to snatch us from danger, we lose trust. We begin to ask questions like, "Why didn't God move the car off the track before it was hit by the train? Why didn't God snatch the toddler out of the swimming pool before he drowned?" *Superman* would never have let the car remain on the track or allowed the toddler to drown. You can see that if we hold such an image of God, we risk becoming alienated or at least we begin to think that God is ineffective.

The Stop-Gap God

Many times people think of God as providing what human beings do not know how to provide. In ancient times as well as modern, people believed that God controlled fertility. If a couple were childless, they prayed that God would make the woman fertile. (It was presumed that infertility was a defect in the woman.) Now, most couples who want to conceive a child but cannot seem to do so visit fertility clinics. Many of these women do become pregnant, thanks to the advances of modern science. So, in a sense, God becomes a little smaller, a little less important in people's lives. Examples can be multiplied. If, during ski season, the snowfall is insufficient to provide good skiing, ski resorts make artificial snow. If a friend needs surgery, we try to find the best doctor. If there is a drought, farmers irrigate. If we want to pass an exam, we study. If one's image of God is that God does what we need done, then every time human beings learn to do what previously they had depended upon God for, then God becomes a little smaller, a bit more peripheral to life.

Most religious traditions value prayer and often include in their rituals petitions to the deity. These petitions request—at times demand—from the deity the fulfillment of the petitioner's desires. Even when farmers irrigate during a drought and couples visit fertility clinics, they still pray for rain or for conception. We quite naturally ask the question, then, do such people pray out of habit or from a superstitious mindset? The response such people often give is this: We experience that God does not intervene in the historical process to answer our individual prayers. Yet, we pray because the act of petition symbolizes our belief that human beings are not in this world alone. God is with us. God expects us to use our intellects to solve problems for farmers and for infertile couples. Yet, we are not totally autonomous; we live in relationship with God.

The Absent God

Many times, God is imaged as being entirely removed from the human scene and totally disinterested in human concerns. This God is sometimes called the God of the Greek philosophers such as Plato and Aristotle. These philosophers ascribed reason to God and described "him" philosophically, as the source of all being or as the undivided one and source of all within the cosmos. It was understood that this God existed in utter isolation from humans, and that our troubles and concerns were of no intrinsic importance to God.

The inception of the Age of Science in the seventeenth century provides us with a modern version of the absent God. The discoveries and methodologies of empirical scientists during this century contributed to the establishment of a new worldview. No longer was God understood to be directly responsible for the governance of the universe; God simply established the rules of nature and left them to work themselves out without intervening. According to this worldview, the cosmos was imaged as a machine, and the rules of mechanics prevailed. One machine that was frequently used as an analog for the cosmos was the clock; God was the clockmaker. "He" wound up the clock and then forgot about it. Governed by this image of God, people could live their whole lives with little involvement with the deity.

The Arbitrary God

The arbitrary God possesses many of the characteristics of the Greek gods and goddesses who were thought to live on Mount Olympus. The mythic actions of these gods often incorporate the loves, passions, and jealousies we humans experience. These gods can be bribed and placated by us. They are willful; sometimes they will respond positively to human entreaties, but often they respond in a spiteful or negative manner, for no apparent reason, and there is nothing that we can do about it. This image of an arbitrary and capricious God is very much operative in the contemporary world. Even though Christians, Jews, and Muslims do not claim the worldview of the ancient Greeks, many attribute these same characteristics to their deity. Uninterpreted and literally read biblical stories, such as that of Abraham and Isaac, contribute to understanding God as arbitrary. As a result, many live in fear of offending this God, not because they act unjustly but because they are not sure how this all-powerful God "thinks." Their concern to stay on the right side of this God sometimes prevents them from assuming responsibility for their own lives. This may have alienating results.

The Ambiguity of God Images

The images of God just described are not alienating for everyone. There exists neither a universally reconciling nor alienating image of God. We are all at different stages of personal development and live within various worldviews. These worldviews often propose divergent understandings of God. These factors affect how one views particular portrayals of the divine. Also, an image that may be alienating at a particular period in life may be reunderstood and found reconciling at a later stage. Women have reported that the image of God as father was alienating at one period in their lives, but at a later time they found it reconciling. They attribute this to the fact that they began to differentiate the image of God as father from the image of their biological father.

In Hindu mythology, there is the saying that there are 333 million gods. Many understand this to mean that Hinduism is a polytheistic religion. Another view understands this statement to mean that there is an infinite variety of ways in which God is experienced and understood. It is unusual for a person to find the same image of God satisfactory throughout an entire lifetime.

THE TENDENCIES OF RELIGIOUS AUTHORITIES TO CONTROL

Those who assume positions of religious leadership, whether they are imams, rabbis, **mullahs,** or priests, share the same human condition that we all do. They experience the same tendencies toward goodness and the same unscrupulous inclinations that all people do. Even though we know this, we sometimes project onto our religious leaders ideals of perfection, which they accept. If such leaders are unsure of themselves or if they develop an unrealistic and inflated understanding of their importance, they often try to control the lives of their coreligionists. Religious authorities exercise control by mandating how people are to organize and manage various aspects of their lives: financial, intellectual, temporal, sexual.

Typically, religions involve their members in good works. This requires investments of money and time on their part. Often these are freely given and flow from a generous spirit. At times, though, religious leaders manipulate members to contribute beyond their means or to spend more time in church activities than their other family and work obligations allow. They are able to do this by speaking in the name of God; that is, they preach and speak as if they know, unambiguously, the mind of God. When they speak in this way, they may provoke feelings of fear and guilt which make it difficult for people to refuse unreasonable demands on their financial and temporal resources. Eventually, people become alienated and may equate religion itself with control. When this happens, they become disillusioned with or alienated from religion generally.

Similarly, our minds are made to seek knowledge and truth. It is true that each religious worldview or tradition has parameters that establish the boundaries of that tradition. If people follow a path that goes outside the tradition's parameters, then it is proper for religious authorities to declare that such people are no longer members of the community. As we saw in Part IV, however, every person and every group is always in the process of developing. Some people are more concerned than others that a community's teachings be expressed in ways compatible with the language of the prevailing culture. Their investigations uncover the disconcerting fact that language and the cultural mindset have changed to such an extent that to continue using the same exact words to express a particular religious teaching would, in fact, be unfaithful to the meaning embedded in the teaching itself. So these scholars enter into the process of explaining or interpreting the tradition in new terms.

A striking example of this phenomenon in the Roman Catholic church was the controversy known as the Modernist Heresy. At the turn of the twentieth century, many Catholic theologians, especially French and German theologians, attempted to bring the fruits of modern scholarship to bear on biblical and theological studies. They saw that the philosophical milieu had changed, and they desired to bring their church up-to-date. Because the language they used was new, it disconcerted many and made them uncomfortable. As a result of a religious leadership that sought unquestioning obedience, many of these men were declared to be heretics and were **excommunicated**. Many of them died alienated from the church which they so much wanted to serve. But not all religious leadership is controlling. A half century later, Pope John XXIII, about whom we read earlier, called a world-wide council of the Roman Catholic church for the express purpose of bringing it up-to-date.

Finally, many religious traditions throughout the world seek to control their members through restrictions on sexuality and procreation. Religious traditions consider marriage and procreation to be important and sacred tasks. Indeed the sexual instinct is among the most powerful forces in the animal kingdom. Indiscriminate sexual expression can have devastating effects on individuals and on society. So it is understandable that religions regulate sexual conduct and procreation. Still, religions may promulgate laws in these domains which go far beyond what is necessary to insure the importance and sanctity of these areas of human experience.

Even though the rules of sexual conduct include both men and women, it is often the case that women bear a disproportionate burden of the law. This is true in Hinduism where, until recently, it was expected that a widow immolate herself on her husband's funeral pyre. This is true in Islam, where divorce is much easier for a man to obtain than it is for a woman. It is true in Judaism and some Christian denominations, where marriage with a person of another faith—if not absolutely forbidden—is discouraged and frowned upon.

RELIGIOUS RESPONSES IN THE FACE OF SUFFERING

Every religious tradition deals with suffering and death. When the various traditions are true to their ideals, they deal with suffering and death through rituals and through reflection on scriptures which support the people affected. Profound loss is a mystery which calls into question our most basic convictions and apparent certitudes about good and evil, reward and punishment, as well as about the image of the deity that informs our living. Truly, there is no explanation that will ever explain suffering, death, and loss in a rationally satisfying way. The study of Job in chapter 7 emphasizes this realization.

We are often told as we grow up that suffering and disease are punishments for sin. This is what the friends of Job believed, and that way of thinking persists even to this day. The inference of such a statement is the belief that if we live honestly, study hard, and are faithful to our commitments that we will live happy lives relatively untouched by deep suffering. Then, at the end of a long, fruitful, and happy life, we will die peacefully amid the comfort of family and friends. Sometimes this happens. It is rare, though, that people live into old age unaffected by suffering. And how can we maintain that suffering is punishment for sin when we read every day of innocent children who die from incurable diseases, inexplicable acts of violence, and neglect. In the novel *The Plague*, the French existentialist Albert Camus (1913-1960) wrote very movingly and courageously of the questions posed to religion by the suffering of innocent children. When all is said and done, when we have tried to relieve suffering and prevent death to the best of our knowledge and ability, perhaps the wisest response is to join Job before this impenetrable mystery.

Even though this may be the wisest response, many times religious

MARYKNOLL PHOTO ARCHIVES/J. PADULA

An image of death in India. What can be said in the face of such suffering?

leaders give facile and superficial answers to explain people's agony and grief. We hear sermons or read books that declare that God knows best, or that this is the will of God. Yet Irving Greenberg, a conservative rabbi who has written extensively on the challenges to religious images of God posed by the Holocaust, asks us, "Can you say these things in the presence of a burning child?" If you can, what kind of monster have we made God to be?

When we suffer the effects of evil or even of natural catastrophes, we know, intuitively, that such responses are too facile and superficial and that, ultimately, they destroy connections between our unconscious and our conscious lives. This separation is alienating. Even when we have not thought through the implications of these facile answers to the extent that persons like Rabbi Greenberg have, we find them repugnant.

Modern psychology has formulated theories that legitimate and verify our intuitive rejection of the facile answers. Psychologists theorize that we must not repress our experiences of suffering and evil. When we do, the feelings attached to these experiences live a subterranean life and affect our consciousness in a debilitating way. We do not need to explain or completely resolve these experiences; in fact, we cannot. We can, however, bring them to the full light of day and find a place for them. Then these feelings of powerlessness and frustration lose their power over us. Religions do not serve us well by offering us easy answers or repeating platitudes when we suffer. Consequently, when this occurs, we sometimes withdraw our allegiance from some part of that religion's worldview.

PERSONAL SOURCES OF ALIENATION

Up to this point, we have investigated sources of religious alienation that are extrinsic to individuals and originate in our culture, in our society, or with religious leaders. But alienation can also result from personal, psychological causes. Before we enter into this discussion, we do well to remind ourselves that none of us is a perfect psychological specimen. We all have our idiosyncrasies and areas of immaturity. The discussion which follows, though, will help us to understand more completely that authenticity is never completely achieved and that inauthenticity cannot be reduced to a single factor, whether social, cultural, or personal.

We assume that as human beings fulfill various life tasks, they develop into increasingly mature persons. Now, let us add to that understanding the fact that development is never simply linear, advancing from one point to another; it is cyclical. We complete a developmental task appropriate to a two-year-old, for example, but we repeat that task at a deeper level during adolescence. Consider this example: One of the tasks of the two-year-old is to develop a sense of identity. The toddler does this by saying, "No." The purpose of this "no" is to discover the boundaries between her-

CNS PHOTO BY DOUGLAS E. KAUP, PITTSBURGH CATHOLIC

Members of the KKK feel they are superior to other groups, and they use religion to legitimate their belief. Notice the cross on their disguise. Members of the KKK separate themselves from others. What is their source of alienation?

self and her parents. This task recurs during the teenage years. At a deeper, more mature level than the toddler, the teenager is faced with questions of identity and must work these out. The implication of this for religion is that we cannot arrive at religious maturity sooner than we arrive at psychological maturity. Religious and psychological maturity are distinct but not separate. They are intrinsically related. So, if we are "stuck" at a particular level of psychological development, we will also be "stuck" at that same level in our religious development.

When we are very young, we learn what we need to do to gain approval and rewards from authorities such as our parents. We also learn what to do to avoid punishment. Even though we may at times throw tantrums, we also know how to act like "good boys and girls" to receive approval. In like manner, in the initial stages of religious development, we transfer this need of approval to the deity. We act to "please" God in order to be rewarded. Of course the stakes are often very high—heaven or hell! As we mature psychologically, we learn that approval must come from within. In our corresponding religious development, we are asked to leave behind seeking "God's approval," because this attitude often alienates us from our deepest wishes and desires. If we are not in touch with what is deeply satisfying to us, our lives will be constricted and barren. We will be alienated from God even as we try to fulfill the demands of religion. We need not draw the conclusion that God does not enter into our decision making, but we do need to consider how we can be true to ourselves, our worldview, and to God. People who remain in the stage of seeking approval outside themselves often become very legalistic. Fulfilling religious laws in order to "please" another relieves one of responsibility. It also contributes to profound alienation from oneself.

As we continue maturing, we reach a stage where we romanticize or idealize our parents and the institutions to which we belong. There is no school like ours; no pet as perfect as ours; no friend as perfect as ours; no religion more true than ours. Gradually, though, we begin to notice that there is no perfect school, parent, friend, or religion. Then, we either accept this in ourselves and others, or we become disillusioned and begin a search for perfect replacements. One sign of maturity is that we acknowledge the ambiguity of life, the give and take of friendships, and the lack of perfection in people and institutions. We can see the implications for religious development. We go through stages when we think God is perfect—according to *our* conception of the perfect God. At this stage, it is often said that human beings make God into their image and likeness. We project onto God *our* needs, much as we project our ideals onto friends, lovers, and spouses. In the case both of God and friends, the time comes when we realize they are different from us. We must allow them to be themselves, not who we want them to be.

RESPONSES TO ALIENATION

When we begin to leave the romantic or idealized stage of religious development, when the realization begins to dawn that our particular religious tradition has lacks, inconsistencies, and errors, we often feel we are not in step with our friends, with our families, with the worldviews of the religious traditions in which we were raised or about which we have read. We begin to feel a dissatisfaction with the way things are. The values and practices that had helped us find our place in the world no longer seem to fulfill that function.

Many writers have described this situation. If it were not for this restlessness, this dissatisfaction with our situation, many of the good things people have accomplished over the ages would have been left undone. For example, health care for the indigent, free education for all children, the abolition of child labor and slavery (if not of prejudice), all this would not have been achieved if some individuals and groups had not looked around and said to themselves and to one another, "I am ill at ease with this situation. This is not the way things ought to be."

Although the people who set about making these reforms may have felt somewhat "outside" their immediate religious communities and families, they often felt deeply integrated with their religious story. In fact it is from these stories that they received nurture and sustenance for actualizing their insights, even when this took years. Stories, because they appeal to the imagination and appeal to us on many levels, have the power to direct and sustain our orientation for long periods of time. Rosemary Radford Ruether makes this very point when she considers her motivation for doing feminist theology. She claims that the Christian story as appropriated in Catholicism has provided her with the very principles she employs to critique the inequities and injustices within Catholicism. Relying on their religious traditions for legitimation, reformers proceeded to rectify situations they viewed as incompatible with human living.

CULTS

People sometimes experience an even deeper, more profound alienation. It is an alienation that causes people to feel that their story no longer works and, in fact, is totally useless in orienting them in the world or in helping them find meaning.

We have seen that religions are ambiguous. They provide us with suggestions of how to live a reconciled or authentic life. We have seen, also, that since religions never exist in the abstract, since they are always inherently cultural and social, affected by historical circumstances, they have within them sources of alienation. At times religions promote inauthentic living. Most people agree that everyone has a tremendous magnitude of psychic energy. Since this energy is immaterial, it is often named spiritual energy. Like any type of energy, it is useful only when it is focused or directed toward a goal—when it is ordered. When religions are perceived as misdirecting this energy toward inauthentic living, many people seek alternate ways of directing this energy. Some participate in political groups and direct this energy toward achieving the goal of the group. Others engage their energy toward accomplishing a particular social good, like securing a better education for the forgotten children of our various cultures.

Adolescents and young adults who are alienated by traditional religions often direct this spiritual energy into a cult. The word "cult" has many connotations. In its most general sense, it represents a minority religious movement, one that separates itself from the mainstream religions to which this text has often referred. If we accept that definition, we can say that—in its beginning stages—Christianity was a cult in relation to Judaism. If, over a period of time, a particular cult grows and becomes the dominant religious group in a particular region, it is no longer a cult. It may, however, give rise to other cults.

The Shakers (The United Society of Believers in Christ's Second Coming) were an English community formed about 1750, when its members seceded from the Society of Friends (Quakers). So intense was their prayer, that their bodies actually shook when they were involved in community worship. Thus, they received the popular name, Shakers.

Under the leadership of Ann Lee, whom the Shakers regarded as the female incarnation of Christ, a group of Shakers established themselves in Massachusetts. There, they promoted the ideals of simple living: hard work, good food which was simply prepared, and good furniture which was simple in style. They cared for orphans and accepted new members, but celibacy was practiced by all members. Naturally, over time, these communities died off. Americans, however, still admire Shaker design in furniture and use Shaker recipes in preparing good, nutritious food.

In the contemporary world, the word "cult" is often used in a derogatory or negative manner. This is not surprising, because the members of a cult deviate from general, more widespread beliefs. Whenever people begin to question the beliefs and practices of the dominant group, members of the dominant group often become defensive. We still see this in regard to the Vietnam War. Although that war forever changed American attitudes toward war, the patriotism of those young men and women who opposed the war remains in question to this very day, thirty or more years later.

In the religious realm, cults of the goddess are often viewed pejoratively. At first, referring to whatever is ultimate in a person's life as "goddess" rather than "god" seems strange and deviant. It is resisted. However, when we reflect that God is also a metaphor for ultimacy and spiritual focus, then goddess cults do not seem as threatening. The principal difference between the God of Christianity and the goddess of cults is the constellation of values that each perceives as ultimate.

There are, however, valid reasons that some cults provoke negative reactions. Some, such as various satanic cults, are destructive not only toward those outside the cult but to the members of the cult themselves. Some cults are benign or beneficial to their members; others are destructive. Implied in that statement are criteria according to which we make that judgment. Strangely enough, the criteria are as psychological as they are specifically religious.

This book is based on several assumptions which are generally accepted but which cannot be conclusively proven. Included among these assumptions are the following: We human beings seek to live meaningful and authentic lives; we live meaningfully and authentically when we try to live justly and honorably with our brothers and sisters; as we mature, we assume responsibility for our decisions, and our vision broadens so that we are able to appreciate our own cultures with their benefits and liabilities and to understand the benefits and liabilities of other cultures. When either religions or cults help us to achieve our humanity, they are deemed good for us, or beneficial. When they cause us to narrow our vision, to give responsibility for decision making over to an extrinsic authority, to see nothing good in the religions and cults of others, then they are viewed as destructive or dangerous. Hitler's cult of Aryan supremacy was a destructive cult, destructive almost beyond imagining.

Why are adolescents and young adults so often the ones who are attracted to cults? This is a complex question, and there is usually no single answer to it. The following characteristics, though, exist in some combination in every cultist. 1) Cultists are idealists; they have little tolerance for hypocrisy and ambiguity and so become disillusioned with traditional religions and other social arrangements when the participants, especially the leaders, do not always live up to the tradition's ideal. 2) Cultists have often grown up in families that were either extremely controlling or exerted no control at all. In either case, these young people have received little or no assistance in discovering and nurturing their uniqueness or personal identity. In fact, the prospect of participating in the creation of their own destiny is often overwhelming. 3) Cultists are naive in that they believe there exists on this earth a group of people with neither guile nor malice who love simply, purely, and unambiguously; they are willing to follow unquestioningly the leader of such a group in order to take on the identity of the cult and live in this idealized state.

The reasons that cults are attractive are not only personal, but social as well. In our contemporary world, the stories and rituals, the myths and values that have traditionally helped young people find their place in the world are falling apart. The English poet Matthew Arnold (1822-1888) poignantly expresses this sense of philosophical despair and dislocation in the poem *Stanzas from The Grande Chartreuse*:

> Wandering between two worlds, one dead,
> The other powerless to be born,
> With nowhere yet to rest my head
> Like these, on earth I wait forlorn.

The religious and social stories that have provided a way of centering our lives are falling apart all around us. In the interim, when new stories are developing, it is sometimes attractive to throw our lot in with any group that promises "salvation."

The center of a cult is always the cult leader. This leader responds to the needs of young people by providing them with instruction on the rules and regulations for living in this ideal state. Often, to promote the formation of a new identity, young cultists are forbidden to have contact with parents or friends or anyone else who would tempt them to return to their former way of life. Many times, they are deprived of sleep or other sensory stimuli because this makes them more receptive to the instruction of the leader and his aides. Often, sacrifices—such as remaining celibate, giving material resources to the community and rendering absolute obedience to the leader—are also demanded.

Thinking about Cults

Muhammad, Jesus, and Siddartha Gautama (the Buddha) were religious leaders whose charismatic preaching attracted groups of followers. In the beginning each of these religious movements could have been called a cult. These cults developed into religions which have members in nearly every nation on earth. Generally, we think of these religions as benefiting our attempts to live authentically. What characteristics do these religious innovators share with the cult leaders described above? What might make you hesitant to compare them with such cult leaders?

There have always been cults. People who have joined cults, for whatever reason, have always been viewed as living on the margin. Today, cults appear to have become increasingly attractive for the reasons we have just discussed, such as disillusionment with well-established tradition, extreme idealism, social disintegration and the government itself. Two recent examples are the Branch Davidians of Waco, Texas, and Heaven's Gate of southern California.

The members of the Heaven's Gate cult believed that in order to prepare themselves to be born again in a new, higher level of being, they must give up their belongings, end personal relationships, and renounce sensual pleasures. Periodically, when cult members were prepared to move to a higher level of existence, a heavenly body would come to facilitate their journey. The thirty-nine members of the cult who committed suicide in 1997 apparently believed that the Hale-Bopp comet was the signal that heavenly beings were coming to lead them to a new plane of existence.

There are cults which help us to live well and those that are destructive. Cults provide some members with a way of filling their emotional needs or their need for identity. Often, when these needs are filled, the members become disinterested in the cult and leave it.

Religion Understood as Totally Alienating

Some people respond to religion by claiming that it totally alienates individuals from their humanity. Two people who maintained that religion, by its nature, was alienating are Karl Marx (1818-1883) and Sigmund Freud (1856-1939). Karl Marx, who along with Friedrich Engels wrote the

INTERNATIONAL PUBLISHERS CO., INC.   A. W. FREUD ET AL.

Karl Marx (left) and Sigmund Freud (right) both found religion to be totally alienating. How do you evaluate their reasons for this alienation?

Communist Manifesto, believed that all historical institutions—economic and political as well as religious—represented human self-alienation. Marx believed that the practice of religion was symptomatic of an unreal or illusory way of perceiving the world. Everything that humans gave to religion—the praise of God, the belief in an afterlife—distanced them from their own selfhood. Further, Marx taught that secular patterns of life, such as the conventional understanding of family, had religious underpinnings and were also alienating. For persons to become reconciled to themselves, Marx thought, all existing systems or institutions, including religion, needed to be critiqued.

One example will show why Marx thought religion was a source of alienation. Marx observed the misery of the factory worker in the wake of the Industrial Revolution and judged that the comfort proffered to these workers in the name of religion was only an illusion. It did nothing to question the fundamental falsity of the economic situation itself. Rather, religion reinforced the status quo. Often, pastors preached that people were born into the situation God willed for them. Therefore, poor people were poor and rich people were rich because God wanted it that way. The marginalized and disadvantaged should endure their situation, placing their hope in the life to come. The powerful and advantaged people should give thanks for their blessings. Religion was certainly not viewed as a help to alleviate material suffering. As a consequence, both rich and poor were confirmed in their illusions about the nature of reality.

Sigmund Freud, the father of depth psychology, was not overly concerned about people's material situation, but he was concerned about their psychological condition. In his medical practice, Freud treated primarily the middle class of Vienna. Listening to their stories and analyzing their dreams led him to believe that institutional religions promoted repressive practices that frequently caused grave psychological damage in his patients. He observed that many people avoided assuming responsibility for personal decision making by abdicating this obligation to institutional Judaism or Christianity. He further noticed that when these same people violated religious taboos, they were consumed by destructive guilt. Certainly, neither Karl Marx nor Sigmund Freud regarded religion as a blessing.

THE AMBIGUITY OF RELIGION

Both Marx and Freud offer valuable critiques of religion. Judaism and Christianity have benefited most from their critiques. **Liberation theologians** who work in less-developed countries have often acknowledged the astuteness of Marx's economic analysis of class conflict. Jewish and Christian psychologists who are assisting their clients to establish a healthy sexuality agree with Freud that religious authorities have often contributed to unhealthy sexual repression. Still, a half century or more since these men called into question the whole notion of religion, there are not many scholars who accept their positions unconditionally.

The human journey is a search for authenticity. We have seen that religion is one way that may help us establish a meaningful way of life, a life that promotes our personal growth, and that is concerned for others. In this chapter, we also learned that established religious traditions, in distinction from our spiritual impulses, do not always assist us in living meaningful lives. This is true whether we are talking about Native American traditions, Buddhist cosmologies, or Christian religions. Each may foster responsibility or dependence, spiritual freedom or subservience, maturity or infantilism. But even these neat distinctions, although true, are misleading. Our development and human flourishing also depends on what we, as individuals, are looking for in a religion. It is not an easy task to live freely and responsibly, and although our religion may urge us to live in such a manner, we may choose to live a legalistic life in order to satisfy our own needs. Then, we interpret our tradition's stories in a way that fulfills these psychological needs.

CONCLUSION

Our conversations about religion have revealed that religion is not only ambiguous; it is complex. To understand it is, in some ways, like studying a gemstone or entering into an ongoing conversation. We can focus on one facet at a time, one topic at a time, like we did in this book. That gives us an in-depth appreciation of a particular part. We also need, however, to see and to appreciate how the various facets fit together to produce one phenomenon. We need to realize that our conversations never end; we merely pause. When we do that, it is difficult to know where one aspect of religion ends and another begins. Our hope is that you will continue your study of religion, turning it over again and again in your imagination, discovering new ways of looking at it and describing it. Our hope is that you will continue your conversations about religion, conversations with yourself, with friends, and with all others whom you trust enough to discuss these important topics.

RESOURCES

Activities

1. As people mature, they assess situations differently than they did when they were younger. Describe a personal, biographical, or fictional situation in which alienation was transformed into reconciliation? To what factors do you attribute this change?
2. For one week, keep a log of TV programs you watch or works of fiction you read. Decide which characters you think are alienated and why? Which are reconciled? Which characters accept the ambiguity of life? Explain and give reasons for your judgments.
3. List ten words or phrases that describe authenticity. List ten words or phrases that describe inauthenticity. Which was easier to do? Why do you think this is so?
4. Listen to the music and lyrics of a currently popular musical group in which the theme of alienation is prominent. How is alienation imaged? Put these lyrics into the historical context of their time period. Given the historical context, do you think reconciliation is possible? What would it require?
5. Hare Krishna, Heaven's Gate, the Branch Davidians (Waco), the Unification Church, and the Church of Scientology are cults that frequently appear in the media. Choose one of these cults, and surf the net to discover the range of material that is available. Then, critique the reports that you find to determine which are more reliable than the others. Give reasons for your critique.
5. Choreograph a dance, create lyrics, or write a series of poems that portray the themes of alienation and reconciliation.

Readings

Mary Daly. *Beyond God the Father: Toward a Philosophy of Women's Liberation.* Boston: Beacon, 1985. Among the books that initiated the feminist movement within Christianity, it presents a philosophy of women's liberation.
Toni Morrison. *Beloved.* New York: Knopf, 1987. This is the profoundly moving

story of the various levels of alienation in the life of a former slave. The author won the Pulitzer Prize for this novel.

Art Spiegelman. *Maus I: A Survivor's Tale, My Father Bleeds History.* New York: Pantheon, 1991, c. 1986. The story of how Vladek Spiegelman, a Polish Jew, and his wife survived the Holocaust.

————. *Maus II: A Survivor's Tale, And Here My Troubles Began.* New York: Pantheon, 1992. This account takes up the story from the end of World War II when Spiegelman and his wife left Germany and settled in New York. Told in cartoons by Vladek's son, the cartoonist Art Spiegelman, *Maus II* explores, with humor and pathos, the tortured relationship in the lives of survivors and their children. The use of the cartoon genre is shocking but immensely effective. *Maus II* won the 1992 Pulitzer Prize.

Elie Wiesel. *Night.* New York: Bantam, 1982. With this book, the Nobel Peace Prize recipient broke ten years of silence following his liberation from a Nazi concentration camp. It is autobiographical and is the first in a series of books by this author which depict his struggles with religious alienation.

Audiovisuals

The Shakers in America. Port Washington, NY: Applause Video, 1991. This video shows the history of the Shakers and the influence of their culture in the United States.

Night and Fog. Chicago: Films, Inc. 1983. French film with English subtitles. This documentary is acclaimed as one of the most worthwhile among the many that have tried to come to grips with the Holocaust.

The Business of Paradigms. Burnsville, MN: Charterhouse International Learning Corporation, 1990. Although the examples are drawn primarily from the field of business, this video provides an excellent portrayal of how we think in paradigms. It is easily applicable to the field of religion, especially such topics as images of God.

Women Serving Religion. Available from Films for the Humanities, P.O. Box 2053, Princeton, NJ 08543. 1995. This traces contemporary women's roles in Judaism, Islam, and Christianity; it also explores the question of ordination in these religions.

A Conversation with Toni Morrison. San Francisco: California Newsreel, 1992. This interview was given as commentary on the alienating themes in her book *Beloved.*

Glossary

Aborigines Literally, "those from the beginning." The word is most often used with reference to the native people of Australia but may be used of any indigenous group.

Acts of the Apostles The second volume of Luke's gospel, it begins with Pentecost and the inauguration of the Christian community and ends with Paul the apostle on his way to house arrest in Rome. A turning point is the council of Jerusalem, a gathering of such leaders as Peter, James, and Paul to determine whether non-Jewish converts to Christianity had to be circumcised and observe the Jewish law before they could be baptized.

Adam In Hebrew, "red, ruddy," perhaps related to the Akkadian word for "creature." Akkadian was the language of Babylon. In Genesis 2:4b-27, the Hebrew word designates the human creature, the first step in the creation of woman and man. The tradition of understanding the word as a proper name traces back to the Septuagint translation (ca. 250). In the Genesis account there is a play on the Hebrew words *adam* and *adamah*, "soil, arable land." The human who is a farmer in Genesis is created out of the land (Mother Earth?) it farms.

Adonai Hebrew word, "my lords," here a plural of majesty, which readers substitute for the personal name Yahweh, considered too sacred to pronounce. The singular *adon* simply means "mister, sir."

Allah In Islam the one undivided God proclaimed by Muhammad who is creator and sustainer of all that is, and who has revealed himself in the Qur'an.

Allegory A method of reading narrative that assigns symbolic meanings to characters, events, and places. In Galatians 4:21-31, Paul interprets the story of Abraham, Sarah, and Hagar allegorically.

Amos An early biblical prophet (eighth century B.C.E., during the reign of Jeroboam II, ca. 786-746); unique because he was a Judahite (from the southern kingdom) preaching in the northern kingdom of Israel. He probably gained his knowledge of international affairs from travels associated with his position as manager of the King of Judah's flocks.

Arhant Literally, a "worthy one" or saint in Theravada Buddhism who has overcome desire and attained enlightenment and will not be reborn.

Ark of the Covenant 1. large niche in the eastern wall of present-day synagogues for the five Torah scrolls; 2. a wooden chest, said to hold a container of manna, the tablets of the covenant, and the staff God gave to Aaron, the spokesperson for Moses (Exodus 25:10-22). In the early stages of Israelite religion, the ark served as God's throne and often played a role in Israelite battles (1 Samuel 4). Once the Jerusalem Temple was built, it was placed in the Holy of Holies as God's footstool. Its fate after the destruction of the temple in 586 B.C.E. is unknown (*pace* Steven Spielberg).

Bar/Bat mitzvah Literally "son/daughter of the commandment"; the Jewish ritual through which one becomes an adult member of the Jewish community.

Bhakti In Hinduism, religious devotion, loving adoration of a god.

Bible Literally, "the book." In Christianity the volume which contains the Jewish scriptures (Tanak) is called the Old Testament, and the canonical Christian scriptures, the New Testament.

Blasphemy Opposite of praise; speech which disparages the deity; punishable by death in the Tanak (1 Kings 21:9-13). According to Matthew 26:65, the Sanhedrin argued that Jesus was a blasphemer.

Boddhisattva Literally, "a being intended for enlightenment"; the moral exemplar in Mahayana Buddhism who, out of compassion, delays his or her own experience of nirvana to help others.

Brahman In Vedic religion and Hinduism, absolute and total reality.

Buddha Literally the "awakened one" or the "enlightened one." This title was first given to Siddhartha Gautama, the founder of Buddhism. Subsequently it was applied to a variety of buddha figures which are manifestations of the buddha nature that is understood to underlie the universe.

Canon From Greek *kanon* and Hebrew *qaneh*, "reed," perhaps used as a measuring stick. Today a canon is the standard by which religious traditions determine whether writings are authoritative for them. It is also the official list of books recognized as genuine and used in teaching and in determining doctrine.

Church 1. The community of all Christians, presented in the New Testament as "the body of Christ." 2. A denomination within Christianity or a local group of Christians. 3. A building used for the assembly and worship of Christians.

Circumcision The cutting off of the foreskin of males or the excision of the labia or clitoris in females. In a number of traditional African and Oceanic societies circumcision is carried out as a religious rite either shortly after birth or at puberty. In Judaism and Islam males are circumcised in commemoration of Abraham's covenant with God (Genesis 17:10).

Code In ethics, the tendency on the part of many cultures to summarize their moral obligations and duties into succinct summaries or laws, such as the Ten Commandments.

Codex A book made up of pages sewn together; this Christian innovation replaced the scrolls on which scriptures had originally been written.

Communist Manifesto Published in 1848 by Karl Marx and Friedrich Engels, it outlines the purposes and objectives of the Communist League.

Confucius (551-479 B.C.E.) A Chinese teacher and public servant whose teachings on the principles of the good life form the basis of Confucianism, a Chinese tradition that is variously described as a religion or a philosophy.

Conscience The internal capacity for moral discrimination which enables moral consistency by prodding us, through powerful emotions, to achieve coherence between our moral knowing and moral doing.

Cosmic law The moral order that some religious traditions see as inherent in the universe. Indian religions, Hinduism and Buddhism, refer to this law as dharma. Chinese religions, Confucianism and Taoism, refer to this law as Tao.

Cosmology An understanding of the structure of the universe.

Council of Chalcedon A meeting of leaders of the Christian church that took place in the city of Chalcedon in 451 to define orthodox teachings about Jesus the Christ in the face of the teachings of the cleric Arius; also determined the four-gospel canon.

Council of Trent Seventeenth-century meeting of leaders of the Roman Catholic church in the city of Trent, Italy, to respond to the reforms which Martin Luther claimed were necessary. The council defined a Catholic canon more inclusive than the canon of the reformers.

Culture A shared way of life that includes material products, a pattern of social relationships, and values and beliefs.

Deuterocanonical Literally, "second canon"; Apocrypha in Protestant traditions. The fourteen pre-Christian books or parts of books found in the Greek Septuagint and some editions of the Latin Vulgate that do not appear in the Tanak or in most Protestant Bibles. The Council of Trent removed 1-2 Esdras and the Prayer of Manasseh from this list.

Dharma In Hinduism, Buddhism, and Jainism the moral order which sustains the cosmos.

Diaspora Literally, "dispersion." The Jewish people who live outside Israel among the Gentiles.

Diatessaron From the Greek, literally, "according to four"; a harmony of the four New Testament gospels, edited and arranged into a single narrative and used widely in northern Syria until the fifth century when all copies were destroyed.

Eightfold Path In Buddhism, the eight steps to overcome suffering and reach enlightenment. They are broken into three instructions in the Theravadin tradition: concentration (right effort, right mindfulness, and right meditation), morality (right speech, right conduct, and right livelihood), and wisdom (right belief and right aspiration).

Eisegesis Reading into the text information or interpretations that are not there. Imposing one's own presuppositions and beliefs on a text. Classic examples are the traditional identification of the serpent in Genesis 3 as the devil, of the Garden of Eden as perfect existence, and of the woman's eating of the fruit as sin. See exegesis.

Encyclical A Roman Catholic document issued by the pope as a foundation for church teaching on matters of faith and actions.

Enlightenment 1. In Buddhism, the realization of insight into the nature of reality achieved by the Buddha; also the passing into nirvana of a person following the Buddha's way who attains release from the cycle of birth and rebirth. 2. In philosophy, a European intellectual movement of the seventeenth and eighteenth centuries which celebrated reason and posited knowledge, freedom, and happiness as the goals of a rational person.

Eve Her name is derived from a Hebrew verb which means "to live"; thus she is "the mother of the living," a frequent title of ancient Near Eastern fertility goddesses. In Genesis 3, she acquires the knowledge necessary to create culture. In the New Testament, Paul holds her responsible for the "fall" of humanity (2 Corinthians 11:3).

Excommunication The action of official religious bodies that excludes individuals or groups from participation in the rituals of that religion. Usually, persons are excommunicated due to perceived heresy.

Exegesis An explanation or interpretation of a text; the application of various methods of interpretation to a text.

Feminist hermeneutics A way of reading texts whose aim is resistance and transformation. It uses historical and literary methodologies, which focus on the text in its historical and rhetorical contexts, but also storytelling, bibliodrama, and ritual for creating a new feminist imagination.

Five Pillars of Islam The basic obligations individual Muslims must observe, including the profession of faith, daily prayer, giving of alms to the needy, fasting during the month of Ramadan, and the pilgrimage to Mecca at least once.

Five Precepts The rules for behavior which all Buddhists vow to keep. They include the precepts to abstain from taking life; to abstain from taking what is not given; to abstain from sensuous misconduct; to abstain from false speech; and to abstain from intoxicants.

Four Noble Truths The basic teachings of Buddhism suggested by Siddhartha Gautama: life is painful; the cause of pain is desire; there is a way to overcome this suffering; and the way is the Eightfold Path.

Genre French, "form" or "type" of literature. A type of literature determined by style, form, or content. A first step in interpretation is to determine the literary form of the text. We read legal material differently than we do poetry.

Gnosticism Early Christian movement whose members claimed they had gained salvation because Jesus had revealed to them special knowledge (Greek *gnosis*); only an elite few were initiated into these mysteries. Eventually condemned as a heresy, perhaps on political grounds. The Nag Hammadi Library contained Christian Gnostic writings.

Gospel The literary form of the writings of the four evangelists; the "good news" of the Christian message.

Haggada Literally, "narrative." The nonlegal part of the Talmud consisting of history, folklore, poems, and sermons. Also, the liturgical text used for the Passover Seder.

Hajj The pilgrimage to Mecca, one of the Five Pillars of Islam, which every Muslim is expected to make during his or her lifetime if possible.

Haudenosaunee Literally, "people of the longhouse." The six nations of the Iroquois Confederacy.

Heresy Religious teaching or opinion that is contrary to accepted religious doctrine. Literally, it means separation from the community. Those who withdraw their allegiance from a particular, essential teaching of a religious worldview are named heretics. At times persons are declared outside the community by religious authorities. Often, those accused of heresy by one age are reincorporated into the community when their work is judged in a larger context by the thinkers of a more historically minded community. The case of Galileo is such an example.

Hierophany Manifestation of the sacred.

Hogan The traditional dwelling of the Navajo. It is a conical house of logs covered by earth. At the top there is a smoke hole. It is entered by a low, covered opening.

Holi Hindu spring festival dedicated to the god Krishna.

Holocaust The genocidal murder of six million Jews, and others who did not fit the Nazi Aryan ideal, by the Nazis during World War II. Many Jews use the term "shoah," meaning catastrophe, when speaking of this event.

Idealism On the popular level, it simply refers to people who profess values which they refuse to compromise. Often, they are intolerant of others who do not hold the same values. Philosophically, it refers to the view that universals or innate ideas exist independently of the individual.

Initiation The ritual process by which one attains a social and/or religious status.

Islam Literally, "submission," that is, to God, who is known as Allah. Muhammad was the founder of Islam, a strictly monotheistic religion.

Jain/Jainism A religion founded by Mahavira ("Great Hero") in the sixth century B.C.E. as an offshoot of Hinduism. Rejecting belief in a supreme deity, Jains seek release from endless reincarnation through a life of strict self-denial, with special emphasis on *ahimsa*, noninjury to another living being. Their teaching of nonviolence influenced Gandhi.

Jerusalem 1. capital of present-day Israel; 2. city-state David conquered and made his religious and political capital ca. 1000 B.C.E.; site of the Temple, the central symbol of Israelite religion; 3. often personified in prophetic literature as Woman Zion, God's faithless wife, or as Mother Zion mourning her lost children.

Jñana In Hinduism, saving knowledge or wisdom, insight into the unity of reality.

Ka'ba Arabic for "cube"; the primary shrine of Islam, located in the Grand Mosque of Mecca. It symbolizes the center of the world and Muslims on the hajj visit there.

Karma In Indian thought, the chain of cause and effect which binds one to endless cycles of life, death, and rebirth.

Kerygma A Greek word meaning "preaching" or "proclamation." Christianity's central kerygma includes the life and ministry of Jesus of Nazareth, especially his death and resurrection (1 Cor 15:3-5).

Kettuba The marriage contract historically used in Jewish communities to provide a sense of equality between the partners and to protect them.

Koan A mind puzzle given by a Zen Buddhist master to students to enable them to break free from the cognitive constraints of their culture and to achieve enlightenment.

Kosher Traditional Jewish dietary laws based on biblical legislation. These laws determine what foods may be eaten, and in what combination they may be eaten.

Krishna In Hinduism, an incarnation of the god Vishnu.

Kwanzaa The ritual celebration developed within the African-American community by Dr. Maulana Karenga in 1966. The celebration enables the participants to celebrate their African heritage while also leading them to reflect on ways to improve their lives and the lives of their communities. The celebration lasts from December 26 to January 1.

Lectionary A book containing readings from the Bible for use in Christian public worship on weekdays and Sundays. Many lectionaries are arranged on a three-year cycle, for weekdays and for Sundays.

Liberation theologians Originally, Christian theologians working in Latin American who reflected on the incompatibility between the practice of the gospel and the existence of mass suffering and poverty. Later, the practice of any religious community in any locale which gives primacy to religious practice to change oppressive structures.

Mahabharata Literally "great epic of the Bharata dynasty." A classic Hindu epic of more than 100,000 couplets, the world's longest poem, which recounts wars between two related families, the Kauravas and the Pandavas. The hero of the epic is Krishna, an avatar ("one who descends") of the Lord Vishnu. The Bhagavadgita (the "Song of the Lord") is a section of the Mahabharata. The Mahabharata, which is thought to be based on events which took place between 1400 and 1000 B.C.E., reached its present form about 400 C.E.

Mahayana Buddhism Literally, "Large Raft" or "Vehicle" Buddhism; one of the two branches of Buddhism, dominant in East Asia and Vietnam. This name refers to the belief that its teachings provide a "large raft" to carry people to enlightenment.

Mana A Melanesian word which describes a mysterious power which inhabits individuals, objects, and events enabling them to be particularly effective. It has been adopted as a general term in the study of religions.

Mass The Roman Catholic form of the Christian Eucharist, the memorial meal of bread and wine that celebrates the sacrifice of Jesus.

Messiah Hebrew term, "anointed"; it designated kings and priests who were consecrated in their special roles by having oil poured over their heads. David and his descendants who ruled in Jerusalem were all messiahs. After the Davidic dynasty ended in 586 B.C.E., the prophets projected promises made to David onto a future figure who would restore the kingdom of David to its original glory (e.g., Daniel 9:25-26). New Testament writers identified Jesus of Nazareth as this figure (e.g., Matthew 16:13-20).

Metaphor Application of a name or descriptive term to an object or state to which it does not literally apply; also a system of thought in which a term evokes a multifaceted experience.

Micah A book contained in Hebrew scripture named for the prophet Micah. He promoted pure worship and spoke out against injustice.

Mitzvah The Hebrew term for commandment. In Judaism, moral obligations and duties are often stated in the form of commandments.

Moksha In Indian religions, release from the cycles of death and rebirth.

Moral perplexity The internal moral conflict and confusion we experience when faced with an ethical choice or dilemma. We cannot make one choice over another without experiencing some moral blame or guilt.

Mullah A Muslim man who is expert in Muslim law and theology.

Muslim Literally, "one who submits," that is, a practioner of Islam.

Myth Greek *mythos* is "story." Today, a narrative expressing a religious truth that cannot be verified by scientific means. Myths are stories about divine beings and national heroes who represent the powers and energies which influence us but which we cannot control. Carl Jung viewed myth as our inherited remembrance of primeval events that live on in our unconscious mind and which we repeatedly enact through ritual.

Natural law According to St. Thomas Aquinas, the moral order in the universe created by God and discernible through reason to guide humanity toward its true end.

Nirvana Literally, "blowing out." In Indian religions the cessation of human desires and absorption into Brahman.

Om Om or Aum is the most important sacred sound in the Vedic and Hindu tradition. It is used as a symbol of Brahman.

Parable From the Greek *parabole*, "comparison." A short narrative that has its hearers/readers pronounce judgment upon themselves through their reaction to its unexpected final twist. Jesus of Nazareth used parables extensively in his preaching (Matthew 13:3-53, etc.). At the same time, this use of parables kept most of his hearers from grasping his message (Mark 4:10-12 and parallel passages).

Passion narrative A symbolic narrative interpreting the suffering, death, and resurrection of Jesus of Nazareth; each gospel interprets the event and the person of Jesus differently.

Passover Seven-day Jewish spring festival which remembers the deliverance from Egypt. The festival begins with a service in the home.

Pharisee A member of an ancient Jewish movement that emphasized the importance of observance of the Torah, the Jewish law.

Polytheism The belief in more than one supreme being.

Prayer Communication with God or gods or spirits, often employing verbal formulas. Prayer may be public or private.

Priest From Greek *presbyteros*, "elder." One authorized to perform ritual, such as sacrifices, for a community, to mediate between God or gods and human beings, or to provide interpretation of tradition. The term "priest" is used in some Christian denominations to designate a minister.

Psalms A series of 150 prayer-poems usually attributed to King David. They are widely used today in both Jewish and Christian worship.

Q/Quelle A hypothetical collection of the sayings of Jesus of Nazareth; perhaps used by Luke and Matthew in the formulation of their gospels.

Qur'an In Islam, the Word of Allah, given as a revelation to the prophet Muhammad. The Holy Book of Islam, it is said to be a faithful copy of the eternal Qur'an inscribed in heaven.

Raja yoga A mental, physical, and spiritual discipline in Hinduism designed to aid in the practice of meditation.

Reincarnation In Indian thought, the endless cycle of birth, death, and rebirth through which all creatures are bound through karma.

Repression A psychological term for a defense mechanism which assigns to the unconscious events and memories so painful that they are neither allowed into consciousness nor recalled at will. Although they are unknown to the conscious subject, they still have effects on conscious life.

Rig Veda Literally, "hymns of wisdom." A collection of hymns, dating from the second millennium B.C.E., dedicated to the gods of the Aryan peoples who settled in northwest India. The Rig Veda is part of the Hindu scriptures.

Rites of passage Significant actions and rituals communities use to mark the process of moving from one status to another throughout the life cycle.

Sabbath The seventh day of the week, observed as a holy day of rest and worship in Judaism.

Sacrament In Christianity, "an outward and visible sign of an inward and spiritual grace" (Book of Common Prayer). Reformed churches count only Baptism and Eucharist as sacraments. Roman Catholic and Orthodox churches add Confirmation, Matrimony, Holy Orders, Penance, and the Anointing of the Sick.

Sacred A modality of human experience which relates to that which is held to have ultimate worth and which is seen to be in a reciprocal relationship with the profane.

Sangha In Buddhism, the community of monks who live together and participate in the practices and rituals which lead to enlightenment.

Sermon on the Mount Found in the Gospel of Matthew 5-7, it contains the Beatitudes. It is depicted by Matthew as the inaugural sermon of Jesus, outlining his teachings.

Seven Principles During the Kwanzaa celebration, the principles of unity, self-determination, collective work, cooperative economics, purpose, creativity, and faith provide the basis for reflection for participants.

Shalako Among the Zuni, an annual winter dance ceremony which renews the life of cosmos and community. Also, the mythological bird figures which come to visit and dance on this occasion.

Shaman Among the Tungu people of Siberia, a religious practitioner who is able to contact and influence spirits. By extension, a similar figure in other religious traditions.

Shari'ah The collection of interpretations and extrapolations from learned members of the Islamic community to make laws for people to abide by.

Sikhism A religion founded around 1500 C.E. by Guru Nanak in northern India; combines the mysticism of Hinduism with the rigid monotheism of Islam, while it rejects their leadership structure and rituals. Noted for its veneration of its scriptures.

Simile A figure of speech which compares two generally dissimilar realities on the basis of resemblance in one aspect. In making the comparison, the writer uses "like" or "as." Example: "My love is like a red, red rose."

Sola Scriptura A Latin phrase associated with the sixteenth-century reformer Martin Luther; it means "only scripture," reflecting Luther's teaching that scripture alone is necessary for belief and church order. Luther rejected the traditional beliefs and practice that the church in Rome recognized to be as binding as scripture.

Son of Man A Hebrew phrase meaning "mortal" or "human being" (Psalm 8; Isaiah 56:2; Qoheleth 3:18-19); the prophet Ezekiel uses it to refer to himself (Ezekiel 2:1). In Daniel 7:12-14, "one like a son of man" refers to Israel itself or to a divinely appointed future rule. In the gospels it is the one title that Jesus of Nazareth consistently uses about himself (e.g., Matthew 8:20; Mark 2:28; Luke 12:8-10; John 3:14).

Sorcery The art and practices of a person such as a magician, especially one supposedly aided by evil spirits.

Southern Baptist Convention The representative body of the various Southern Baptist congregations.

Stupa Bell-like or dome-shaped structure found in Asia which houses objects of religious veneration and devotion.

Sufi A Muslim who follows the more experiential and mystical teachings of the prophet Muhammad.

Sun Dance Traditional renewal ceremony of the Plains peoples of the United States and Canada.

Suppression A psychological term which names the defense mechanism of refusing to think about unpleasant events or feelings.

Symbol In a religious sense, a word, object, or action which evokes awareness of ultimate values or concerns. More generally, that which evokes or stands for something else by virtue of analogous qualities.

Synagogue Literally, "assembly." The meeting of Jews for study and prayer, and the building in which the assembly takes place.

Synoptic gospels The first three gospels; they share so much material in common that their texts may be viewed together as if "with one eye."

Synoptic problem Term for the problematic relationship, that is, the nature of their literary dependence, of Matthew, Mark, and Luke. Although Mark was once viewed as a condensed version of Matthew, today most scholars agree that both Matthew and Luke depend upon Mark, which is then the first attested gospel that we know.

Tallit The prayer shawl used by Jewish men and women during ritual prayer. They are received at one's bar/bat mitzvah and used in other rituals as well.

Talmud A collection of Jewish writings made up of the Mishnah, written editions of ancient oral interpretations of the Torah collected by Judah haNasi in Palestine in the early third century C.E., and the Gemara, further commentaries on the Mishnah. There are two Talmuds: an incomplete Palestinian Talmud compiled ca. 450 and the longer Babylonian Talmud compiled around 500.

Tanak An acronym for the Hebrew words Torah (Instruction), Nebe'im (prophets), Ketubim (writings); the Jewish bible.

Tao Literally, "the way" or cosmic order which underlies all reality in Chinese religions.

Taoism Founded by Lao Tzu in sixth century B.C.E. China; its main scriptures are the *Tao Te Ching* and the *Chuang-tzu*. Its ethical ideal is *wu-wei*, "active non-striving." By nonaction, the wise seek to come into harmony with the Tao, the self-generating organic course of the universe, which itself accomplishes by nonaction.

Tatian A second-century defender of Christianity and antagonist of Greek culture; produced a harmonized gospel, the Diatessaron.

Ten Precepts The rules a Buddhist monk vows to keep to become a member of the monastic community. In addition to the Five Precepts, they include the precepts not to take food from noon to the next morning; not to adorn their bodies with anything other than the three robes; not to participate in public entertainments; not to use comfortable beds; and not to use money.

Theology Systematic enquiry into matters of ultimate concern and, in particular, study of the nature of God.

Theravada Buddhism Literally, "Way of the Elders"; one of the two branches of Buddhism, found in Southeast Asia. It claims to be the oldest form of Buddhist teaching.

Torah 1. A Hebrew word meaning both "instruction" and "law," specifically the body of law associated with Moses and found in the first division of the Tanak. 2. The books of Genesis, Exodus, Leviticus, Numbers, and Deuteronomy. In the Christian canon, these same books are called the Pentateuch (Greek *pente* = five).

Tradition 1. Customs, beliefs, and practices transmitted orally from generation to generation and embodying the religious history and beliefs of a community. In the seventeenth century, Martin Luther rejected the claims of tradition in favor of scripture alone. An example of Catholic tradition is mandatory celibacy for priests and permanent deacons. 2. In Judaism, oral explanations and interpretations of the Torah eventually collected in the Mishnah. 3. Recollections about Jesus of Nazareth preserved orally in various communities and later used as sources by the gospel writers.

Umma Arabic for "community"; it refers to the entire world community of Muslims.

Vatican II A worldwide council of Catholic hierarchy called by Pope John XXIII (1962-1965). In its sixteen official documents it brought Catholic liturgy and theology more in line with the insights of contemporary culture and made major changes in the church's modes of engaging the world.

Veda Literally, "knowledge." One of the four collections of hymns to the Aryan gods. The term also applies to the corpus of Indian sacred literature, which includes the four Vedas, plus the interpretations of them which are constituted by the Brahamanas, Aranyakas, and Upanishads.

Vedanta In Hinduism, the main philosophical tradition, which believes that there is only one reality and that the individual self is identified with the absolute and with every other individual self.

Vishnu In Hinduism, the life-giver and preserver of the cosmos. Vishnu appears on earth from time to time as an avatar ("one who descends") to remind people of the ways to salvation.

Yoga In Hinduism the way of salvation through inner discipline. It has eight stages: restraint, discipline, posture, breathing, detachment, concentration, meditation, and trance. There are four main styles of yoga which correspond to personality types: *karma yoga,* the path of action, *jñana yoga,* the path of knowledge, *bhakti yoga,* the path of devotion, and *raja yoga,* the path of insight. In postclassical Hinduism *yoga* also refers to a philosophical system that teaches a dualistic worldview.

Zoroastrianism According to legend, begun three thousand years ago in Iran by the prophet Zarathustra. Stresses living a moral life with concern for ritual purity in worship and in daily life and the worship of its God Ahura Mazda and the good spirits through sacrifice and praise. In addition to a deity who controls good, Zoroastrian theology also identifies a deity who controls evil.

Zuni A multistoried masonry pueblo (town) in New Mexico near the Arizona border and the more than 5,000 Native Americans who inhabit it.

Index